AF881980

TRANSITIONAL AND RETROSPECTIVE JUSTICE IN THE BALTIC STATES

More than twenty years after the fall of Communism, many countries in Central and Eastern Europe are still seeking truth and justice for the repression suffered under communist rule. This search has been particularly notable in the Baltic states, given the three countries' histories as both former Soviet republics and later member states of the European Union. On the one hand, the legacy of Stalinist oppression was more severe in these countries than elsewhere in Central Europe, but on the other hand much of this past could more easily be externalized onto the former Soviet Union (and by extension Russia) following re-independence.

Transitional and Retrospective Justice in the Baltic States develops a novel conceptual framework in order to understand the politics involved with transitional and retrospective justice, and then applies this outline to the Baltic states to analyze more systematic patterns of truth- and justice-seeking in the post-communist world.

EVA-CLARITA PETTAI is Senior Researcher at the Institute of Government and Politics, University of Tartu, Estonia.

VELLO PETTAI is Professor of Comparative Politics and Director of the Institute of Government and Politics, University of Tartu, Estonia.

TRANSITIONAL AND RETROSPECTIVE JUSTICE IN THE BALTIC STATES

EVA-CLARITA PETTAI

and

VELLO PETTAI

CAMBRIDGE
UNIVERSITY PRESS

CAMBRIDGE
UNIVERSITY PRESS

University Printing House, Cambridge CB2 8BS, United Kingdom

One Liberty Plaza, 20th Floor, New York, NY 10006, USA

477 Williamstown Road, Port Melbourne, VIC 3207, Australia

314-321, 3rd Floor, Plot 3, Splendor Forum, Jasola District Centre, New Delhi - 110025, India

79 Anson Road, #06-04/06, Singapore 079906

Cambridge University Press is part of the University of Cambridge.

It furthers the University's mission by disseminating knowledge in the pursuit of education, learning and research at the highest international levels of excellence.

www.cambridge.org
Information on this title: www.cambridge.org/9781107627581

© Eva-Clarita Pettai and Vello Pettai 2015

This publication is in copyright. Subject to statutory exception and to the provisions of relevant collective licensing agreements, no reproduction of any part may take place without the written permission of Cambridge University Press.

First published 2015
First paperback edition 2018

A catalogue record for this publication is available from the British Library

ISBN 978-1-107-04949-9 Hardback
ISBN 978-1-107-62758-1 Paperback

Cambridge University Press has no responsibility for the persistence or accuracy of URLs for external or third-party internet websites referred to in this publication, and does not guarantee that any content on such websites is, or will remain, accurate or appropriate.

To Amma and Raul

CONTENTS

FIGURES AND TABLES

Figures

Tables

ACKNOWLEDGMENTS

If we were to explain how this book project came about, it would definitely be a case of social science overkill to say that it resulted from both "distal and proximate causes." Still, it is true that already in the early 1990s both of us had a strong interest in the politics of the past in the Baltic states. Whether it was a concern with the "democratization of history" in Latvia (Eva-Clarita) or a fascination with the doctrine of "legal continuity" in Estonia (Vello), there was a strong overlap in the questions we were asking about how the past is played out in contemporary politics. In 2008, these two trajectories merged into one, when Carlos Closa Montero invited us to contribute to a European Union commissioned project entitled "How the Memory of Crimes Committed by Totalitarian and/or Other Repressive Regimes in Europe Is Dealt With." We agreed to prepare jointly the national report on Estonia. And when in 2009 this research was completed, our appetite had been whetted for a more extensive and comparative study of the Baltic states.

While we drew some inspiration from the other project reports on Latvia and Lithuania that had been written (and kindly shared with us) by Andrejs Plakans (Latvia) and Tomas Balkelis and Violeta Davoliūtė (Lithuania), we realized that there was much more that could be researched on these issues, particularly from a political science perspective that was our own. We therefore examined the broad array of conceptual and theoretical frameworks that have been put forward to make sense of the politics of truth and justice in post-communist societies. We also harnessed our combined language skills (in Estonian, Latvian, Russian, French and German) to access as many additional archival, legal, scholarly and media resources as possible. Where our own language skills were not enough (i.e. in Lithuanian), our quick and abiding research assistant Lukas Pukelis helped made up the difference. The core of our endeavor was complete.

Along the way, however, we also benefited from other help. One of these impulses came from the participants in the workshop "Between Retribution and Restoration: Explaining the Politics of Transitional

Justice" organized by Klaus Bachmann and Adam Czarnota at the 2012 Joint Sessions of the European Consortium for Political Research. Although our final conceptual framework bears only a partial resemblance to what we presented there, this is perhaps the finest tribute that we can pay to the Workshop, since its participants helped alert us to many initial weaknesses in our argument. Other readers such as Lavinia Stan and, again, Klaus Bachmann helped to refine our thoughts at different stages, especially with regard to the conceptual parts of our book.

In 2012–13, as we entered the *tous azimuts* stage of data collection and fact checking, Mārtiņš Kaprāns kept us abreast of a number of additional sources and developments in Latvia. Aigi Rahi-Tamm offered her insights on Estonia. And a number of key interviewees in all three countries (see our list after the References) provided even more perspective on the very diverse realms of truth and justice. Maija Skurska also supplied additional research assistance for Latvia.

Eventually, when authors begin to think that they know enough about a topic to start writing about it, they inevitably look for support from institutions and other kind folk to facilitate their textual creativity. Our primary source of support came, of course, from the University of Tartu and two important research grants from the Estonian Ministry of Education and Research (Targeted Finance Project nr SF0180128s08 and Institutional Research Grant nr IUT20-39). Our thanks also go to the European University Institute (and here in particular to Andreas Frijdal, László Bruzst and their support staffs) for making possible two weeks of intensive writing at the Villa San Felice during March–April 2013. Another absolutely blissful period of creative writing was enabled by Vieda Skultāne, who graciously offered her flat in Riga to Vello during two weeks in January 2014 so that two more chapters could be brought across the finish line.

When all of our analyses, arguments, claims and conclusions were complete, it remained for people like Lina Strupinskienė, Rein Taagepera, Lukas Pukelis and Dovilė Budrytė to assess our work as collegial critics, and for Cambridge University Press' own reviewer to have his/her say. We integrated their comments as extensively as we could. Many were extremely thorough and insightful! Our thanks also go to Elizabeth Spicer at Cambridge for her generosity when it came to extending deadlines and to the editing team at the Press.

Needless to say, our closest help for this project came from our son Jakob who, amidst his seven years of age, endured valiantly each time his mom and dad started debating 'Box 2' vs. 'Box 3' in a language (English) he had yet to master. We trust, however, that he will eventually come to understand this tongue, as well as the import of this book, for as an Estonian-German his heritage, too, encompasses the many issues dealt with on these pages. We also take the opportunity to thank Jakob's grandparents, Adam and Verena, who on many occasions helped pass their grandson's time as different chapters came into being.

Lastly, it bears mentioning that just as key parts of this work were being completed in Florence, one of the people to whom we dedicate this work, Clarita von Trott zu Solz (or Amma) departed this world. Because totalitarianism, loss and remembrance were all a part of Amma's remarkable life, her example was forever present in our minds as we tackled these difficult issues. Similarly inspirational was the story of Raul Pettai, who in 1944 was forced to leave his homeland just as the most anguishing clash of two totalitarian powers took place. That he moved on with his life while maintaining his national identity is a testimony to the Baltic peoples' ability not to be crushed by the weight of the past, but always to push forward with an enduring sense of character and purpose.

ABBREVIATIONS

CoE	Council of Europe
EC	European Commission
ECtHR	European Court of Human Rights
ECHR	European Convention on Human Rights
EPP-ED	European Peoples Party-European Democrats
EU	European Union
IKUERK	*Inimsusevastaste kuritegude uurimise Eesti rahvusvaheline komisjon* (Estonian International Commission for the Investigation of Crimes Against Humanity)
JHA	Justice and Home Affairs
KAPO	*Kaitsepolitsei* (Estonian Security Police Board)
KGB	*Komitet gosudarstvennoy bezopasnosti* (Soviet Committee on State Security)
LAF	*Lietuvos aktyvistų frontas* (Lithuanian Activists Front)
LDDP	*Lietuvos demokratinė darbo partija* (Lithuanian Democratic Labor Party)
LGGRTC	*Lietuvos gyventojų genocido ir rezistencijos tyrimo centras* (Lithuanian Genocide and Resistance Research Center)
LOM	*Latvijas Okkupācijas mūzejs* (Occupation Museum of Latvia)
LPKTS	*Lietuvos politinių kalinių ir tremtinių sąjunga* (Lithuanian Union of Political Prisoners and Deportees)
LPRA	*Latvijas politiski represēto apvienība* (Latvian Association of Victims of Political Repression)
LVK	*Latvijas vēsturnieku komisija* (Commission of the Historians of Latvia)
MGB	*Ministerstvo gosudarstvennoi bezopasnosti* (Soviet Ministry of State Security)
MEP	Member of European Parliament
NATO	North Atlantic Treaty Organisation
NKGB	*Narodnyi komissariat gosudarstvennyi bezopasnosti* (People's Commissariat for State Security)
NKVD	*Narodnyi komissariat vnutrennykh del'* (People's Commissariat for Internal Affairs)

ORURK	*Okupatsioonide repressiivpoliitika uurimise riiklik komisjon* (State Commission for the Examination of Repressive Policies Carried Out During the Occupations)
PACE	Parliamentary Assembly of the Council of Europe
SAB	*Satversmes aizsardzības birojs* (Latvian Constitutional Protection Bureau)
STS	*Specialiųjų tyrimų skyrius* (Special Investigations Division, Lithuanian Prosecutor General's Office)
SWC	Simon Wiesenthal Center
TKNSORNLI	*Tarptautinė komisija nacių ir sovietinio okupacinių režimų nusikaltimams Lietuvoje įvertinti* (International Commission for the Evaluation of the Crimes of the Soviet and Nazi Occupation Regimes in Lithuania)
TRNIK	*Totalitāro režīmu noziegumu izmeklēšanas komisija* (Investigative Commission for the Crimes of the Totalitarian Regimes)
TRNIN	*Totalitāro režīmu noziegumu izmeklēšanas nodaļa* (Investigative Division for Crimes of the Totalitarian Regimes, Latvian Prosecutor General's Office)
TSDC	*Totalitārisma seku dokumentēšanas centrs* (Center for the Documentation of the Consequences of Totalitarianism)
TS-LDK	*Tėvynės sąjunga-Lietuvos krikščionys demokratai* (Homeland Union-Lithuanian Christian Democrats)

Introduction

The imposing, 130-year-old building on the front cover of this book encapsulates all of the facets of transitional and retrospective justice that we aim to cover in this study. The building, located on Gediminas Avenue in the center of Vilnius, has an infamous history of having been the headquarters of terror for two murderous regimes that controlled Lithuania from 1940 to 1991. Both the Nazi Gestapo and the Soviet KGB operated their central command from this building. From here leaders planned their mass crimes of rounding up and deporting hundreds of thousands of Lithuanians, Jews, Poles and other nationalities, either to concentration camps in the Reich or to the Gulag in Siberia. Many have qualified this genocide – in relation to both totalitarian regimes.

Having originally been built as a court house for the Czarist empire, the building naturally had in its basement a prison, where especially pilloried political prisoners were detained. "Detention," of course, was usually a transitory state. During Nazi rule, but especially under the Soviets immediately after the war, prisoners were regularly executed in a special chamber, where bodies could easily be thrown on to trucks for transport to a special mass grave not far outside of Vilnius (Tuskulėnai).

During the 1950s, when the worst of the Stalinist era had passed, but also a 50,000-man Lithuanian partisan movement had been crushed, the Soviets seemed to declare victory with the erection of a huge statue of Lenin in front of the KGB building and the renaming of the entire square in honor of the Soviet leader. The KGB itself settled down to a more conventional mode of surveillance, manipulation and intimidation. The service's network of collaborators grew. So did the number of files on people: young and old, men and women, urban and rural, prominent and humble.

Some three decades went by like this, when all of a sudden the roles began to reverse. Those who had been imprisoned, deported, repressed, subjugated, intimidated all came out to the streets and squares of

Lithuania. They came to express their repugnance and rejection of the Soviet regime. And they did so on very special days of the year – June 14, August 23, March 25 – when the pain of their memories was strongest. The victims were beginning to vanquish the perpetrators.

At first, the victims gained "rehabilitation," or what some would see as an almost perverse situation where the Soviet state acknowledged the fact that these people were no longer criminals for having been killed, repressed or deported by a foreign occupying power. Still, the initiative was gratefully received. Victims were given legal status, some property was restituted and eventually a number of compensatory benefits enacted. Yet, the chief perpetrator of all this repression, the KGB, wasn't at all a part of this process. Rather, it was the three democratizing Soviet Baltic governments who were attempting to do some good for their citizens.

Still, on Gediminas Avenue, the KGB's leaders were becoming uneasy. The political winds were changing too rapidly. Their operations were no longer secure. Better to remove the more sensitive files and materials to Omsk, Ulyanovsk or elsewhere in Russia. If the USSR's occupation in the Baltic states were to end, these materials could become important for future Baltic–Soviet relations. Needless to say, some of the files would also simply go up in smoke right there in that famed building.

The dénouement to this gradual turnaround – in the form of the attempted anti-Gorbachev coup – was, of course, relatively unexpected. All the more reason for the KGB to act quickly during those days in August 1991 to make sure it could shut down its operations with maximum advantage in the face of eager commissions appointed by the Baltic governments and parliaments to take over Soviet property. Eventually, the KGB even relinquished its grand headquarters in central Vilnius. It was now up to the Lithuanians to decide what to do with it.

One outcome was to return the building to its old Czarist function, as in 1993 the Vilnius District Court took up residence on the third and fourth floors. However, it seemed only fitting that the basement area, which had served as the Gestapo and KGB prison and hence as a place of death, should be turned into a commemorative site. In October 1992, the Lithuanian Museum of Genocide was opened on several floors of the building to enlighten the public about the terror that had taken place there as well as to explain the broader repression the KGB had wrought in Lithuania. When in 1997 the museum was made a subsection of the Lithuanian Genocide and Resistance Research Center, the Gediminas Avenue building became even more an emblematic part of Lithuania's quest for truth and justice. In the course of ten years, its function in fulfilling the repressive aims of the KGB had been completely inverted.

Moreover, in 1994 the building would be put to even more use as a site of truth and justice when the Resistance Participants Rights Commission was relocated to the first floor of Gediminas Avenue 40/1. Now victims were awaited at the building, not only to visit the museum but also to organize their legal status as "Participants in Armed Resistance," "Independence Defenders," "Political Prisoners," "Deportees." A staff was set up, whose main responsibility would be to issue identification cards and social benefit certifications to more than 80,000 individuals, depending on their eligibility under nearly forty categories of repressed person's status.

Finally, in the other wing of the building that had been handed over to the Vilnius District Court, another two dimensions of transitional justice would play themselves out. In 1992, the Lithuanian parliament passed a law establishing criminal sanctions for those convicted of involvement in "genocide." Within three years, the Vilnius District Court would open a trial against three former Soviet security agents accused of genocide because of their actions in crushing anti-Soviet partisans in 1945. All three men would be found guilty. Meanwhile, some years later the Court would be the site for more contestation, as a number of former agents or informants of the KGB would challenge accusations leveled by the country's Lustration Commission that they had once worked with the secret Soviet agency. In a most poignant manner, many of the most difficult issues of complicity and collaboration were now being adjudicated in the same rooms once used by this regime to repress the Lithuanian people.

In these opening pages we have taxed the patience of our reader with a long overview of repression and justice in Lithuania in order to illustrate many of the conceptual and theoretical arguments to be presented in this book. First, it is not a coincidence that Lithuania decided to pack so many aspects of truth and justice into one building. Indeed, in this book we will argue that all of the realms of truth and justice are connected and that it is important to examine them as a whole. This is exemplified not least by an institution such as the Lithuanian Genocide and Resistance Research Center, which has been involved in not only organizing remembrance activities and engaging with former victims of repression, but also in preparing victim status applications, reviewing lustration convictions and gathering materials for the successful prosecution of ex-KGB operatives for nothing less than genocide. In our view, the reason why such activities sometimes come together – and sometimes do not – relates to politics. We want to see why this is so. Likewise, we are keen to ask what is the consequence of having constellations of this kind or another? Are there effects on, say, popular satisfaction with democracy, respect for rule of law or social memory more generally? Are societies that take on broad-scale truth and justice policies different from those that do so less?

Whereas previous research into truth and justice issues has generally been limited to single policy domains, we will aim to show that activities in one sphere are often linked to developments in another. And what is more important: politicians and legislators who have to decide on these policies often navigate these terrains simultaneously. We believe that achieving truth and justice in post-authoritarian or post-communist societies is a multidimensional process.[1] Our objective is therefore to open up this complexity with a new set of conceptual and analytical tools, as well as a rigorous application of those tools to the three Baltic states. Our result will be an ability to evaluate each country's *pattern* of truth and justice policy along with providing some indications as to why these patterns differ across these three states and what effects these patterns have on actually "overcoming" the past.

The politics of truth and justice

Taken in broad terms, this book examines the politics of truth and justice in post-communist countries. All of the words selected in this formulation have meaning in terms of delineating our subject matter and showing how we contribute to the study of specific social science phenomena. In relation to how other scholars have treated these issues, our work will reveal itself to be at times wider, at times narrower in scope. At each stage of the explication, however, we will attempt to justify our approach on conceptual and theoretical grounds.

We begin with 'the politics of truth and justice'. This notion denotes for us the struggles waged by political and social actors to influence the role the state plays (a) in setting prevailing truth discourses about a non-democratic past and (b) in passing measures to enact some interpretation of justice in relation to this past. By citing specifically the role of the state, we indicate that we are interested above all in the power of

[1] A fact underscored by other recent research such as Olsen et al. (2010a) and Binningsbø et al. (2012), both of which look for combinations of truth and justice measures as opposed to single policies.

government authority to influence these two processes of truth establishment and justice enactment. By this statement we do not wish to deny the increasingly important role played by external, international actors in the field of truth and justice, through international criminal tribunals, truth commissions or other forms of truth establishment and justice enactment in post-conflict societies. This "exogenous" type of transitional justice (Elster 2004) has indeed seen a proliferation of studies over recent years. Likewise, we acknowledge the important role played by civil society not only in instigating domestic policies of redress or punishment but also in liaising with international agencies to bring about the desired results (Boesenecker and Vinjamuri 2011). However, we do believe that it is still the post-conflict or post-dictatorial state that these external truth and justice efforts are aiming at, that is, the "endogenous" truth and justice process. And it depends ultimately on the degree of cooperation of domestic political and social actors whether or not international intervention contributes to truth and justice.

There are certainly many levels on which these two phenomena take place. On the level of direct social relations, for example, individuals might exchange in a one-on-one fashion their understandings about the past and thereby mold a form of interpersonal truth discourse. Likewise, they may see as their own kind of justice measure a decision to shun someone perceived as having been responsible for past repression, or conversely they may accord someone particular respect for their suffering. Furthermore, truth and justice about the past may operate via cultural artifacts that surround us. For instance, material media such as films or books often project a certain understanding of earlier eras as well as send messages about the justice that is due. In noting these other forms of truth and justice formation, we echo the categories of "communicative," "social" and "cultural memory" brought out by Aleida Assmann (2004) and others.

However, our choice here is to focus on the power that the modern state has when engaging in these processes, since this authority can have the greatest impact on other venues of truth and justice creation, and it can often be final in its consequences. By extension, therefore, we are interested in the efforts of political and social actors to influence the ways in which this state power might be exercised. This represents the "politics." We are not focused solely on what measures the state adopts or their success but also on which actors push for which measures and how they wage their struggles. Moreover, such actors can be formal political ones such as parties, prime ministers or presidents. They may also be social actors like social movements or civil society groups. In any regard, our concern is with how these actors determine the uses of state authority in setting truth discourses about the past and enacting justice measures.

We acknowledge that there is a certain overlap between what we term the politics of truth and justice and what is often referred to as the politics of memory. Yet, we see a danger of analytically blurring these rather distinct political phenomena. The politics of memory remains a rather vague field of study that looks at a wide range of mechanisms and processes by which very different "mnemonic actors," possessing myriad different motives, constraints and opportunities, seek to influence and shape public perceptions of the past and to forge historical memory and shared meaning in society. Such mnemonic actors can be elected leaders and political and civic organizations, but also representatives of various social and professional groups such as journalists, academics (in particular historians), intellectuals and artists, as well as religious leaders. Thus, studies of the politics of memory encompass a conceivably wide range of activities and issues, from measures and policies implemented by the state, to public speeches and commemorative practices that offer interpretations of past events all the way to history education and textbooks, monuments and museum exhibitions. We would therefore claim that while truth and justice measures do to a certain extent contribute to collective perceptions of the past and to the forging of shared historical narratives, their primary and defining purpose remains that they are serving justice to particular individuals or groups who have been defined by legislative Acts as either perpetrators or victims of past wrong.

Taking a more holistic view of transitional justice

The politics of post-communist truth and justice (as we have delimited it) is a field that has expanded almost exponentially over the last two decades. Not only has the range of available empirical case studies grown considerably, but also the causal models for explaining different varieties of this phenomenon have become more refined and overarching. In this book, however, we argue that scholars have lost sight of the proverbial forest through the mass of trees that have been documented. Moreover, we will claim that by taking a moment to map out more accurately the full landscape of truth and justice measures, scholars will be able to grasp more substantively the inter-connections existing between these varieties and across country-cases. Our task of arriving at more purposeful comparative and causal analyses will be bettered if we have a clearer conceptual framework through which to both distinguish individual measures and outline country patterns.

We begin by arguing that existing studies of post-communist truth and justice processes suffer from three shortcomings. The first involves authors who have predominantly focused on single measures of transitional justice (most prominently lustration policies) and have tried to explain their variation in the region by identifying the determinants for the adoption or rejection of specific lustration mechanisms (Moran 1994; Welsh 1994; Nedelsky 2004; Williams et al. 2005; Nalepa 2010; David 2011). Yet the models developed in this vein have usually not been transferred (nor are they always transferable) to other areas of justice such as the criminal prosecution of past wrongdoers or restitution policies targeted at victims of past injustice. Hence, while these works have a clear causal research ambition, the dependent variable as such is relatively narrow, and therefore these studies say little about other justice types or the way in which a society might have to deal interactively with many justice forms at once. Moreover, what if, say, high levels of lustration in a country were actually being driven by a broader-scale pattern of crusading across all fields of truth and justice? What would the causal explanation then be? In our view, studies of single phenomena related to post-communist truth and justice are easily susceptible to Galton's problem, where inferences are made without understanding wider, environmental factors that may be actually instigating the process.

The second (to our mind incomplete) approach concerns those authors who have, indeed, sought to capture a more diversified range of truth and justice measures, and yet have failed to provide a comprehensive and truly typological model that might enable further comparative causal analysis (McAdams 2001; Calhoun 2004; Appel 2005; Offe and Poppe 2005; Stan 2009c, 2013). While these works do make an effort to differentiate between certain justice measures, they do not go very far in laying out a full analytical framework. Either they leave their inventory as a taxonomical roster or they fail to test their model with a rigorous empirical case.

Lastly, what we believe is entirely missing in the literature is a solid incorporation of temporality into the analysis of truth and justice processes. Moreover, by temporality we mean three separate time perspectives. If we take as our Archimedean point the moment of a society's transition to democracy (i.e. the removal of the non-democratic rulers and the instauration of democratic leaders), the first temporality relates to what most scholars know as "transitional justice" or efforts to deal with the repression and wrongdoing carried out by the regime that has just been toppled from power. A second temporal dimension arises when the previous regime lasted for many decades, and truth and justice issues emerge with regard to its early wrongdoings. Here the challenges of achieving truth and justice are different in that few victims, eyewitnesses or perpetrators may be left in society, and documentation is hard to obtain. At the same time, these more historical wrongs are still part of a new democracy's task of dealing with its antecedent regime. The adjudication and redress of such wrongs can give rise to real politics and affect the new democracy's political development. We believe that this perspective deserves to be treated in its own right, with the name "retrospective justice."[2] Thirdly, a number of scholars have already observed how truth and justice processes can emerge or intensify long after a democratic transition is over (Elster 2004; Horne 2009b). Here the temporality shifts to a later starting point, but still reverts back to the moment of democratic transition and asks whether enough has been done to overcome the legacies of the previous regime. In conceptualizing this time perspective, we follow scholars who have spoken of "post-transitional justice" (Collins 2010; Raimundo 2012). However, we will also modify some of their parameters to make the concept more operative.

A final point concerns differentiating these three temporalities. As we will explain further in Chapter 1, transitional and retrospective justice are similar in that they can take place at the same time; they simply look back at either closer or farther moments in the past when alleged injustice was done. Post-transitional justice, by contrast, happens at a later period in time – we argue as of the moment that democratic electoral politics have taken hold – and looks back at what for transitional justice was the present. As a result, post-transitional justice should not be seen as simply a third type of justice, but rather as a phenomenon that might arise as a function of the other two, and indeed, as an essential revision of those earlier decisions.

Previous regime type vis-à-vis truth and justice

Before we outline our book in its entirety, we present a short excursus on the relevance of past regime type for analyzing transitional and retrospective

[2] With this we deliberately distinguish the phenomenon not just from transitional justice, but also from "historical justice," the latter being rather disconnected from post-regime contexts and reaching even farther back in time to "repair historical injustice" such as black slavery, imperial-colonial rule or the suppression of indigenous populations. For a flagship publication in this field, see Berg and Schaefer (2009).

justice. While many recent studies have ventured into bold comparisons of transitional justice around the globe, encompassing post-authoritarian, post-conflict and post-communist political regimes (Barahona De Brito et al. 2001; Elster 2006; Olsen et al. 2010a; Grodsky 2011), our preference in this regard is to limit the conceptual scope to a single regime type, since in our opinion the contextual conditions that each regime sets up for latter-day transitional justice challenges are too varied to provide for meaningful comparison.[3] To take but the most palpable example, not only have post-communist regimes had to deal with a seemingly greater range of justice issues, but they have also had to manage these matters across a broader spectrum of people (that is, past wrongdoers as well as claimants to rectification). For instance, the Communist regimes that took power during the 1940s in Eastern Europe (but also elsewhere) frequently began their rule with large-scale property nationalization. This issue has resurfaced as property restitution in almost all of the countries since 1989, becoming a major focus of transitional justice that is less present elsewhere (Offe 1997; Tucker 2006b; Kuti 2009). Likewise, the scale of communist-era repressive acts, such as forced deportations or the resettlement of entire populations, has been greater than in many other repressive regimes. These parameters are to our mind substantive in terms of how we analyze truth and justice processes.

Of course, our objective here is not to argue in favor of post-communist exceptionalism. It is merely to pick up on the point echoed by other scholars (Offe 1997; Kuzio 2001) that post-communist regimes have faced a "simultaneity" of problems involving political, economic, social and sometimes even national identity related challenges. This, we argue, is reflected also in the range of transitional justice issues confronting these societies. Likewise, it is possible to maintain that because the past regime's repressive measures affected a wider section of the population, the political demand for dealing with these issues will be greater. Individual politicians are more likely to feel a need to take up these pressures. There are more interest groups, injustice categories, remembrance moments or other aspects that will trigger a politics of truth and justice.

The analytical model we propose thus has an interesting methodological consequence of pleading in favor of more delineated case selection, primarily because the model makes us more sensitive to all of the precise processes that may be going on in a certain post-regime category,

[3] Recently this preference has also been echoed by other researchers. For example, Binningsbø et al. (2012) limit their study of the effects of transitional justice measures to uniquely post-conflict situations and defer including all new democracies.

therefore prompting us to want to control for the effects of these background conditions when selecting our cases.

Outline of the book

In this book we have challenged ourselves with a tricky balancing act. On the one hand, we were motivated to undertake this project because of the paucity of information about the Baltic states that we discovered in the existing literature.[4] Either Estonia, Latvia and Lithuania have been overlooked because they fall out of the mental picture of Central and Eastern Europe, or they have been examined on the basis of very limited and inadequate sources that have led to superficial assessments being made. Above all, scholars have frequently been tempted to treat the three countries as simply one entity. Somehow being able to reduce them to a single category – "the Baltics" – often seems easier that treating them as separate cases (something that people from the "Balkans" and the "Caucasus" can probably relate to). Of course, the Balts themselves are partly to blame here: efforts to portray the unity of the three states either during their common struggle for re-independence from the Soviet Union or as a regional bloc thereafter logically prompt observers to perceive Estonia, Latvia and Lithuania as uniform societies and polities. However, as our empirical analysis will show, there are very tangible differences in the politics of truth and justice that have emerged in these three states. These dovetail with many other divergences that have already been observed in terms of constitutional structures (Vaičaitis 2012), party development (Pettai et al. 2010), economic development (Norkus 2012; Kattel and Raudla 2013) and minority policy (Vihalemm 2011).

Yet alongside the need to fill this empirical gap, we have increasingly been drawn to making a statement also on theoretical grounds. The way in which the Gediminas Avenue building in Vilnius exemplifies for us the need to think in a more holistic conceptual manner illustrates how

[4] Only in the course of the last five years have certain comprehensive case studies emerged. See first and foremost the reports contracted by the European Commission as part of the project "How the Memory of Crimes Committed by Totalitarian Regimes in Europe Is Dealt with in the Member States" (Balkelis and Davoliūtė 2009; Pettai and Onken 2009; Plakans 2009). Subsequently, the 2013 *Encyclopedia of Transitional Justice* features entries about all three countries (Budryte 2013a; Pettai 2013a; Wezel 2013). And separate overview articles on Estonia and Latvia have appeared from Tamm (2013) and Švarca (2012). However, none of these works has attempted to put forth a synthesized analytical model.

empirical investigation can lead to theoretical revelation. Hence, instead of simply describing truth and justice politics in the Baltic states across some set of conventional rubrics, we have been pulled into generating a more overarching analytical model, which we are then obliged to relate back to our empirical cases as illustratively as possible.

We therefore end up with a dual task: to provide comprehensive background information on the Baltic states across a wide range of truth and justice phenomena for empirical readers, while at the same time testing the coherence and validity of our conceptual model for comparative scholars. This naturally puts a premium on how we structure our book and its chapters. We hope that readers interested in the basic facts about property restitution, criminal trials against Stalinist executioners or the Baltic history commissions will find these readily in the text. At the same time, we invite more theoretically driven scholars to examine the innovativeness of our model and the insights that our analytical matrix might bring. Both types of readers should benefit from our Conclusion, which provides visualized summaries of the patterns of truth and justice politics in each Baltic state, while also offering reflections at an inferential level as to what the causes and consequences of such patterns might be.

Turning to the individual chapters, we begin inexorably in Chapter 1 by presenting our conceptual framework, meaning a more detailed exposition of how we propose to overcome the three shortcomings in the existing literature that we noted above. Our basic argument is that many of the elements we need in order to achieve a more holistic understanding of truth and justice politics are already there. We simply need to see how these elements fit better together. As we review the contributions of Claus Offe, Noel Calhoun, Jon Elster, Brian Grodsky and others, we will arrive at our synthetic model, which will take the form of a twelve-cell analytical matrix. While this may seem unruly as a future conceptual tool, we will argue that this combination allows us to classify a wide range of phenomena that currently are all too often lumped into a single gigantic category called "transitional justice." Our goal, however, is not only disaggregation but also the notion of examining *combinations* of these disaggregated measures (or patterns), which we claim represents a more substantive epistemological category than looking simply at single measures.

In Chapter 2, we tilt back to an empirical approach by reviewing the geographic and historical context of the Baltic states, and in particular their period of Soviet and Nazi rule. Our objective here is not to provide a comprehensive historical overview, but rather to place the Baltic states' experience with totalitarianism and repression in a comparative Central

European and post-Soviet context. While these countries share many similarities with Central Europe, they also face particular legacies because of their Soviet past. Additionally, our aim is to bring out differences in the degree of historical complexity among the three states, something that has notable consequences for today's truth and justice processes.

The subsequent four chapters (Chapters 3–6) represent an attempt to cover expediently the twelve cells generated by our matrix and in empirical terms. These can also be seen as reference chapters for those seeking specific information about certain justice measures. Thus, Chapter 3 covers criminal trials against accused perpetrators of the former Soviet and Nazi regimes. We will examine here not only criminal justice legislation and a number of actual court proceedings, but also their breadth in terms of the criminal charges brought against the accused and the political-prosecutorial strategies that evolved over time. The Baltic cases are particularly interesting, because they have pushed the limit in terms of how crimes such as "genocide" should be defined and prosecuted.

Chapter 4, meanwhile, turns attention to both political-administrative and symbolic-representational measures that might be applied against erstwhile perpetrators. Here we actually cover two levels of our analytical matrix together, because these are often interlinked. In empirical terms, we will review the use of lustration policies such as purging and vetting, but also more symbolic measures such as providing incentives for self-reporting or making public the names of ex-KGB agents as well as adopting political declarations that condemn former political rulers.

Likewise, Chapter 5 will constitute a composite account of two analytical levels from our matrix. Here we will turn our attention to victim-related truth and justice measures, and look at policies that are at the criminal-legal and political-administrative levels. In other words, our focus will be on rehabilitation policies and different legal statuses for repressed persons, along with the social benefits the Baltic states have decided to accord such persons. At the same time, we will also cover property restitution, since this represents an equally political-administrative measure that states can undertake to redress victims of exproriation policies.

Chapter 6 rounds out the operationalization of our analytical matrix by looking at symbolic measures aimed at victims. These include the enactment of official commemorative days, the establishment of investigative commissions and institutes as well as state-sponsored memory collection. We will also profile the major victim organizations in the Baltic states, especially those that receive significant state funding, along with the more important government-funded museums and other historical research institutions.

Across all of these empirical chapters we take care to delineate measures that we see as representing either transitional or retrospective justice. This means, for example, that while there may have been many criminal trials against Stalinist-era repressors (retrospective justice), little has been undertaken in relation to Brezhnev-era leaders (transitional justice). Likewise, we distinguish between compensation payments that have been paid out to deportees from the 1940s as opposed to honors or benefits accorded individuals killed or injured during the 1988–91 independence struggle. These two types of benefits also say something about how the state has defined victims in historiographical terms.

Our final empirical section, Chapter 7, does not stem from our analytical matrix, but rather seeks to add an international dimension to the analysis. Namely, we will look at how Baltic truth and justice politics have reverberated in the three countries' bilateral relations with Russia, the European Union and international institutions such as the European Court of Human Rights. In this respect, we turn somewhat to the "exogenous" aspect of truth and justice politics, for many external actors have indeed taken an active interest in how the Balts have dealt with their past. At the same time, we will see how the Balts have had some success in pushing their own agenda in these international contexts. The flow of influence has not always been one-way.

In our Conclusion we will present empirical summaries of our analytical matrix for each Baltic country and then comment on the final patterns of truth and justice politics that we see. We will formulate a typological distinction between possible "etatist" vs. "inactive" patterns of truth and justice politics, and then observe where the Baltic states fall on this continuum. Foreshadowing our final empirical outcome, we will see that while Lithuania falls more toward the etatist model, Estonia leans in the other direction (though being by no means completely inactive) and Latvia exhibits a mixed pattern. With these empirical values at hand, we will reflect on what accounts for the variance across these countries as well as whether there are any consequences from these differing patterns. We will close with the observation that whereas finding determinants for diverging patterns of truth and justice politics is possible, speculating on the effects of such phenomena is a more hazardous enterprise.

1

Post-communist transitional justice: framing the subject

The model we present in this book for understanding the politics of truth and justice in post-communist societies draws on a wide range of existing strands in the literature that we argue can be brought together in a more enlightening and analytically fruitful manner than previously done. In this chapter we will outline this synthesis as well as show how it builds on the work of others. The essence of our approach is to examine the politics of truth and justice from a more holistic perspective by combining three of the phenomenon's dimensions that we believe have not been synthesized enough. While none of these dimensions is completely new in itself, the process of refining and combining them yields in our view a more powerful analytical tool for examining the politics of truth and justice.

We will start by re-examining two well-known analytical parameters in the field: the perpetrator/victim and the criminal/non-criminal dimensions of transitional justice. We will show in a first instance how these two categories can be refined and better cross-matched. Thereafter, we will outline different temporal dimensions to the politics of truth and justice, showing how it matters when a measure is passed and what kind of time period it is targeting. Alongside conventional "transitional justice," we will therefore delineate "retrospective" and "post-transitional" justice, both of which we will relate back to our matrix model. While this will turn our analytical framework into an even more intricate set of categories, the result will be a more precise and discriminating understanding of how truth and justice measures are related to each other and how they should be viewed as broad patterns of societal coming to terms with the past.

Crafting a comparative matrix of truth and justice measures

We begin with one of the more widespread dichotomies in the literature on transitional justice, that of retributive vs. restorative justice (Elster

2006; Cesarini 2009). This pair refers essentially to the fact that any instance of justice pertains by definition to both a perpetrator and a victim. Hence, it implies an obligation to examine measures that have been undertaken both to exact "retribution" upon the perpetrators and to accord "restoration" to victims. As Jon Elster (2004: 7) puts it, new regimes emerging from authoritarian rule are faced with a rather binary decision, namely "whether [or not] leaders of, collaborators with or agents of the former regime should be brought to court or otherwise penalized, and whether and how the victims of the regimes should be rehabilitated and compensated." Aviezer Tucker makes the same distinction across a pair of publications, when he speaks of "negative justice" against perpetrators and "positive justice" in relation to victims (2006a, 2006b).

We acknowledge the fact that sometimes the distinction between perpetrator and victim becomes blurred, as erstwhile perpetrators of state crimes become victims of repression themselves, or as criteria for what is right or wrong shift over time. Totalitarian regimes, especially if their rule extends over a longer period, give rise to situations that cannot be easily categorized in binary terms. However, our aim is not to put forward a normative assessment of any single perpetrator's or victim's behavior, nor is it to discuss ethical aspects of democratic state response to the many ambiguities of past wrongs – "the many shades of defeatism and opportunism" as Elster (2004: xi) calls it. Instead, the purpose of our conceptualization is to make sense of the various state measures of truth and justice and to analyze the politics of their emergence and implementation. For us, how the targets of these measures are defined and how wrongdoer and victim categories are delineated relate precisely to the political struggles that we are keen to examine.

A second classificatory axis that emerges from the literature is a distinction based on the degree to which a measure is formalized in a criminal-judicial sense. In his path-breaking compilation of transitional justice sources, Neil Kritz suggested just such a differentiation when he spoke of 'criminal' and 'non-criminal' sanctions against perpetrators (Kritz 1995a: xxv–xvi). This has been echoed across other works with the terminological pair "judicial/non-judicial," especially by scholars who juxtapose criminal trials with truth commissions (United Nations Secretary General 2004: para. 8; Bisset 2012). The essential dividing line here concerns whether the measure involves judicial (i.e. court) procedures that examine issues of criminal prosecution, or the measure enacts procedures outside the realm of formal legal accountability. Yet, whereas

Table 1.1 *A matrix interpretation of Offe's justice categories*

	Actors	Victims
Criminal law	punishment	–
Civil law	deprivation	compensation

Source: Offe (1992)

the perpetrator/victim dichotomy described earlier is relatively binary, the criminal/non-criminal pair actually leaves the second half of the distinction rather open. Indeed, there is a wide range of measures that are outside the strict criminal-judicial realm and that in our view merit additional differentiation. In our model, we will aim to enhance this parameter.

Having distilled from the literature two often-used parameters, it is striking to see how few scholars have attempted to bring these dimensions together. Claus Offe has been perhaps the most systematic thinker to contemplate the connections between these dimensions. In a relatively short 1992 publication, he mapped out the basic permutations between what he called actor/victim and criminal/civil measures. Rendered as a matrix in Table 1.1, we see how Offe delineated the ways in which a country might choose between "punishment" as a criminal measure against perpetrators, "deprivation" as a civil law approach toward perpetrators and "compensation" as non-judicial restitution for victims. Using these code words, he made sense of many of the well-known truth and justice measures such as trials, lustration and reparations.[1] However, interestingly, Offe excluded as logically impossible the fourth combination of judicial measures for victims, arguing at the time that criminal justice "is as a rule restricted to negative sanctions," hence only toward perpetrators (Offe 1992: 195).

Roughly a decade later, Noel Calhoun (2004) attempted to clarify this approach by not only presenting a formal matrix but also illustrating how rehabilitation could fall under the category of judicial measures enacted for victims. In visual form, her model is presented in Table 1.2. It conveys in a very useful manner the ways in which well-known truth and

[1] In a later publication, Offe (1997) outlined these phenomena again, although this time he referred to them as "retribution," "disqualification" and "restitution." Why he did so is unclear.

Table 1.2 *Calhoun's forms of legal redress*

	Perpetrators	Victims
Criminal law	trials	rehabilitation
Civil law	lustration	compensation

Source: Calhoun (2004: 8)

justice measures differ from each other in substantive terms. More specifically, the categories allow us to pinpoint more precisely *where* and *how* the politics of one or another measure is likely to take place. We are able to identify more immediately the likely parameters of such political struggles. We can ask questions such as what will be the stakes involved in adopting certain measures and for whom will these decisions be important?

Unfortunately, Calhoun in her work did not adopt this matrix as a formal analytical tool for evaluating her comparative cases of Eastern Germany, Poland and Russia. For example, she could have used the matrix to assess the degree to which each country engaged in the four different categories of truth and justice.[2] Thereafter, on the basis of these single measures she could have generated a composite assessment of each country's pattern of truth and justice across the matrix as a whole. Instead, Calhoun presents more stylized portrayals of the three countries and treats the notion of transitional justice overall as more a normative-philosophical issue. The potential of her matrix model remains unrealized.

At about the same time, Offe, too, began to re-craft his original insights. Writing now together with Ulrike Poppe, the two presented a re-conceptualization of the phenomenon by adhering more inherently to Kritz's distinction of criminal/non-criminal (Offe and Poppe 2005, 2006). That is, the vertical axis of the authors' new matrix no longer merely differentiated between types of law, but began with the category of what they termed "legal" measures, and then pointed to a residual category, which encompassed everything outside this point of departure. The result was a renewed reminder of the fact that states can also adopt

[2] Indeed, Jaskovska and Moran (2006) attempt to use this framework in their analysis of the Baltic states.

Table 1.3 *Types of response to past injustices, Offe and Poppe*

	Perpetrators	Victims
Legal sanctions	criminal punishment	restitution/compensation
Political sanctions	disqualification from public sector employment	"recognition"

Source: Offe and Poppe (2005: 132)

what Offe and Poppe would end up calling "political" measures, that is, measures which often have more political rather than judicial or legal meaning. This dimension was particularly relevant for highlighting the many non-criminal measures states can enact in relation to victims and which do not have direct procedural forms. Thus, in Offe and Poppe's final model, the measures illustrating each combination of axes became as shown in Table 1.3.

For Offe and Poppe, the emblematic measure involving political (non-criminal) measures for victims involved "recognition." This was in contradistinction to Calhoun's model, which contained no reference to symbolic measures. Likewise in contrast to Calhoun, compensation for victims became for Offe and Poppe a "legal" measure, alongside restitution, while rehabilitation remained outside the scope of Offe and Poppe's framework.

The outcome from these different contributions is a sense that truth and justice measures actually vary along *three* levels of consequence: criminal-judicial, political-administrative and symbolic-representational. By delineating measures in this way, we can see that there are two realms of policy outside the formal legal-judicial domain. Calhoun leads us to one (the political-administrative), and Offe and Poppe to the other (the symbolic-representational). We therefore find this combined version of the matrix to be the most useful in being able to holistically analyze the politics of truth and justice in post-communist countries.

It remains for us within this first section to note two more contributors to our thinking. Needless to say, perhaps the most comprehensive thinker on transitional justice has been Jon Elster, whose 2004 framework for studying the phenomenon encompasses no less than three "institutions of transitional justice," four "levels of transitional justice," six "decisions of transitional justice," eight "agents of transitional justice" and eleven different ways in which individuals can overlap in these agent roles and/or shift from one to another (Elster 2004: 79–135).

From our perspective, Elster's identification of three "institutions of transitional justice" appears to hint at many of the analytical categories we are aiming at. Indeed, at one point he refers to these as "explananda, or dependent variables" (2004: 116). As he writes:

> We may distinguish three institutional forms of justice: legal justice, administrative justice, and political justice. Better perhaps, we may conceptualize the institutions of justice as a continuum, with pure legal justice at one end and pure political justice at the other. Administrative justice may be closer to the legal or to the political end of the spectrum, depending on the extent to which the officials to be purged have the benefit of due process. Moreover, legal justice may be impure and still recognizably legal. Also, some forms of political justice share important features with legal justice.
>
> (Elster 2004: 84)

While on the surface it would seem that Elster is talking about categories similar to our own in terms of legal vs. political measures, the difference soon becomes apparent when we note some of the examples Elster brings. As Elster goes on to say:

> What I shall call "pure political justice" occurs when the executive branch of the new government (or an occupying power) unilaterally and without the possibility of appeal designates the wrongdoers and decides what shall be done with them.
>
> (Elster 2004: 84)

Against this backdrop we see that in reality Elster is using the word "political" to draw attention to how mercurial a transitional justice decision might be as opposed to being grounded in a certain process. Hence, his whole spectrum is about assessing the procedural integrity of a measure, not its qualitative nature.

Likewise it is worth examining Elster's six "decisions of transitional justice," which might equally serve to taxonomize the phenomenon in a more methodological manner (2004: 116–35). These decisions begin with the question of whether to engage at all in transitional justice. If so, then whether to go for "justice or truth." If it is justice, then which of the regime's previous deeds is declared as having been a crime? Do harmful acts carried out by opposition forces also count? If certain acts are punished, then in what form and with what degree of severity? If victims are compensated, then for what types of suffering, how far back in time and with what means? Although the string of choices Elster compiles is extensive, it is presented in a manner resembling a decision

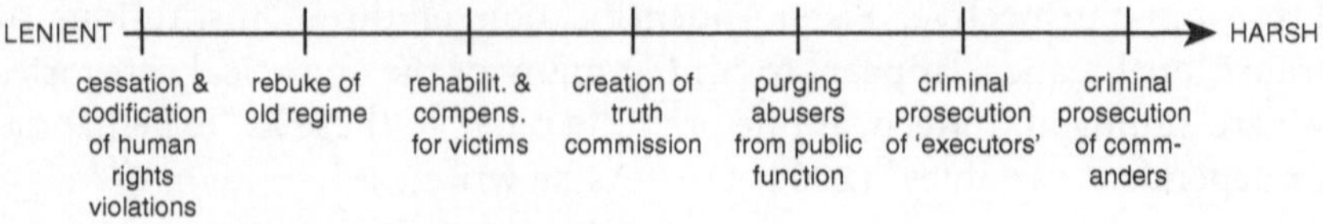

Figure 1.1 Grodsky's "Justice spectrum"
Source: Grodsky (2011: 38)

tree and therefore implies that the choices are successive. Elster also does not consider "recognition" modes of transitional justice, which may end up being a default option for democratic politicians if all other measures are precluded.

Brian Grodsky (2011) offers a similarly elaborate range of justice measures spanning from "most lenient" to "most harsh." In what he calls the "transitional justice spectrum," Grodsky ranks seven policies of post-authoritarian justice based on "the degree to which they personalize responsibility as well as by the severity of each policy's repercussions for the perpetrators" (2011: 38). Thus, his key criterion is the "severity" of justice mechanisms according to the degree of risk that new leaders take by implementing particular mechanisms vis-à-vis the former regime elites. His result is a spectrum that ranges from the most lenient "cessation and codification of human rights violations" to the harshest "criminal prosecution of commanders" (see Figure 1.1).

On the one hand, Grodsky acknowledges that this ranking allows us to organize justice measures along a victim–perpetrator continuum, since clearly the further right one moves on the scale, the more the measures begin to target perpetrators as opposed to victims. On the other hand, the real objective of Grodsky's spectrum is to incorporate the logic of power politics that stands behind each measure. With each progression from lenient to harsh measures, the risk that new governments take in possibly provoking resistance on the part of former power-holders rises.

While we find Grodsky's model a very insightful operationalization of risk and relative power arguments, it is somewhat akin to Elster's in that it focuses mainly on individual leaders' decisions to engage in transitional justice, albeit across a more operationalized spectrum. Because of this, Grodsky's notion of truth and justice politics becomes relatively narrow and does not answer the broader question of what a country's full pattern of truth and justice might be. It also implies that countries move up or down this scale of truth and justice, obscuring the fact that countries might combine measures in varying sequences.

Table 1.4 *An integrated analytical model of truth and justice measures*

	Perpetrators	Victims
Criminal-judicial	trials	rehabilitation
Political-administrative	purges/vetting	compensation/restitution
Symbolic-representational	voluntary self-reporting	recognition/truth-telling

Equally, we find incomplete the fact that Grodsky's spectrum does not include any political-administrative justice measures, such as the vetting and purging of former administrative personnel and secret police members from the new state system. To be sure, Grodsky acknowledges the importance (in both negative and positive normative terms) of lustration policies in the post-communist transitions. Yet the aim of his justice spectrum is to test the model equally on post-communist as well as post-conflict and post-authoritarian countries. Indeed, his comparative cases stretch from post-communist Poland to post-conflict Serbia/Montenegro and Croatia to post-Soviet authoritarian Uzbekistan. Although this contextual breadth is impressive, it can also be seen as problematic. As we noted in our Introduction, we believe that different non-democratic regime types contain different constellations of political actors, risks and tasks in relation to truth and justice. Hence, post-communist and post-conflict situations definitely involve differences. Likewise, it is difficult to see the merits of including a country like Uzbekistan, which has not even seen a change in leader since the Soviet era.

Drawing on the combined insights of the authors noted above, we arrive at an initial three-by-two matrix, which encompasses on the one hand the conventional perpetrator/victim distinction, while differentiating on the other between three substantive levels of truth and justice measures: criminal-judicial, political-administrative and symbolic-representational. In Table 1.4, we can see how these categories help to flesh out in a more vivid manner the way in which truth and justice measures differ from each other.

As noted above, the analytic leverage gained via this model lies in its ability to discriminate more clearly across substantive categories of truth and justice (i.e. the vertical axis). Within the realm of measures enacted against perpetrators, we know, for example, that the range of policies commonly belonging to the category of "lustration" varies widely. By differentiating between political-administrative and symbolic-representational, we can better situate measures such as the Czech Republic's very extensive vetting and purging procedures for the civil service versus more lenient systems such as Poland's "ritual of confession" (self-declarations) with minimal sanctions (David 2011: 86). Our contention is that the latter type of measure is more symbolic-representational, since it rarely has substantive political-administrative consequences.

A second advantage of our preliminary model is gained within the domain of victim-oriented measures. When comparing the two models suggested by Calhoun and Offe/Poppe, we notice that three broad categories of victim measures emerge: rehabilitation, restitution and recognition. Using our matrix, we can place these measures in separate categories, based precisely on the premise that the first involves the rectification of criminal-judicial records, the second a political-administrative decision to compensate victims or return confiscated property and the third a symbolic-representational acknowledgment of past suffering. Property restitution represents a particularly tricky type of measure in the Offe/Poppe model, since it sits uneasily in their "legal category" (as it is not comparable to court-based rehabilitations). At the same time, it is not a symbolic measure, since the return of property nationalized during the communist era can often be quite extensive and, second, it is as a rule carried out by precise administrative steps.[3]

Temporal dimensions of truth and justice

The matrix of truth and justice measures that we have outlined so far accords very well with the way "transitional justice" has been treated in a large number of countries and against the backdrop of different types of non-democratic regimes. Be it trials against former military leaders in Guatemala and Bolivia, political bans for former Nazi collaborators in postwar Belgium or Stasi informants in reunified Germany, rehabilitation of political prisoners in the Czech Republic, or forms of official recognition of victims through truth-seeking in post-apartheid South Africa, our classificatory matrix allows us to see what *combined* patterns of truth and justice measures a country might exhibit in relation to its previous regime.

[3] To be fair, Offe did treat very extensively the issue of property restitution in his 1997 book *Varieties of Transition*. However, he wrote about it as a chapter separate from his discussion of transitional justice and embedded most of the discussion within the context of economic reconstruction.

Yet embedded within this matrix are, in fact, three temporalities, or time frames, that we believe deserve further elucidation, as they inform additionally the political dynamics around specific truth and justice choices. A useful manner in which to approach this point is to disaggregate one of the more vivid understandings of "transitional justice" as put forward by Samuel P. Huntington (1991). Writing about the "torturer problem," Huntington noted that new democracies always face the difficult decision of whether or not to go after the perpetrators of abuse under the previous regime. In raising this dilemma, however, Huntington actually pointed to two temporal issues. The first involves the manner in which new democratic leaders attempt to deal with justice issues stemming from the immediately banished repressive regime. The temporal quality here involves the fact that justice is being served in relation to acts that are relatively proximate in time as opposed to those that may go back several decades. Thus, any attempt to put behind bars the last cohort of leaders of the previous regime and/or to vindicate their victims represents a focus on dealing with the recent past. By contrast, truth and justice efforts may also turn toward crimes and abuses from the more distant past, a temporal dimension that we propose to call *retrospective justice.*

Clearly the degree of retrospective justice in a given country will depend on how long the previous non-democratic regime was in power. In short-lived junta regimes (like Greece from 1967 to 1973), there will be little, at least during the early years of transition. Hence, it is all the more likely that retrospective justice issues will be present in post-communist countries, since as a rule communist domination lasted for fifty years or more, and more often than not it was accompanied by a particularly brutal period of repression during the late 1940s and early 1950s coinciding with the rule of Josif Stalin in the Soviet Union. However, this does not make retrospective justice merely a regional phenomenon or one contingent on the type of non-democratic regime that was in power. The processes of re-examining historical justice issues, for example in Spain in relation to that country's civil war as well as the subsequent Franco regime, quite readily qualify as retrospective justice (Aguilar 2008). Efforts to memorialize victims or perhaps even still find and prosecute perpetrators from some of Latin America's erstwhile military regimes would also count.

Analytically it is important to stress that where countries do have longer histories of non-democratic rule, they may actually witness truth and justice struggles in relation to *both* conventional transitional justice as well as possible retrospective justice (Grodsky 2009). Moreover, not only might both processes exist, but also their politics will likely be different. The political objective of conventional transitional justice is to sideline or vanquish those who might actually endanger the nascent democratic regime. Likewise, its objective may be to bring back into democratic society all those who until recently suffered under direct repression. In any case, it is aimed at locking in the democratic victory.

Retrospective justice, meanwhile, turns the focus toward those who also deserve justice, but who are not consequential for securing the democratic transition. Perpetrators of abuse from decades ago may still deserve to be punished, but they may by now be old and retired from active professional life. Likewise their victims may have long since been released from their imprisonment or repression, and they may have been able to resume some semblance of regular life; hence, for them, too, the justice that comes is with considerable delay. Moreover, where victims have been killed or have disappeared, the justice that is rendered is even more post-factum. Nonetheless, it is often undertaken, because it is considered right and proper by the new democratic regime. Hence, to reiterate the key point, retrospective justice can span all of the categories of our previous matrix; however, it takes place in relation to events that are in the more distant past (beyond a single generation) and involves individuals (particularly on the perpetrators' side) who are not directly linked to the viability of the new democracy.

Recalling here Grodsky's analytical spectrum, we see that transitional and retrospective justice differ also with respect to how much political capital is required to effect one or the other. It is clearly easier for nascent democratic leaders to undertake trials against long retired, low-level regime oppressors or to rehabilitate victims of repression from thirty or forty years earlier than it is to pursue powerful leaders of the previous regime or to glorify erstwhile political prisoners, who may still be controversial. Where retrospective justice issues exist, new democratic politicians may find it preferable to pursue only these measures given their lower political costs. This would seem to diminish the significance of retrospective justice as a phenomenon. However, this is precisely the point: the existence of this kind of additional or alternative realm of justice issues may help to explain why more immediate transitional justice measures are *not* pursued. Where such dual domains are present, it is important to examine both of them and be mindful of possible links between the politics within each domain. Both time frames deserve, therefore, to be brought more directly into the analysis.

It should be noted that sometimes transitional and retrospective justice may seem to overlap. An illustrative case here involves the criminal trial of Erich Mielke in Germany after reunification. As an East German police inspector during the postwar Stalinist period, Mielke was instrumental in establishing the totalitarian system, building up the *Staatssicherheit* (Stasi), of which he was head from 1957 to 1989. Mielke was thus clearly more responsible than almost anyone else for gross human rights violations carried out by the regime. However, in 1992 he was convicted not for his human rights violations during the fifty years of GDR rule, but for the murder of two police officers he had committed as a Communist activist in 1931 in Berlin. While this was clearly an example of how prosecutors at the time chose to pursue a safer strategy and prosecute for simple murder instead of framing communist-era misdeeds in terms of gross human rights violations, it was also an example of how sometimes crimes that lie farther back in time serve as substitutes for what is actually being punished. The real objective of the trial was to see one of the most notorious repressors of the East German regime behind bars and thereby also bolster the consolidation of democracy in the former GDR (Bruce 2009: 27). The Mielke trial, in our view, can therefore still be counted as a case of transitional justice.

A second temporality that is contained within Huntington's depiction of the "torturer problem" is the speed with which such initial transitional justice measures should be adopted. Huntington famously recommended that such steps should be taken within the first year of democratic rule, especially if the previous regime had been removed through "displacement" or collapse. In relation to victims, however, there are also immediate tasks such as the release of political prisoners or the need to repudiate in symbolic terms the earlier regime. The essence of the temporality here lies in the desire to leverage the political moment as much as possible. In this respect, it echoes the way in which "transitional justice" originally got its name, since most of the time these measures are adopted in the midst of a regime transition with a view to strengthening the chances of democratic consolidation. Ruti Teitel epitomized this perspective in her book *Transitional Justice*, by examining "how various legal responses *in periods of substantial political change* [emphasis added] enable the construction of normative shift" (2000: 7). She sought to highlight the way in which "[l]egal measures during such periods follow a distinctive paradigm, guided by rule-of-law principles tailored to the goal of political transformation"

(p. 213). Much of the legal acrobatics one sees when countries attempt to fashion legal-criminal cases against former regime leaders for abuses that were not so culpable during non-democratic rule illustrates the unique nature of this time period within the broader search for truth and justice.

Yet following this immediate period of reckoning, societies often return to these questions sometime after the initial democratic transition is over. As Naomi Roht-Arriazza (2006: 13) notes, "certain aspects of the transitional justice agenda will endure for many years. Transitions may happen in bouts and waves, as new generations come of age and as the international context changes. A long-term perspective is therefore essential." Struggles over issues of truth and justice may re-erupt either because of new factual revelations about the past, changing political calculations or because of evolving public opinion. Irrespective of the reason, however, it is clear that this phenomenon constitutes a second temporality as it is removed in time from the initial period of reckoning. It stretches forward in time and asks the question, with what tempo or pace do political leaders or their societies decide to attempt to come to terms with their repressive past.

Elster (2004: 75–76) sought to elucidate this dimension by drawing out three variants, calling them "protracted," "second-wave" and "postponed" transitional justice. The first characterizes for him a situation where "the [transitional justice] process starts up immediately, but then goes on for a long time until the issues are resolved." The second maintains that "[a]fter a process of immediate transitional justice, there is a latency period during which no action is taken, until, decades later, new proceedings are initiated." And the third argues that "the *first* actions are undertaken (say) ten years or more after the transition," hence after considerable delay. Unfortunately, Elster did not elaborate on these types nor did he actively incorporate them into an analytical framework for transitional justice. He noted that most post-communist countries would fall in his view into the "protracted" transitional justice category. This would imply that the disputes in the region over transitional justice constitute more or less a single stream of contestation. It would not, however, make any qualitative distinction as to how the political game might shift as these countries exit the immediate regime transition period and enter a new period of nascent democratic politics, a point to which we will return shortly.

Equally intrigued by the comparative speed and duration of truth and justice seeking have been Cath Collins (2010) and Filipa Raimundo

(2012), each of whom has sought to coin a special term for this phenomenon, "post-transitional justice." Collins' inspiration for proposing the term comes from the cases of Chile and El Salvador, in which civil society groups allied with international organizations and through the use of the domestic judicial system have challenged the legitimacy of military amnesties agreed during the initial period of democratic transition. According to Collins, these struggles represent a new type of politics of truth and justice because they take place in a new democratic context.

> [W]here transitional justice is centrally concerned with attaining and preserving the minimum institutional requirements of formal democracy, post-transitional justice focuses on subsequent questions of the quality, reach, and perfectibility of that democracy.
>
> (Collins 2010: 22)

As a consequence, Collins argues, post-transitional justice is more "multi-sited, multi-actor, and multi-referential." Raimundo, meanwhile, offers the following conceptualization:

> Post-transitional justice [is] defined as the re-introduction of the issues of the past onto the political agenda and/or the judicial sphere with the intention of changing the dominant narrative of the past, revisiting the memory of the transition and addressing the insufficiencies of transitional justice, all in compliance with the rule of law. In this conceptualization, post-transitional justice represents the adoption of measures that are meant to change the status quo on the state's approach to the past, regardless of an emphasis on the wrongdoers or the victims of the previous regime.
>
> (Raimundo 2012: 274)

With this Raimundo runs directly counter to Collins' narrow understanding of post-transitional justice as confined to (civil society) challenges in relation to initial democratization settlements as well as vis-à-vis issues of accountability. Instead she takes a much wider perspective on the purposes of later waves of transitional justice as being about changing narratives in relation both to the pre-democratic past and its collapse and to transitional justice. Moreover, her concept remains open to include measures that pertain to victims and victimizers alike. She thus offers a framework that is in many ways more suitable to accommodate the idiosyncrasies of diverse transitional justice cases. It also clearly advances our understanding of the politics of truth and justice in states that emerge from more extended authoritarian and communist regimes, both in temporal terms and in terms of the number of people involved in past wrongs.

In this book, we acknowledge these different approaches by adhering most of all to the temporal baselines highlighted by Collins, while adopting some of the analytical substance offered by Raimundo. This means that we suggest a starting point for cases of post-transitional justice as soon as the basic tenets of democracy have been established in a country (echoing Collins', "the minimum institutional requirements of formal democracy"). At the same time, we seek to assess each change in transitional justice measures against a backdrop of how significantly it alters either a historical narrative or past political agreements on truth and justice.

The reason for the first criterion comes again from the literature on democratization. More than two decades ago, Guillermo O'Donnell (1992) reminded scholars that there is a difference between the initial assumption of power by democratic political forces in a country, the subsequent period of initial stabilization among those forces and finally the eventual consolidation of the democratic system.[4] All too often scholars have divided democratization into merely two phases, seeing the initial power triumph by democrats and the stabilization of their power as one stage, while consolidation represents (depending on the strictness of one's definition) a period that starts right after the initial phase is over (Raimundo 2013: 138). We believe that in fact a tripartite temporal distinction is crucial in order to see how the politics of truth and justice change once political and social actors begin to shift their mental perspective from the immediate need to secure a democratic transition to one of operating in a nascent, but not yet necessarily stabilized, democratic political environment. The rhetoric, allies and resources that various political groups will draw upon to begin a new effort at truth and justice at this point will be different from the previous period. However, this should not be confused with democratic consolidation, since most definitions of this phenomenon require (and rightly so) more substantive institutional or behavioral thresholds to be reached (Valenzuela 1992). In short, rather than take the state of consolidation as our reference for identifying cases of post-transitional justice, we take the *end of transition* as the basic separation point for

[4] See also Schedler (2001).

delineating a new period in the political dynamics surrounding truth and justice issues.[5]

At the same time, we are sensitive to Raimundo's more substantive definition of post-transitional justice as it derives from the desire to give the phenomenon empirical import and to avoid characterizing any small change in truth and justice measures as post-transitional. In this respect Raimundo's selection of Spain (2007) and Poland (2005–2006) as cases allows her to profile a seemingly new concept, since the countries represent an extreme value on that phenomenon. We see with greater clarity the ways in which political struggles for post-transitional justice can have far-reaching consequences for truth discourses and broader narratives. Still, it is worth acknowledging that such instances of extensive post-transitional justice as in Spain and Poland are rare.

The relevance of these different nuances of post-transitional justice for our empirical analysis is twofold. First, because we take a composite view of truth and justice measures in a country, our unit of analysis is slightly different from when one applies the concept merely to a single measure such as lustration. When looking at patterns of truth and justice, post-transitional justice would seem to have to mean that all of the measures in such a composite should involve a reformulation of existing narratives or a transformation of the status quo. This, however, would clearly be too high a benchmark to make such a concept useful. We therefore prefer to operationalize the concept in our context by asking whether one or more realms of truth and justice indeed undergo major transformation, and also whether other realms see at least an intensification of policy measures, which taken together show that a major reassessment of *Vergangenheitsbewältigung* is going on. In the chapters that follow, we will see that only Lithuania comes close to having a period of

[5] In this respect, we critique Raimundo's work (2012) for an incorrect determination of the proper starting point for Poland's case(s) of post-transitional justice. Her temporal criterion for post-transitional justice is in reality democratic consolidation, which she then dates in the case of Poland to 1997 when the country adopted a new constitution. By doing so, however, she characterizes the adoption of a lustration law in that same year as part of the end of the "transition" and not as part of "post-transition." We find this arguable, since in fact there is plenty of evidence to argue that despite the lack of party system consolidation throughout the 1990s, Poland's initial transition to democracy ended in the mid-1990s (with the acceptance of the ex-communists' return to power and their subsequent adherence to the basic democratic rules) and that therefore the 1997 lustration law was Poland's first instance of post-transitional justice. The 2005/2006 campaign started by the Kaczynski brothers thus constitutes a second wave of post transitional justice. See also Raimundo (2013).

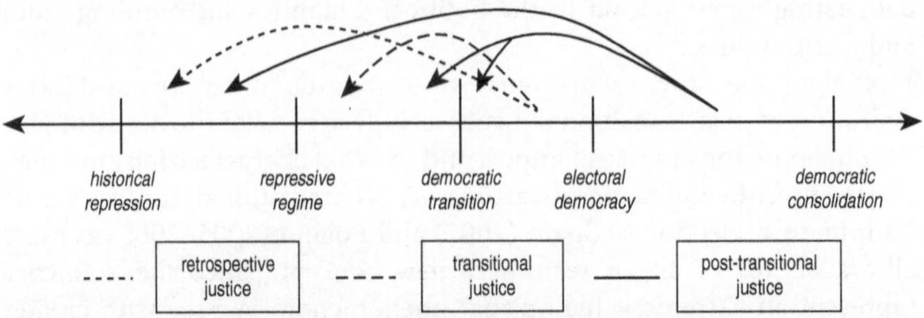

Figure 1.2 Three temporalities of post-communist truth and justice

post-transitional justice when, beginning in November 1996, the new national-conservative government in power undertook a major overhaul of victim-oriented measures, and most importantly, introduced for the first time a broadscale lustration policy that included targeting the private sector. These changes constitute for us an important reorientation of both previous policies and understandings of truth and justice in the country. We will return to this evaluation in the Conclusion.

Summarizing our argument about the three temporalities of truth and justice policies, we may note that the first two, retrospective and transitional justice, differ in character from the third one, post-transitional justice. Whereas the first two serve to delineate distinct temporal perspectives toward the past, the third actually denotes the same phenomena of retrospective and transitional justice, but simply from the standpoint of when, in relation to the initial transition, these efforts take place (as well as their intensity). Under our definition of post-transitional, this phenomenon may take place repeatedly and in relation to both retrospective and transitional justice; however, the point is that it takes place after the end of the initial establishment of a democratic regime. In graphic form these perspectives are depicted in Figure 1.2.

The final piece in our puzzle involves relating these temporalities back to the analytical matrix presented earlier. If we acknowledge that democratic regimes may undertake truth and justice measures in relation to both their recent and their distant non-democratic past, we must proceed to split our matrix into additional parts. We propose to do this as represented in Table 1.5, where we have now divided the perpetrator and victim columns to differentiate between retrospective and transitional justice variants. Needless to say, this change doubles the size of our matrix. However, it allows us to render more accurately the range of measures available to politicians as well as the relationships between them.

Our third temporality of truth and justice, that is, changes in these policies during the years and decades following democratic transition, is embedded within each cell of our final matrix depending on whether years later political leaders decide either to initiate, intensify, soften or abandon a certain class of measures. To depict this temporality in a visual manner (and thereby be able to better compare countries) is more complicated without establishing a clear scale on which to assess the intensity of a particular measure. It is, of course, a well-known approach in political science to rank qualitative phenomena using ordinal scales. This is, indeed, the essence of Grodsky's scale depicted in Figure 1.1. However, even with a sequential ordering of values, we are never quite clear whether the distance between any given pair of measures is the same as the distance between any other pair. In the Conclusion of our book, therefore, we limit ourselves to evaluating changes in truth and justice policies in descriptive terms.

A final dimension concerning the coding or classification of measures across our matrix relates to the legal level at which a measure is adopted. Whereas most truth and justice measures are enacted at the level of national parliaments (and are then implemented through government decrees or even local government regulations), it is possible to enshrine certain truth and justice principles in a country's constitution. This pertains particularly to political measures (such as office bans) or symbolic gestures (such as a national condemnation of the past regime). Needless to say, it is more difficult to imagine this degree of codification for measures such as property restitution or criminal trials. However, it is true that the politics of truth and justice has often become constitutionalized in many post-communist countries. Both Poland's 1997 constitution and Hungary's more recent 2011 constitution contain explicit references to truth and justice issues. In our analysis of the Baltic states, we will come across this phenomenon when we examine how Estonia tried to institute an office ban within its new constitution in 1992. However, apart from this particular policy, constitutionalization has not been a relevant phenomenon.

Mapping out the full matrix

The twelve boxes that are generated by our reconstitution of key parameters of truth and justice (Table 1.5) deserve examination one by one in order to appreciate the usefulness and diversity of the model. We have labeled the cells with numbers and letters to make referencing easier. We

Table 1.5 *A full matrix of post-communist truth and justice*

	Perpetrators		Victims	
	Retrospective	*Transitional*	*Retrospective*	*Transitional*
Criminal-judicial	1a • Establishing legal frameworks • Criminal investigations and prosecutions of "historical" perpetrators	1b • Establishing legal frameworks • Investigations and prosecutions of erstwhile regime perpetrators	4a • Legal rehabilitations (incl. posthumous) of victims of decades-old political trials and repression	4b • Legal rehabilitations of recent political convicts • Release of political prisoners
Political-administrative	2a • Removing privileges or benefits for former regime oppressors or officials	2b • Purges, office bans, and vetting of former secret police agents (and informers) and/or high regime officials	5a • Awarding of special benefits for victims of decades-old repression • Restitution of property nationalized decades earlier	5b • Awarding of special benefits for political prisoners and other recently repressed victims • Restitution of their property, if confiscated
Symbolic-representational	3a • Condemnation of past regime and/or crimes • Non-judicial determination of responsibilities for historical crimes; disclosure of names	3b • Voluntary self-reporting, name disclosure (public shaming); official condemnation of Communist Party • non-judicial investigations revealing mechanisms of abuse	6a • Public remembrance days and rituals for victims • Official apology / declaration of regret • Historical truth-seeking, research and remembrance	6b • Official truth-seeking and truth-telling • Public remembrance • Access for victims to personal secret police records

will also refer to these boxes continually in our chapters. Boxes 1a and 1b define criminal-judicial measures against perpetrators accused of repression either in the distant past or more recently. We have already noted that for new democratic leaders it is often difficult to exercise criminal justice against more recent leaders of a non-democratic regime. Indeed, in many cases these ex-leaders will have negotiated for themselves explicit amnesties before leaving power. Thus, this box frequently becomes a case of post-transitional justice or policies undertaken many years after democracy has been established, when activists demand that amnesties be rescinded and/or trials initiated. Still, the whole question of amnesties becomes an interesting conceptual issue from the perspective of our matrix as well. In essence, an amnesty represents a legal commitment *not* to engage in a certain justice measure. It goes beyond a decision to simply forgo any trials; it constitutes a public agreement to take a certain measure off the table. We note, therefore, that amnesties are embedded in our matrix as something more than simply the absence of any trials in Box 1b. However, we do not bring it out as explicitly as some other researchers.[6]

In terms of empirical reference points within Central and Eastern Europe, the criminal proceedings and trials against Erich Honecker and Willi Stoph in Germany, Generals Czeslaw Kiszczak and Wojciech Jaruzelski in Poland or Todor Zhivkov in Bulgaria come to mind, but also the various trials against higher- and lower-rank German officials, who ordered and carried out the shooting of people trying to cross the German–German border (Quint 2000). Interestingly, we see relatively few cases of criminal-judicial retrospective justice in Central Europe (Box 1a). The Stalinist period clearly brought great repression to the region, including show trials, political imprisonment, executions, torture and deportation; however, so far few of these countries have been able to prosecute these crimes with any systemic effort. Legislative initiatives were made in Hungary during the immediate transition period, when members of the Democratic Forum proposed a bill that would amend the criminal code to lift statutes of limitation for past offenses that amounted to crimes even by the legal standards under Communism, yet had not been prosecuted previously for political reasons. Though the law covered

[6] See Olsen et al. (2010a). For example, the Transitional Justice Database lists trials and amnesties as separate measures, and Olsen and her colleagues find that it is the combination of trials and amnesties that works best for promoting human rights and democracy. From the perspective of our matrix, however, these two measures are essentially one and the same box.

crimes committed as far back as the immediate postwar years, most of the crimes that would have fallen under the law had been committed during and after the failed uprising in 1956 (Stan 2009b). The law never came into force as it was struck down by the Constitutional Court that took a rather legalistic approach, referring to principles of rule of law as well as an insufficient legal conception of treason employed in the law (Sadurski 2003). In 1993 the parliament adopted the much narrower Law on Procedures in the Matter of Certain Criminal Offenses during the 1956 October Revolution and Freedom Struggle (Law 90/1993), the basic provisions of which did succeed in passing constitutional scrutiny. It allowed prosecutors to file charges against individual perpetrators of violent acts (e.g. shooting into crowds of protesters) on the basis of international humanitarian law and universal norms, framing these acts of violence as crimes against humanity and even war crimes for which statutory limitations do not exist (Kiss 2013: 233). However, the number of criminal proceedings started on the basis of this law has been small, and even fewer court convictions have followed. Likewise, Romanian authorities pressed charges in September 2013 against Alexandru Visinescu, who at the age of 88 was indicted for nothing less than "genocide" for his role in running the Ramnicu Sarat prison from 1956 to 1963 and thereby being responsible for the systematic repression of regime opponents (Higgins 2013). However, here too the indictment represented an isolated case, since very few retrospective justice trials have taken place in Romania; instead, the country focused on repression connected with the December 1989 revolution (Stan 2013: 29–57).

All of these cases highlight a special characteristic of retrospective justice in the criminal-judicial domain. On the one hand, these attempts at justice are often severely hampered because of statutes of limitation or constraining principles of the rule of law, such as the prohibition of retroactive punishment (*nullum crimen sine lege*). As a consequence, prosecutors sometimes attempt to base their investigations on charges that are in fact much more controversial or far-reaching, such as genocide or crimes against humanity. As we will note later in Chapter 3, there are trade-offs to this kind of prosecutorial approach. While the publicity and appearance of resolve that is gained from such indictments is very powerful, it is not always evident that prosecutors will actually succeed in proving such charges in court. To be sure, the definitions of genocide and crimes against humanity have become more diverse over the last two decades, not only because of investigations into horrific cases like Rwanda or Srebrenica, but also because some of the Balts' investigations into their era of Stalinist repression have shown that such judicial categories are not merely hyperbole or political rhetoric. Hence, one of the ironies of criminal-judicial retrospective justice in post-communist Europe is that where it emerges, it is likely to take precisely such extensive prosecutorial dimensions because the degree of repression during the Stalinist era was so severe and systematic. It becomes almost incumbent upon prosecutors to charge such perpetrators with genocide or crimes against humanity because the repression was so methodical. Naturally, there are also lesser degrees of criminal-judicial retrospective and transitional justice in that politicians may establish the necessary legal frameworks for such inquiries or even indictments, but prosecutors never take up such efforts. Likewise, prosecutors might agree to open up a few investigations, but they never actually press charges, either because of political timidity or because prosecutors are simply overwhelmed by the resource requirements of investigating such cases (given the need to find surviving witnesses and securing testimony, archival documents or other evidence). Lastly, of course, prosecutors may go to trial, but know already that their arguments are weak and therefore they ultimately lose their case. In Chapter 3 we will see that the Baltic states (and in particular Lithuania) have pursued quite an extensive policy of criminal-judicial retrospective justice. Part of this is explained by the extreme severity of Stalinist repression (to be outlined in Chapter 2). Equally, the fact that this repression was carried out by an external force (the Soviet repressive regime), under what has since been internationally acknowledged as an illegal occupation, has allowed charges such as genocide or crimes against humanity to be applied with much greater ease, as they could be cast in terms of universal jurisdiction enshrined in international humanitarian law. Stalinist repression was not simply a national communist regime suppressing its own people; rather, it was arguably a foreign power subjugating neighboring nations through systematic killing and terror. At the same time, these facts notwithstanding, the Baltic states' decision to pursue perpetrators of repression from the 1940s and 1950s has been a conscious policy choice, the origins and evolution of which we will examine.

Turning to Boxes 2a and 2b, we see that political-administrative measures may also vary across efforts at retrospective and transitional justice in a way that is not merely a function of the time the repression was committed. Clearly, the more familiar of these two boxes is 2b, which covers many of the measures of purging, vetting, screening and disclosure often referred to as "lustration." In this book we will disaggregate the phenomenon analytically by using the distinction between political-administrative and symbolic-representational policies. We will see that the purging of former regime officials from political office or civil service constitutes a very obvious case of political-administrative justice against perpetrators in that these people are directly deprived of a livelihood in positions of public trust. By contrast, measures such as voluntary self-reporting by former regime operatives (together with, for example, promises by the authorities to keep the details of these past deeds a state secret) are often included under the umbrella of lustration but are, in fact, symbolic actions, since persons who refuse to self-report their past involvement with the secret police are not actually prevented from pursuing public office in the future. They are merely shamed by having their names revealed in public.

In Box 2a, we see that policies of purging or vetting (familiar in the cases of transitional justice) are unlikely to take place vis-à-vis perpetrators of decades-old misdeeds, since these individuals are unlikely to be in public office anymore, nor are they likely to want to pursue such office. At the same time, democratic politicians may want to recompense their inability to press criminal charges against such perpetrators by stripping them of whatever privileges or benefits they may still enjoy. For example, Elster (2004: x) notes that in 1990 the Polish Sejm reportedly decided to downgrade the special state pensions previously awarded to Communist Party members to those given to average citizens.

At the symbolic-representational level (Boxes 3a and 3b), we record those measures that are aimed at bringing out the names of perpetrators as well as describing their role in repression, but without inflicting greater retribution toward them apart from public disgrace. Such policies often start with official condemnations of either the past regime or of specific past crimes and then stress in particular the moral responsibility held by former regime officials. The objective is to cast an unequivocal reproach toward all those associated with the past system (and not just to commemorate victims, as will be discussed later). As noted earlier, those policies that call on former regime operatives to make themselves known to the democratic authorities constitute also a symbolic approach to transitional justice, especially if they are accompanied with a promise not to take any punitive action. These policies cause discrete embarrassment and perhaps even contrition on the part of the perpetrator, but have no professional or criminal consequences.

Farther down this scale are policies aimed at publicizing the names of former regime operatives, irrespective of their consent. A mild version of such a policy involves naming special state commissions to detail the mechanisms of regime repression as well as to bring out the involvement of certain individuals. This kind of method would pertain relatively equally to both retrospective and transitional justice with the main difference being that the individuals named in relation to decades-old crimes are likely to have already passed away. Nonetheless, the main tenet of such a policy would be to entrust the publication of names to a group of experts, at whose discretion it would be to present the information. A more radical approach involves the proverbial "throwing open of the files," in which authorities decide to make all existing documentation available to the public with little supplementary screening or contextualization. Here there is an interesting difference between retrospective and transitional justice. As we will see in Chapter 4, it is one thing to make public thousands of names and documents involving the KGB and its operations during the 1940s and 1950s (as has been done in Lithuania); it is quite another to decide to open recent KGB files unselectively (as was temporarily decided in Latvia).

Switching now to the victims' dimension of truth and justice, we note that Boxes 4a and 4b share the same legal-procedural objective of clearing the names of those falsely convicted by the past regime. However, the people involved are different. Those individuals who suffered from decades-old repression will frequently see their rehabilitation as taking place long after the fact. For more recent political prisoners or dissidents, the righting of their criminal record may carry greater import, since other legal restrictions may continue to apply to them as long as these prior convictions remain on the books. One good example here is that alongside convictions for criminal offenses such as anti-regime activities (often termed in the communist context "hooliganism"), many regime opponents were also punished through psychiatric diagnoses and incarceration in mental institutions. Such offenses are frequently more difficult to rehabilitate; however, they may have equally serious consequences for victims later on if, because of these false diagnoses, such individuals are prevented from applying for certain jobs or obtaining a driver's license.

In the case of rehabilitation under retrospective justice, it is worth noting that the politics behind this kind of measure will often follow a collective logic. Initially, democratic politicians will adopt blanket rehabilitation measures in order to cover as many people as quickly as possible. This is clearly an indication of the fact that such measures have low political costs for politicians, as posited by Grodsky. But they also have pitfalls if the rehabilitation is done too hastily or indeed too superficially. On the one hand, certain people who did violate laws may slip through the cracks and be accorded recognition they do not deserve. Likewise, genuine victims may be at a loss when trying to obtain a formal certificate of their rehabilitation, since politicians and government officials have not bothered or have been unable to work out precise administrative procedures after solemn restorative proclamations have been issued.

Indeed, a logical next step for many democratic regimes is to follow up their legal-criminal rehabilitation procedures with political-administrative compensation or benefits for such victims (Boxes 5a and 5b). In its more systematized and individualized form, victims may be accorded a special "repressed person's" status, which may include not only an official identification card but also any range of social or medical benefits. The latter might encompass supplementary pension payments, free or reduced-cost medical treatment and/or special privileges as part of privatization. (For example, time spent as a repressed person counts extra in terms of calculating the length of a person's period of adult employment and therefore his/her eligibility for privatization vouchers.) An additional aspect here involves whether the spouses or children of victims are covered under such benefits, and if so, in what regard. From a political point of view, democratic politicians may be in a better position to undertake political-administrative measures for more recent regime victims (transitional justice), since their number may be smaller and the precise details of injustice clearer. Political-administrative justice in relation to retrospective suffering may end up costing the nascent democracy much more financially, although many victims may already be of old age or passed away. Much of the outcome here will depend on the strength of civil society organizations representing such victim groups. Likewise, the structure of the party system will be important, that is, whether anti-communist parties are strong enough to mobilize such groups electorally.

A much more serious dilemma arises in the juxtaposition of political-administrative retrospective and transitional justice when we consider how to restitute property nationalized or confiscated by the earlier regime. For dissidents or other recent political prisoners, it is likely that their property will have remained intact and can be immediately returned or will at least be subject to easy assessment for purposes of compensation. In cases of retrospective justice, democratic politicians may feel obliged to restitute or compensate property lost by those repressed or deported, even if this repression took place decades ago and assessing the value of such property becomes extremely difficult. It is important to note here how the political dynamics are linked. The rehabilitation of past victims on a legal-criminal level rarely stops with just that. It often becomes an irresistible consequence that the new democratic state takes on responsibility for also righting property injustices.

Moreover, in the post-communist context property restitution goes one step further, involving the way in which all of the communist regimes of Central and Eastern Europe began their rule by nationalizing most types of private property, be it businesses, homes or land. Dealing with this aspect of retrospective justice has meant broadening the category of victim to still more people, many of whom may not have been repressed in any other way except for having lost property to nationalization. What is more, since property is subject to inheritance, its restitution can bring into play the offspring of those originally victimized. Put most starkly, certain people may only realize their "victim" status once a restitution policy is passed, and with that second- or even third-generation claimants are made eligible. For democratic politicians, this represents an important policy choice.

Our final boxes, 6a and 6b, examine state-led policies involving the symbolic-representational acknowledgment of victims. Our aim here is to be as clear as possible in our usage, since we are cognizant of the fact that this final category opens a gateway to a number of phenomena, which our study will not cover. First, we know that by developing and promoting policies acknowledging the victims of a past repressive regime, democratic governments are also influencing historical narratives and memory discourses in society. Indeed, more broadly one could say that states are even engaging in national myth construction when they choose to officially memorialize certain types of victims and not others. Our analysis, however, will not take the discussion to this level, since our objective is to map out the politics surrounding the genesis and implementation of policies involving retrospective and transitional justice. The broader implications of these policies for national identity construction must remain outside our purview. A second borderline involves the way in which state recognition of victims influences the development of social memory or the manner in which the past is understood by society. By instituting certain remembrance policies and commemorative practices, the state is helping to determine the elements of the past that citizens will retain in their consciousness. When the state establishes certain commemorative days or allocates money for the erection of a monument to families deported from a certain village, it is signaling to the populace at large that these facts should be retained in their social memory. At the same time, we know that social memory as such is a much broader construct, involving influences from civil society groups (say, erecting their own private monuments), the media and pop culture (via special broadcasts, documentaries, cinematic productions, stage performances or literature), as well as from family interactions and communicative patterns. In short, while recognizing that state policies in the symbolic-representational realm are part of a wider phenomenon of social memory, our analysis will not extend to how truth and justice issues evolve within this overarching sphere.

These points raise some tricky questions about what to include in Boxes 6a and 6b. First and foremost, the two boxes encompass any kind of official statement expressing condemnation, regret or apology for the suffering of victims under the previous regime. Needless to say, such statements can occur repeatedly, especially if they are linked to commemorative days or driven by political motives. By the same token, they are collective in that they usually address all victims in equal measure. Moreover, because they are issued as public documents, their effect is felt by not only individual victims but also society as a whole. By contrast, policies that acknowledge victims individually through specific ceremonies or acts of remembrance get much closer to the heart of the matter. They aim at creating a direct link between the new democratic polity and the victim of the prior regime.

An equally ambiguous mode of state recognition involves the creation of truth commissions or historical commissions. For simplicity's sake, we use the first term to refer to commissions established for the purposes of transitional justice, while the second is linked to retrospective justice. In other words, truth commissions are about recognizing more recent victims of the repressive regime and investigating their patterns of suffering, while historical commissions are focused on more distant periods or sometimes specific instances of state abuse. Irrespective of their temporal perspective, however, such commissions can also work on both the collective and the individualized level. Their final reports will often summarize the past regime and thereby influence the national narrative on the past. At the same time, state commissions, especially those concerned with more recent human rights violations, can be tasked with (or they can take on the role of) truth-telling, where victims are allowed to describe the nature of their suffering directly to the body. If the state establishes commissions with such powers, it is contributing very tangibly to helping victims obtain justice. The only qualification here is that historically (or retrospectively) oriented truth bodies may be limited in their ability to speak to primary witnesses or obtain victim statements given that many of these victims will have passed away. In such instances, commissions end up having a rather academic character as well as a more collective effect by focusing on the development of a historical narrative concerning past injustice (Pettai 2015).

Other individualized measures include allowing victims to see the information or files gathered about them by the erstwhile security service. This is perhaps one of the most immediate ways of individual-level truth-revelation as former victims of interrogations, torture, manipulation or surveillance by state organs learn about what was done to them and, in some cases, by whom. The often cathartic effects are palpable as victims can "re-appropriate stolen aspects of their lives" and get a sense of closure (Lewis 2003). From this perspective formal regulations of file access for individuals who suffered under the previous regime clearly belong among the essential, albeit symbolic, measures of truth and justice.

Few post-totalitarian states have allowed access to personal secret police files in as comprehensive a fashion as Germany with the establishment of the *Stasiunterlagenbehörde* in 1992. Then again, in few other cases have the records of the former state security apparatus been so completely preserved as in the former GDR. In most other states files were either destroyed or secretly removed by outgoing authorities. Moreover, any remaining interrogation protocols, monitoring reports or secret agent/informant lists are usually encoded and sorted in a way that makes their exact content hard to decipher. Thus, apart from general issues of reliability and the value of such documents that is usually discussed in the literature on lustration (Grodsky 2011: 58–73), allowing access to these files requires the installment of proper mechanisms and personnel, an expense which affects policy choices in this domain.

Summary

An important analytical premise of this book is that democratic polities that seek to "come to terms with their past" often face a wide range of questions and dilemmas. Multiple levels of policy choice and consequence are involved, not only in the immediate transition period but also years later. These should not be kept in isolation or examined as discrete phenomena. Rather, we should seek to bring them together as a whole. In 2004, Jon Elster offered a magisterial overview of these issues in his work *Closing the Books*. However, in our view the analysis remained under-systematized, particularly in terms of how we might be able to relate different truth and justice measures to each other. Most precisely, we lacked a framework for discerning *patterns* of truth and justice in different countries, which would allow us to begin the process of comparison across countries and across erstwhile non-democratic regimes. The twelve-box matrix that we gradually developed in this chapter and that we summarize in Table 1.5 takes us a step further toward this goal.

This conceptual matrix does not yet generate the patterns themselves, since these can only be determined via empirical investigation. Thus, for example, the answer to the question, to what extent will democratic politicians faced with issues of both retrospective and transitional justice end up privileging one domain over the other, will depend on multiple factors yet to be explored. However, it is important to begin by bringing the relevant analytical dimensions together. This has now been done, and we have in hand a conceptual tool with which we can conceivably analyze any country that faces issues of truth and justice. These measures can be mapped across our matrix and then compared to other country cases or over time. To be sure, some countries may face fewer challenges concerning retrospective justice, since the number of more distant human rights abuses may be lower. Post-authoritarian democracies may also differ from post-communist democracies (not to mention post-conflict situations) in terms of the proportions of different measures. However, through our matrix these cases do become broadly comparable across a set of baseline parameters.

In the next chapters we will attempt to illustrate this via the three Baltic states. Estonia, Latvia and Lithuania afford particularly good cases for this task, since all too often they have been seen as a single identity. Yet by using our analytical model, we can discern in a ready and precise fashion how different they actually are. This, in turn, offers an opportunity to explain these differences and to clarify interrelationships between individual measures. Yet before entering into this empirical analysis we provide in the next chapter a historical overview of the Baltic states and in particular an examination of how their status as former Soviet republics has affected their politics of transitional and retrospective justice.

2

Comparable or incomparable: placing the Baltic states in context

The Baltic states are often difficult for scholars to place in a comparative context – both historically and politically. For some, they are part of the swath of Central and Eastern European countries that became free with the collapse of communism, began a transition to democracy via open elections, eventually joined NATO and the European Union, and by now are partially integrated into the Eurozone. In other words, they are readily comparable to the better-known Visegrad countries or to the Balkans. For others, the point of departure is the Baltics' history as Soviet Socialist Republics, their more direct subjugation to Soviet Russian rule, and hence a more indecipherable image as post-Soviet states easily lumped together with the Commonwealth of Independent States. Each of these two portrayals is partially right; the Baltic states cannot be put unambiguously into one category or the other. Indeed, as we will see in this chapter, this duality becomes particularly clear in the case of post-communist truth and justice. However, because we aim to contribute to the comparative study of this phenomenon, these similarities and differences require elucidation. This chapter will thus provide a comparative contextualization of the Baltic historical trajectories as well as of key political aspects that are important for understanding these countries' post-communist truth and justice processes.

There are many points and experiences of history which align the Baltic states to those of Central Europe. For one, the advent of modern statehood for practically all of the peoples of the region was a product of the near simultaneous collapse of the Ottoman, Habsburg and Czarist empires. The histories of contemporary Latvian or Czech, Estonian or Polish statehood all date roughly from 1918–20. Modern political development for these nations started largely along similar trajectories. This parallelism includes the travails of trying to establish democracy when no such prior experience existed. In this sense there is nothing particularly surprising about the fact that the democracy of one Central

European nation and one Baltic nation were among the first to collapse when, in 1926, Józef Piłsudski and Antanas Smetona staged military coups in Poland and Lithuania, respectively, and established authoritarian dictatorships. In Latvia and Estonia democracy lasted slightly longer, but in 1934 these countries, too, succumbed to breakdown, as Kārlis Ulmanis and Konstantin Päts seized control of their countries' presidencies and installed similarly personalistic authoritarian regimes. If viewed from the perspective of the late 1930s, therefore, nearly all of the countries in Central and Eastern Europe shared an ambivalent legacy of democratic dawn and authoritarian twilight.

It was only with the events of the 1939–40 period that the Baltic states would come to endure a particular fate – one that would also have a distinct effect on their future politics of truth and justice. The agreement between Hitler and Stalin on August 23 (or rather September 28) 1939 to divide up Finland, Poland and the Baltic states as part of a secret annex to their official Non-Aggression Pact led to the Baltic states falling under Soviet Communist rule earlier than the rest of Eastern Europe.[1] After first forcing Estonia and Latvia to sign "mutual assistance treaties" with the Soviet Union in September and finally Lithuania in October 1939 and then establishing, on the basis of these treaties, military bases in all three countries, Moscow ultimately launched a full-scale occupation of the territories in June 1940. This complete military control of Estonia, Latvia and Lithuania then allowed the Soviets to rig special elections in July, which finally led to puppet governments "requesting" to become part of the USSR in August (Hiden and Salmon 1994).[2] For Lithuania the mutual assistance pact with the Soviet Union held yet another

[1] In the wake of the Hitler–Stalin Pact, Nazi Germany concluded agreements with the independent Baltic states to bring the national minorities of Baltic Germans "*heim ins Reich*," which in reality meant the resettlement of tens of thousands of people to the newly German-occupied territories of Poland, the so-called Warthegau. An estimated 14,000 people from Estonia and 52,000 from Latvia left the region, not all of them voluntarily as they had to give up properties and social positions (Kasekamp 2010). In 1941 another 52,000 Germans, mostly farmers of East Prussia, were "repatriated" from Lithuania.

[2] The 1939–40 decision-making processes and the question of why the Baltic leadership "meekly acquiesced to Soviet demands" (Kasekamp 2010: 127) still preoccupies historians and social scientists wondering why the Baltic leadership did not go the Finnish way or at least show more substantial resistance to the forced takeover. The weakness of the authoritarian governments that had successfully paralyzed civic and political life in the countries and a lack of strong international alliances, combined with a realistic assessment of the countries' military and civil capacities to resist without enormous human costs are usually seen as the main reasons (Senn 2007).

dimension, as it included negotiations over the fate of Vilnius, then part of Poland, which had been occupied by the Soviet Army in September 1939. Watching Poland collapse under the German attack and the Red Army taking over the Vilnius region, the political elite saw a prospect of "regaining Lithuania's capital," which was widely seen as having been occupied by Poland since 1920–22. The eventual acceptance of Soviet troops on Lithuanian territory was later justified, at least partially, with this aspiration (Senn 2007: 25). Indeed, in late October 1939 Vilnius was "given" to Lithuania by the Soviets. One could thus say that the country's occupation by the Soviet Union was somewhat sweetened by the fact that Vilnius finally became part of the independent state – albeit only for a short period, as in the space of barely a year Lithuania itself was annexed to the USSR.

Today, "near universal academic and international consensus" reigns about the illegal character of the events of 1939–40 and the overall process of Baltic incorporation into the USSR (Purs 2013: 19). Already at the time neither the US nor the British governments would recognize the annexation of the Baltic states into the USSR, and both countries would maintain (together with many other Western governments) a so-called "non-recognition policy" throughout the Cold War period (Van Elsuwege 2003; Plakans 2011: 346). Hence, this fact, too, would become part of the Baltics' perspective on their past. More specifically, it would be molded into a special doctrine of "legal continuity" of statehood, to which we will return later.

The relevant point at this stage is that the Soviet Communist experience for the Baltic states not only started earlier than in other Central European states, who experienced the terror of Stalinization only after the war, but was also more immanent and direct. The Soviet occupation in 1940 started with widespread extra-judicial arrests, political trials, executions and disappearances of military and political opponents, including government ministers and even presidents, who were either sentenced to death or imprisonment for alleged "anti-communist crimes" or simply interned in faraway regions within the USSR (Šneidere 2005). Real estate and private savings above a specified level together with large industrial enterprises, banks and agricultural lands were nationalized, religious organizations were put under special scrutiny and freedom of expression was severely restricted. Any form of protest against these measures was suppressed through "a steady rate of monthly political arrests," carried out by the Soviet security organs (Õispuu 1996a; Anušauskas 2003a; Šneidere 2005; Purs 2013: 25).

The widespread terror inflicted on these countries during the first year of Soviet rule – still called in Latvia "the year of horror" or *baigais gads* – culminated in June 1941 in a mass deportation of several thousand more "dangerous elements" from all three republics. This first mass deportation is perhaps the most thoroughly researched event in Baltic historical scholarship, as for Baltic historians and politicians it constitutes "the first clear proof of the Soviet Union's intent to destroy Estonia, Latvia and Lithuania" (Purs 2013: 27). It targeted the politically and economically active elites of the three states (Lithuanians, Latvians and Estonians) as well as members of minorities, especially many Jews. Many of these people, mostly men, were imprisoned without any official charges; many more were later killed in Russia without trial or died of deprivation and hardship. Few returned from this first mass deportation (Plakans 2011: 347). As we show in Table 2.1 below, the estimated number of people that suffered massive human rights violations, including imprisonment, torture, extra-judicial execution, deportation and forced exile between June 1940 and June 1941 reaches over 17,500 in Estonia, 22,000 in Latvia and 30,400 in Lithuania. These numbers do not include several tens of thousands of men forcefully recruited into the Red Army (many of whom perished in labor battalions), last-minute executions of political prisoners as well as 85,000 people evacuated to the USSR, many of them under threat of imprisonment by the Soviets (Plakans 2011: 349). In sum, this particular year of Soviet reign would become the first period of repressive rule which would enter the Balts' later politics of truth and justice.

On the heels of this devastating oppressor, however, another would quickly follow, as on June 22, 1941 Nazi Germany invaded the USSR and by extension the Baltic territories. Thus, whereas for many of the other Central and Western European states for whom Nazi occupation would be their first encounter with totalitarian oppression, for the Balts it would be their second. This well-known historical fact is still often insufficiently considered in historical studies that focus on either the Stalinist or Nazi mass crimes in the region, ignoring their particular interactions and the considerable demoralizing and, in fact, brutalizing effects on the local populations, who were confronted with difficult, often impossible, choices as their lives were invaded by two alternating murderous regimes within only a few years (MacQueen 1998; Snyder 2012). The weeks following the German attack on the Soviet Union would indeed epitomize the whole drama of dual occupation that played itself out in these years and continues to haunt today's processes of retrospective truth and justice, especially in Lithuania. Research by the International Commission for the Evaluation of the Crimes of the Soviet and Nazi Occupations in Lithuania has shown that the highest number of civilian casualties caused by Soviet military and security forces during the first year of Soviet occupation occurred during the very last weeks of Soviet rule, as the Red Army and Security organs retreated from Lithuania in June/July 1941 and murdered several thousand political prisoners and other civilians in the process (Anušauskas 2003b).

These acts alone were enough to drive people to join the national resistance against the Soviets during this time, resulting in an uprising that took place just one day after Nazi Germany launched its attack on the Soviet Union. The leading force behind this "June Uprising" was the Lithuanian Activist Front (*Lietuvos aktyvistų frontas*, LAF) that managed to mobilize over 10,000 people in its anti-Soviet fight, causing substantial damage to the retreating Soviet Army. On June 23, 1941 the LAF proclaimed Lithuania an independent state, and despite the ensuing German occupation, a provisional government would exist until August when it was dissolved by the German occupation authorities (Plakans 2011: 348). For many nationally minded Lithuanians, the June Uprising and the independence declaration of 1941 remained an important anchor throughout the Soviet period and in today's remembrance culture (Girnius 2011; Landsbergis 2012). In recent years, however, the activities of the LAF have been discussed more critically given the organization's association with the Nazis. Lithuanian Jews have, in particular, pointed to the resistance's deeply anti-Semitic stances and involvement in anti-Jewish pogroms that took place during the same period.[3] Indeed, over 1,500 local Jews were killed in the same week that the uprising took place, and the Nazi *Einsatzgruppe A* reported to Berlin that the killing had been carried out with the help of "Lithuanian partisans" (MacQueen 1998). Though these early reports from the eastern front need to be read with caution as to their description of actual events, especially with regard to local self-initiative, there is no denying that Lithuanians were actively participating in arresting their Jewish fellow citizens and turning them over to the Nazi death squads. Some

[3] In this the Lithuanian anti-Soviet resistance fight during this period resembles that of the Organization of Ukrainian Nationalists and Ukrainian Insurgent Army (*Orhanizatsiia ukraïns'kykh natsionalistiv – Ukraïns'ka povstans'ka armiia* – OUN-UPA), albeit on a slightly smaller scale, that collaborated with the Nazis in the fight against the Soviets and committed mass crimes against the civilian population, especially Jews, in the process. See Snyder (2003), Davies (2005).

blame in particular the LAF itself for having cultivated "the specter of Judeo-Bolshevism" and the myth about Jews having been mainly responsible for the 1941 deportations, thus instigating several anti-Jewish pogroms in the summer of 1941 (Arad 2004).

Many people fell victim to the German attacks, especially in the early days of the war on the USSR; however, the main target of the Nazi racial extermination policies that were immediately pursued upon taking control were the roughly 200,000 Lithuanian, 75,000 Latvian and 1,000 Estonian Jews, the majority of whom were rounded up and shot in mass killings in the first seven months of Nazi German occupation. The scale of mass murder in such a short period of time was due to the tight organization of the *SS Einsatzgruppen* and their local auxiliaries (MacQueen 1998). Fueled by Nazi propaganda about the involvement of Jews in the Soviet terror of 1940–41, but also by home-grown anti-Semitism and baser motives such as greed and opportunism, local authorities and individuals cooperated in the Nazi policies of discrimination, expropriation and enslavement that often preceded the murder (Maripuu 2001; Truska and Vareikis 2004; Reichelt 2010; Zuroff 2011). The number of those Balts who actively participated in the shooting actions organized by the *SS Einsatzgruppe A* (in Estonia and Latvia) and *Einsatzkommando 3* (in Lithuania) reached several thousand across the region, organized mostly in special mobile execution units such as the *Arājs kommando* in Latvia and the *Rollkommando Hamann* in Lithuania. Apart from the Jewish populations, the Nazi policies of labor exploitation and extinction also targeted the Roma population, an estimated 60–70 percent of which perished, along with other "enemies of the Third Reich," mostly Communists (Zimmermann 2008; Kasekamp 2010; Plakans 2011: 354).

While the issue of local collaboration in Nazi crimes was a widespread phenomenon across Nazi-occupied Europe, it was only in this region (including Belarus, Eastern Poland and Ukraine, which Timothy Snyder has termed the "Bloodlands of Europe") that the distinctions between collaborators and resisters, victims and victimizers become highly complex and sometimes hard to determine. This is because working against the criminal Soviet regime often meant some degree of collaboration with the no less criminal Nazi occupiers. On the whole, of course, this ambiguity did not pertain to those who committed murder or otherwise actively helped to realize the Nazi extermination policies. As historians have already shown, in all three Baltic states several hundreds of volunteers joined the local auxiliary police battalions, many of which were dispatched to guard concentration camps and ghettos, participate in shootings as well as fight against anti-Nazi partisans both inside and outside the countries' borders, involving some of them in mass crimes (Ezergailis 1996; Birn 2001; Arad 2004a; Bubnys 2004; Reichelt 2010).

More controversial, however, is a proper evaluation of the role played by the Estonian and Latvian so-called "voluntary *Waffen-SS* legions." These units encompassed some 5,300 Estonian and roughly 100,000 Latvian men, who were drafted in 1943 in order to fight the rapidly approaching Soviet Army.[4] As Plakans maintains, only about 15–20 percent of these men joined the divisions truly voluntarily; most others were recruited under threat of severe punishment (Plakans 2011: 357). Still, the implication that Estonians and Latvians had fought actively on the Nazi German side was difficult to blend with a counter-narrative that such combat had nonetheless helped to forestall the return of an equally deadly regime in the form of the Soviet Union. Moreover, both the Estonian and Latvian *Waffen-SS* battalions included individuals who had previously served in local police units or as military staff and as such had been involved in mass crimes (Ezergailis 1997; IKUERK 2001). This blurring of otherwise clear distinctions between resisters, perpetrators and victims recurs when we read about anti-Soviet partisans fighting in all three Baltic states, but in particular in Lithuania long after 1944. Today these individuals are often considered national "freedom fighters," yet some of these men had previously participated in murder and pogroms or in the guarding of prison camps during the Nazi occupation. Likewise, some of these "freedom fighters" brought terror to the local countryside as they punished those who would not join their ranks or otherwise support them. These acts would, in turn, drive others to collaborate with the Soviet authorities or even work as so-called agent-combatants, infiltrating the ranks of the partisans and reporting their movements to the NKVD (Bergmanis et al. 2005). Today many of these collaborators have been prosecuted by Lithuanian courts for having participated in genocide, as we will examine in Chapter 3. It is, indeed, these historical ambiguities, not particular to but certainly

[4] In the last year of the war, a total of about 40,000 Estonian men were enlisted into military units of the German *Wehrmacht*, and a small number into the *Waffen-SS*. Lithuanians successfully boycotted the formation of a *Waffen-SS* unit. However, about 125,000 Balts, most of them Lithuanians, were subsequently conscripted into labor services in Germany (Kasekamp 2010: 137).

most evident in the Baltic cases, that will surface time and again during the countries' post-1991 search for truth and justice.

Indeed, Baltic investigations into past wrongdoing and public-political debates about accountability and remembrance regarding Nazi-era crimes have been often highly controversial. Moreover, debates about local collaboration with the Nazi occupation were further obscured by forty years of both Soviet historiographical distortions and open misinformation as well as by subjective and often imprecise accounts from survivors of Nazi atrocities who had fled the region after the war. In this again, the Baltic post-1991 processes of truth and justice about the Nazi era differed from similar post-1945 debates in Poland or Romania. They were perhaps as much affected by the lack of factual knowledge as they were constrained by competing myths and accusatory narratives built up over the course of four decades, rendering the process of coming to terms with this period of history extremely difficult.

Upon the return of the Soviet Army in the fall of 1944, Stalinist terror was revived. The years 1945–53 saw renewed waves of arrests, political trials and deportations. Based on a 1943 decree by the Supreme Soviet of the USSR "on the penalties for German-fascist wrongdoers, guilty of murdering and torturing the Soviet civilian population" ad hoc military tribunals started prosecuting actual and alleged Nazi collaborators in all three re-occupied Baltic republics, many of whom were sentenced on questionable grounds to years of forced labor, while others received death sentences and where executed right away (Liivoja 2013: 251). The Soviet security organs (now known as the MGB), moreover, executed an unknown number of "enemies of the Soviet people" without granting any right to a trial. In 1994 the remains of over 900 individuals were found on the grounds of the Tuskulėnai park, not far from the Vilnius city center. Among those buried there were both Nazi collaborators and murderers as well as anti-Soviet resistance fighters and other "hostile elements" such as Catholic priests. In Latvia, too, hundreds of individuals were put on trial and convicted for collaboration with the enemy, or "counterrevolutionary crimes" as it was called in the Soviet Russian Criminal Law of 1926, a notoriously broad legal concept that allowed prosecutors to punish people for whatever trespasses (Liivoja 2013). Many of these individuals were sentenced to years in the Gulag; others were executed still in the Baltic republics. The exact number of victims is unknown (Bergmanis et al. 2005). Only with regard to the notorious Arājs Kommando have more detailed investigations been carried out on the basis of criminal records of the KGB in Latvia. While many of the estimated 1,200–2,000 members of this killing squad were killed during the war or postwar partisan battles or committed suicide (and some, including Arājs himself, successfully escaped to the West), over 350 individuals ended up facing Soviet trials between 1944 and 1967. Most of them received sentences of between ten and twenty-five years in prison camps, and forty-four were sentenced to death (Vīksne 2005: 204). In Estonia, several hundred individuals were similarly prosecuted for alleged or actual collaboration with the Nazis, often on the mere bases of their belonging to certain official bodies such as the *Omakaitse* (Home Guard). In the post-1991 Baltic states, these trials and sentences would often serve as the reason prosecutors would give to explain their relative inactivity with regard to prosecuting surviving Nazi collaborators (see Chapter 3). Moreover, from a legal perspective all of these postwar trials were most questionable, as they were often based on exaggerated charges and coerced confessions, and the accused were not given any opportunity to defend themselves (Liivoja 2013). Meanwhile, the Soviet security forces continued where they had left off in the summer of 1941 and arrested any remaining political leaders and other representatives of pre-war states. Within one year between the fall of 1944 and 1945, over 10,000 people were arrested in Estonia alone, many of whom died. In September 1944 a group of former leaders headed by the former minister of internal affairs, Otto Tief, tried to regain control of the country in the wake of the German retreat. In a desperate move, Tief proclaimed Estonia's re-independence and attempted to form a provisionary government. However, the move lasted for just four days; on September 22 the Soviet Army re-occupied Tallinn and arrested most of the members of this government. Those captured were subsequently taken to Moscow and sentenced to many years in the Gulag. Moreover, twelve other former ministers of Estonian pre-war governments, who had managed to avoid capture during 1940–41, were now arrested and sentenced to long-term imprisonment or death (IKUERK 2008). In re-independent Estonia, the short-lived attempt to restore state sovereignty would later be venerated as an additional symbol of national resistance. (See Chapter 6.)

Armed opposition to the restored Soviet regime raged in all three countries throughout the second half of the 1940s, yet in Lithuania it assumed the dimensions of a full-scale guerilla war (Kuodytė and Tracevskis 2004). Here the partisan movement against Soviet security forces was highly organized with a central command held by the Council of Lithuanian Freedom Fighters that oversaw an estimated 50,000 men and women in their fight against the Soviet regime across various districts of the country (Morkus and Burauskaite 2002). In 1949 the joint staff of the armed resistance under Brigadier General Jonas Žemaitis signed a declaration that reinstated independent Lithuania and further consolidated the structural organization of the anti-Soviet resistance.

During this guerilla war, which lasted into the mid-1950s, an estimated 20,000 partisans were killed (Kuodytė and Tracevskis 2004). Likewise, local collaborators with the Soviet regime were organized into ad hoc "people's defense brigades" that would infiltrate the partisan ranks in order to then betray them to the Soviet security forces. Oftentimes they were involved in the shootings themselves (Purs 2012: 30). Numerous civilians ended up being killed or abused by both the MGB and the anti-Soviet partisans for lack of support or for alleged collaboration with the other side, as noted earlier. Attempts by the Soviets to crush these resistance activities or to offer amnesties largely failed, leading Moscow to draw up even harsher plans for deporting the families of the partisans. The largest of these operations was carried out in May 1948 when almost 40,000 Lithuanians, representing the families of killed or convicted partisan fighters, as well as other "enemies of the people" were rounded up and deported toward Siberia (Purs 2013: 31). In the aftermath of this repression, the resistance fighting was considerably weakened, though not extinguished. It therefore went on to hinder another major goal of the Soviet authorities, the collectivization of agriculture. This defiance prompted another mass deportation in March 1949, now encompassing Estonia and Latvia as well. Under the codename *Priboi* (coastal surf), an estimated 21,000 Estonians, 42,000 Latvians and over 32,000 Lithuanians were put on freight trains and "resettled" to faraway Siberian localities, mainly around Krasnoyarsk, Omsk, Irkutsk and Novosibirsk. More than two-thirds of those deported were women and children under the age of 16, some of them without parents (Strods and Kott 2002: 20; Õispuu 2003; Anušauskas 2005).

With this series of large-scale repressive actions, the nature of Soviet rule dramatically changed. Whereas during the first year of occupation in 1940–41 the targets of Soviet mass terror had been mainly the political, military and intellectual elites of the three states (liquidated with the objective of decapitating the newly absorbed societies), after 1944, Soviet repression turned to crushing a deeper undercurrent of national resistance and to radically changing the social fabric and economic structure of these countries. The deportees were declared "nationalists", "fascists" and "bandits" (anti-Soviet partisans) as well as "kulaks," the latter being independent farmers who refused to join the collective farms as part of collectivization. Official Soviet reports show that already by late 1950, some 4.4 percent of the 1949 Baltic deportees had perished because of extremely harsh living conditions and starvation (Strods and Kott 2002: 17).[5]

Eventually a sizable number of deportees returned to their homelands, after their residency restrictions were eased, and some were granted amnesty ("rehabilitation") in the wake of de-Stalinization (Plakans 2011). However, those who returned often remained stigmatized as "enemies of the people," since their criminal records were not necessarily wiped clean. For some, the return home was also very slow, sometimes impossible, since although they were released from their direct confinement areas after 1956, they were often not allowed to return specifically to the Baltics until the 1960s and 1970s (Rahi-Tamm 2005).

Today, some Baltic scholars, but also an increasing number of Western historians, have come to the conclusion that the 1948–49 mass deportations can be considered genocide, owing to an understanding that these forced resettlements were ordered and carried out in a way that clearly suggests that they were aimed at harming particular national and ethnic groups, thus falling under the definition of the 1948 Convention on the Prevention and Punishment of the Crime of Genocide (Snyder 2010). As we will see in Chapter 3, in legal terms all three Baltic states would classify the Soviet-era mass deportations as genocide in their newly adopted criminal law. Whether or not the "genocide paradigm" can be used to understand the entire Soviet occupation of the Baltic region remains highly contested among historians and lawyers (Strods and Kott 2002; Mertelsmann and Rahi-Tamm 2009). It is also, needless to say, a heated element of the politics of truth and justice.

Even though research into Stalinist-era repression has been considerable over the past twenty years, especially in the countries themselves, the exact numbers of those deported, murdered and otherwise repressed during this time are extremely hard to determine. Historians are often faced with incongruent documentation or still lack access to crucial archives in the Russian Federation (Rahi 2003). Estimates of the total number of Baltic inhabitants repressed, executed or deported to remote

[5] Other estimates state that about 10 percent of those deported in 1949 died in Siberian exile, most of them in the first years. See Mälksoo (2001: 765).

regions of the USSR between 1940 and 1953 diverge considerably, ranging from several hundred thousand to over a million, depending on how they define the various categories of "repressed."[6] Add to this the number of those killed by execution or in postwar partisan battles (especially in Lithuania) as well as the estimated 80,000 Estonians, 160,000 Latvians and 64,000 Lithuanians who fled the returning Soviet Army in 1944–45 westward (an estimated 7,000 of whom perished in the Baltic Sea), and the full amplitude of the loss inflicted on the Baltic populations by Stalin is made clear (Rahi 2003: 29; Kasekamp 2010: 139; Plakans 2011: 358).

In Table 2.1 we attempt to bring together some of these various figures, although we recognize the hazardous nature of this endeavor. Our aim is not to provide a definitive tally of human losses during the period 1939–53 but, rather, to give the reader a basic sense of the magnitude of repression as a guidepost for better understanding the politics around this history. The data are compiled on the basis of official assessments by Baltic historians and other experts, as published by state commissions or other research institutions. Despite the considerable divergences in the numbers to be found here, we have tried to be as precise as possible about the kind of repression and crime.

To be sure, Stalinization after 1945 precipitated massive rights abuses in other Central European countries, including mass arrests, show trials, population transfers and expulsions (Naimark and Gibianskii 1997; Tismăneanu 2009). Yet communist consolidation of power did not include the same degree of mass terror and the removal of a significant and tangible portion of the local populations. Soviet policies targeted the majority population rather than a minority and thereby caused greater damage in total numbers to the Baltic populations than Stalinism did in the Soviet-dominated states of Central Europe.

The conclusion from this historical overview is that the nature of what we call post-communist retrospective justice, that is, justice aimed at crimes that were committed decades before the collapse of the regime, was comparatively stronger in the Baltic cases. It included the notion

[6] For Estonia alone, Mertelsmann and Rahi-Tamm (2009: 309) estimate that "[r]oughly 12–14 percent of the population" fell victim to persecution. Based on mostly Lithuanian historians' estimates, Dainius Žalimas (2010: 50) suggests that 300,000 Estonian citizens (one-third of the pre-war population) were "affected by arrests, mass murder, deportation and other acts of repression." Likewise, he puts the Lithuanian losses at about one-fifth of the population at the time, or some 900,000 people affected by repressions, deportations and exodus.

Table 2.1 *Estimated human costs of Soviet and Nazi occupations 1940–1956*

Period/ action	Estonia	Latvia	Lithuania
Population	1,126,413 (1934)	1,905,000 (1935)	est. 2,575,400 (1938)
First Soviet occupation June 1940 – July 1941			
June 1941 mass deportation	9,267 *(of whom 2,409 were later executed and 4,264 returned home)*	15,424 *(incl. family members arrested before or after 14 June; < 6,000 killed or died en route; 3,400 perished in labor camps*	17,500
Victims of repressions (arrest, torture, political trials, imprisonment or other sanctions)	*c.* 8,000	< 20,000–21,000	12,900
Extra-judicial executions	< 2,000	Not known	< 3,000
Nazi occupation July 1941 – May 1944			
Mass killing of local "racial" minorities during 1941–44	992 Jews < 300 Roma	65,000–70,000 Jews < 1,900 Roma	196,000 Jews *Number of Roma killed estimated at several thousand*
Killing of Jews from outside	7,000–8,000	20,000	Not known
Killing of other civilians	< 7,000	16,300	45,000
Forced labor	est. 3,000	16,800	36,500
Second Soviet occupation fall 1944–1956			
Mass deportations 1948–49	March 1949: 20,702 *3,000 died en route or in exile* *10,331 non-deported individuals suffered repressions by the KGB*	March 1949: 42,231 *8,000 died en route or in exile*	1948: 41,000 1949: 32,735
Other deportations between 1945 and 1956	< 650	500–1,700	< 59, 200
Arrests and political imprisonment (outside the country)	25,000–30,000 *c. 11,000 perished*	< 32,000	186,000
Post-war partisans killed or imprisoned during 1945–56	8,468 *< 4,000 killed*	8,000 *2,500–3,000 killed*	21,500

Sources: Estonia: IKUERK 2001; IKUERK 2004; IKUERK 2008, Rahi-Tamm 2005; Õispuu 2007. Latvia: Nollendorfs and Oberländer 2005, especially the chapters by I. Šneidere; R. Vīksne; D. Bleiere; J. Riekstiņš; A. Bergmanis, R. Jansons and I. Zālīte. Also: Pelkaus 2001; Šķinķe 2007; Riekstiņš 2000. Lithuania: Kuodytė and Tracevskis 2004; Morkus and Burauskaitė 2002; Anušauskas 1996, 2003a, 2003b; Bubnys (1998).

that as part of otherwise pervasive Stalinist terror individuals, relatives and fellow countrymen had been taken en masse far outside the borders of these homelands and subjected to physical and emotional hardship. To be sure, historical inquiries based on archival documents may yet prove that these mass deportations, though clearly ordered and planned by the USSR state security organs, could not have taken place without high levels of local complicity and participation (Strods and Kott 2002: 30; Rahi 2003). Hence, a moment of deeper reckoning with how such mass terror could have happened may yet come. Still, it does not change the degree of national trauma engendered as a result of the mass deportations and Stalinist terror, which was stronger than in many of the other post-communist Central European cases. As will be discussed later on, this, too, has had significant implications for the post-communist process of truth and justice.

During the post-Stalinist period, we come to a final element of difference with regard to the Baltic cases. This concerns the deeper nature of the regime and of the repressive services operated by it. Although we know that the structure of the Communist regimes across the region was largely analogous – characterized by a single, leading communist party having a leadership structure of a politburo, central committee and local committees largely paralleling the structures of state administration – the Baltics were, again, different in that they were a part of the core Soviet system. This concerned both the Communist Party structures as well as the repressive apparatus of the state security service. In other words, the various local organs of both the Communist Party of the Soviet Union as well as the KGB were not fully or even partially autonomous, but rather were fulfilling (more directly than those in any of the Central European regimes after 1956) the direct orders of Moscow (Senn 2007: 18–20; Burinskaitė 2011). There was little opportunity for national deviation from the system as would be experienced during successive cycles in 1953, 1956, 1968 and 1980 in Central Europe. At best there would be efforts to mitigate individual policies of the regime, most notably the degree of Russification in the republics (Plakans 2011). In this Lithuania would be the more successful, being able to prevent the large-scale migration of Russian speakers to its republic in contrast to Estonia and Latvia, where hundreds of thousands of mostly Russian Soviet citizens would settle during the 1950s, 1960s and 1970s. Not only did these settler populations dramatically alter the ethno-demographic balance in the two republics (reducing by 1989 the proportion of the titular populations to just 61.5 percent in Estonia and 52 percent in Latvia), they also generated strong socio-linguistic tensions, since rarely would these settlers learn the local languages and would instead increasingly oblige Estonians and Latvians to communicate in Russian (Maripuu 2004). Part of this skewed ethno-political transformation was caused, furthermore, by the fact that among both the Estonian and the Latvian nations there were sizable co-ethnic communities deep in Russia – a result of peasant migrations to these areas in search of land during the nineteenth century as well as during World War I and the Russian Revolution. Many of these heavily Russified Estonians and Latvians would subsequently be hand-picked to serve as trusted Soviet administrators after 1944. These would include high-level officials such as Johannes Käbin and Karl Vaino in Estonia, Arvīds Pelše and Augusts Voss in Latvia. All of them contributed especially to fostering an image of Soviet rule as imposed, alien and foreign. The situation was somewhat different in Lithuania, where after 1953 the Lithuanian Communist Party "quietly initiated a nativisation campaign," increasing the number of ethnic Lithuanians among party officials from one-third in 1952 to two-thirds in 1965 (Kasekamp 2010: 148). The more native character of the Communist leadership remained constant throughout the Soviet period (Burauskaite and Morkus 2002). According to some, this helped, notably, to fend off some of Moscow's policies with regard to ethnic demography in the non-Russian Soviet republics. It would also create a degree of legitimacy for the Lithuanian Communist Party once the re-independence struggle had begun (Purs 2013). This, in turn, would foster the well-known bipolar ex-communist/anti-communist cleavage in the Lithuanian party system with repercussions not least for the country's truth and justice process. Yet there were also clear limits to how much local communist leaders could do to initiate national policies of their own, a fact evidenced by the purges among Estonian and Latvian party elites (in 1950 and 1959, respectively) for allegedly "bourgeois nationalist" activity.[7]

[7] Then chairman of the Council of Ministers of Latvian SSR, Eduards Berklavs together with several other Communist Party officials attempted to limit the influx of Russian-speaking labor that was accompanied by massive linguistic Russification of Latvia. In 1959 a massive internal purge took place and Beklavs was removed from office on the charges of being "bourgeois nationalist" and exiled in Russia (Prigge 2004). In a similar fashion nine years earlier, the Estonian Communist Party had carried out major purges against "bourgeois nationalists." In its March 1950 Plenary Session, the Central Committee of the Estonian Communist Party launched a campaign that included not only several Communist Party members alleged to pursue a nationalist agenda, but also members of the national intelligentsia. Some 200 university lecturers were "repressed" and about 1,000 university students expelled from their university (Rahi-Tamm 2005: 32).

We come therefore to a final historical parameter of the Baltic cases, which involves this same degree of outright Soviet Russian domination, yet seen from another angle. Namely, while this repression was more severe and total, it was also imposed almost directly from outside and indeed in many cases carried out by individuals brought in from outside. To be sure, there remain issues of Baltic collaboration with both the Stalinist repressions and the later KGB persecution, to which we allude above. Yet however mythologized it may be, there remains a strong sense in the Baltic states of being able to treat the entire Soviet era and regime as an externally inflicted tragedy. There is, paradoxically, a greater feeling of distance from the Soviet experience in the Baltics than perhaps elsewhere in Central Europe toward the communist period, because there is a greater possibility of externalizing the phenomenon. One might even venture to say that the politics of truth and justice in the Baltics has been akin to that experienced in countries formally occupied by the Nazis during World War II and for whom the repressive regime was likewise a foreign imposition. To be sure, there are limits to this analogy, not the least of which being the length of the occupation itself. However, let us begin with the first parallelism, which is legal-judicial.

When Mikhail Gorbachev came to power in the Soviet Union and proclaimed *glasnost* and *perestroika*, the Baltic states, too, opened up with lively debates about the state of their society. As has been well documented (Taagepera 1989; Lieven 1994; Dreifelds 1996), this mobilization soon led to mass popular movements against the Soviet regime, first bringing down the Brezhnevite leaders in these republics in summer 1988 and later leading to democratic popular movements (the Estonian *Rahvarinne*, the Latvian *Tautas Fronte* and the Lithuanian *Sąjūdis*) taking power after free elections held in February and March 1990. In terms of the politics of truth and justice, however, a corollary to this democratization was a deeper examination of the legitimacy of the Soviet regime itself. As early as 1988, a number of more radical Baltic activists as well as some moderate politicians questioned the bases of Soviet rule not only in terms of it being non-democratic or repressive but also in terms of it having been from the outset in breach of international law. These perspectives found wide popular support within the populations, for whom the search for "historical truth" had become central in the struggle for more freedom and self-determination. Indeed, campaigns by newly created victim organizations and popular movements in all three countries to reveal often unknown facts about Soviet mass atrocities had a strongly mobilizing effect on the population and, as we will see in later chapters, the grassroots-level truth-seeking of political activists foreshadowed later official measures established by the re-independent states. Yet in the late 1980s, instead of simply confirming the fact that intimidation, coercion and violence had been used to establish communist rule in the Baltic states, the Balts were able to expand the narrative to speak about wholly illegal occupation and annexation in the eyes of international law. Increasingly through 1989 and 1990, the discourse about democratization and possible autonomy within the Soviet Union shifted to not only calls for independence but also demands for a specific end to the unlawful annexation of the Baltic states and a "restoration" of their *de jure* never interrupted statehood. This narrative was bolstered no less by the West itself and its years of "non-recognition policy" toward the Soviet incorporation of Estonia, Latvia and Lithuania. But it was equally propelled in organizational terms by movements like the Citizens Committees in Estonia and Latvia and the Freedom League in Lithuania. And eventually when independence was regained in August 1991 the principle of "legal continuity" and "state restoration" was enshrined in all of the Baltic countries' declarations concerning the end of Soviet rule (Pettai 2007).

The politics of truth and justice in the Baltic states had suddenly assumed an eminently legal and international character, one that brought in very particular terms like "occupation" and was unabashedly meant to echo interpretations of the Nazi occupation of, say, Denmark or the more contemporaneous Iraqi occupation of Kuwait. From the perspective of our analysis, we will see how this would modify particularly Boxes 1 and 6 of our matrix, since the trials of former regime perpetrators could now be cast as involving crimes against humanity and outright genocide along with other aspects of international law. Likewise, symbolic policies aimed at acknowledging and remembering the victims as well as truth-seeking efforts by historical commissions would be deeply imbued with the illegal occupation frame.

Ultimately, the legal restorationist doctrine would be carried through all kinds of policy areas in the Baltic states, including determining the degree of property restitution, regulating bilateral relations with Russia and establishing overarching state identities (such as celebrating the ninety-fifth anniversary of statehood in 2013). An additional and highly controversial extension of the legal restorationist doctrine concerned citizenship policy. Here Estonia and Latvia in particular decided to apply a very strict interpretation of the doctrine to mean that all Soviet-era settlers to their two republics and their descendants could not be granted automatic citizenship in the newly restored states. Rather, as people having settled in the area during an illegal occupation, these individuals could only be given the right to become naturalized citizens after having passed relevant language exams and other procedures. Moreover, such rules would apply even if these people had been born in the respective republics (to settler parents) and lived there all their lives. The upshot was that in late 1991, when these rules were adopted, there were in Estonia and Latvia, respectively, some 400,000 and 700,000 "non-citizens" (Pettai 2001). Although initially this did not seem to be a problem, since the individuals remained Soviet citizens, when the USSR itself was dissolved in December 1991, these people became individuals without any citizenship, unless they went through the process of naturalization or acquired Russian Federation (or some other Soviet successor state) citizenship.

The ethno-political motives behind this policy were evident in that the large-scale influx of these mostly Slav settlers over the last forty years had dramatically changed the ethno-demographic balance in these two societies. Had the entire resident population in Estonia and Latvia been made citizens, it would have effectively transformed these countries into bi-national states, akin to Belgium. For the Estonians and Latvians, however, the analogy was more to Fiji, where the native Fijian population had been overrun by Indian-born migrants during British colonial rule and where ethnic politics has never been stable since independence was acquired in 1970. In this respect, legal continuity and the extension of this principle to citizenship policy was an important element of ethno-political justice for the Estonian and Latvian populations. It was also highly effective, in that once founding parliamentary elections were held in the two countries in 1992 and 1993, the share of ethnic Estonians and Latvians within the citizenry would be dramatically in their favor. Of a population in Estonia that was just 65 percent ethnic Estonian in 1992, the citizenry was nearly 90 percent Estonian, while comparable figures for Latvia were 53.5 percent and 75 percent. Given such shifts in ethno-political weight, the new parliaments in these two countries were also heavily skewed toward the titular populations, and over the next two decades party formation would also be strongly affected with minority Russian parties being weak, particularly in Estonia (Arter 1996; Pettai et al. 2010).

Analogous citizenship measures were never adopted in Lithuania, since the Soviet-era influx of settlers had been significantly less, affecting less than 10 percent of the population by 1991. Lithuanians represented nearly 80 percent of the population, and the next sizable minority constituted Poles, who had also been autochthonous to the region for centuries. While ethno-political disputes did exist between Lithuanians and Poles, they were of lesser consequence and had little importance for truth and justice involving the Soviet past.

We come therefore to a final implication of the citizenship issue, which will receive greater treatment in Chapter 4. The issue concerns whether citizenship legislation in Estonia and Latvia constituted an oblique form of lustration. All of the different parameters that we have sought to bring out concerning the externalized nature of the Soviet regime – the ethno-political (Russian-Baltic) undertones of the regime, the ethno-demographic changes wrought by the regime and the citizenship policies imposed after the regime – have led some scholars to see a direct relationship between the severity of citizenship legislation in Estonia and Latvia and the leniency of lustration policy in these countries (Jaskovska and Moran 2006; Stan 2009c). The argument runs largely as follows: to the extent that the Soviet regimes in these two republics were dominated politically by settler Russians and to the extent that this was especially the case within the structures of the KGB (where Estonians and Latvians might not have been fully trusted), the need to cleanse the state of collaborators was dramatically reduced in Estonia and Latvia once it became possible to declare most of these people non-citizens and thereby make them ineligible for civil service appointment and even elected office (Stan 2009c: 254). The externalized dimension of the Soviet regime had come full circle: it was no longer necessary to look for collaborators if most of these people could be extracted from the state and society through alternative legal grounds – citizenship. This would explain (as we will see later) why Estonia adopted a very mild system of self-reporting for ex-KGB agents and also never followed this up with any post-transitional justice, while Latvia, similarly, never implemented any direct lustration policies, although it did have fierce debates about releasing the names of former agents. Meanwhile, Lithuania, which had many fewer settler Russians in its Soviet regime, would be confronted much more with Lithuanians who had themselves run the KGB and served in high posts of the Soviet system. Hence, the pressures for lustration would be greater.

There is certainly some truth to this deduction if we consider the portrayal of Russian-speaking Soviet-era settlers to Estonia and Latvia as "occupants" or at least as the most visible remnants of the illegal Soviet occupation in the media in both countries. Thus, as a rather radical interpretation of this, we could say that by virtue of excluding these people from citizenship, both Estonia and Latvia inflicted "punishment" on a rather fuzzy perpetrator group defined by a collective notion of guilt for past regime abuses. However, as we will show in Chapter 4, this kind of conclusion does not reflect the reality of post-Soviet lustration policies in the two states in empirical terms, and neither does it serve the goal of having a nuanced and conceptually informed analysis of various lustration measures as they were eventually adopted in the two states.

Coming finally to one of the most practical dimensions of truth and justice in post-communist societies, it is important to point out two additional consequences of the fact that the Balts were under the subjugation of a Soviet KGB that was part of a larger organization located in a neighboring, now foreign, territory. First, beginning in 1989 when democratization commenced in the Baltic republics and the Soviet authorities grew more uneasy about the long-term prospects for these regions, the KGB began systematically moving operational files to the Russian Federation, where they remain today. To be sure, repressive agencies across the Communist bloc began destroying sensitive materials just as soon as they realized their regime was collapsing. This leads, in turn, to the fact that in none of the post-communist countries would the files of the former regime ever be integral or complete. Still, in the Baltic cases this incompleteness would be caused by having had almost entire archives removed from these countries and transported across borders to another country. As will be detailed in later chapters, only some historical files from the Stalinist era as well as some 1980s files concerning foreign travel applications, surveillance reports and some interrogation records (in Latvia) would be returned or recovered in these countries. In other words, a particular Baltic disparity with the rest of Central and Eastern Europe was again evident in the fact that their opportunity for a more complete *Auseinandersetzung*, or accounting with the past, was curtailed not least because the actual files have been withheld from their possession.

Secondly, in contrast to the other Central and East European countries, the Balts could not simply storm their secret service headquarters or change interior ministers and thereby place the repressive apparatus under democratic control. Rather, as independent states they had to *negotiate* the takeover of KGB offices, equipment and other practicalities with the Soviet authorities. The importance of this point becomes evident in terms of the sheer time that it would take to carry out these procedures. Several rounds of talks, lasting weeks (sometimes months), entailing numerous interim agreements and formal protocols, both at the interstate and local-regional levels – all of this would become a major task for the new Baltic governments during the fall of 1991. Needless to say, in the course of this interlude, still further materials would be removed, lost or destroyed. Moreover, according to one source, the Estonian government during this period (led by Edgar Savisaar) felt so unsure as to how to deal with the ex-KGB that it agreed preliminarily to a special draft accord with the Soviet Minister of Internal Affairs that would have formally offered social benefits, protection from retributive measures and other guarantees to all former KGB employees in the country (Mägi 2012). Had such an agreement actually come to pass, the possibility for any kind of punitive measure against these people would have been ruled out from the start. In sum, the flipside of the coin concerning the Balts' opportunity for externalizing their fifty years of repressive rule was the fact that the actual information about this former regime would also remain largely outside their borders.

Summary

The overview of Baltic history that we have offered here is far from complete and has been tailored in particular to bringing out those elements which we see as relevant for understanding the three countries' post-communist politics of truth and justice. We have highlighted both those elements that have made Baltic truth and justice more complicated, and those that seemed to have simplified the process.

On the level of social memory, the greater distance that the Balts could place between themselves and the Soviets would also help foster a greater sense of pure victimhood. There is a certain paradox in the fact that as countries more directly subjugated to Soviet Communist rule, the Baltic states also had an easier time of shedding that yoke, since this rule – when viewed as an illegal occupation and annexation – was so much easier to characterize as wholly alien. As such, one could also feel how the regime had seemingly left much of the national fabric untouched. The overarching victimhood paradigm has allowed Baltic policy-makers to project issues of culpability on to an "other," thus externalizing questions of moral accountability for the wrongs of the previous Communist regime. This made the transitional justice process somewhat less wrenching than in some of the other post-communist states of Central and Eastern Europe, but also in Ukraine. Baltic elites and populations were somewhat relieved from going through a deeper process of soul-searching regarding questions of home-grown wrong and local involvement in the excesses of the Communist regime. To be sure, some ambiguity exists among Balts in terms of *de facto* complicity with past repressive policies, not least concerning the later decades. As we shall see in our empirical chapters, there is also slightly more complexity to this dimension in Lithuania, precisely because the Soviet regime contained fewer externally imposed Russian leaders and was therefore more "national-communist"; hence, the debates over certain Lithuanians having operated within the Soviet system have been more acrimonious. Yet, on the whole the duality of full-scale Soviet control leading to more massive Stalinist and post-Stalinist repression *alongside* a greater degree of international-legal condemnation as well as ethno-national victimhood has constituted an all-pervasive parameter of truth and justice politics that is particular to the Baltic states.

On a practical level, meanwhile, the challenge of coming to terms with the past has been more difficult for the Balts, since neither the Soviet Union nor its successor the Russian Federation has been in any mood to agree to the new legal framework of restored Baltic independence, and neither would Moscow accept responsibility for the Soviet past and engage in redress policies. This has been manifested, for example, in the reluctance of Russian ministries and state archives to allow Baltic historians and prosecutors access to relevant KGB files. The disagreements have also permeated many other bilateral issues, such as concluding formal border treaties as well as starting any kind of historical dialogue and rapprochement over the past (Ehin and Berg 2009). We will come back to this issue of external reverberations of Baltic truth and justice policies toward both Russia and the European Union in Chapter 7.

3

Punishing the perpetrators: criminal investigations and trials

In March 1994 Latvian prosecutors arrested the former head of the Latvian SSR People's Commissariat for Internal Affairs (NKVD) Alfons Noviks. Noviks, an ethnic Latvian, had served as head of the NKVD between 1940 and 1953, and since his retirement had lived a comfortable life in Soviet Latvia. On the March day in question, Noviks was taken into custody and charged with crimes against humanity and genocide for having signed thousands of deportation orders, especially during the later Stalinist period. In addition, he was accused not only of having ordered the torture of political prisoners, but also of having taken an active part in that torture. A third charge involved engaging in property confiscation. In December 1995 the then 88-year-old was found guilty of having committed "genocide against the Latvian people" and sentenced to life imprisonment. He died three months later in prison (Jakobsone 2001: 68; Švarca 2012).

The story of Alfons Noviks illustrates three things about forms of criminal-legal punishment of perpetrators in the post-communist world and in the Baltic states in particular. The first concerns who Alfons Noviks was not. Noviks was not a recent leader of the Soviet Latvian regime when he was arrested. He was an octogenarian long in retirement. In other words, the Latvian state was not prosecuting the key communist-era rulers who had kept the country under Soviet repression over the last decade. This was not a case of transitional justice in the form we have elaborated in this book. Rather, secondly, Noviks epitomizes the phenomenon of retrospective justice. Latvian prosecutors were targeting a series of crimes committed by the prior Soviet regime that were clearly heinous, but involved a time period that was far in the past and for which a limited number of eyewitnesses and victims existed. This was a political choice. Thirdly, the fact that the charges levied against Noviks involved nothing less than genocide and other crimes against humanity indicates that retrospective justice involved atrocities of almost unimaginable proportions in this post-communist context. Trials such as these were about mass murder.

These three points begin to lay the groundwork for understanding how Estonia, Latvia and Lithuania have dealt with the criminal-judicial punishment of perpetrators of repression during the Soviet era. Yet, we will see that within the context of our analytical framework (Boxes 1a and 1b of our matrix) the Baltic states have pursued relatively little transitional justice and much greater amounts of retrospective justice. The three states have not attempted to criminally punish high-ranking leaders of the former Communist Party or other officials who were responsible for maintaining the Soviet system. While prosecutors have gone after some of the individuals who engaged in acts of repression during the three states' independence struggle (to be described below), these endeavors constituted a kind of second-order transitional justice when compared to efforts in other countries to put senior Communist officials on trial, such as Wojciech Jaruzelski in Poland or Erich Honecker in Germany.

Instead, the Baltic states have engaged very widely in the pursuit of retrospective justice by carrying out investigations, indictments and trials of dozens of individuals accused of having participated in Stalinist-era repressions during the 1940s and 1950s. Alfons Noviks was a premier example of this pursuit, but there have been many others. Moreover, we will see that of the three Baltic states Lithuania has pursued these matters the most by far, in terms of not only numbers but also the range of past incidents investigated as well as the severity of criminal charges levied.

We will begin with a reflection on how the Baltic states faced the overall question of pursuing post-communist criminal justice in comparison to other Central and Eastern European countries. Thereafter we will turn to an examination of those cases of transitional justice that have taken place, namely the investigations and trials of individuals accused of repression and treason during the re-independence movement in 1990 and 1991. By far the bulk of the chapter, however, will examine retrospective justice toward Soviet-era perpetrators in the Baltic states. Moreover, given the breadth of these efforts we will divide the account into three analytical dimensions. First, we will examine the criminal-legal framework that was set up by Baltic legislators in the early 1990s and how this evolved over time. Our aim will be both to outline the emergence of political and legal strategies toward taking up individual-level judicial action against Stalin-era perpetrators and to examine the particular issues and challenges arising for legislators in formulating the necessary legal framework.

A second important requirement for enacting retrospective justice involves setting up a proper investigative infrastructure for prosecutors to do their job. In this vein we will examine the institutional arrangements (and/or divisions of labor) that were established by legislators in order to organize the criminal justice process. How functional were the institutional settings for guaranteeing the efficiency of the investigative and prosecutorial process? What does the institutional arrangement tell us about political attitudes with regard to the retrospective criminal justice process?

Finally, we will outline the full range of investigations and trials that have taken place in the three states. We will see that the three states have differed considerably in terms of the kinds of past criminal incidences they have investigated, the legal interpretation they have given to these acts and the number of cases in each category they have decided to pursue. Moreover, we will observe temporal shifts in how the three countries have pursued these efforts. Whereas all three countries initiated their retrospective justice measures with more or less the same intensity, Latvia and later Estonia saw this zeal taper off after 2000. Lithuania also exhibited different lulls in prosecutorial activity. However, in 2008 the pace dramatically quickened, as conservative political forces in parliament demanded greater action by the prosecutor, and actually allocated considerable funds for the hiring of additional investigators and the start of new trials.

General reflections on criminal justice in the post-Soviet context

Across post-communist Central and Eastern Europe, the criminal-legal punishment of perpetrators of past repression has been hampered by what Calhoun has described as the "dilemma of justice" or the need to reconcile the "moral desire to punish the guilty . . . [with the] legal requirements of a liberal democratic state" (Calhoun 2004: 2). This second half of the equation constitutes the crux of the problem. The principles of modern, democratic legal justice do not allow for revenge prosecution or subjective retribution. The rigors of democratic rule of law mean that most of the repressive acts committed during the communist era cannot be easily prosecuted by simply creating new law. This would constitute retroactive punishment. Additionally, although many communist-era leaders committed acts of administrative wrongdoing, such as abuse of power or corruption, these crimes would generally fall under statutes of limitation, thus closing off yet another avenue of pursuit.

One of the few remaining responses to this dilemma was to examine communist-era crimes from the perspective of international humanitarian law and the principles of universal jurisdiction. These would bear no statutes of limitation and could be pursued with vigor. However, this approach was also applicable above all in relation to the worst crimes (deportations, mass arrests, acts of torture and mass murder) of the Stalinist years, meaning upwards of a half-century ago. Hence, the upshot of any desire to carry out criminal-legal prosecution of perpetrators from the communist era was to engage solely in what we have called retrospective justice, and this on a relatively challenging level of prosecuting crimes against humanity and other egregious offenses.

The Baltic states represented a relatively distinctive and interesting combination of these circumstances. On the one hand, as former Soviet republics, they faced particular difficulties in contemplating any kind of direct, criminal prosecution of their erstwhile Soviet leaders. Not only had many pro-Soviet leaders (such as Karl Vaino from Estonia or Boris Pugo from Latvia) left the country for Russia by 1991, Soviet authorities also took much of the potential evidence for legal prosecution (such as KGB files) with them. Meanwhile, many of the Soviet-era leaders who were left in the Baltic states had actually come to play an important role in facilitating the democratization and re-independence of the three republics as such. Algirdas Brazauskas in Lithuania, Arnold Rüütel in Estonia or Anatolijs Gorbunovs in Latvia are among the most well known. Although all three men had been high-ranking communist-era functionaries and hence deeply implicated in the operation of the old regime, they skillfully transformed themselves into heroes of the democratic transition by turning in the right direction at the right time. Indeed, two out of the three leaders (Brazauskas and Rüütel) would go on to become president of their country following re-independence. Criminal-legal prosecution of these erstwhile regime figures was out of the question.

In this respect, we see that the nationalism involved with the Baltics' transition to democracy and the way this would allow some of the erstwhile leaders to recover a degree of political capital meant that transitional justice vis-à-vis perpetrators would be limited from the outset. The only exception involved those former figures who stayed in the Baltics and continued to defend the Soviet system. As we will see below, one such person was Alfreds Rubiks, who (together with another conspirator Ojārs Potreki) would be tried and sentenced to prison for having participated in an attempted overthrow of the democratic Latvian government in January 1991. However, even here the exception was ambiguous, since Rubiks had sought to thwart the Latvian independence movement. He was not accused of any wrongdoing when he served, for example, as Mayor of Riga during the 1980s or when he was a communist party functionary before that.

Hence, the Baltic states figure more prominently in Box 1a of our matrix, as their focus was mostly on perpetrators of mass repression during the Stalinist era. In fact, they were the only countries from among those who emerged from the rubble of the Soviet Union to prosecute the crimes of the Soviet Communist regime by way of criminal law (Satkauskas 2004). Again, nationalism was a factor here, since the re-independence movement of the late 1980s had featured not only anti-Soviet sentiment but also a more solemn wave of public remembrance and investigation of the deportations and other Soviet crimes of the 1940s and 1950s (see Chapter 6). This public focus on past repression was part of the reason why retrospective justice would become a very substantive part of the process of dealing with the past in the Baltic states.

Punishing erstwhile regime leaders: Baltic cases of transitional justice

Under classical transitional justice, the three Baltic states would be expected to investigate and eventually put on trial leaders from the Soviet era who had been centrally responsible for maintaining Soviet rule and repression. The fact that the Balts had developed a particular understanding of their Soviet period as one of illegal foreign occupation meant that conceivably they could have even tried these leaders as quislings and punished them for treason. The long duration of the Soviet occupation had, of course, meant that no one necessarily saw the issue of transitional justice in such stark terms. Nonetheless, a loathing did exist for those leaders who had been appointed by the late Soviet leader Leonid Brezhnev and were therefore particularly associated with the stagnation and conservatism that had embodied the end of the Soviet era. These leaders might well have been the ones subsequent democratic leaders would have wanted most to pursue under a form of transitional justice.

However, in each republic these leaders had either passed away or been transferred out by Mikhail Gorbachev before they could fall into the hands of the newly re-independent governments. In Lithuania, this prospect extinguished first when Lithuanian Communist Party chief Petras Griškevičius, in power since 1974, died in November 1987, right at the start of the nationalist reawakening. Moreover, Griškevičius had himself replaced the even longer-serving Lithuanian Communist, Antanas Sniečkus, who had died in 1974 after having run the Lithuanian Communist Party since 1940. Ringaudas Songaila, an apparatchik who would succeed Griškevičius in 1987, wasn't even given a year to lead the party before the more reformist Algirdas Brazauskas seized the reins and helped steer the entire republic toward independence.

In Estonia and Latvia, Brezhnev-era leaders hung on for much longer. Karl Vaino, appointed as Estonian Communist Party chief in 1978, relished his job of keeping the republic under tight Soviet control. He opposed Mikhail Gorbachev's calls for democratic and economic reform and dismissed open declarations of no-confidence in his leadership within Estonia until he was ousted from office in June 1988. Gorbachev elevated Vaino to a job in the Communist Party Central Committee in Moscow, where he later retired and never again set foot in Estonia. Gorbachev also helped to extricate the last Brezhnevite leader of Latvia, Boris Pugo, by appointing him to the full Politburo of the Communist Party in Moscow and eventually to the post of Interior Minister of the USSR. As is well known, however, Gorbachev would later regret this move, when in August 1991 Pugo would play an active part in plotting the *coup d'état* against him. In the event, Pugo successfully evaded any consequences for his actions by committing suicide two days after the coup had failed.

Another echelon of Soviet rulers who might have been pursued by latter-day democratic leaders concerned the local heads of the KGB. However, here too the main officials were removed early during the democratic transition. For example, Boris Pugo had pursued part of his earlier career in the Latvian KGB and had even headed the organization from 1980 to 1984, but he would never be held accountable for his deeds after his suicide. Estonia's KGB chief from 1961 to 1982, August Pork actually decided to stay in Estonia after retirement and even remained through independence, but according to one news report left for Moscow in 1996 (Brinkman 2007). In Lithuania, Juozas Petkevičius headed the Soviet security service for over twenty years from 1967 to 1987. Under his tight-fisted rule, Catholic Church activists and other dissidents were consistently repressed (Burinskaitė and Okuličiūtė 2010). Following his departure from office in 1987, Petkevičius stayed in Lithuania, but died in September 1991, barely a month after the country restored its full independence. His successor in office, Eduardas Eismuntas, was suspected of having destroyed KGB materials and undermining the independence movement before his removal in 1990; however, no formal investigation was ever launched into his past.

The Baltic states, therefore, had few recent Soviet-era leaders who had been truly repressive and whom independent governments might have wanted to pursue and prosecute. Yet this only covered some of the options for transitional justice vis-à-vis perpetrators. Democratic leaders may also pursue transitional justice against those who opposed the democratic transition through violence and who it is thought need to be sidelined in order to secure the new democratic order. In the Baltic states pro-Soviet and anti-independence forces had been quite strong from 1988 to 1991, encompassing not only recalcitrant Communist Party members but also the managers of major Soviet enterprises and some Soviet military officials. These dense networks were used not only to organize a number of anti-independence demonstrations during these years but also to provide civilian cover when the Soviet military was used directly to quell Baltic independence aspirations in 1991. During the first such attempt in January, Soviet paratroopers occupied the Lithuanian television tower in Vilnius as well as many other buildings, and in the process killed fourteen demonstrators in what threatened to be a full-scale crackdown on the three states.

In sync with these events, the head of the pro-Soviet Lithuanian Communist Party, Mykolas Burokevičius, was among those who formed a Lithuanian National Salvation Committee (*Nacionalinio gelbėjimo komitetas*) intent on seizing power once the Soviet troops had removed the pro-independence government. In the end, the military action failed and Burokevičius went into hiding. However, Lithuanian prosecutors immediately began gathering materials against him. When in August the full-scale *coup d'état* was attempted in Moscow, pro-Soviet forces in Lithuania were subdued. Yet as soon as the events cleared, Lithuanian prosecutors indicted Burokevičius for sedition and other acts linked to the January 1991 assaults. Burokevičius became the first high-level pro-Soviet official in Lithuania to be charged in an act of transitional justice. However, he could not be taken into immediate custody as he had in the meantime fled to Belarus. It was only in January 1994 that Burokevičius together with another defendant, Juozas Jermalavičius, would be returned to Lithuania to stand trial.

The court proceedings – soon to be dubbed the "January 13 trial" by the media – were initiated against a total of six anti-independence activists in November 1996. Because of repeated delays requested by the defendants for reasons of ill health, the trial would last more than two and a half years. However, it would also grow in magnitude, as Lithuanian prosecutors would attempt to link the defendants to a whole series of anti-independence actions stretching from April 1990 to August 1991. Moreover, in a twist of fate prosecutors would indict the accused on the basis of the same sections of the Soviet Lithuanian criminal code that had been used to convict dissidents during the Soviet era, namely provisions against "publicly urging the forceful overthrow of the sovereignty of the state" (Article 68) and "the creation [of] and participation in anti-state organizations" (Article 70) (European Court of Human Rights 2008b). In other words, prosecutors took the issue much farther than the single events of January 1991 in order to seek a more principled ruling against the anti-independence leaders. Transitional justice was being served upon individuals viewed as having been intimately bound up in the repression attempted at the very end of the old regime.

In August 1999, all of the defendants in the January 13 trial were convicted. An appeals court later circumscribed some of the convictions and reduced the sentences, but it upheld the fundamental principle of punishing the pro-Soviet activists for defying Lithuanian sovereignty and belonging to a banned organization.[1] Mykolas Burokevičius was sentenced to the longest prison sentence, twelve years, but was released early in January 2006. Burokevičius (along with two other defendants) would go on to contest their convictions in the European Court of Human Rights. However, these petitions were denied in February 2008. (See Chapter 7.)

In all, Lithuania would pursue the criminal prosecution of a range of anti-independence forces, including erstwhile Soviet military personnel involved in the January 1991 killings, but also those who carried out

[1] Specifically, the Court noted that the Lithuanian Criminal Code had been amended in November 1990 in order to turn both Article 68 and 70 into statutes especially applicable for actions against the new Lithuanian state. Clearly, Lithuanian legislators had approved these changes with a view to having legal-criminal recourse against pro-Soviet activists. However, the appeals court noted that because of the later date of these amendments the defendants could not be charged with any anti-independence actions they had committed before November 1990. This extenuated the criminal circumstances for some of the defendants, but didn't override the basic conviction in relation to those acts committed after November 1990 (European Court of Human Rights 2008b).

several violent attacks against nascent Lithuanian border posts in which nearly a dozen border guards were murdered (15min.lt 2013). Yet in most cases investigations have been severely hampered by the fact that the suspects have fled to Belarus or Russia, and authorities in these two countries have refused to help Lithuanian prosecutors (European Court of Human Rights 2008b). The efforts at transitional justice in relation to specific perpetrators of repression during the independence struggle were thus very tangible, although the effectiveness of these actions was mixed.

The other Baltic state to pursue a kind of transitional justice against Soviet-era perpetrators was Latvia. As in Lithuania, attention focused on those who had actively defied the new pro-independence government after May 1990. This again involved the pro-Soviet wing of the local Communist Party, which had given support to Soviet military violence in the republic in January 1991, but in particular had served as a local coordinating base for the August 1991 conservative coup against Mikhail Gorbachev.

Specifically, the last head of the Latvian Communist Party, Alfreds Rubiks, had taken up the cause to defend Soviet rule in Latvia. He was no outsider in the republic, in contrast to some of the other Russified Baltic leaders (particularly in Estonia and Latvia). Born in the eastern city of Daugavpils, he had served as mayor of Riga from 1984 to 1990. Yet he remained committed to the Soviet system, and as pro-independence sentiment began to rise, he became more reactionary. During 1990 Rubiks headed up a number of shadowy groups formed to uphold Soviet rule. Most critically, in January 1991 he chaired the pro-Moscow All-Latvian Societal Salvation Committee (*Vislatvijas sabiedrības glābšanas komiteja*) and coordinated the actions of Soviet paratroopers and other forces meant to topple the Latvian government just as similar events were taking place in Lithuania. Rubiks and his deputy Ojārs Potreki issued an ultimatum to the Latvian parliament to dissolve itself and later declared during a public rally on January 15 that the Committee had taken over power in the republic. When the Soviet crackdown subsided (due to international pressure), Rubiks suspended his committee's activities. However, in August he sprang into action again by forming the Latvian State Committee on the State of Emergency as a mirror organization to the illegal putschist group in Moscow. After this coup attempt again failed, Latvian state authorities no longer tolerated Rubiks and arrested him (together with Potreki) almost immediately on August 23. As in the case of Burokevičius, Rubiks was charged with undermining the sovereignty of the Latvian state and was sentenced to eight years in prison. However, in contrast to Burokevičius, Rubiks became much more of a martyr for those nostalgic for the Soviet era. He was repeatedly championed by the Latvian Socialist Party or successor to the Latvian Communist Party, including being nominated for president of Latvia while still in prison. In November 1997 he was released early from incarceration and immediately became re-engaged with politics. He was a prominent member of a coalition of Russian-based political parties called For Human Rights in a United Latvia, and he continued to speak out in public. Although he was prevented by lustration laws from running for elective office in Latvia (see Chapter 4), he took advantage in 2009 of Europe-wide rules to run and gain a seat in the European Parliament, which the Latvian authorities could not deny him. There he joined the European United Left party group and has continued not only to criticize Latvian post-independence politics, but also to openly challenge Baltic historical narratives by justifying Stalin-era deportations and other repressions against Latvians (see Chapter 7).

Estonia's absolute lack of transitional justice toward pro-Soviet activists during 1990 and 1991 stems partly from the fact that the military crackdowns in Lithuania and Latvia never reached the northern-most Baltic state with such intensity. As a result, openly seditious "salvation committees" never formed in Estonia, and the pro-Moscow activists who did stage demonstrations and strikes in 1989 and 1990 were never charged with any wrongdoing.

Establishing the legal framework for prosecuting communist-era crimes

The understanding that independent Estonia, Latvia and Lithuania could and should find a judicial response to mass crimes committed during the Soviet era and for going after individuals who had been involved in those crimes emerged in close conjunction with the three states' claims regarding the illegal and illegitimate character of their Soviet rule. As described in Chapter 2, Baltic independence activists argued successfully that their states had continued to exist in international law throughout the Soviet period because of the illegal nature of the 1939 Hitler–Stalin Pact and the events that followed. The forced seizure of power by the Soviet authorities and their local supporters was thus an illegal act. What is more, the acts of repression and abuse committed by that regime should be qualified in terms of international, and not just domestic, law (Mälksoo 2003a).

Baltic legislators worked largely on their own initiative in examining the different options for classifying Stalinist crimes such that these could be made subject to latter-day prosecution. Victim organizations and other "accountability actors" (Collins 2010) also supported them, primarily by pushing not only for the swift rehabilitation of former political convicts but also for criminal-legal justice against perpetrators. As Lauri Mälksoo (2001: 760) has remarked, the temporal distance to some of the worst crimes committed by the previous regime made it extremely difficult to apply legal principles in a consistent manner. A broad range of taxonomic terms were available for these crimes: deportation, genocide, crimes against humanity, ethnic cleansing, gross human rights violations.

An important background orientation for dealing with these issues was set by the Baltic states' abiding belief in their doctrine of legal continuity and the inclination that this would give toward further applying international law when dealing with domestic political issues. In the realm of retrospective justice, an important cornerstone was laid with the three states' quick accession to the 1948 Convention on the Prevention and Punishment of the Crime of Genocide and the 1968 Convention on the Non-Applicability of Statutory Limitations to War Crimes and Crimes Against Humanity. These international legal norms would provide a blueprint for Baltic legislators to formulate new laws and/or amendments to existing criminal codes that would allow for the prosecution of Stalinist crimes of the 1940s and 1950s.

However, in some instances these frameworks would be modified or even sharpened in order to stress particular aspects of the Baltic context. Thus, Lithuania decided to augment its April 1992 ratification of the two international conventions with a special Law on the Liability for the Genocide of the Lithuanian People (Lietuvos Respublikos Seimas 1992b). While the Law declared that both Nazi Germany and the Soviet Union had committed crimes against humanity, its main focus was on defining the crime of genocide with a clear view to prosecuting Soviet crimes. On the whole, the definition provided was very close to that contained in Article 2 of the Genocide Convention. However, in a slight qualification Article 2 of the Law explicitly classified as genocide "the killing and torturing and deportation of Lithuanian inhabitants committed during the occupation and annexation of Lithuania by Nazi Germany and the USSR" (Lietuvos Respublikos Seimas 1992b). According to Žilinskas, this choice of formulation was not the result of any substantial legal discussion, but rather driven by the political intention of the legislators at the time to make a strong statement with regard to the Soviet Communist past. As he observes, "the title of 'genocide' itself has a much stronger impact on public opinion, especially when dealing with historical injustices, unlike 'crimes against humanity' whose nature is much less understood by the public" (Žilinskas 2009: 338). At the same time, with its rather categorical nature the 1992 law set the tone for subsequent legislative acts and public-political discourses on the Soviet-era crimes. Moreover, it would actually create complications for prosecutors seeking to render justice for past mass crimes, for in addition to its ad hoc nature the law essentially established only a single avenue for prosecution (genocide).

It was only in 1998 that the Lithuanian Seimas would come around to at least regularizing this codification of genocide when it decided to create a special section on "State Crimes" within the Soviet Lithuanian Penal Code still in force. Article 71 of the Code would henceforth include reference to the crime of genocide, and the special 1992 law was repealed. Moreover, the crime of genocide was declared punishable also retroactively (Lietuvos Respublikos Seimas 1998a). Yet this formal adjustment did not mean a change in the overall perception of Soviet crimes, since the wording used for Article 71 was the same as that in the 1992 law. As one Lithuanian prosecutorial official, Rimvydas Valentukevičius, noted, Lithuanian lawmakers aimed "to correct the error" made in international law in the definition of genocide; thus, the new provision continued to include "annihilation of people on social and political grounds in the concept of genocide" (Valentukevičius 2004). A few months after the adoption of the genocide provision, the Seimas adopted another amendment to the Code, inserting a separate section on war crimes, listing *inter alia* the "deportation of civilians from an occupied country" as among the offenses falling under this category (Article 100) (Lietuvos Respublikos Seimas 1998b). Yet, despite these amendments Lithuanian legislators failed to institute crimes against humanity as an alternative legal category for adjudicating Soviet-era crimes outside the category of war crimes. This would be achieved only in 2003 when a new national criminal code would be adopted in which a broad definition for genocide was provided together with a codification of other crimes against humanity and war crimes (Articles 99–113).

Both Estonia and Latvia pursued a rather different path in developing a legal framework for prosecuting Soviet-era mass crimes. To be sure, both would begin with the adoption of the relevant international conventions. In fact, Latvia would be the first to declare its adherence to these treaties when it proclaimed the restoration of its independence in May 1990. In March 1992 the Supreme Council would follow up with a decision (*lēmums*) "on the enforcement of conventional legal norms in relation to crimes against humanity," in which it established that according to the UN Convention of November 26, 1968, "crimes against humanity do not fall under any [statutory] limitations and where such crimes have been committed they shall be called to criminal accountability" (Latvijas Republikas Augstākā Padome 1992d). Based on this ruling, in April 1993 the Latvian Supreme Council passed an amendment to its Soviet-era Criminal Code, adding a comprehensive set of provisions to deal not only with genocide but also with crimes against humanity, crimes against peace and war crimes. Yet, in an interesting twist, Paragraph 68.1 of the new Code would carry the title "Crimes Against Humanity and Genocide" and contain only a single definition:

> an intentional act for purposes of the destruction in whole or in part of any group of people identifiable as such by nationality, ethnic origin, race, social class or a defined collective belief or faith, killing members of the group, causing them serious bodily harm or causing their mental illness, deliberately creating conditions of life that result in whole or in part, in physical destruction, as well as for the same purpose by limiting or depriving indigenous economic, political and/or social human rights.
>
> (Latvijas Republikas Augstākā Padome 1993)

Estonia was the last Baltic country to update its criminal legislation with new provisions regarding punishment for mass human rights abuses. For although as early as December 1988 one parliamentary document had called on the Estonian SSR prosecutor general to investigate any reported incidents of "mass murder or other crimes against humanity,"[2] there was no formal legal provision for prosecuting such crimes until nearly six years later. In November 1994, the Riigikogu passed a special law on the criminal accountability of individuals responsible for crimes against humanity or war crimes (Eesti Vabariigi Riigikogu 1994a). In it, Estonia renewed its pledge to uphold the relevant UN conventions it had ratified back in August 1991. It also, however, followed Latvia's example and inserted a formal chapter into its Soviet-era Criminal Code containing four paragraphs that codified, among

[2] See Point 3 in the Estonian SSR Supreme Soviet law "Kohtuväliste massirepressioonide kohta Nõukogude Eestis 1940–1950-ndail aastail" (Eesti NSV Ülemnõukogu 1988).

others, crimes against humanity and war crimes. Paragraph 61.1 now defined "crimes against humanity, including genocide" as:

> any willful act, the objective of which it was to completely or partially destroy a national, ethnic, racial, religious, anti-occupation resistance or other social group, or acts involving the killing or severe or very severe bodily injury or mental injury or torture of any member of such a group, or acts involving the forcible separation of children [from their parents] or in the event of armed attack, occupation or annexation the deportation or expulsion of native residents as well as any deprivation of their economic, political and social rights or any restriction of these rights.
>
> (Eesti Vabariigi Riigikogu 1994a)

As we will show in the later section on prosecutorial strategies and case law, the codification of two distinct offenses within one single article in both the Latvian and the Estonian criminal laws of the early 1990s caused considerable confusion in terms of the distinct features of each offense. Some of the first judgments, indeed, remained rather ambiguous as to whether or not the genocidal intention of the defendant – a crucial element of the legal conception of genocide – had been sufficiently established by prosecutors with regard to specific acts of deportation or other forms of repression.

Hence, reviewing these early legislative settings from a comparative perspective, we see that while Lithuanian legislators classified Soviet crimes exclusively in terms of the "crime of crimes," genocide, both Latvian and Estonian lawmakers conflated the two rather different international crimes of genocide and crimes against humanity into one. All three initial legal frameworks, however, suggested a political will by Baltic legislators to amend established conceptions in order to fit the particular offenses committed under Soviet rule (Satkauskas 2004: 397). Whether this diversion from international customary law was the result of "*lacunae* in the knowledge of international law" among Baltic legislators and scholars, as Lauri Mälksoo (2001: 761) suggests with regard to Estonia, or a deliberate political statement as suggested by Žilinskas (2009) in the case of Lithuania, Baltic legislation and jurisdiction have become the subject of much scholarly debate as well as some prosecutorial confusion especially among Latvian and Estonian authorities over the course of the 1990s.

Moreover, relatively little of this confusion would be cleared up after 2000, despite the adoption of wholly new Criminal Codes in all three countries. The relevant legislation that would enter into force in Latvia in

1999, in Estonia in 2002 and in Lithuania in 2003 continued to show legislators' preference for qualifying Soviet repressions and crimes above all as genocide. All three Criminal Codes continued to define the crime of genocide as broadly directed against a group of people defined by nationality, ethnic origin, race, religion, social or political beliefs.[3] And in the Estonian case the latter category was again specified as "group(s) resisting occupation" (Division II, Article 89). Only the Estonian law offered an additional definition of offenses under the code of "crimes against humanity" (Article 90), while Lithuania outlined crimes against humanity under two articles: no. 100 "Treatment of Persons Prohibited under International Law" and no. 101 "Killing of Persons Protected under International Law," among them also the offense of deportation. The Latvian Criminal Code of 1999 did not provide a separate codification of crimes against humanity. Instead, chapter IX of the Criminal Code defines only the offenses of "genocide," "crimes against peace" and "war crimes" (Articles 71, 72 and 74).[4] As we will see in our later discussion of prosecutorial choices and outcomes, this would have a considerable effect on the number of criminal proceedings newly initiated by the Prosecutor General's Office in Latvia after 2000, since the limitation to genocide as the sole prosecutorial option meant trying such cases would be more daunting.

Baltic scholars of international humanitarian law tend to point out that the broad definition of genocide adopted by Baltic legislators is by no means unprecedented (Mälksoo 2001; Satkauskas 2004). An increasing number of states, among them Austria, France and Finland, have "opted in their national law for an extended list of [protected] groups," thus aiming to go beyond the still dominant international understanding of the concept (Žilinskas 2009: 337; see also Bruun 1993: 210–18). In fact,

[3] In 2014 the Lithuanian Constitutional Court confirmed this interpretation, maintaining that the state has the right to adapt the definition of genocide to its own cultural-historical context and to extend the definition of genocide to relevant groups. At the same time, the Court cautioned against the retroactive application of this extended definition of genocide to crimes committed in the 1950s. It urged state prosecutors and courts to assess Soviet-era crimes strictly on the basis of universally recognized norms of international law (Constitutional Court of the Republic of Lithuania 2014).

[4] Only in May 2009 did the Latvian Saeima finally introduce a separate criminal provision for crimes against humanity (para 71.2). The amendments to the law were done in the context of adopting EU regulations on hate speech and xenophobia into national criminal law. Together with the introduction of a definition of crimes against humanity, the genocide definition was changed to parallel that in international treaties. See also Chapter 7.

some scholars argue that this growing number of states worldwide is indicative of a widespread dissatisfaction with existing legal conceptions of the international crime of genocide as adopted in customary law (Schabas 2000). Some have even claimed an "international trend" is afoot to change this (Mälksoo 2001: 771).

Proponents of a legal redefinition of Stalinist crimes argue both historically and legally. For example, based on an ever more thorough analysis of the historical facts that show the inhumane methods and destructive outcome of Stalin-era forced resettlement of large parts of the Baltic populations, historians and legal scholars have argued for seeing the mass deportations of the 1940s as directed against the Baltic nations rather than just particular politically or ideologically opposed groups (Strods and Kott 2002; Constitutional Court of the Republic of Lithuania 2014: 39). Others have argued that the 1948 Genocide Convention was itself flawed, as it was a compromise "born of politics and the desire to insulate political leaders from scrutiny and liability" – in this case especially Stalin (Van Schaak 1996: 2261). Indeed, some maintain that Raphael Lemkin, the brain behind the term "genocide" and one of the fathers of the 1948 Genocide Convention, had originally proposed a much broader understanding, seeing genocide as effected through "a synchronized attack on different aspects of life of the captive people," including in the "political and social field" (cited in Quigley 2006: 5). Moreover, Lemkin is said to have actively lobbied for the inclusion of political and social groups in the list of protected groups during the treaty negotiations, and there is evidence that he personally considered Soviet repressions against the Baltic populations (especially the mass deportations) as falling under the category of genocide (Weiss-Wendt 2005). Thus, although there may be strong arguments in favor of rethinking historical and judicial presumptions, the Baltic approach of "model[ing] the respective definitions [of genocide] according to their applicability to repressive acts committed during the Soviet occupation" (Satkauskas 2004: 397) remains a highly controversial and politically contested issue mirrored also in prosecutorial strategies and choices made during the past twenty years.

Establishing the investigatory infrastructure

In addition to establishing a proper legal basis for punishing communist-era crimes, prosecutors tasked with pursuing retrospective criminal justice also required an institutional infrastructure in order to investigate cases and be successful in court. Here, the historical character of the crimes under consideration only added to the need for resources, since vast amounts of archival work needed to be done, excavations and forensic work carried out, elderly witnesses questioned and other materials collected. When comparing the Baltic states in this domain, we will see that whereas Lithuania and Latvia established special subdivisions within their Prosecutor General's offices to deal solely with wartime crimes and postwar Soviet abuses, Estonia assigned this investigatory responsibility to the country's internal security service, the *Kaitsepolitsei*. Moreover, the extent to which each country has linked professional historians capable of doing the relevant research with criminal investigators ready to assess the information from a legal point of view goes some way to explaining the scope and also success of the retrospective criminal justice process.

Lithuania was the first to move on this score as early as October 1991 when under the center-right government of Gediminas Vagnorius a Special Investigations Division (*Specialiųjų tyrimų skyrius*, STS) was established within the Prosecutor General's Office. The division was tasked with working closely with both the State Security Department and historians to identify individuals involved in the mass deportations and other Soviet-era crimes as well as the anti-partisan repressions carried out by the Soviet security forces (NKVD and its successors). While the Prosecutor General's Office would become the sole agency empowered to conduct pre-trial investigations into crimes against humanity, genocide and war crimes, it had a clear political mandate to do so, and all the more so after the 1992 Law on Genocide in Lithuania was adopted. After 1998 these powers were granted also to the Lithuanian State Security Department as well as territorial offices of the regular police. Nonetheless, the STS continued to monitor all investigations in order to ensure the correct application of the code of criminal procedure (Balkelis and Davoliūtė 2009).

The investigatory capacities of the STS were considerably bolstered by a restructuring in 1997 of the Genocide and Resistance Research Center of Lithuania (*Lietuvos gyventojų genocido ir rezistencijos tyrimo centras* – LGGRTC). This was a research institution that had been established already in 1992 to continue the work of earlier grassroots initiatives in collecting data about former deportees and other victims of Soviet repression (see also Chapter 6). The changes to this institution that were implemented in 1997 involved giving more weight to historical investigations that focused on perpetrators. As a parliamentary resolution at the time stated:

> seven years after the re-establishment of the independence of the Republic of Lithuania, the consequences of the Soviet and Nazi occupation have not yet been systematised and evaluated, the structures of occupational regimes which organized and perpetrated mass repressions, deportation and genocide of Lithuanian population, war crimes and other crimes against humanity have not been identified.
>
> (Lietuvos Respublikos Seimas 1997c)

Thus, a special investigations unit for crimes against humanity, genocide and war crimes was established and its collaboration with judicial institutions was formalized. As a specialized subdivision of the LGGRTC, this new office actively supported the STS by supplying material for proceedings, offering advice on historical matters, securing documents, and at times initiating its own investigations into specific cases. During the early 2000s the LGGRTC became a very close partner of the Lithuanian Prosecutor General's Office in carrying out pre-trial investigations and other tasks. Its role could be seen in many of the cases that would eventually come to trial.

Latvia's first attempts at providing an institutional infrastructure for criminal proceedings started slightly later than those in Lithuania. In March 1992, the Saeima established an Investigative Commission for the Crimes of the Totalitarian Regimes (*Totalitāro režīmu noziegumu izmeklēšanas komisija* – TRNIK) in order to lay the groundwork for the establishment of a special investigative arm of the Latvian Prosecutor General's Office, the Investigation Division for Crimes of the Totalitarian Regimes (*Totalitāro režīmu noziegumu izmeklēšanas nodaļa* – TRNIN) as well as for the creation of a Center for the Documentation of the Consequences of Totalitarianism (*Totalitārisma seku dokumentēšanas centrs* – TSDC). Thus, the Prosecutor General's Office had a separate subdivision to deal with Stalinist-era crimes, and additionally its activities were, from the beginning, formally complemented by a research institution that employed professional historians. The TSDC was mainly tasked with preserving and reviewing leftover KGB material (see Chapter 4). However, as of 1995 it would also play a critical role in carrying out pre-trial investigations in relation to criminal proceedings against alleged perpetrators of crimes against humanity. For this to be possible, in 1995 the TSDC was moved from its previous subordination under the Ministry of Justice to become a structural unit of the Constitutional Protection

Bureau (*Satversmes aizsardzības birojs*, SAB), the Latvian domestic intelligence service (Latvijas Republikas Saeima 1994b). In contrast to the Ministry of Justice, the SAB was formally authorized to carry out pretrial criminal investigations, but the move was also motivated by security considerations regarding the activities of the TSDC's investigators (Zālīte, e-mail correspondence, 2013). These concerns probably related primarily to the Center's political-administrative tasks in the realm of lustration and regulating access to KGB files. However, this institutional arrangement resulted in a remarkable intensification of prosecutorial activities after 1995, as the TSDC worked most closely with the TRNIN. Its staff members received subpoena powers and special training in interrogating witnesses for trial purposes. The TSDC thus became a key actor in the criminal-legal truth and justice process. Indeed, according to one of the former employees of the TSDC, the Center's team of historians instigated most of the criminal proceedings by the Prosecutor General's Office, among them the most prominent case of war crimes committed by Soviet army sergeant Vassily Kononov (Jansons, e-mail correspondence, 2013). In 2008, after a longer period in which historical investigations into the mass crimes of the 1940s had already slowed down and the cooperation between TRNIN and TSDC markedly diminished, the Center's historical research activities ceased completely. The main reason for this concerned strict austerity measures in the wake of the 2008 economic crisis. However, a lack of interest on the part of the SAB leadership to deal with historical crimes as well as decreasing political support also played a role in this. Indeed, the institutional restructuring of the TSDC in 2008 was seen by some media commentators as proof that investigations into historical crimes were no longer seen as necessary and even regarded as "a waste of time" (Sprūde 2009a). The Center was eventually moved to the outskirts of Riga, its archive partially transferred to the State Archive, most of its employees laid off and its tasks reduced to providing lustration-related information upon request (Pettai 2013a). In an unrelated move, the TRNIN at the Prosecutor General's Office was also abolished a few years later.

In Estonia, yet a different institutional constellation was found. Alongside the Prosecutor General's Office, the main responsibility for carrying out criminal investigations was placed with the Estonian Security Police Board (*Kaitsepolitsei* – KAPO). This meant that even if formal investigatory capacity was enhanced by having two institutions work on the issue, the fact remained that neither would actually possess immediate expertise in the historical domain. To be sure, KAPO would eventually liaise with historians working for the International Commission for the Investigation of Crimes Against Humanity created in 1998 by President Lennart Meri (see Chapter 6). However, the Police Board would never develop as close a bond with the historians working for the Commission as the Lithuanian STS would with the LGGRTC, or the Latvian TRNIN with the TSDC.

In comparing these institutional arrangements, we may say that while Estonia's institutional settings suggest an approach that links the investigation into totalitarian regime crimes with national security,[5] the Lithuanian way of placing sole responsibility for criminal investigations within the Prosecutor General's Office and providing historical support via the LGGRTC indicates a more historical justice-oriented approach. The Latvian model is more ambiguous and perhaps involves both methods at once. On the one hand, the TSDC's investigators operated under the Latvian intelligence service (SAB) similarly to those working within the Estonian KAPO. Yet this has not lent a strong security character to the TSDC's work. On the contrary, for the first fifteen years of its existence the TSDC remained an organization strongly focused on historical analysis and even public dissemination. Its members have participated actively in interpretive debates over the character of the Soviet regime and in discussions over historical justice.

Prosecutorial choices and outcomes: the ups and downs of the criminal justice process

The preceding overview of legal frameworks and investigatory infrastructures indicated that Lithuania stands out among the Baltic states for having a relatively assertive focus on genocide as the key legal lens through which to pursue retrospective criminal justice as well as for developing an extensive and financially sustained network of investigatory agencies to prepare cases. These impressions are borne out by Table 3.1 in which we have summarized the entire list of investigations, trials and convictions related to Stalinist-era crimes in the Baltic states. The table shows that not only does Lithuania contain the most names, it also features the most cases of genocide and in particular in relation to Soviet security operations against Lithuanian postwar partisans. The

[5] This view was strongly voiced by the Deputy Director of the KAPO, Martin Arpo, during an interview, October 4, 2013.

Table 3.1 *Comparative table of criminal-legal trials against Stalinist-era perpetrators*

Legal provision	**1940–41** (1941 deportations & killings of civilians)	**1941–44** (Holocaust; wartime killing of civilians)	**post-1945** (civilian and partisan killings)	**1945–56** (1949 "Priboi" and other deportations of civilians)
ESTONIA				
1994 CC amendment §61.1: CaH/genocide	*V. Riis* (1996); *I. Jakobson* (1996)		**K.-L. Paulov** (1999); **V. Penart** (1999) / **R. Tuvi** (1999; §136 (a))	**J. Klaassepp** (1999); **V. Beškov** (1999); **M. Neverovski** (1999); **V. Loginov** (1999); **P. Kislyiy / A. Kolk** (2003); **V. Kask (2006)**
2002 CC §89: CaH				**J. Karpov** (2006); *A. Kolga*; *R. Sisask* (2010); *S. Nikejev* (2010); *B. Loho*; *V. Martson*; *H. Laus*; *O. Adamson*; *L. Maikov*; *N. Žerebtsov*
§90: genocide				*A. Meri* (2003); *V. Paltmann* (2008); *J. Pähna* (2008); *V. Pehk* (2012)
§95: war crimes		*H. Männil* (2005)		
LATVIA				
1993 CC amendment §68.1: CaH/genocide	**M. Farbtuhs** (1999); **Y. Savenko** (2000); *Kirsanovs* (1999); *S. Murin* (1995); *M. Šustins*; *Ž. Sprūde*; *A. Zvejnieks*		**J. Kiršteins** (2005); *J. Lukaševics*; *M. Vītoliņs*; *A. Bundulis*; *L. Fomins* (1998)	**A. Noviks** (1996); **N. Tess** (2003); **N. Larionovs** (2005); *I. Mašonkin* (2006); *T. Jakušonoks* (1998); *I. Reisners*; *J. Dzintars*
§68.3: war crimes		**V. Kononov** (2004)		
1999 CC §71 genocide				
§73 war crimes		*K. Kalejs* (2000)		
LITHUANIA				
1992 special Law on Genocide	*A. Surin* (1998)	**K. Gimžauskas** (1998); *A. Lileikis* (1998)	**K. Kurakinas / P. Bartacevicius / J. Šakalys** (1995) / *J. Š.*	*J. Baranauskas* (2001)

Table 3.1 (*cont.*)

Legal provision	**1940–41** (1941 deportations & killings of civilians)	**1941–44** (Holocaust; wartime killing of civilians)	**post-1945** (civilian and partisan killings)	**1945–56** (1949 "Priboi" and other deportations of civilians)
1998 CC amendments §71: genocide	**P. Raslanas** (1999); **I. P.** (1999)	*Gudelis* (1999)	*Z. K.* (1999); **B. Viater / K. Kregždė / A. Lapinskas / P. Preikšaitis / I. Tamošiūnas** (2000); **R. J. Š.** (2001); **V. Vasiliauskas / M. Žukaitienė** (2001); **J. Dabulevičius** (2003); **J. Juškauskas / J. Navickas** (2006); *B. B.* (2008); *J. Naubaras* (2009); **P. A. Povilaitis** (2009); **M. Misiukonis** (2014); *S. Tichomirov; R. Kublicka; P. Laguckas* (2009); ***J. Karpavičius*** (2010)	
§334: deportation from occupied state				**F. S.** (2001); **V. Misiūnas** (2002); *A. Surin* (1999)
2003 CC §99: genocide			**M. Bulatovas** (2010); **P. Preikšaitis** (2012); **V. J. Petronis** (2013); **V. Vasiliauskas** (2011); *V. Valkavicas* (2009); ***P. J.*** (2010); ***V. Š.*** (2010); ***B. Blazys*** (2010); ***J. Kuprėnienė / I. Vorobjov*** (2010)	
§102: deportation from occupied state; §101: killing of persons protected under int'l law; §100: treatment of persons prohibited under int'l law		**A. Dailidė** (2005)	**I. L.** (2012)	**V. Kojalis** (2010); **Z. D.** (2007); **A. V.** (2004); **J. S.** (2008); **M. Tabakajev** (2012); ***T. P.*** (2010)

KEY: **Bold**: cases that resulted in a court verdict (both guilty and not guilty); ***bold/italics***: court proceedings are still ongoing (as of 2014); *Italics*: investigations were discontinued (due to the death or ill health of the defendant) before the case was taken to court or during court proceedings.

latter fact is especially interesting in that Lithuanian prosecutors have clearly framed their investigations into what in many other countries would be considered simple counter-insurgency efforts as genocide. Meanwhile, Estonia and Latvia concentrated their efforts on pursuing the perpetrators of mass deportations from the 1940s and mostly issued indictments for crimes against humanity, although especially Latvian prosecutors also framed some deportation cases in genocide terms.

Table 3.1 also demonstrates a temporal dimension by sorting cases according to when they were taken to court or, in the case of a concluded trial, when a verdict was reached (indicated by the year). This is particularly useful as it allows us to trace the prosecutorial development (the ups and down of the criminal justice process) over time. In the sections that follow, we offer a more detailed profile of each country's investigations and trials. While it is not possible to outline each and every case that has been initiated, we do highlight those that have been emblematic of the way in which retrospective justice has been rendered on a criminal-judicial level.

But before we continue to discuss Baltic case law regarding communist-era crimes, a word needs to be added about Baltic prosecutors' activities in pursuing criminal justice for Nazi-era crimes, in particular those committed by local collaborators with the Nazi *Einsatzgruppen* in killing Jews. Throughout their first decade of re-independence, the Baltic states were much criticized for not doing enough to bring the last surviving Holocaust collaborators among their populations to justice. The Simon Wiesenthal Center (SWC), in particular, lamented the lack of criminal prosecutions of Nazi-era crimes in all three Baltic states after 1991, implicating a conscious neglect by Baltic governments of the issue of local Nazi collaboration (Onken 2003: 198). In the early 2000s the SWC further increased its pressures by launching a campaign entitled "Operation Last Chance" across the Baltic states and Central Europe calling on people to come forward if they knew of anyone who had collaborated with the Nazi occupation authorities in the killing of civilians during World War II (Zuroff 2011). The campaign was met with considerable indignation by the Baltic populations where the sense of loss with regard to their own family members was dominating discourses about the war. Any suggestion of the historical guilt of fellow countrymen was therefore strongly rejected as unjustified and wrong in view of the nations' victimization under Stalin.

In responding to the accusations of inactivity, Baltic prosecutors argued that many Nazi-era collaborators had already been prosecuted and punished right after the war by Soviet war crimes tribunals (Jansons 2002; Valentukevičius 2004). Indeed, thousands of people, among them both German POWs and actual and alleged Nazi collaborators among the local populations, were charged with war crimes. Many had been convicted and subsequently executed or deported to prison camps in the Gulag (see Chapter 2). Nevertheless, several individuals had managed to escape Soviet criminal justice during the postwar years either by fleeing to the West or by hiding out, thus living lives without ever being held to account for what they had done during the war. Whether or not the activities of Soviet postwar military tribunals can be accepted as a sufficient argument for not pursuing any further justice for those former Nazi collaborators, some of whom still lived in Western emigration, is an open question. To give priority to cases of Soviet regime crimes in pursuing criminal justice was certainly a political choice by Baltic prosecutors and governments.

Irrespective of these arguments, Lithuanian prosecutors had already in the early 1990s started to look into some of the cases of Nazi-era crimes, as indicated in Table 3.1. Based on the 1992 special Law on Genocide two individuals, the former deputy chief of the Vilnius Security Police, Kazys Gimžauskas, and his superior, former member of the Nazi-sponsored Lithuanian Security Police Aleksandras Lileikis, were formally charged for complicity and participation in the genocide of Jews in Lithuania. Both men had fled to the United States after the war and had been previously, yet unsuccessfully, investigated for wartime crimes by US authorities. After his US citizenship was revoked, Gimžauskas fled to Lithuania in 1996 (US Department of Justice 2001). His trial started in 1998 yet was repeatedly postponed due to health issues of the then 90-year-old. In 2000 the Seimas adopted an amendment to the procedural law to allow defendants to be absent from their trial for health reasons. This provision allowed the court proceedings to continue and to result in a conviction of the defendant in 2001. However, at 91 and with severe health problems, Gimžauskas was ruled unfit for punishment. His was the first successful Holocaust-related conviction in a former Soviet state. Indeed, the trial against his former superior, Lileikis, was less successful. Accused of having been in charge of several operations of the Lithuanian security police (the *Saugumas*) to capture and hand over Jews to the German authorities to be murdered, Lileikis was formally charged with genocide in 1999. However, he died shortly after his first court hearing in September 2000.

The only other successful trial against a Nazi perpetrator in the Baltic states took place in 2005 against Algimantas Dailidė, a former member of the Nazi-sponsored Lithuanian Security Police. After having been extradited to Lithuania from the United States in 2003, court proceedings began in November 2005 with charges for war crimes pursuant to Paragraph 100 ("Treatment of Persons Prohibited under International Law") of the 2003 national Criminal Code. In 2006 the Vilnius District Court found him guilty of taking part in the arrest of tens of thousands of Jews. His sentence was, however, suspended due to his advanced age and poor health. Apart from these more prominent cases, Baltic prosecutors would also investigate and sometimes seek the extradition of a handful of other individuals residing outside the three states (one more in Lithuania, two in Latvia and one in Estonia). In all of these instances, however, investigations would be closed either because of lack of evidence or because the accused had died or was no longer considered fit for trial.

In September 2000 the Latvian Prosecutor General's Office did bring charges for war crimes against a former Nazi-sponsored security police member, Konrads Kalējs. The move came after almost twenty years, during which Kalējs as an Australian citizen had repeatedly evaded prosecution by moving between five different countries. Over the years he had gone through several extradition proceedings where his past misdeeds had been revealed by US and Canadian courts. Yet he could not be prosecuted as his case fell outside US or Canadian jurisdiction and Australian authorities were slow in pursuing his case. According to Indulis Zālīte, whose team of historians at the TSDC investigated the case, Latvia's judicial authorities were under considerable political pressure during the mid-1990s as the need to demonstrate Latvia's readiness to prosecute Nazi collaborators had grown thanks to campaigns like the Wiesenthal Center's "Operation Last Chance." Yet the evidence found in this case by Latvian investigators did not suffice to file charges of genocide. Instead, the prosecutor chose to indict Kalējs for war crimes in connection with his role as a commander of the Salaspils prison camp during the war. Finally, in May 2001 Australian authorities ordered the extradition of Kalējs to Latvia; however, he died during the appeals procedures (Barkham 2001).

In Estonia, only one case of Nazi-era crimes was ever investigated by prosecutors; however, it never reached the stage of formal indictment. Already during the early 1990s the Wiesenthal Center had drawn the Estonian government's attention to the case of former Nazi Security

Police member Harry Männil, who the Center claimed had participated in the murder of numerous civilians, among them about a hundred Jews, in 1941. Yet investigations by Estonian prosecutors, some of them carried out at the request of Männil himself, came to the conclusion that there was insufficient evidence to support possible prosecution. In 1995 the director general of the Estonian Security Police Board, Jüri Pihl, commented on the case saying that "Harry Männil has no connections to any war crimes committed in Estonia during the Second World War; there was nothing criminal in his actions" (Luup 1998). Finally in 2001 the Prosecutor General's Office reopened criminal investigations into the case. This came not only after the Wiesenthal Center had increased its pressures, but also after the Estonian International Commission for Investigation of Crimes Against Humanity had established, in early 1999, that even though no evidence could be found for Männil's direct involvement in the killing of civilians, several of the Jews that he had interrogated were later killed. Thus, similar to the case of Dailidė in Lithuania, Männil was investigated with regard to his involvement in the arrest of a range of people (including Jews) during the Nazi period and their handing over to the Nazi security forces. After five years of investigating the case, however, Estonian prosecutors again declared that there was insufficient evidence to support prosecution. On the contrary, officials reported, investigations appeared to indicate that Männil had not been aware that the people he had interrogated in the early days of the German occupation would later be murdered. In December 2005 the investigations were discontinued.

Whether or not Baltic prosecutors could have shown more determination in pursuing criminal justice for Nazi-era crimes cannot be further discussed in this book. The cases briefly outlined here were important to show that alongside communist-related truth and justice, some effort was made to address Nazi-era crimes. The politics related to these cases was, however, above all international, since this issue would be closely monitored by Western countries as part of the Balts' re-integration with Europe (see also Chapter 7). For the remainder of this chapter, we now turn to look at cases brought by Baltic prosecutors in relation to Soviet-era crimes.

Lithuania

Between 1997 and 2014 Lithuanian prosecutors managed to prepare criminal cases for prosecution against forty-seven individuals indicted for crimes against humanity, genocide and war crimes relating to the Soviet period.[6] Several of the suspects died either before their cases could be sent to court or during the court proceedings. Of the remaining individuals, twenty-two were ultimately convicted. However, many prison sentences have also been suspended due to ill health, or they were shortened thanks to particular amnesty laws.[7] Eight cases have ended in acquittal. As can be seen in Table 3.1, cases relating to the postwar partisan wars in the Lithuanian countryside have far outnumbered cases concerning the mass deportations during the early and late 1940s. Only five cases have concerned killing or premeditated murder during the war; four of these related to the Nazi occupation period, and the other to the first Soviet occupation. Among the cases still being processed in various Lithuanian courts, those relating to genocide as part of the killing of anti-Soviet partisans after 1945 continue to dominate.

The problematic nature of Lithuania's 1992 Law on Genocide can also be seen in our table. Prosecutors initiated only very few cases on the basis of this statute, one concerning the Nazi period and two more (involving five individuals) relating to crimes of the postwar Soviet regime. All other court proceedings were launched based on the 1998 amendment to the Criminal Code and under improved investigatory conditions (i.e. after the restructuring of the LGGRTC).

An important theme that we try to capture in Table 3.1 is the evolution of Lithuanian prosecutorial activity over time. While we have already noted that all three Baltic countries were able to pick up the pace of their investigations and indictments as soon as proper legal frameworks and investigatory mechanisms were in place, the Lithuanian case features additional fluctuations. One conjunction of factors emerged in 1998, when the number of criminal investigations rose notably due to the creation of a special investigatory unit within the LGGRTC that began to supply prosecutors with additional historical information.[8] Likewise, alongside amendments to the Criminal Code passed in 1998, a new

[6] Many more initial investigations were carried out, yet never resulted in formal charges. See Generalinės Prokuratūros STS (2011).

[7] In June 1993 a special amnesty law was adopted to mark the new Constitution of Lithuania. The law granted a reduction of or exemption from prison sentences for certain groups of people, among them men over the age of 60. (See Lietuvos Respublikos Seimas 1993.)

[8] While between 1994 and 1997 an average of three new investigations were started per year by the Prosecutor General's Office, in 1998–99 this number rose to ten and sixteen and has remained on that level since (Generalinės Prokuratūros STS 2011: 4)

Criminal Procedure Code was adopted that increased the scope of investigatory and prosecutorial activities by regulating institutional cooperation between the State Security Department, the Prosecutor General and district and county prosecutors in cases of alleged historical crimes (Valentukevičius 2004).

A final, more political fluctuation emerged in 2007, when in response to a renewed decline in investigations and indictments, parliamentarians questioned the Prosecutor General's Office about this falloff. Coming during a pre-election period when center-right political forces were hoping to regain a parliamentary majority, conservative MPs queried the state of investigations into communist-era perpetrators. In two separate parliamentary debates in March and June 2007, they discussed the prosecutor general's report and his claim that investigations were winding down because few perpetrators were still alive or fit enough for trial. The authorities' report also detailed the difficulties involved in obtaining relevant material from the Russian Federation as well as a lack of interest both among some local prosecutors to conduct investigations and among the population to come forward with information (Generalinės Prokuratūros STS 2008). Parliamentarians, however, were not satisfied. MPs from the Homeland Union-Lithuanian Conservatives (TS-LK) party demanded an increased effort to identify and arrest still surviving perpetrators (Lietuvos Respublikos Seimas 2007).

The outcome of the deliberations was the passage of an amendment to the state budget allocating increased funds to the Prosecutor General's Office in order for the latter to hire seventy-two new prosecutors (Generalinės Prokuratūros STS 2008: 3). This had an effect in terms of increasing the number of not only newly started pre-trial investigations but also cases being sent to the courts. If before 2009 there had been an average of one or two trials per year, then in 2009 the number of court cases jumped to five and in 2010 to eight (Generalinės Prokuratūros STS 2011: 5).

From among the individual cases listed in Table 3.1, it is worth highlighting five that characterize some of the broader processes that we have been describing. As with Latvia's case of Alfons Noviks, Lithuania also kicked off its retrospective justice process with a high-publicity trial of three defendants accused of indiscriminate killing right after the end of World War II. In October 1995 the Vilnius District Court opened a trial against Kirilas Kurakinas, Petras Bartasevičius and Juozas Šakalys, all of whom had been members of a special NKVD unit called the "Fighter

Battalions" (*Istrebitelnye bataliony*). The battalion had been tasked with crushing anti-Soviet resistance in Lithuania right after the war, and specifically the three defendants were accused of having executed two women, one of them nine months pregnant, and a child in May 1945. The case was significant as it set a precedent for many more cases to follow, in which the killing of anti-Soviet partisans by NKVD operatives was classified as genocide. Crucial for the court in establishing genocidal intent among the defendants was their membership in the special battalion that, according to documents from the Soviet Ministry of Internal Affairs, had been tasked with the "mass killing of the Lithuanian population" (Satkauskas 2004: 393). The actions of these battalions were thus seen as part of a broader "genocidal campaign" launched against the Lithuanian people by the Soviet Security forces, which was enough to prove genocidal intent among the accused (Žalimas 2010). Kurakinas, who was in charge of one such battalion and admitted to the execution of the women and child, was sentenced to seven years' imprisonment (reduced later to two years thanks to amnesty rules), while the other two defendants received prison sentences of two years and four months each (Vilnius District Court 1998).

In 2001, another member of the Soviet security forces, the former head of the Telšiai NKGB, Petras Raslanas, was convicted *in absentia*[9] for genocide for having been involved in organizing the killing of seventy-six Lithuanians in 1941. In this instance the mass crime had been carried out not against anti-Soviet guerillas or their supporters, but against political prisoners (classified as unarmed civilians) during the chaotic days of late June 1941 and the German invasion. Relying on the new 1998 genocide amendment to the Criminal Code, the court qualified the particularly brutal executions of the prisoners as an effort to eliminate "a part of civilian unarmed inhabitants of Lithuania belonging to a separate political group [that was opposed to the Soviet regime]" (Žalimas 2010: 18). From a legal point of view, both the Kurakinas et al. and the Raslanas judgments were remarkable in that they not only stretched the legal conception of genocide established in international law but also punished acts of genocide that were committed prior to the drafting of any international convention or legal norms regarding this crime. Only the 1998 amendments had explicitly regulated the retroactive character of

[9] Raslanas resided in the Russian Federation at the time and the Russian government refused to extradite him for prosecution.

the crimes of genocide. Yet in neither case did the Lithuanian courts feel the need to allude to these facts in their judgments. Moreover, in stark contrast to other cases in Latvia and Estonia, none of the convicted individuals ever appealed this issue to the European Court of Human Rights (Quigley 2006: 44).

In 2004 the Kaunas District Court found former MGB officer Vytautas Vasiliauskas and his informant Martina Žukaitinė guilty of genocide for instigating and carrying out the killing of two partisans in January 1953. Again the court relied on Lithuania's particular definition of genocide that includes political groups. It argued that under Article 71.2 of the Criminal Code, Vasiliauskas had committed an act of genocide by virtue of having worked for the Soviet Security Forces whose main purpose at the time was to physically destroy the political resistance of the Lithuanian people. The accused was seen as having been fully aware of this purpose and having committed some of the killing himself (European Court of Human Rights 2009b). Yet other than in the case of Kurakinas, the judgment here took specific note of the expanded nature of this definition of genocide, acknowledging its divergence from the 1948 Genocide Convention and other international treaties. At the same time, the court confirmed the state prosecutor's assessment that the extension of the definition was "founded and in line with reality" and referred to similar jurisdiction in other countries (European Court of Human Rights 2009b). Moreover, the Appeals Court of Lithuania argued in a follow-up ruling that "although the [Genocide] Convention does not contain provisions on possible broader interpretation of the definition of genocide, it does not contain any prohibition of such an interpretation either."[10] Vasiliauskas and Žukaitiene were sentenced to six and five years respectively, yet only Vasiliauskas lodged a complaint to the European Court of Human Rights (ECtHR) arguing that the wider definition of genocide in Lithuanian law did not comply with international laws at the time when the offenses were committed, thus claiming a violation of Article 7 (prohibition of retroactivity) of the Convention. This was thus the first, and so far only, case that has challenged Lithuanian legislation with regard to Soviet-era crimes, in particular its interpretation of the crime of genocide. In June 2009 the ECtHR decided to communicate the application back to the respondent state, Lithuania, for commentary. It

[10] Judgment of Apeals Court of Lithuania in the case no. 1A-392 of Zukaitiene and Vasiliauskas, September 21, 2004, cited in Žalimas (2010: 14–15).

thus indirectly hinted that it would consider the case in greater depth at a later point in time (European Court of Human Rights 2009b).

An example of acquittal in relation to alleged postwar anti-partisan acts involves the joint case of Pranas Preikšaitis, Ignas Tamošiūnas and Algirdas Lapinskas, all of whom were former agents of the Soviet Security forces after the war and, like Vasiliauskas, were charged with genocide for their involvement in the killing of fifteen partisans in 1952 and 1953. The material for this case had been collected primarily by researchers at the LGGRTC and the charges had been laid on the basis of Article 2 of the 1992 Law on Genocide. Preikšaitis, in particular, rejected the allegations by pointing out that his participation in the Soviet security forces had been necessary to protect himself, since anti-Soviet partisans were known to have been killing people for not joining their ranks. Moreover, he pointed out that the so-called forest brothers had been killing innocent civilians, so he saw a necessity to fight them (Satkauskas 2004: 393). Both arguments are notable in that they contradicted the dominant narrative in Lithuania today of the heroic freedom fighters defending the country against Soviet occupation. In the end, however, what proved decisive for the case was that not enough evidence had been provided to prove the defendants' participation in the actual executions. Their mere participation in the arrest of people did not constitute sufficient grounds for the crime of genocide according to Lithuania's 1992 law.[11]

What is interesting about these partisan-related cases is the historical and legal interpretation of the postwar guerilla struggles against Soviet rule. For the state prosecutor, the defendants' membership in institutions or units that had had as their primary purpose the destruction of the armed anti-Soviet resistance was often enough to assume a genocidal intent and to classify the defendants' participation in killings of partisans as collaboration in genocide against the Lithuanian people. In more than a few cases, the courts followed this argumentation and expressed no reservations about this interpretation. Yet as Gailius points out, there is good reason to question this view of the partisan battles as a form of extinction and to see in them instead an armed conflict between the Soviet state and anti-Soviet guerilla fighters (Gailius 2005). Still, the Lithuanian Constitutional Court reaffirmed the predominant genocide interpretation by ruling in 2014 that:

[11] Judgment of Vilnius Regional Court, June 4, 2002, as reported by Satkauskas (2004).

> under the universally recognised norms of international law, actions are considered to constitute genocide if they are deliberate actions aimed at destroying, not only in whole but also in part, any national, ethnical, racial, or religious group; when a part of the protected group is targeted, that part must be significant enough for its destruction to have an impact on the group as a whole; actions may also be recognised as genocide if they are deliberate actions aimed at destroying certain social or political groups that constitute a significant part of any national, ethnical, racial, or religious group and the destruction of which would have an impact on the respective national, ethnical, racial, or religious group as a whole.
>
> (Constitutional Court of the Republic of Lithuania 2014: 39)

Thus, while charges of genocide have prevailed in relation to anti-partisan acts, it is interesting to note that Lithuanian prosecutors have hardly ever pressed charges of genocide in relation to individuals involved in mass deportations. An illustrative trial in this regard is that of Vincas Misiūnas, which took place in 2002. This former officer in the MGB was accused of having organized the deportation of a Lithuanian family in 1951 during the anti-"kulak" policies of the Soviet Union. Although this was an incident that took place long after the end of the war, the prosecutors charged Misiūnas for war crimes, pursuant to Article 334 of the 1998 amendments to the Lithuanian Criminal Code. According to this provision the act of war crimes could be extended to the postwar period, since for Lithuania this crime included the "deportation of civilians from occupied or annexed territories to the territory of the state responsible for occupation or annexation or to the territory of a third state" (Lietuvos Respublikos Seimas 1998a).

Thus the prosecutor could have, in theory, argued in the same vein as in the anti-partisan cases that Misiūnas had acted with full awareness of the destructive purpose of the deportations, and therefore the crimes could have been linked to genocide instead. Yet according to Gailius (2005), the prosecutor opted for an "easier" charge. The interpretation of historical circumstances was again somewhat bent in order to allow for charges of war crimes, thus legally defining the postwar period as constituting a state of war in Lithuania. While this understanding of the partisan struggles may be disputed, legally this interpretation certainly made up for the lack of a relevant provision in the 1998 law that would provide a definition of deportations as a crime against humanity. In the case of Misiūnas and one other defendant, this prosecutorial strategy worked out. In 2002 the court found Misiūnas guilty and sentenced the

77-year-old to three years in prison. Subsequently the sentence was commuted on the basis of amnesty laws.

Latvia

In Latvia the first criminal proceedings against Soviet-era perpetrators started soon after the necessary legal provisions were in place; at the same time, they also concluded relatively quickly within a few years. When we look at Table 3.1 for Latvia, we notice not only the relative dearth of cases in comparison to the other two countries but also the fact that not a single trial took place based on the new 1999 Criminal Code. Finally, we notice that almost all of the cases relate to the mass deportations of 1941 and 1949. Indeed, only one trial concerned a case of postwar anti-partisan actions, and it ended in acquittal due to a lack of evidence.

Overall, the Latvian criminal justice process appeared to come in two waves. Starting in 1994, criminal charges were levied against mostly higher-ranking former NKVD officials accused of having been instrumental in organizing the mass deportations and political terror. The individuals in question belonged to the generation of Soviet security agents who had actively helped to establish Soviet rule in Latvia, either because they were already living in Latvia at the time of the Soviet takeover or because they were sent in as security agents immediately following the 1940 occupation. Not surprisingly, few of these individuals were really fit to stand trial by the mid-1990s. Indeed, in only two of these cases did the prosecutors manage to prepare actual court proceedings. Alfons Noviks was one, standing trial in 1995 for genocide, as we noted earlier. The other case involved Mikhails Farbtuhs, a former lower-rank NKVD official in the region of Daugavpils, who stood trial only in 1999 following several postponements related to poor health. He, too, was eventually convicted for "crimes against humanity, genocide."

By the late 1990s, however, judicial activities intensified thanks to the improvement in investigatory infrastructure that we noted earlier, namely the closer level of cooperation between the TRNIN and the TSDC. The new series of indictments was now aimed at more lower-ranking former NKVD operatives, most of them were charged for having been involved in the 1949 deportations, and all of them (with one exception) charged on the basis of Article 68.1 of the 1993 Criminal Code.

Still, court proceedings continued to drag on for many years. In one case (regarding Ilya Mašonkin) proceedings lasted almost a decade. In other instances, the trials never got started because the suspects either died or committed suicide upon being presented with the charges (e.g. Solomon Murin and Leonīds Fomins). Lastly, in several cases the accused either fled to Russia or were already residing in the Russian Federation, which refused to cooperate with Latvian prosecutors and would not respond to extradition requests.[12] Thus, relatively few trials against communist-era perpetrators of mass crimes actually took place in Latvia (altogether ten), and those that did often stretched out over many years. Where they did result in conviction, the sentences were usually suspended in view of the advanced age of the convicts.

In Table 3.1 we therefore see that curiously enough no new Soviet-related criminal proceedings have been started in Latvia based on the new 1999 Criminal Code and its provisions concerning mass crimes. The reason for this is both legal and institutional. On the one hand, the new Code failed to include a separate category for crimes against humanity; instead, only "genocide" was included. As a result, prosecutors were extremely limited in their indictment strategies, especially given the difficulties of proving genocidal intent if someone had, for example, participated in the deportation of just one family. Indeed, according to the former head of the TSDC, Indulis Zālīte, the new state prosecutor grew rather wary of filing genocide charges in such cases (Zālīte, Interview, 2013). This put a heavy burden on any kind of prosecutorial activity. Moreover, investigations themselves would be hampered by new procedural laws adopted in the late 1990s that would restrict the use of documentary evidence in cases of crimes against humanity and war crimes (requiring prosecutors to rely more on eyewitnesses and other sources). As a consequence, several cases that were submitted to local courts in 2002 never resulted in actual trials (Delfi.lv 2006).

On the other hand, the limited institutional capacities of the TRNIN as well as a change in the Prosecutor General's Office's leadership played an institutional role in the rapid decline of new criminal proceedings. In 1999 Uldis Strēlis, the chief prosecutor and head of the TRNIN, resigned. As a former deportee himself, he had been a staunch advocate of retrospective truth and criminal justice (Titavs 1997). His successor, Jānis Osis, was much more cautious in indicting former perpetrators for genocide and more wary about the political fall-out (both domestic and international) from the many ongoing cases. As our overview of

[12] These concerned the cases of Semjons Šustins, Ivāns Reisners, Žanis Sprūde, Alfrēds Zvejnieks and Jānis Dzintars.

individual cases will show, several of these trials involved Russian citizens, and the Russian Federation not only strongly protested these proceedings but also actively assisted the defendants.

The case that characterizes the evolution of Latvian prosecutorial strategy the most involves the trial against Alfons Noviks. In 1995 Noviks was convicted for having "committed genocide against certain groups of Latvia's population that were regarded by the totalitarian regime to be socially dangerous and detrimental to the existing regime" (Supreme Court of the Republic of Latvia 1996). The ruling was based on the finding that as the People's Commissar for Public Security in the Latvian SSR between 1940 and 1953 Noviks had signed thousands of deportation orders as well as participated in "unlawful executions," torture and other human rights violations. The sentence became a precedent as it sent out the signal that Latvia would bring to justice not only those who had executed grave human rights violations, but also those who had ordered those acts (Satkauskas 2004). It was also the first of several convictions that would define the forced resettlement of people as genocide. What was crucial for the legal argument was not only the number of victims deported and their belonging to a particular social or political group defined as dangerous but also the conditions under which the arrests and resettlement took place, that is, the harsh living conditions in remote and scarcely populated areas of the Soviet Union that would eventually cause the death of many of the deported. Relying on Soviet documents and official directives, the prosecutors could show that the ordering of deportations was done "with the view to complete extermination" of a particular group defined according to social class or political conviction, thus constituting genocidal intent (Satkauskas 2004: 263).

Indeed, this line of argument resulted in several other deportation-related cases that would follow in subsequent years against both high-ranking officials, who gave the order to deport people, and lower-ranking operatives like Mikhails Farbtuhs. Moreover, the Noviks case became politically important in later years, as more and more trials would involve Russian Federation citizens. The fact that the first genocide conviction had been spoken in a case against an ethnic Latvian thus became a frequent reference to refute accusations from Russian officials that Latvia was only prosecuting perpetrators of non-Latvian origin.

The first of the several cases against Russian Federation citizens involved Ilya Mašonkin, a former operative agent of the NKVD. In 1998 the prosecutor opened criminal proceedings against Mašonkin for having been responsible for the deportation of at least a hundred families in March 1949, many of whom later perished. Mašonkin was arrested in March 1998 and kept in custody despite his advanced age for fear that he would flee to the Russian Federation as others had done before him (Puķītis 1998). The concern was all the more reasonable as Mašonkin requested and received active assistance from the embassy of the Russian Federation in first negotiating his release from custody and later in his court defense. Considerable media attention accompanied the trial, as Mašonkin's lawyers requested repeated delays in order to carry out medical examinations and other procedures. In 2006 the Riga Regional Court finally decided that the 91-year-old Mašonkin was no longer able to stand trial due to deficient mental and physical health.

In other cases involving Russian Federation citizens, Latvian prosecutors were more successful in achieving convictions. One of these was against Yevgeny Savenko, a former investigator within the NKVD. The accusations leveled against him involved not only deportation but also other acts of repression carried out during the first year of Soviet occupation. Savenko was accused of having fabricated false accusations against at least sixty individuals, who were subsequently executed or deported. Among his alleged victims were members of the pre-war Latvian government, military and police (Quigley 2006: 45). Moreover, the charges included responsibility for the deportation of at least forty-three women and children to Siberia in 1941. In Savenko's case, there were no delays, and court proceedings began in February 2000. Nevertheless, the Russian embassy and Russian-language media in Latvia continued to express concern over the trial, and during the hearings the courtroom was filled with mostly Russian supporters of the defendant, accusing the Latvian court of "taking revenge against old men" (Goldbergs 2000). Indeed, Savenko was one of several cases where the courtroom was crowded with local Russians who, encouraged by Russian media, saw the trials as political. In the particular case of Savenko, however, the defendant admitted to the allegations, albeit claiming that he had only followed orders, and even apologized to his victims, some of whom were present during the proceedings. This fact was, according to one Latvian journalist, never reported in the Russian media (Fridrihsone 2000b). Savenko was found guilty of the charges, but his sentence was reduced to his pre-trial imprisonment on account of his advanced age and admission of guilt. He was released on the day that his verdict was announced.

Latvia's remaining deportation cases have all concerned the 1949 deportations. The defendants in these proceedings were charged with crimes against humanity and genocide pursuant to Article 68.1 of the Latvian Criminal Code. The argument was that the accused had not only executed the arrests and deportation of people based on their class (or social) belonging, but also known and accepted the fact that deportation for these people would almost certainly lead to death. Most of the accused were defended by one and the same defense lawyer, Aleksandr Ogurcov, whose main line of defense was that the acts for which his clients were being charged had not constituted an offense at the time of commission, thus involving a case of retroactive justice incompatible with the rule of law.[13] Moreover, in the case of Nikolajs Tess, another Russian Federation citizen accused of having signed deportation orders for forty-two Latvian families in March of 1949, Ogurcov stressed the incompatibility of Latvian criminal law with international legal instruments such as the European Convention on Human Rights (ECHR) and the Genocide Convention. Specifically, he argued that the deportation of wealthy farmers in the 1949 deportation did not fall under the conventional definition of "genocide" (Švarca 2012: 72). In both cases, however, the Latvian regional and higher courts dismissed these arguments and found the defendants guilty of crimes against humanity and genocide.

The Russian Federation again actively supported the defendants' cause through both legal and practical assistance. The Russian Ministry of Foreign Affairs and other state representatives also periodically released statements critical of the proceedings. In the trial against Nikolajs Larionovs, a former NKVD operative accused of having issued over 150 deportation orders in 1949, Russia declared the charges ill-founded as the defendant had in fact only compiled lists of persons "as part of the struggle against Nazi accomplices, robbers, murderers and bandits from the criminal confederacy of the so called 'forest brethren'" (Ministry of Foreign Affairs of the Russian Federation 2003). In addition to blaming Latvian courts and prosecutors for historical misperceptions and "deliberate forgetting," the statement also voiced concern about the evidence used in the proceedings, pointing to a lack of witnesses present at the trial and lamenting the lack of international legal basis for the allegations. A year later the Russian Ministry of Foreign Affairs issued another statement on the case of Nikolajs Tess,

13 Aleksandr Ogurcov was the main or second defense lawyer in the cases of Vassilij Kononov, Ilja Mašonkin, Mikhails Farbtuhs, Nikolajs Larionovs and Nikolajs Tess. He also defended Alfreds Rubiks, that is, a case of transitional criminal justice, as discussed earlier in this chapter.

whose appeal in a very similar court case had been rejected by the Latvian Supreme Court. Russia portrayed the entire prosecution as "fabricated and politically motivated," calling Tess "innocent" and accusing Latvia of violating the European Convention (Ministry of Foreign Affairs of the Russian Federation 2004).

Both Tess and Larionovs eventually appealed their sentences to the ECtHR with the allegation that Latvia had violated the principle of *nullum crimen sine lege* (Article 7) of the ECHR. Yet both defendants died before the ECtHR Chamber reached a conclusion on the cases, Tess in December 2006, Larionovs in 2005. In both instances the appeal to the Court was upheld beyond the deaths of the convicts – in the case of Tess by his wife, in that of Larionovs by his son. In 2008 the ECtHR rejected most of the applicants' complaints. Regarding specifically Article 7, the Court decided to defer a decision and to communicate the case back to the Latvian government, thus indicating that a later ruling on the case was not excluded (European Court of Human Rights 2008d). However, probably because of the death of the defendants, no further proceedings have since taken place.

Concerning cases brought in connection with the postwar killing of anti-Soviet partisans (or "Forest Brethren"), Latvian state prosecutors have managed to bring only one such instance to the courts. In October 1999 Jānis Kiršteins was arrested and charged with genocide for killing an anti-Soviet partisan in 1948. He was also accused of having facilitated military tribunals during which fabricated evidence was used to have several other partisans and their supporters (including whole families with children) be sent to prison camps in the Gulag (Cīrulis 2007). Kiršteins, an ethnic Latvian, vehemently rejected the idea that he had intended to destroy the Latvian nation when as a 19-year old he had signed up for service with the MGB and participated in anti-partisan operations. Again, the case dragged out for many years only to finally end in April 2005 with an acquittal due to insufficient evidence of genocidal intent. Later prosecutorial attempts to achieve the resumption of proceedings came to naught due to Kiršteins' deteriorating health (Cīrulis 2008).

Arguably the most notorious case of Latvian retrospective criminal justice did not even involve accusations of crimes against humanity or genocide, but rather of war crimes. These charges were brought in 1998 against a much decorated veteran of the Soviet Army, Vassily Kononov. As a sergeant Kononov had been deployed in eastern Latvia during the German occupation and operated behind the front lines against the

Nazis and their local collaborators. The charges brought against him involved having led a Soviet partisan brigade that, disguised in German uniforms, brutally killed nine people in the village of Mazie Bati, among them a pregnant woman who was burnt to death on 27 May 1944. The specific incident of a wartime killing of civilians had been brought to the attention of the Prosecutor General's Office by the historians at the TSDC. Over the course of the next six years, the case would pass through two contradictory judgments by different Latvian courts as well as various appeals by both the defendant and the prosecutor general before finally reaching the Latvian Supreme Court in 2004. The case became an outstanding example of judicial error, but also of the struggles involved with achieving retrospective adjudication of some of the worst crimes committed during the war and under conditions of double (Nazi/Soviet) occupation. One participant in this process, former TSDC head Zālīte, has suggested that the problems arose in part because of Latvian inexperience in prosecuting cases of war crimes (Zālīte, Interview, 2013). At the same time, the notion that Latvia might pursue the conviction of a decorated veteran of the victorious Red Army for war crimes was sufficiently audacious to bring on a fair amount of difficult re-examination of prevailing historical-legal interpretations. This latter observation related not only to Latvian courts, who would have to navigate this argumentation, but also to the ECtHR, who would hear the case on appeal no less than twice before finally finding in Latvia's favor. The details of this European level of adjudication will be discussed in Chapter 7. Here we will introduce the domestic Latvian wrangling.

Court proceedings against Kononov started in January 2000. Kononov pleaded not guilty, as he claimed the events of that day in 1944 had been a justified act of retaliation against armed Nazi collaborators. Kononov denied any direct involvement in the killing of the villagers and affirmed that his order had been to capture the "traitors" (the male villagers) for a war tribunal. Yet after reviewing the evidence brought against him, including eyewitness accounts as well as Kononov's own postwar writings, in which he had boasted about the killing of the villagers, the Riga Regional Court in 2000 found that Kononov had indeed perpetrated acts prohibited by several international conventions, among them the Hague Convention of 1907 and the Geneva Convention of 1949. He was thus found guilty of war crimes pursuant to Article 68.3 of the Latvian Criminal Code and sentenced to six years' imprisonment. The judgment was met with sharp protests from the Russian embassy, calling the conviction of a war hero in the fight against fascism a "humiliation of the millions of victims of Nazism" (Fridrihsone 2000a). Shortly after the court decision was announced, Kononov was awarded with Russian citizenship, and Russian President Vladimir Putin himself declared that the incarceration of a war veteran could seriously damage Russian–Latvian relations (Antonevičs 2000).

After appeals of the sentence were lodged by both Kononov and the Latvian prosecutor, the Criminal Division of the Supreme Court decided in 2001 that the Riga Regional Court had argued hastily in its judgment and that the case needed to be further investigated. Among the gaps in reasoning according to the higher court was the fact that the lower judge and prosecutor had not answered clearly enough the question of whether or not the village of Mazie Bati was on occupied territory in 1944 and whether or not the villagers could be defined as combatants or civilians. Thus, in October 2003 the trial reopened, now at the Latgale Regional Court. This time the Court acquitted Kononov of war crimes, but found him guilty of "banditry," an offense under Article 72 of the former Soviet-era Criminal Code still in force. The judge argued that because Latvia had been incorporated into the USSR in 1940, the applicant's conduct had to be considered in the light of Soviet law. Moreover, the court accepted Kononov's argument that the villagers had been collaborators with the Nazi occupation authorities and that the death of the male villagers "could be regarded as having been necessary and justified by considerations of a military order." This did not, however, apply to the women killed or to the burning of their houses, hence the conviction for banditry (European Court of Human Rights 2008a). As a consequence, Kononov was released from custody, since the statute of limitation for banditry as an offense had long since expired.

Unwilling to give up, the Latvian Prosecutor General's Office appealed this ruling anew, arguing that the Latgale court had insufficiently considered the fact that Latvia had been illegally occupied in 1940, and thus Kononov's actions in 1944 should not be assessed against Soviet law, but against international law. In this case, the events in Mazie Bati would be seen as constituting a violation of several customary laws of war and other international conventions in force at the time. Agreeing with these arguments, the Criminal Affairs Division of the Supreme Court quashed the Latgale Regional Court's verdict and found Kononov guilty of war crimes (Article 68.3). The ruling was also upheld in April 2004 by the Senate of the Supreme Court (Cassese et al. 2011: 68).

At the conclusion of all of these proceedings, Kononov was finally released from custody, given his deteriorating health by then. Yet at this stage it was Kononov who decided to continue pursuing his acquittal, and a complaint was lodged with the ECtHR. This already highly political case of a war crimes trial against a former veteran of the Red Army now became an issue of European concern, as never before had the Court ruled on such an allegation against a former member of the Allied powers. The case now took on a whole new international dimension, which we will examine in greater detail in Chapter 7.

Estonia

The Estonian approach to retrospective criminal justice has not shown the kind of fluctuation or abrupt end of prosecutorial development that we observe in our other two cases. In Estonia, the process started slightly later than in the two other Baltic states because of its later adoption (in 1994) of a legal framework, but then it proceeded with relative speed, albeit at a low level of intensity in terms of actual court cases. As we can see in Table 3.1, the Estonian criminal justice process mirrors the Latvian one in that the overall number of cases brought to the courts has been limited, and most of them have related to the 1949 mass deportations. Moreover, as in Latvia most cases that resulted in criminal convictions were initiated on the basis of the 1994 amendments to the Soviet-era criminal code. Yet differently from Latvia, Estonia's prosecutor general continued to open new criminal proceedings against those involved in deportations also after the new Criminal Code came into force in 2002, and indeed brought individual cases to trial as late as 2008.[14] In contrast to Lithuania, however, there was no major fluctuation in the Estonian retrospective criminal justice process, rather there has been a continuous decline in the number of cases due to the passing-away of possible defendants and a rather slow pace of prosecutorial work to begin with.

The first wave of criminal investigations and proceedings initiated by the Estonian Prosecutor General's Office focused on criminal acts in connection with both the postwar deportations and partisan struggles as well as the first year of Soviet occupation. Indeed, the very first couple of cases brought to the courts involved two former leading officials of the NKVD in Estonia accused of having been responsible for the mass

[14] Thus, the case of former NKVD operative Jaan Pähna was brought to the Haapsalu County Court as late as 2008. Accused of having been responsible for the deportation of sixteen families or forty-six individuals, Pähna could not stand trial and the proceedings were ended in 2011 (Postimees 2011).

deportations of 1941 (Vassili Riis) as well as for fabricating false accusations for trials against opponents of the Soviet regime (Idel Jakobson) during 1940–41. Neither man could be brought to justice as they both died during court proceedings. Between 1996 and 2000 criminal prosecution was initiated against a total of nine higher- and lower-ranking NKVD operatives accused of having ordered and/or carried out repressions against civilians and/or people resisting the occupation regime.

A second wave of criminal proceedings started in the early 2000s and was based on the new national Criminal Code. This second wave of indictments for crimes against humanity targeted predominantly individuals accused of offenses in connection with the 1949 mass deportations. As we can see from our table, most of these cases dragged out considerably as defendants struggled with deteriorating health. Thus, the overall number of actually concluded court cases remains very limited. Between 1995 and 2011 a total of fourteen cases involving twenty-four individuals eventually reached the trial stage resulting in eight convictions for involvement in the mass deportations of 1949 and three convictions for taking part in anti-partisan killings (Arpo 2012: 103). In the majority of cases, court proceedings had to be terminated prematurely on account of the defendant's bad health or death. Moreover, where verdicts were reached, sentences had often to be suspended due to old age. None of the cases involving crimes against humanity ever ended in acquittal.

Collectively, Estonian retrospective justice cases did not attract much media attention, nor did they stir the kind of public protests by Russian minority representatives or Russian Federation officials as in neighboring Latvia. The fact that these cases were primarily investigated and handled by the Security Police Board might have contributed to a certain degree of secrecy surrounding the process. Other than the historians involved in pre-trial investigations in Latvia and Lithuania, KAPO employees would not publicly engage in the broader academic or media discourse about the moral implications of these trials or their interpretation of Soviet crimes.

What we can also deduce from Table 3.1 is the fact that after the new Criminal Code came into force in 2002, Estonian prosecutors chose in a majority of cases to charge defendants with crimes against humanity rather than genocide, even though both were now codified separately. The reason for this prosecutorial choice may have been the considerable confusion that the previous legal provision (combining both offenses) had caused. As Lauri Mälksoo (2001: 778–80) points out, in many of the early cases against former NKVD agents involved in the 1949 deportations the courts did indeed come to rather ambiguous conclusions with regard to whether or not acts committed by the defendants could be classified as genocide. Instead of taking a clear stance, the courts simply followed the prosecutor's formulation defining deportations already as "deliberate acts, the purpose of which was to destroy a national group, a group offering resistance to the occupation regime and a social group declared 'kulaks'" (Indictment of Klaassepp, cited in Mälksoo 2001: 779). At the same time, little attention was paid to the question of the individual defendant's past genocidal intention and, according to Lauri Mälksoo, none of the earlier deportation-related judgments mentioned the term "genocide" at all. Instead, they mentioned in more than one case that the defendants had followed orders rather than planned or organized the crime themselves. Yet this obvious lack of "intent to destroy" notwithstanding, all of the deportation trials resulted in convictions pursuant to Article 61.1 of the Criminal Code "Crimes against humanity, including genocide."

A case that exemplifies this kind of seemingly contradictory ruling is that of Johannes Klaassepp, a former agent of the NKVD in western Estonia. In 1999 the prosecutor general indicted him for "crimes against humanity, including genocide" for having deported twenty-three Estonians and for participating in the deportation of nine additional people, all classified by the Soviet system as "kulaks" in March 1949. The Lääne County Court found Klaassepp guilty of the charges and sentenced him to eight years in prison with a probation period of two years. In its judgment the court considered the age of Klaassepp's victims, the youngest of whom was 4 years old as well as the fact that he followed orders. The judgment against Klaassepp set the precedent for several other deportation-related cases that followed the same year against former NKVD operatives, including the Russian Federation citizen Vassili Beškov, for deporting civilians from different parts of Estonia in 1949.

The prosecutorial strategy to ignore the ambiguities of the specific legal provision of "crimes against humanity, including genocide" came under criticism in a case not relating to deportations, but to the postwar killing of anti-Soviet partisans. Karl-Leonhard Paulov, a former agent-combatant of the NKVD right after the war, was accused of having killed three men, who had acted as partisans against the re-established Soviet regime in 1946. The indictment made the argument that Paulov "had killed . . . in order to destroy a group offering resistance to the occupation regime," an offense clearly codified in Article 61.1 in the 1994 Estonian criminal law (cited in Mälksoo 2001: 776). In its judgment of October 1999, the Põlva County Court found that Paulov could not be charged with crimes against humanity and re-qualified the crimes as simple murder due to the fact that Paulov had been paid for killing the men. The court also established that the "Forest Brethren" had been armed and therefore should be considered a political resistance group rather than as civilians; hence, a genocide indictment could not apply. In this respect, the court gave priority to international definitions of genocide that do not include acts against political groups. It concluded that Paulov could not be convicted for allegedly destroying the Estonian nation simply by killing three people.

When Paulov was found innocent also by an appeals court, the prosecutor general appealed these decisions to the Estonian Supreme Court. In March 2000 that court overruled both of the lower court rulings. The Supreme Court took note of the fact that Article 61.1 of the Estonian legal code contained in reality two distinct crimes and that because the lower courts had mixed the two together, their rulings were inapplicable. The Court ruled further that even though the three partisans had hid in the forest to avoid Soviet repression, the regime had decided to deny them the right to a fair trial and instead killed them, thus committing not just simple murder, but a crime against humanity. The execution of the partisans, according to the Court, had been committed with an intention to kill not just these three men, but "anybody, whose killing would have come within the scope of the operations planned by the NKVD" (Eesti Vabariigi Riigikohus 1999). The Court sent the Paulov case back down to the Põlva County Court, which convicted the defendant in July 2000 for crimes against humanity in accordance with international law. Paulov received a sentence of eight years' imprisonment in a maximum-security prison. He died in February 2002, and to this day remains the only person in Estonia to have actually received and served a prison sentence for his crimes.

The judgment reached in the case of Paulov served as a precedent for subsequent rulings concerning both the postwar killing of partisans as well as participation in deportations. Indeed, from then on the courts were more careful in differentiating the two crimes embedded in Article 61.1 of the 1994 law, often bolstering their judgments with references to the relevant international treaties and conventions such as the Charter of the International Military Tribunal (Nuremberg Tribunal) and the 1949 Geneva Convention. Thus, in only one other partisan-related case against Vladimir Penart, a former head of the Elva District Department of the ESSR Ministry of Internal Affairs, did the final judgment of September 2003 stress the fact that the defendant had actually planned and organized the killing of three partisans, for which Penart was then convicted under the crimes against humanity formulation.[15]

The Estonian courts' legal interpretation of postwar Stalinist repression as crimes against humanity received an affirmation from the European Court of Human Rights in 2006, when it rejected the appeals of Vladimir Penart, as well as those of two other convicts, August Kolk and Petr Kislyiy.[16] All three had asserted that their convictions had been unlawful, since the acts for which they were tried were not considered criminal at the time of their commission and therefore the convictions violated Article 7 of the ECHR. The ECtHR rejected this argument and largely followed the reasoning of the Estonian Supreme Court in saying that the Soviet authorities had been a part of drafting the Nuremburg and other principles that prohibited crimes against humanity. Hence, these principles were a firm part of international law at the moment when the men had committed their acts (Cassese 2006). As we will discuss in Chapter 7, all three applications to the ECtHR were rejected on admissibility grounds for being "manifestly ill founded" (European Court of Human Rights 2006a).

We can thus see a learning process in Estonia in terms of how the insufficient legal provisions of 1994 were being applied on cases of historical mass crimes and abuses. While in earlier cases the courts often chose to ignore the implicit contradictions in the prosecutor's arguments borne out of the combined codification of two distinct offenses, the judgment in the Paulov case would set a new tone. Judgments following this precedent case would more carefully distinguish between offenses that qualified as crimes against humanity vs genocide, usually arriving at convictions in relation to the former. The later 2002 Criminal Code finally resolved the earlier legal ambiguities by clearly separating the two offenses. This only further strengthened the predominant prosecutorial strategy to indict former NKVD/MGB operatives for crimes against humanity rather than participation in genocide,

[15] A co-defendant in the case, Rudolf Tuvi, was found guilty only for murder, since he had been hired by Penart to do the killing. Because this offense was covered under statutory limitations, Tuvi did not serve any prison time.

[16] In Estonian court documents and media outlets, the Russian name Kislyiy is transliterated as Kislõi.

the way Latvian courts had done. This did not mean that Estonian prosecutors would completely abandon the option of prosecuting mass deportations as genocide; they were simply more cautious in doing so.

One of the more notable cases involving genocide was that against Arnold Meri, a decorated Soviet war veteran and former commander of Soviet security forces in charge of the deportations. He was also cousin of former president Lennart Meri, although the two were not close personally. In 2003 the prosecutor general charged Meri with genocide for participating in the deportation of 261 people from the island of Hiiumaa in March 1949, among them many children and women. Meri admitted to his involvement in organizing the deportations, yet denied responsibility for the consequences of the operation, as he claimed that he was only monitoring an action that was in accordance with the law at the time. His case attracted much public attention not least among Russian officials and the media who attempted to portray the trial as an attack on a hero of the Soviet Union. Meri's lawyers managed to delay court proceedings considerably by requesting repeated medical examinations of the then 84-year-old. When the hearing finally started in May 2008, Meri's health had so far deteriorated that barely a year later, in March 2009, he died while the court proceedings were still ongoing. The case was subsequently discontinued.

Comparative summary

This comparative analysis of efforts in the three Baltic states to pursue retrospective and transitional justice against perpetrators at the criminal-legal level over the past twenty-five years reveals many similarities in terms of the legal provisions and prosecutorial strategies adopted above all in Estonia and Latvia. The caution that prosecutors have shown in these two countries (albeit for different reasons) stands in contrast to some of the bolder approaches launched in Lithuania in terms of either Lithuania's early 1992 definition of "genocide" or its politically driven effort to ramp up prosecutions after 2008. Our analysis, however, also reveals some striking differences. The first concerns the overall number of cases that made it to the courts. Likewise one sees variation in the historical periods prosecutors have decided to pursue for prosecution. Lastly, we may note the different investigative infrastructures set up to support the judicial process, as well as the prosecutorial strategies and legal arguments employed.

With regard to the overall number of cases, we have seen that while Latvian prosecutors managed to bring a few individuals to justice up until 1999 and failed to initiate any new criminal proceedings thereafter, Estonian prosecutors have been only slightly more successful in prosecuting perpetrators of Soviet mass crimes. Yet here as well the number of actual trials consistently decreases over the course of the 2000s. The slow Estonian decline of court proceedings has been mostly explained by the passage of time that works in favor of those being investigated for crimes against humanity. In Latvia the relatively sudden decline of prosecutorial activity after 2000 has been explained based on both legal and political reasons. While the limited scope of legal options provided by the new Criminal Code certainly contributed to the slowdown, the political noise surrounding several of the trials against former war veterans or NKVD agents of Russian background also impacted on prosecutors' willingness to pursue further retrospective criminal justice. According to Indulis Zālīte, dragged-out cases like that of Mašonkin and Kononov, but also the case against Nazi collaborator Kalējs, required considerable attention and additional investigations, taking up much of the already limited resources at the TRNIN and TSDC (Zālīte, Interview, 2013). The rather confrontational approach taken by Russia with regard to some of the trials was certainly an additional reason why the new state prosecutor in charge of the TRNIN after 1999 was more cautious in pursuing genocide charges against former members of the Soviet repressive apparatus. Thus, despite the fact that Russian citizens were also prosecuted in Estonia (though somewhat fewer in number), the Latvian trials ended up being much more constrained by politics than those in Estonia. What is more, Latvia stands out as the only case among the Baltic states where trials against former NKVD agents involved public expressions of protest, mostly by local Russians. These were stirred not least by frequent reports in the Russian media. Indeed, a study in 2008 revealed that "Latvian court proceedings against former Soviet military or KGB veterans" ranked among the three top themes covered by the Russian media in the mid-2000s (Petrenko 2008: 46). Thus, neither Estonian nor Lithuanian judges and prosecutors were confronted to the same degree with – and perhaps constrained by – public opinion and foreign policy considerations.

As we indicated at the start of the chapter, Lithuania displays a rather divergent pattern of criminal-judicial truth and justice vis-à-vis Stalin-era perpetrators. In terms of the number of cases and prosecutorial development over time, we see a much more dynamic process that started with relatively few trials in the mid-1990s only to considerably speed up after 1997. Thereafter, we see a continuously high level of new criminal proceedings initiated each year. Moreover, criminal prosecution of postwar regime crimes remained high on the agenda of the country's center-right political parties, resulting in a renewed intensification of prosecutorial work after 2008. Thus, in contrast to Estonia and Latvia, Lithuania does not seem to be over with retrospective criminal justice issues but, rather, seems determined to seek out every last surviving perpetrator of Soviet crimes.

The three Baltic countries also differ in terms of the historical crimes or incidents that were targeted by criminal investigations. Again Estonia and Latvia are similar here, as prosecutors and their support institutions focused most of their investigatory resources on finding and prosecuting individuals who had been responsible for the deportations carried out in 1941 and 1949. By contrast, the number of deportation-related cases in Lithuania seems rather small. Instead, cases relating to postwar killings and anti-partisan operations dominate the criminal justice picture. This divergence is, of course, primarily explained by the historical circumstances of World War II and the postwar period that saw a considerably stronger and more organized anti-Soviet resistance in the Lithuanian countryside than there ever was in Latvia or Estonia. In consequence there is also more material about counterinsurgency measures by the Soviet regime left in Lithuanian archives as well as more witnesses still alive and ready to testify. However, the significantly higher number of charges against former NKVD operatives involved in anti-partisan operations as opposed to those involved in deportations around the same time indicates also a political choice behind prosecutorial strategy. In the end the criminal-judicial process of reckoning with past crimes has a considerable impact on the social processes of remembering and the development of a shared narrative of the nation's recent past. In this context it seems far more rewarding to draw public attention to historical cases of resistance against foreign rule via the partisan-related "genocide trials" than to focus exclusively on acts of passive victimization.

In both the Lithuanian and the Latvian cases, the periods of increased prosecutorial activity in the late 1990s came about in part thanks to an improvement in the investigative infrastructure available to prosecutors via closer cooperation with historians. Thus, Latvia saw most of its cases that later resulted in court proceedings initiated by the historians of the TSDC during the second half of the 1990s. Likewise, the first wave of arrests and indictments in Lithuania came after the restructuring of the

LGGRTC in 1997 and the institutionalization of collaboration between the STS and the newly established special investigation unit at the Center. Our empirical findings do not necessarily support the claim that the intensity of cooperation between legal and historical experts in the retrospective criminal justice process has an immediate impact on the success rate of trials. However, the lack of an institutional infrastructure that encourages cooperation between the judiciary and professional historians does hint at an overall different political approach to the matter. Thus, the Estonian arrangement of leaving criminal adjudication of Stalin-era crimes with the Prosecutor General's Office and the Security Police Board served in many ways to frame the issue of retrospective criminal justice as a matter of national security. Though national media would report on individual trials and their outcomes, this rarely went beyond mere statements of facts, and the criminal justice process remained rather disconnected from broader historical and moral discourses on the Soviet period. This was rather different in the other two states, as we will show in the coming chapters, and the fact that historians were intimately involved in the criminal investigations certainly contributed to the broader public visibility and debating of Soviet-era wrongs.

A comparative look at the precise legal provisions that were implemented in order to facilitate the criminal justice process reveals, again, similarities between Estonia and Latvia. Both countries adopted amendments to the old Soviet Criminal Codes instituting legal provisions that would collapse both crimes against humanity and genocide into a single code. In both cases, consequently, the charges filed by prosecutors sought to frame the involvement in deportations in whatever capacity (either by giving orders or by carrying out concrete operations) as attempted "genocide" against a (politically or socially determined) part of the nation. While Latvian courts mostly went along with this line of argument, Estonian judges felt the need to differentiate between the two offenses and to embed national law more within international law. This led to a situation where most individuals who had been indicted pursuant to Article 61.1 of the 1994 Estonian Criminal Code for their involvement in deportations and anti-partisan repressions ended up being convicted for crimes against humanity (Liivoja 2013). In Latvia, by contrast, several of the men accused of ordering the deportations were convicted for "genocide against the Latvian people," thus following the broad definition provided by national law. The shift to a new Criminal Code after 2000 would further deepen these divergences, as Estonian prosecutors would continue to file indictments for crimes against humanity, now clearly codified in the law. Latvian law enforcement officials, on the other hand, would not have this option, leading to a complete halt in new indictments.

In Lithuania the legislators' determination to classify Stalin-era crimes against the Lithuanian population both during and after the war as genocide, and nothing but genocide, was even more pronounced. Yet despite the rather one-dimensional and insufficiently drafted special Law on Genocide from 1992, as well as later amendments to the existing criminal code, prosecutors restrained from classifying acts relating to the mass deportations as genocide. Instead, they indicted individuals who had ordered or carried out deportations for war crimes, as this particular offense would be codified in Article 100 of the 1998 Criminal Code ("deportation of people from occupied countries"). Concerning the 1948 and 1949 deportations, officials had to considerably stretch their definition of "war condition" in Lithuania. At the same time almost all acts of repression against anti-Soviet resistance groups and their supporters were framed in genocide terms, taking the broad definition of the crime provided by national law. Thus, we see a mirror image of prosecutorial strategies with regard to the application of genocide when comparing Lithuania to the other two countries.

The broad definition of genocide codified in all three Baltic Criminal Codes (in Latvia after 2009) has attracted considerable scholarly attention, as we noted in the earlier sections of this chapter. Although an increasing number of scholars of international law have pointed to insufficiencies within current definitions of genocide in postwar international conventions, the generous application of this "crime of crimes" in Lithuania should still be regarded with caution, and further judicial scrutiny may yet come via the ECtHR. Nonetheless, it is unlikely that the European Court will have any impact on prosecutorial strategies in Lithuania. The ECtHR can only determine whether Lithuanian jurisdiction violates Article 7 of the ECHR, and thus whether Lithuania is allowed to retroactively prosecute crimes committed before 1948 when "genocide" entered international criminal law. This, however, is clearly confirmed by legal experts who maintain that "Lithuania and Latvia did not violate the principle of legality by prosecuting for acts committed in the early 1940s. Genocide was recognized by the UN General Assembly in 1946 as an offense that already existed in international law and thus pre-dated 1946" (Quigley 2006: 71). We see, therefore, once again that Baltic processes of truth and justice have often had effects that go beyond their borders.

4

Truth or punishment: purges, bargains and exposure of wrongdoing

"The whole system attacked a person's brain, a person's thinking, a person's family, a person's personality. How can we now say that that doesn't mean anything?" asked imploringly one of Estonia's most revered poets, Hando Runnel, as he addressed colleagues in Estonia's Constitutional Assembly on February 28, 1992.

> I am talking . . . about the Communist Party as a system, because I think that our problem right now is that we want to reduce the history of communism, the history and essence of the regime to simply an individual-psychological level . . . We are tiptoeing past this historic evil and horrible phenomenon to the point that we don't even dare to put the word communist or communism into our Constitution . . . This is a path of sin.
>
> (Peep 1997: 885–86)

Runnel was defending an implementation provision for Estonia's new constitution, which would collectively bar a range of former functionaries of the Estonian Communist Party and its Communist Youth League from running for elective office at both the national and the local levels until December 31, 2000. The measure would have propelled Estonia to the forefront of "decommunization" efforts in Central and Eastern Europe or, in other words, the campaign to sideline indiscriminately the entire political class of the former regime. Only in Czechoslovakia had something similar been adopted by that time. Certainly among the republics of the former Soviet Union this would have been an earth-shattering move.

Yet just seven weeks later, Estonia found itself at the opposite extreme of dealing with erstwhile Communist power-holders. Legislators approved a proposal to impose on future elected officials and civil servants a mere "oath of conscience," in which individuals would declare that they had never worked for the security services of an occupying power and that they had never participated in the surveillance or repression of their fellow citizens. Hence, the new provision was limited to acts of actual repression and no longer involved working within the Communist regime itself. Moreover, the oath would not be examined or screened by any official body. Only if a person's oath was formally challenged in court could that person risk losing their office or position. In other words, Estonia went from having a proposal to bar thousands of former Communist functionaries from political life in the newly re-independent state to a final policy that ended up barring no one.

Abrupt shifts like this are, of course, nothing surprising in politics. Political forces rise and fall, and public debate often shifts opinion toward alternative decisions. Moreover, in the given instance it was the case that two separate bodies made these decisions: the Constitutional Assembly proposed the decommunization measure, while the actual national legislature, the Supreme Council, dropped the proposal in favor of a milder provision. Yet, what this story is meant to show is that a broad range of approaches exists in terms of dealing with those perpetrators of a former regime, who are not guilty of directly criminal acts like mass deportation or terror, but who are seen as guilty of complicity with the old system. What to do with the broad array of people who ran the regime day to day and were therefore implicitly responsible for maintaining (in the case of the Baltic states) a foreign occupation? Were these individuals all quislings? What to do with those people who essentially repressed others through spying, informing or betraying confidence?

Because these particular actions are difficult to cast in a criminal-judicial form (i.e. it is not possible to criminalize membership in the Communist Party or the KGB *post hoc*), there remain only the political-administrative and symbolic-representational levels, at which democracies can attempt to enact measures that provide at least a modicum of justice for these perceived transgressions. It is, therefore, to these measures that we turn in this chapter. Moreover, in the case of former Communist Party officials or secret police agents the wrongdoings are of the recent past; hence, they involve *transitional* justice in the sense we outlined in Chapter 1. Referring back to our analytical matrix, we will be talking here about Box 2b, and we will therefore spend the first section of this chapter laying out the different decommunization and lustration measures that are conceivable under this category. In a second extensive part of the chapter, we will outline how each of the Baltic states approached these options, starting with a discussion of the fact that at least in relation to identifying former KGB operatives the three countries were much more in the dark about these matters than elsewhere in Central and Eastern Europe, since the Soviet secret police had removed most of its operational files to Russia already in 1989. This did not stop Latvia and Lithuania from carrying out, in 1992, an immediate attempt at purging suspected KGB agents from their parliaments – a period we will also examine briefly. However, as the Baltic countries settled down to pass more long-term lustration policies, we will see how varying degrees of turmoil would accompany them on this path.

As one might guess from our opening vignette, Estonia emerges as the Baltic country that has implemented the mildest set of lustration measures, even though its initial decommunization plans seemed foreboding. Latvia has maintained a steadier policy of screening both electoral candidates and high state officials for former KGB ties; but it has also been caught up in repeated debates over whether to make the names of former agents and informants public based on a limited set of KGB documents that it did recover. Lithuania, finally, has lurched back and forth the most, with intense debate over lustration arising in 1992, 1998–99 and 2005. Its legal framework has also come under the most scrutiny, including several challenges to the main lustration law being lodged in the European Court of Human Rights (ECtHR). Yet some analysts of the Baltic states have seen this rank order in a reverse manner. The primary reason for this is the link they see between the restrictive citizenship laws that Estonia and Latvia passed in the early 1990s and the way in which these laws actually served to cut out of political life many of the same KGB agents that conventional lustration legislation would cover. As a result, the argument runs that Estonia and Latvia did not need to adopt very extensive lustration measures, since in fact they took care of the problem already by simply denying Soviet-era immigrants and their descendants automatic citizenship after August 1991 (Jaskovska and Moran 2006). We will address this claim and the way it might fit into our analytical matrix in a separate section.

In this respect, the bulk of the foregoing chapter will be devoted to Box 2b issues. Retrospective justice or political-administrative measures against perpetrators from the more distant past (Box 2a) have been less prevalent for the obvious reason that many of these individuals were of advanced age in the 1990s, and there was little perceived need to target them with special policies. Needless to say, any lustration measures that were imposed on more recent KGB operatives applied just as much to those in retirement. The only conceivable additional justice measure to adopt would be to remove higher-grade pensions or other benefits from such retirees (also from the Communist Party). This was also done in the three Baltic states.

A second nuance to this chapter will involve covering both political-administrative and symbolic-representational sanctions against perpetrators at once. The reason is that these two levels of justice measures are often much more interwoven than, say, the criminal-legal and political-administrative. This is true not only conceptually (as will be described in the first subsection), but also empirically. For example, in the case of Latvia we will see how debates over the effectiveness of political-administrative policies against former KGB agents often teetered on the verge of adding symbolic-representational measures to the mix (in the form of a wholesale opening of the old files), before figuring out ways to tighten the existing political-administrative policies. As a result, Boxes 2b and 3b of our matrix deserve to be studied simultaneously.

Lastly, when we get to purely symbolic measures, we will examine how over the years the parliaments in all three countries have adopted a number of resolutions and declarations not only remembering victims (to be discussed in Chapter 6) but also condemning specifically the former regime and its repressive organs. Although these statements do not mention any specific individuals, we interpret them as belonging to our Boxes 3a and 3b, since they are declarative actions against what is essentially defined as a collective perpetrator – the regime. In a similar manner, efforts have been made (particularly in Latvia and Lithuania) to ban the use of Soviet regime symbols such as the hammer and sickle or the red star. On the one hand, these are symbolic acts, since they do not impinge on any single perpetrator's livelihood or well-being. On the other hand, they are administrative policies, not least in the sense that they restrict rights and permit fines to be imposed on anyone violating the ban.

Alongside such blanket measures, we also have individual-level symbolic policies such as state-led efforts to reveal posthumously the names of those who carried out historical repression (Box 3a). In Estonia, for example, the International Commission for the Investigation of Crimes Against Humanity (*Inimsusevastaste kuritegude uurimise eesti rahvusvaheline komisjon* – IKUERK) focused much of its attention on identifying the specific individuals who were responsible for Soviet (and Nazi) repression in the country. None of these people could be brought to justice, as they were all deceased. However, making their names clear for the historical record was an important measure of symbolic justice that could be pursued.

Unpacking the concept of lustration

When we exit the realm of formal criminal-judicial justice for perpetrators and turn toward other possible measures that could be taken against former oppressors, the complexity of policy choices and nuances expands considerably. For one thing, culpability outside directly criminal acts like murder or torture becomes a much more normative question to determine. It involves deciding which types of people should be seen as having helped to maintain the regime and what their level of responsibility for that regime maintenance was. Thereafter, it involves determining a commensurate form of punishment in terms of restricting these individuals' opportunities in the democratic system (short of imprisonment). This latter process is also meant, by extension, to protect the new system from the potentially self-interested, deleterious behavior of these former regime operatives. Hence, punishment concerns not only making the perpetrators endure deprivation of certain rights or opportunities, but also separating those persons from the system so that the system can grow without their seemingly harmful influence.

The notion of lustration formally encompasses all of these considerations, which is why the term has come to mean many different things and has therefore lost part of its analytical clarity.[1] The word itself, of course, comes from the Latin root "to cleanse" and therefore alludes most of all to the third dimension of justice mentioned above, namely purifying and protecting a new system from certain detrimental individuals. This serves as a good starting point for unpacking the concept in real terms. That is, we may ask the question, what areas of a new democracy are seen as needing to be purified or protected from ex-regime persons? The most obvious realm of protection is, of course, the political sphere. Individuals, who were responsible for running a previously repressive regime, should be quarantined from having an opportunity to influence the new democratic system. Moreover, this can be viewed on two levels: electoral-representative politics and bureaucratic civil service. In other words, protections for a nascent democracy can include restricting the opportunity of former regime individuals either to run for elected office and/or serve in administrative posts. In both of these areas, deposed officials might influence policy, control public resources or might be

[1] Recent works (within political science) include Letki (2002), Appel (2005), Williams et al. (2005), Sadurski (2005: ch. 9), Czarnota (2009), Horne (2009b), Nalepa (2008, 2010), David (2011), Grodsky (2011), Haughton (2013), Szczerbiak (2014). See also Pettai (2012).

vulnerable to blackmail by others if their past is kept secret. In certain cases, moreover, the civil service dimension of state purification can reach far down into society depending on whether, for example, school teachers or university faculty are also seen as civil servants and therefore likewise subject to removal.

Alongside this broad domain of what could be called the state, we can delineate a second realm of possible cleansing, which is the economy. To be sure, one classic form of a grand bargain between former regime officials and the new democratic community is to say that former officials will be allowed to fade freely into economic society if they agree to relinquish the political realm. However, this may not always be the agreed-upon outcome. Forces in society may militate for the protection of the economic sphere as well, at least in those domains that appear to be most critical for economic development such as banking and finance, key industrial sectors or service areas such as the legal profession or security companies. This may mean that society is depriving itself of people, who are frequently quite entrepreneurial and could contribute to economic growth. However, the danger of these people engaging in self-interested, deleterious behavior in these economic areas may be seen as too high to risk their participation.

Lastly, new democratic societies often engage in practices to purify themselves of former regime individuals on the community level as well. This involves, for example, purposefully not offering such people any recognition for whatever good they may have done in society; instead, however well these individuals may have subsequently behaved, society-level actors such as the media but also average citizens among themselves may continue to remind each other of what role these individuals did at one point play. To take the most obvious example, journalists may decide to intermittently recall the fact that a successful businessperson was once a member of the Communist Party. Likewise, residents in an apartment block may gossip disparagingly for years about how a fellow tenant used to work for the KGB. Needless to say, these behaviors take us relatively far from the conventional understanding of lustration. However, they still reflect the original, broader meaning of cleansing and purifying.

The second major decision point for a new democratic regime (alongside the question of which realms of the community need to be purified) concerns how many official levels of the former regime should be punished or quarantined from the new system.[2] The question starts

[2] See also Elster (2004: 119) on "categories of wrongdoers."

with a broad distinction between direct and indirect oppressors within the old regime. The former are, unsurprisingly, members of the erstwhile security services, who were directly responsible for subjugating the population. The latter are, by extension, those who served in the political structures of the former regime, such as leaders of the Communist Party or ancillary groups like the Communist Youth League (Komsomol). We call these individuals indirect oppressors (or *Schreibtischtäter*), for although they often stood at the very top of the power pyramid, their role in actually carrying out repression was limited. Obviously, some may see these designations in a reverse light: high-level Communist Party members were actually more responsible for overall subjugation than the individual KGB agents who were simply following orders. However, we note as our justification the fact that Communist Party officials often saw their job as helping to simply administer society and do good (at least in their minds), whereas secret security operatives willfully engaged in sowing distrust and exercising coercion in the population.

Another important distinction between these two groups is that political officials from a former regime are all publicly known, whereas repressive officials are usually not. This means that if a new democratic society aims to purify itself of one or the other group, it must reckon with this distinction. It is possible to easily identify, for example, those individuals who were Communist Party apparatchiks. However, determining who was an agent, informer or simple collaborator of the KGB may be much more difficult. The point is that lustration policies will need to figure out how to entice those people with a more shadowy past to divulge their past activity.

A final parameter for understanding the range of purification measures in a society is to examine whether policies aimed at removing secret service operatives from the system rely more on state enforcement or self-enforcement. (See also Kaminski and Nalepa 2006; Nalepa 2008.) Here we come to what is conventionally referred to as lustration, that is, the different procedures for verifying, vetting or purging individuals who previously worked with the state security services. The point is that all of these approaches generally involve heavy state enforcement. Agencies are created to examine whether existing officials or other individuals are mentioned in whatever files remain from the former security police (screening). This may or may not be followed by banning them from office (purging). Agencies may also be involved with reviewing new candidates for elective or appointed office against old files (vetting). Lastly, agencies may be called into being in order to allow people to obtain an official certification that they are not mentioned in any files (accreditation).

By contrast, new democracies can also decide to take a bargaining approach with former direct repressors. They may offer them an opportunity to confess all of their activities in the former system in exchange for a pledge to keep all such information confidential and thereby avoid any public humiliation, thus prioritizing truth over justice. In this case, enforcement is mutual, since the former agents and collaborators can decide for themselves whether they want to own up to their past; the state becomes involved only in listening, and also potentially outing those agents who refused to come clean voluntarily but are later identified nonetheless.

The weakest enforcement option for new democracies seeking to cleanse erstwhile secret service agents from the new regime is to require individuals to submit a written oath or affidavit that they have never participated in the repression of others. This approach epitomizes self-enforcement, since the state does not get involved in the verification of this oath unless a challenge is made by a separate person. The broad effect of such a policy may be that many former agents do feel that giving such an oath may be too risky and therefore they voluntarily exit politics, civil service or any other spheres where this requirement may be enacted. However, they may also try to get away with submitting a necessary oath based on a calculation that very few third parties will bother to undertake a contestation of their oath. They hope they can fly under the radar.

Table 4.1 summarizes these different approaches to justice vis-à-vis non-criminal perpetrators of a former regime. The upper left-hand cell represents the most severe type of political-administrative measure, where a new democracy decides to ban all former regime party members from being elected to public office or serving in the civil service. De-Nazification in Germany and de-Baathification in Iraq come to mind. Needless to say, there are numerous degrees to which this principle can be enacted. Democratic leaders may decide to impose their ban not on all members of, say, the former Communist Party, but only those who were full-time employees at the regional or Central Committee level. Likewise, they may choose to limit the ban on elective office to just the national parliament or on employment in the civil service to high-level ministerial positions. Lastly, there may be a time limit for any ban of, say, ten years. All of these qualifications aside, however, this kind of measure is severe, since it targets a collective group and is not

Table 4 1 *Types of political-administrative measures against perpetrators*

		Indirect repressors *former members of Communist Party & other regime orgs.; generally known*	**Direct repressors** *employees, agents, informers, collaborators of the state security service; generally unknown*		
			State enforcement	Bargaining	Self-enforcement
Purifying repressors from:	**State**	*Political decommunization*: formal prohibition of ex-regime officials from state office	*Screening and purging*: background checks & possible dismissal of standing officials *Vetting*: background checks of new officials *Accreditation*: verification certificates required for employment	*Self-reporting*: voluntary confession to state authorities of prior collaboration; may or may not be kept confidential; periodic release of non-self-reported collaborators' names	*Oath of conscience*: required for existing and new state officials; may expire after time; possible punishment for perjury
	Economy	*Economic decommunization*: formal prohibition of ex-regime officials from certain sectors of private enterprise	*Screening and purging*: background checks & possible dismissal of individuals in key economic positions *Vetting*: background checks for new individuals in key economic positions *Accreditation*: verification certificates required for employment in key economic positions		*Oath of conscience*: required for individuals in key economic positions; may expire after time; possible punishment for perjury
	Society	*Ritual stigmatization*: former regime officials are continually reminded of their past positions	*Indiscriminate outing*: blanket publication of former operatives' names and/or files		*Withdrawal*: individuals avoid public attention because of their past

necessarily linked to any individual wrongdoing or directly repressive activity. It has therefore often been called decommunization, as opposed to simple lustration, precisely because it goes so far (Sadurski 2005; Czarnota 2009). Moreover, it often covers both indirect and direct repressors, since many KGB employees or agents were Communist Party members, and hence would be equally covered under such rules.

Taking the decommunization principle still further, a new democracy may also decide to impose some kind of ban on former regime officials participating in certain economic fields. We call this economic decommunization. Empirically we know that no post-communist country has ever considered such a ban. At the same time, countless analyses of public opinion have shown that popular resentment over ex-communist officials using their old contacts and networks to get rich in the market economy abounds. The impression that former Communists have taken control of different sectors of the economy is in some countries widespread. Hence, as a current of public opinion the issue continues to exist, even if most democratic politicians have shied away from legislating on these impulses.

The final manner in which indirect repressors from a former regime might be chastened in a new democratic society is via ritual stigmatization by other politicians over these individuals' past political careers. As noted above, this involves repeated public reminders of someone else having been a former Communist, even if this fact has nothing to do with a given issue at hand. Admittedly, this kind of practice goes beyond the realm of state policies that we are examining in this book. However, the point is that if we talk about the purification of society, then this more discursive dimension is also there and may even become that much more prevalent if more extensive decommunization efforts are not possible. Certainly in the Baltic states, a case in point is the degree to which Arnold Rüütel, Anatolijs Gorbunovs and Algirdas Brazauskas have had to endure attempts to taint whatever they did after re-independence with the simple epithet that they had once been high-ranking Communist leaders.[3]

In sum, given the complexities of establishing across-the-board punishments for Communist Party members and other indirect repressors,

[3] Even during his nine years in power (from 2005 to 2014), Estonia's Prime Minister Andrus Ansip (a member of the center-right Reform Party) had to respond several times to detractors, who tried to revive discussion of what he had done when he worked in the Tartu city committee of the Estonian Communist Party in 1988.

most post-communist countries have preferred to focus on isolating direct repressors, who are often seen as being more dangerous for nascent democracy because of their wily past, even though identifying these individuals may be more difficult. Yet what is typically conjoined into a single, broad-scale phenomenon of lustration actually contains a range of substantive variations that are explained in the right-hand side of Table 4.1. The key element here is that conventional policies of lustration involve heavy involvement by the new democratic state in terms of implementing and enforcing lustration measures. Purging, vetting and accreditation all involve long hours of review by government-appointed bodies. However, as we shall see in the case of the Baltics, a number of other, milder methods were applied that relied much more on self-reporting and self-enforcement. The reasons for this will be examined shortly. What is important to note here is that these policies often served just as well in terms of keeping ex-KGB elements out of the state (and partly the economy). They gave the unmistakable signal that former security operatives were not welcome in the new system, and most of these people got that message. What these policies did not do, however, was inflict direct humiliation on these individuals, since in most cases the measures allowed these persons to fade into the woodwork. In other words, the new democracy was protected, but the perpetrators were not made to suffer directly.

Placing the Baltic states into Table 4.1, we will see that the three countries have followed varying paths in terms of enacting transitional justice toward perpetrators. We will also observe that at different times each country has lurched toward a particularly radical form of justice. Most of the time the countries have stepped away from the brink; at other times, however, external restraint has been imposed in the form of the ECtHR. As described in the introduction to this chapter, Estonia's headlong plunge into transitional justice took place in 1992, when it became the only Baltic state to consider for a time a broad-scale framework of decommunization or a plan to actually ban high-ranking former Communist Party members from elective office. The decision to desist from this approach came fairly quickly. However, the way in which this event became almost a reverse pendulum swing is captured by the fact that by the end of that year the country ended up with the enactment of a very mild oath of conscience policy. Hence, Estonia went from the left-hand side of Table 4.1 all the way to the right-hand side. A few years later, the country would attempt to fortify this approach with a self-reporting law for ex-KGB employees that we call, in Table 4.1, bargaining. And although this law worked fairly well, it still highlighted the fact that in comparison to the other two Baltic states, Estonia would enact the weakest set of political-administrative measures against former regime elites.

Latvia's lustration policies have seemingly been more consistent, as the country has sought to gradually functionalize a core policy of vetting in relation to electoral candidates and higher state officials concerning possible past links to the KGB. To some extent this approach has been facilitated by the fact that Latvia was able to actually seize a portion of the KGB's more recent files in the country, whereas Estonia and Lithuania never did. Nonetheless, these files have also proved to be a torment in two ways. First, they have generally not been sufficient to actually prove individuals' conscious cooperation with the KGB. Second, they have led twice to the country wavering on the edge of another radical form of justice, namely, the temptation to throw open all of the files and impose societal lustration on all those contained within them.

Lastly, Lithuania's oscillations in the realm of lustration have involved two types. Namely, a clear temporal wave appears, when early efforts in 1991 to purge electoral bodies of ex-KGB agents are then followed-up with no policy at all after the ex-communist Democratic Labor Party (LDDP) returned to office in 1992. This, in turn, is followed by an ardent effort by conservatives to pass a lustration law in 1998–99, once they come back to power. However, here we see the country taken to its second threshold, when the conservatives pass a law that imposes lustration requirements on not only the state, but also areas of the private sector economy. These provisions would also wreak confusion until they were finally struck down by the ECtHR. Nonetheless, they were in effect for a time, and they have served to keep the lustration issue hot on the political agenda. Hence, in our comparison of the three Baltic states we will observe that Lithuania has ultimately been the strongest in terms of Box 2b of our overall matrix. This stark pendulum swing toward intense lustration in 1998–99 will also qualify the country as a case of "post-transitional justice" that we outlined in Chapter 1, but will also summarize in our Conclusion.

KGB materials recovered and processed

The Baltic states faced a considerable challenge in confronting their Soviet KGB legacy since the repressive apparatus was not of their own making but, rather, was imposed and steered from Moscow. Hence, as soon as the Soviet system in the Baltics began to crumble around 1989, the KGB and other Soviet security services (the military intelligence agency GRU, units of the Soviet Interior Ministry, etc.) began to take extra care with their activities, files and archives. Recognizing that the region was becoming more unstable and that a displacement of Soviet authority was a distinct possibility, various anecdotal accounts talk about the KGB removing most of its more sensitive materials from the three states already in 1989 and early 1990. One report on Estonia recounts that the KGB packed up and had transferred to Ulyanovsk the bulk of its "operative" files in January 1990 (Sildam and Mattson 1997). Later, the agency would also use Soviet military convoys in order to spirit away sensitive materials. Scholars working on Lithuania report similarly that the Soviet security services are thought to have removed key files in early 1990 (Skucas 2004; see also Misiunas 1994). At the same time, some flight might have been stemmed from the fact that Lithuania was much bolder in declaring its independence in March 1990 and thereafter attempted to tackle much more immediately the issue of neutralizing the work of the KGB, including encouraging ethnic Lithuanian agents to leave the organization and work for pro-independence forces. The situation in Latvia was more precarious, as the pro-independence government after May 1990 was much weaker and Moscow's control over the KGB was much stronger.[4] Nonetheless, one Latvian politician involved with shutting down the KGB in August 1991 recounts that KGB materials from Latvia were probably shipped out in 1989 (Muciņš, Interview, 2013). In mid-1990, the Latvian Supreme Council also set up a commission to prepare a set of interim agreements with the KGB; however, these accords never came to fruition (Bukovskis 1994).

A second moment of alarm occurred in the days following the failed anti-Gorbachev coup on August 19–21, 1991. In all three countries, the KGB then realized that its operations would now cease entirely and that any remaining compromising materials needed to be destroyed or removed as fast as possible. Hence, witnesses report seeing smoke rising from the KGB headquarters in Tallinn on the weekend of August 24–25, when allegedly 30,000 registry cards of persons known to have worked

[4] For example, there are reports that Latvia's Prime Minister Ivars Godmanis got along well with the Latvian KGB chief Edmunds Johansons, allowing him to sit in on meetings of his cabinet. Apparently the two men also had discussions about transferring the KGB to local Latvian control (Bukovskis 1994). However, this was seen as extremely dangerous, as this would have allowed all kinds of KGB operatives to infiltrate the new Latvian democracy.

for or been in contact with the KGB were burned in a large chimney (Sildam and Mattson 1997). Ashes from burnt files and other materials were also reportedly found in Vilnius (Skucas 2004).

Yet in Latvia, parliamentary deputies who demanded entry to the KGB headquarters in Riga on August 28 were able to seize roughly 4,500 KGB registry cards similar to the ones reportedly incinerated in Tallinn. Because the cards were discovered in a pair of burlap bags, the find would come to be dubbed the "Cheka bags" (*čekas maisi*) in an allusion to the KGB's pre-war predecessor.[5] Moreover, this phrase would become a code word for the entire lustration dilemma in Latvia, that is, whether to "open the Cheka bags" or not. Alongside these registry cards, however, the Latvian authorities also seized fifty-three ledgers that had logged the creation of each individual registry card (Rancāns 2006). The ledgers dated back to 1953 and ran up to 1987. They contained the registry number of each individual card, the code name of each contact listed on the card, the date that person had been recruited and information about whether the contact had become inactive. Indeed, because contacts changed over time, the ledgers recorded entries for over 12,000 different people. The 4,500 index cards that were recovered therefore represented only those people who were active in the late 1980s.[6] (The cards for inactive contacts had been sent to Moscow.) Lastly, a partially destroyed KGB electronic database called "Alfa" also fell into the hands of Latvian officials after the 1991 coup. In painstaking work over several years, researchers and technicians managed to recover a good deal of the data stored there, containing agent reports on up to 80,000 people monitored by the KGB since the 1960s and all the way to 1991. The information was systematized in such a way that it employed different numeric codes as shorthand for characterizing the nature of the person in question and the reason for their surveillance, that is, they had relatives abroad, were known to have nationalist views, etc. (Upleja and Titavs 1998). There was relatively little operational information contained in the files, apart from a few occasional notes added by regular KGB employees. Moreover, the real names of the KGB operatives were encoded. Still, by allowing single individuals to gain access to whatever information was there on them and subsequently talking with those targeted by the KGB,

5 "Cheka" stood for the Russian letters ЧК, which was the abbreviation for *чрезвычайная комиссия* or Extraordinary Commission, the forerunner of the NKVD and the KGB.

6 Mägi (2012: 18) reports a comparable number of active agents having been in Estonia at the end of the Soviet period: between 2,500 and 3,000.

researchers at the Center for the Documentation of the Consequences of Totalitarianism (TSDC) managed to identify a considerable number of former informants, if not always their officers. By 2013, information about 35,656 former KGB informants was gathered and about 8,000 of their reports had been deciphered (Langa and Kalpiņa 2013; Zālītis, Interview, 2013). In any case, the most important consequence of all this was that of the three Baltic states only Latvia would have an actual set of KGB materials on which to draw as part of a lustration process. Over the years, officials confirmed that the card catalogue they had obtained was complete, that is, all of the cards matched the ledgers and were in proper sequential order. At the same time, they were merely a set of names. The cards said nothing about what the individual had actually done for the KGB. Moreover, as one Latvian official confirmed, it was entirely possible that a person was listed in the registry without them ever knowing it (Ābola 2014). For many people, therefore, the "Cheka bags" seemed as much a curse as they were a treasure.

In the weeks following re-independence, all three Baltic governments took steps to formally liquidate the KGB on their territory. For example, in Lithuania a special parliamentary commission was formed to monitor the takeover of KGB property and materials across the country. This transition was also facilitated by the fact that the country had already set up its own nascent national security service in 1990. Meanwhile, in Latvia, the Supreme Council formed two working groups tasked with overseeing the transfer of property and materials. Parliament also took the lead in concluding formal transition agreements with the KGB in August (Johansons 2006). Lastly, Estonian Prime Minister Edgar Savisaar formally agreed to handover protocols with the KGB chief Vadim Bakatin in September and October of 1991. A third accord was concluded in mid-December, just days before the end of the Soviet Union itself.[7]

[7] Although in all three Baltic states these efforts to deal with the KGB immediately after re-independence appeared to be earnest, this would not prevent a series of inquiries from taking place years later into whether this work had truly been done correctly and honestly. In both Estonia and Latvia, special parliamentary commissions would be set up to examine (among other things) how the KGB was dismantled in those countries. Latvia's Prime Minister Ivars Godmanis would be accused of dragging his feet for more than six weeks before appointing an official to oversee the takeover of KGB property. Moreover, this official would be reproached for having allowed the KGB to continue destroying materials after August 1991 (Bukovskis 1994). Meanwhile, the head of Estonia's commission to take over KGB property, Hardo Aasmäe, was later vilified for sloppy documentation and for actually returning to the KGB sacks of material the Estonian government had already seized (Pruuli 1993; Mägi 2012).

While this dissolution of the USSR appeared to throw the situation into even greater flux, the new successor state, the Russian Federation, actually turned out to be an advantage for the Baltic states at least during the first few years. With Boris Yeltsin at its helm, the Russian leadership proved relatively cooperative in terms of giving back certain KGB materials already in 1992. The Estonian government formed a special commission to oversee the return of some 50,000 separate materials, including roughly 29,000 criminal files (or files on people believed to have engaged in anti-Soviet activities) (Sildam and Mattson 1997). Lithuania succeeded in negotiating an analogous recuperation of materials in 1992 and 1994, the latter batch involving information on KGB pensioners left in the country (Skucas 2004; see also Wolff 2006).

Immediate investigations and purges

Once the initial whirlwind of regaining independence and securing KGB property had passed, the next step in solving the question of former agents was to purge them from high political positions. Lithuania launched this process on December 17, 1991 with a law mandating a review of all members of parliament and their possible connections with the KGB and other security services (Kritz 1995b: 428–31). If any former agents were discovered, they were to be subject to a special by-election. The Gajauskas Commission (named after its chair, Balys Gajauskas, a former political prisoner and dissident) undertook a series of investigations, eventually raising suspicion against five individuals, including the former prime minister, Kazimiera Prunskienė, and a prominent leader of the pro-independence *Sąjūdis* movement, Virgilijus Čepaitis (Misiunas 1994; Anušauskas 2006: 198; Stan 2009a: 50). While Čepaitis ended up withdrawing from politics voluntarily, Prunskienė went on to contest in court the Commission's accusations against her (which involved mainly her having written reports for the KGB after trips abroad in the 1980s). In September 1992, she lost her case, but by that time new parliamentary elections were about to be held and she was not formally expelled. Moreover, Prunskienė continued to profess her innocence, arguing that the accusations were all part of an effort to discredit her. Indeed, the Prunskienė case would come to epitomize the degree to which the unmasking of Lithuanian politicians with former KGB links would quickly become a repeated and hotly contested political affair, for during the next fifteen years Prunskienė would undergo additional reviews of her past, including another court challenge in 2009 when she would run for president.

In Latvia, the task of screening parliament for former regime operatives took a slightly different form. As we saw in Chapter 3, the country had been consumed in August 1991 with arresting hardline pro-Soviet leaders like Alfreds Rubiks for their involvement in shadowy anti-independence organizations like the All-Latvian Committee of Public Salvation responsible for the attempted Soviet crackdown in Latvia during January 1991 and for aiding the recent anti-Gorbachev coup attempt. While Rubiks would go on trial for treason, other members of his group were subjected to a ban on running for political offices that was passed through a series of resolutions in the following weeks. In addition, in June 1992 the Latvian Supreme Council adopted amendments to the main law defining the status of parliamentarians and local government council members that would allow parliament to disbar any such legislator, if it were proven that he or she had been a member of these pro-Soviet organizations after January 15, 1991 (Latvijas Republikas Augstākā Padome 1992b; see also Latvijas Republikas Satversmes Tiesa 2000). The expulsion procedure was to be based on a prior parliamentary report detailing the activities of these organizations and their members. Any final decisions would have to be confirmed by the full Supreme Council membership. Yet just ten days after adopting these amendments, the Supreme Council approved the disbarment of fifteen elected representatives at the national and local levels. This was one of the few times in the Baltics that elected officials were actually removed for repressive (and indeed anti-constitutional) activities.

By contrast, in Estonia no attempts were ever made to re-examine sitting legislators and their possible KGB ties. There was also no disqualification of people associated with pro-Soviet groups. On the contrary, some of the most vociferous anti-independence deputies in the Estonian Supreme Council (like Vladimir Lebedev and Sergei Petinov) were even included as delegates to the newly created Constitutional Assembly. True, three local councils in northeast Estonia were disbanded for having obliquely supported the August 1991 attempted coup. However, following fresh elections a few months later, many of these suspect councilors regained their seats and thus remained in office.

Before turning to an examination of the formal lustration policies in each Baltic country, we want to clarify the relevance of one more set of laws adopted in late 1991, namely those on citizenship. As we outlined in Chapter 2, Estonia and Latvia adhered to a very strict implementation of the Baltic states' doctrine of legal state continuity by adopting, in October and November 1991, legislation that restored the citizenship only of those who had been citizens of these two states before June 1940 along with their descendants; automatic citizenship was denied to those who had settled in these republics during Soviet rule and to their descendants. These policies had clear ethno-political motives (since the Estonians and Latvians had seen a dramatic decrease in their share of the population as a result of Soviet colonization policy) as well as stark ethno-political consequences (since the denial of automatic citizenship meant hundreds of thousands of mostly Russian residents in the countries would end up being cut out of the political system). However, what concerns us here is the possible link or effect that these policies had on transitional justice and lustration. A number of scholars have concluded that because Estonia and Latvia passed restrictive citizenship legislation, the two countries obviated the need to adopt more extensive lustration measures (as in Lithuania), since the majority of KGB agents and other suspect individuals became non-citizens and had therefore already been purged from the state and political system. As Jaskovska and Moran (2006: 498) argue, the citizenship laws "served a purpose similar to that of lustration in CEE [Central and Eastern Europe], namely barring individuals associated with the former occupiers or oppressors from holding vital political posts in the new regime." (See also Ellis 1997; Letki 2002; Stan 2009a; Švarca 2012.)

We acknowledge the prima facie validity of this deduction. However, we caution against reading too much causal influence into the connection. First, the Estonian and Latvian citizenship laws were adopted in their day with no reference, consciousness or intent as to their possible impact on weeding out former KGB operatives. Estonian and Latvian legislators did not see citizenship policy as a tool for addressing lustration. Rather, the *raison d'être* for this legislation came purely from the broader framework of legal continuity. Second, the argument implying a causal link between citizenship and lustration is premised on an empirical claim that Estonia and Latvia implemented substantially less rigorous (or even no) lustration procedures as compared to Lithuania. (It is only in this way that the correlation "strict citizenship, low lustration" and vice versa can stand.) However, as we will show in the next section, all three countries adopted different kinds of lustration procedures. And while Estonia is, indeed, perhaps the weakest of the three, it was still the first to implement a self-reporting system that Lithuania adopted only four years later. Likewise, Latvia maintains a relatively robust system of vetting electoral candidates and high state officials for ex-KGB ties, which has led to numerous resignations and court cases. Hence, the empirical relationship is also not there.[8]

These problems notwithstanding, we do see merit in considering for a moment the citizenship issue within the framework of our analytical matrix. Interestingly enough, it would be possible to interpret the restrictive citizenship principles in Estonia and Latvia as a Box 2b political-administrative transitional justice measure against a whole class of perpetrators, namely all Soviet-era settlers in the two republics. The perpetrator designation would come from the fact that these settlers had indirectly helped to implement the Soviet occupation. Indeed, within Estonian and Latvian nationalist rhetoric the word "occupier" has often been used to refer to those who came to the republics during the Soviet period, however injurious this may seem to those actual people. Yet here again we are wary of construing our model to such an extreme, since were we to make this designation it would radically skew the conclusions we would draw in terms of Box 2b across the three Baltic states. Estonia and Latvia would be catapulted to a maximum level of transitional justice, even beyond decommunization! It would also greatly overshadow the differences that exist across the conventional lustration legislation in the three countries. Hence, the notion is better left as a thought experiment.

Lustration laws

Beginning in 1992, the Baltic states would turn toward adopting more systematic lustration legislation that would concentrate on ferreting out any leftover furtive KGB elements in their political systems as well as on preventing these elements from entering their systems in the future. In

[8] In the end, there is also a rather prosaic reason for these misinterpretations, and that is the simple failure by some authors to present accurate research on these two countries. Neither Ellis, Letki nor Jaskovska and Moran provide any information on the actual lustration policies in effect in Estonia and Latvia at the time of their publications. For example, none of these authors talks about the Estonian oath of conscience. Ellis is sketchy on the Latvian procedure for vetting electoral candidates, while Letki and Jaskovska/Moran ignore these policies completely. Hence, because the authors appeared to believe that these countries had no lustration policies, it is easy to draw spurious links to other factors. Stan (2009a) is much more thorough in her exposition of the facts, but still concludes with the same correlative inference between citizenship legislation and level of lustration. Švarca, although a Latvian researcher herself, relies mainly on the conclusions drawn by Stan (2009a) in order to link citizenship with lustration in her analysis.

the sections that follow, we will profile each country separately in order to form a composite view of each case that we can then link back as closely as possible to Table 4.1.

Estonia

Although we have already indicated that Estonia's overall configuration of lustration measures is weaker than in Latvia or Lithuania, the country remains the only one (indeed, across all of post-communist Europe), where a lustration measure has actually been incorporated into the Constitution. Admittedly, this provision would be part of the Implementation Act or transitional annex to the Constitution and would be limited in time (nine years). However, its existence points to the fact that issues of transitional justice were on the minds of members of the Constitutional Assembly as they weighed the most important legal-institutional choices to be made for the newly restored state. These politicians' decision to write in provisions for an oath of conscience to be given by all future elected and appointed public officials would symbolize their desire to not let this level of institutionalization for lustration pass. Needless to say, the idea of having an oath of conscience came against the backdrop of a failure to implement decommunization. Moreover, we will see that the oath of conscience itself had a very limited effect on truly cleansing the body politic. Still, in comparative terms it would represent an interesting foray into long-term truth and justice measures in a situation where the political system itself was not at all yet in place.

The final text of the oath (as stated in the Implementation Act) would require individuals to swear that they had never been "in the state security organs or military intelligence or counter-intelligence services of a country that has occupied Estonia nor participated in the surveillance or repression of other citizens for their political beliefs, disloyalty, class affiliation or prior employment in the civil service or defense forces of the Republic of Estonia" (Eesti Vabariik 1992: §§6–7). The Act stated that both new officials and those in office were obliged to sign such an oath. The procedure would remain in force until December 31, 2000.[9] Within ten

[9] Why this particular date was chosen is unclear. For example, other transitional periods in the Implementation Act were counted in full years beginning from the date of adoption of the Constitution. The deadline chosen for the oath of conscience was a specific day and had no implicit link either to any other transitional period or, for instance, to any future parliamentary election.

days of the Constitution being approved by referendum, the Estonian Supreme Council passed a follow-up law laying out further procedural rules (Eesti Vabariigi Riigikogu 1992). By the end of 1992, thousands of politicians and civil servants had submitted their oath of conscience.

In theory, one might have expected the oath of conscience to have had at least a slightly disruptive effect within the political class and the civil service. After all, the law required already employed state officials to present such statements, whereupon one might imagine at least a temporary increase in the number of people suddenly declaring their resignations and opting for another career. However, no such wave of departures was ever reported. If the oath of conscience had any kind of cleansing effect on the Estonian political and government system, it was gradual and undetectable to the naked eye.[10] Clearly the system also had a deterrent effect into the future, since we will never know how many former KGB operatives decided to stop thinking about a possible political career or employment in the civil service because of the oath of conscience. However, the lustration policy was also weak because of its enforcement procedure, since at no point was consideration given to creating any kind of agency that might quickly and cleanly examine suspect oaths.[11] Rather, the position was that any such contestations should be channeled into the court system.

Indeed, even this detail appears to have been botched, since at the moment when the first challenge was made to a prominent politician's oath of conscience, it would turn out that the July 1992 procedural law on the oath had forgotten to specify which court should actually hear such complaints. The matter arose in relation to none other than Estonia's first president after 1992, Lennart Meri, and his declaration in

[10] In part, of course, the system was designed to work this way, since a subsequent (1994) amendment to the Oath of Conscience Submission Act allowed the Prosecutor General's Office to keep confidential the name of any individual who came to it and voluntarily confessed to their collaboration with the KGB, but had also at some point signed an oath of conscience. This was important, since in that case the Prosecutor General's Office could decide not to support any attempt to contest that person's oath of conscience in court, and thereby actually protect that individual.

[11] The only improvement was the 1994 amendment (mentioned in the previous footnote) that allowed the Prosecutor General's Office to begin an independent investigation into someone's oath of conscience and to later file suit in court if relevant materials were forwarded to it by a third party. The aim of the amendment, however, was not to have the prosecutor actively check everyone's oath of conscience, but rather to relieve the burden on individuals having to go to court alone and bear all of the court costs themselves, if they wanted to contest someone's oath.

1996 that he intended to stand for election to a second term. During the Soviet era Meri (b. 1929) had been an internationally known documentary film producer as well as fiction writer. His father had been an Estonian diplomat, and therefore Meri had actually spent part of his childhood in Paris and Berlin. Following the Soviet takeover, his family was deported to Siberia, from where he would not be allowed to return until 1948. Later, as his literary and film career began to grow, Meri was allowed to travel abroad, where he also visited émigré Estonians (see also Lepassalu 2005).

It was these last two aspects of Meri's biography which were taken up by three plaintiffs in September 1996 when they attempted to contest Meri's oath of conscience. Meri had, of course, given the oath in August 1992 when he first ran for president. Moreover, it had not been an issue in that campaign. However, four years later two members of the Estonian parliament, Eldur Parder and Villu Müüripeal, as well as an émigré Estonian journalist and political activist, Jüri Estam, submitted a formal lawsuit to the Tallinn City Court claiming that Meri had given a false oath. In a somewhat sprawling submission to the court, the plaintiffs raised doubts about how Meri could have been allowed to return from Siberia before Stalin's death if he had not collaborated with the regime in some way. Moreover, the journalist Estam insisted that during Meri's visits with émigré Estonians he must have written reports for a special Soviet Estonian bureau charged with keeping an overview of émigré activities. In either instance, the plaintiffs maintained, Meri had lied in his oath, as he must have cooperated with the security authorities.

To the plaintiffs' dismay, however, the Tallinn City Court refused to hear the case, claiming it had no formal jurisdiction in the matter. In a rather surprising conclusion, the court noted that while the 1992 Procedure for Taking the Oath of Conscience Act had reiterated that challenges to a person's oath of conscience would be heard in the courts, the law did not specify which court – criminal, administrative or civil – would have precise jurisdiction. Arguing that it did not have the legal authority to unilaterally take on this function, the court rejected the case.

Determined to push their point, however, Parder, Müüripeal and Estam appealed the decision ultimately to the Civil Chamber of the Estonian Supreme Court, which ruled in February 1997 that indeed the Procedure for Taking the Oath of Conscience Act had a major flaw in it because it did not specify which court should hear such cases. In order to resolve the issue, the justices ruled that because the oath was meant to protect the public interest, it was a matter of public law, which therefore should henceforth belong to the administrative courts. With this major legal clarification, the plaintiffs appear to have gained enough satisfaction, as they did not pursue their original complaint against President Meri in a new lawsuit.

A second major contestation of an oath of conscience came in September 2006 after the procedure itself had formally expired. In this respect, it was not a formal charge. However, it concerned again a sitting president, this time Meri's successor Arnold Rüütel, and again at a time when the president was seeking re-election. An investigative article published in the weekly newspaper *Eesti Ekspress* alleged that Rüütel, while serving as a deputy prime minister in the Soviet Estonian government, had given orders in March 1981 to intensify KGB monitoring of a special biotechnology company called *Desintegraator*. The company's founding engineer, Johannes Hint, was renowned for his scientific work. However, he was also known for holding dissident political views. In November of that same year Hint was arrested on what many saw as trumped-up charges relating to mismanagement at the company. Following a lengthy trial, Hint was convicted in 1983 and sentenced to fifteen years' imprisonment. Hint died, however, just two years later in 1985.

The archival documentation of Rüütel's involvement with the KGB crackdown on *Desintegraator* – and by extension the repression of Johannes Hint – raised questions about the truthfulness of the president's one-time oath. Rüütel issued a public statement denying any formal involvement in repression, saying that his 1981 letter and any other communications he may have made were simply part of Soviet bureaucratic procedure at that time. The controversy still resonated with many commentators, including a former chief justice of the Estonian Supreme Court, Rait Maruste, who publicly cast doubt on Rüütel's ethical integrity on the issue. The charges also surfaced just three weeks before a special electoral college would decide whether to re-elect Rüütel or appoint his challenger, former MEP Toomas Hendrik Ilves. On the one hand, the controversy had no legal standing, since the oath of conscience procedure had run out six years earlier. Rüütel could no longer be removed from his post on these grounds. However, the issue was one which drew attention once again to Rüütel's long career in the Estonian Communist Party and Soviet Estonian government, which in turn served to reinforce the contrast between him and his challenger Ilves, who was much younger and an émigré Estonian raised in the United States. In the event, Rüütel lost the presidential race to Ilves on the first ballot.

Apart from these two more prominent cases, only a few other oaths of conscience were ever contested, and only one led to a formal dismissal from office. In the waning days of the procedure, in March 2000, the Prosecutor General's Office issued a charge against a member of the Narva City Council, Vadim Tomilov, accusing him of having worked in the Narva city KGB during 1984–88 and thereby having violated the oath of conscience he gave as part of his candidacy for the city council. In March 2001, an administrative court upheld the charge and ordered the Estonian National Electoral Committee to annul his local council mandate.

By late 2000, as the formal deadline for giving oaths of conscience was coming to a close, voices in parliament began to rise for an extension of the procedure. MPs like the former dissident Enn Tarto, but also members from the national-conservative Pro Patria Union, began to draft legislation to this effect. However, numerous legal authorities as well as even the prime minister at the time, Mart Laar, concluded that because the oath had been instated via the Implementation Act of the Constitution and approved through a referendum, the only way one could alter the impending expiration would be to hold a new referendum or amend the Constitution. This they concluded, however, was impractical.[12]

Instead, government officials began working on means to tighten the screening process for top state officials. In June 2001, parliament passed a series of legislative amendments requiring candidates for the positions of chancellor of justice, member of the board of the Bank of Estonia and commander of the Estonian Defense Forces to submit to a special national security screening to be carried out by the Security Police Board. This new system naturally did not cover anything like the range of positions previously mandated by the oath of conscience. But as many politicians and commentators would note in late 2000, the oath of conscience had by then served its main purpose: to lay down a moral

[12] This was the same opinion that had been given to an attempt by Enn Tarto in 1994 to actually criminalize violations of the oath of conscience. Here, too, the argument was that basic law cannot go beyond what is in constitutional law. In addition, it should be noted that the United Nations Human Rights Committee (1995) had voiced a cautionary opinion vis-à-vis Estonia's oath of conscience in 1995. The Committee worried that the oath inhibited individuals' rights "to have access, on general terms of equality, to public service" as stipulated in the International Convention on Civil and Political rights (Art. 25). Although Estonia appears not to have followed up on this opinion (essentially because doing so would have meant amending the Constitution's Implementation Act), MPs were conscious of this international delicacy when considering whether to continue the oath beyond 2000.

guideline that people previously involved with the Soviet repressive regime were undesired in Estonia's new government system and politics. As Chief Justice of the Estonian Supreme Court, Mart Rask, would say in 2007, "The oath of conscience was a cautionary, not a repressive measure, but its message was clear that Estonia's civil service would disavow itself of those people, who had actively been in the service of the foreign power." Rask added that the true effect of the oath should not be measured in terms of how many people had had their oath contested or were removed from office, but rather what indirect effect it had had in terms of breaking any continuity on a personal level with the Soviet era. This, he felt, had been significant (Rask 2007). Perhaps, of course, one could interpret Rask's remarks as trying to put a brave face on a rather timid legacy for the oath of conscience. At the same time, his opinion may also have been buoyed by the knowledge that Estonia's second lustration policy of self-reporting for ex-KGB operatives had actually been a more marked success in terms of identifying true repressors and their past.

The impetus to bolster Estonia's oath of conscience with other lustration measures surfaced in the Estonian parliament just weeks after the restored Riigikogu convened for its first session in October 1992. Lingering doubts that the KGB in Estonia had been shut down under suspicious circumstances prompted newly appointed Prime Minister Mart Laar to form a special cabinet commission to look into the matter. When the commission reported its first findings in February 1993, a public scandal erupted that made many realize that additional legislation was needed (Muuli 1993; Pruuli 1993; Mägi 2012). On May 18, 1993, parliament formed a special temporary commission to look into KGB and other Soviet intelligence agency activities in Estonia (Eesti Vabariigi Riigikogu 1993a). The eight-member group of MPs was given relatively broad powers to subpoena all documents pertaining to the former Soviet secret services from both governmental and other sources as well as to conduct hearings and to commission other studies where necessary. The members of the commission were obliged to keep sensitive information confidential; however, they could contact law enforcement authorities if they discovered material that indicated that a person had lied on their oath of conscience. The most important task of the commission, however, was to prepare a series of additional legislation that would take Estonia's lustration process further. The first such act was passed in March 1994 and regulated the procedure by which all documents from the Soviet security services would be archived (Eesti Vabariigi Riigikogu

1994b). The materials would be deposited in the State Archives, and the law mandated that any private individual still in possession of such documents was required to hand them over to the Archives. In terms of disclosure, all persons were given the right to see information pertaining to themselves in the files; this right was also given to the relatives of such persons in cases where the person was deceased. By April 1996 nearly 4,000 people had requested such access (Padrik 1996).

During the rest of 1994, the commission labored mostly over preparing the new self-reporting law. The commission had hoped initially that the Estonian government would take the lead in preparing a draft; however, when this did not materialize, the commission took it upon itself to finish the task, knowing that parliamentary elections would be due in March 1995 and that after that the commission would be disbanded (Tarto 1994). After relatively little debate in parliament, the Procedure for Registration and Disclosure of Persons who Have Served in or Co-operated with Intelligence or Counter-intelligence Organizations of Security Organizations or Military Forces of States which Have Occupied Estonia Act was passed on February 6, 1995 (Eesti Vabariigi Riigikogu 1995).

As indicated by the long title, the key tenets of the new law involved both registering and potentially disclosing the names of those people who had served in the security agencies of either the Soviet Union or Nazi Germany. Specifically, individuals who had worked for or collaborated with the Gestapo, the KGB, the Soviet military intelligence agency (GRU) or any of their predecessors, were given until April 1, 1996 to register themselves with the Estonian Security Police Board (*Kaitsepolitsei*, KAPO) and to disclose in a written affidavit their full past involvement with such organs. If they did not do so and sufficient evidence was gathered against them by KAPO, their name would be published after the deadline in the *Riigi Teataja* (or State Gazette) as a past agent or accomplice of a foreign occupier. As would become custom in such laws, the net was cast fairly widely to include those people who had served not only as agents of such security services, but also as "a resident, a keeper of a conspiratorial flat or being a trustee of security or intelligence organizations or knowingly and voluntarily co-operating in any other manner with such organizations" (Art. 4, para. 4). As one State Security Police employee would later specify, this provision would even extend to tourist guides, for example, who used to have dealings with foreigners and would report to the KGB, or to long-distance truck drivers on international routes, who would also have had contacts with the KGB (Sildam 1996). In return for such disclosures, the law promised that if such information did not constitute a criminal act, it would be kept confidential in perpetuity as a state secret and no harm would come to the confessor. Moreover, where evidence was obtained on someone who had not registered themselves, that person would still be given a month's notice to contest the available charges in front of a confidential court of law before his/her name would be released to the public.[13]

With these offers of absolution, the Security Police began to await its sinners to the confessional. Although many KGB experts had estimated the total number of individuals encompassed by the law's different categories to be as many as 20,000, by April 1, 1996 only 1,153 people had contacted the Security Police and registered their past sins.[14] Needless to say, there was a surge of people contacting KAPO in the weeks and days prior to the deadline, their ranks including a number of business people, politicians and other public figures (Padrik 1996). At the same time, many people clearly seemed to think they had not been involved in any serious collaboration with the KGB, or felt that they would await the presentation of evidence against them by the Security Police. The last head of the KGB in Estonia (appointed in 1990), Rein Sillar, told one journalist that he had not bothered to contact KAPO. "How many people still doubt that I ever worked in the KGB?" boasted Sillar. "I will be happy to read my name in the *Riigi Teataja*, if such a list should ever appear" (Sildam 1996).

Sillar's skepticism about any KGB names being published was disproved in January 1997, when KAPO published its first, modest list of seven former KGB agents. Over the next eleven years, however, the Board would release thirteen lists of agents with a total of 647 individuals disclosed, 146 women and 501 men.[15] Each list averaged around fifty

[13] Strictly speaking, Estonia's self-registration policy of 1996 would count as a measure falling within Box 3b, given its non-consequential character for those disclosed by the Security Police Board. The fact that we nevertheless included this measure among our discussion of political-administrative transitional justice policies aimed at perpetrators (Box 2b) owes mostly to practical considerations as both administrative and symbolic sanctions against erstwhile regime supporters are often connected – not least in regard to the politics involved.

[14] KAPO has generally declined to talk about how many people it has registered as former operatives, but this number was widely reported in the media and later confirmed by Estonia's Chancellor of Justice (Jõks 2005: 2).

[15] KAPO provides the citations to each issue of the *Riigi Teataja* on its webpage, www.kapo.ee/eng/areas-of-activity/disclosure-of-employees-of-security-organisations-of-the-states-that-have-occupi/procedure-for-registration-and-disclosure. For more analysis of these lists and the categories contained within them, see Pettai and Onken (2009).

names and was published roughly once a year. Significantly, all of the named individuals were linked to the Soviet security services. No names were ever issued of individuals allegedly linked to the Nazi secret services. In part, this is understandable given the shorter duration of the Nazi occupation and its greater distance in the historical past. However, it is unclear to what extent KAPO has pursued investigations of possible Nazi collaborators or whether any of the 1,153 people who confessed their past activities did so because of links with the Nazi regime. Equally telling is the fact that KAPO's lists contained only full-time KGB employees and no lower-rank collaborators or informants, even though the law allowed KAPO to reveal these persons as well. This may have been a political decision to go after only professional KGB operatives. And yet from the perspective of letting people know who collected more casual repressive information on fellow citizens, this goal remained unmet.

As prescribed by law, KAPO not only published the names of these individuals, but also the exact years of their service in different KGB departments. In this respect it appears that KAPO had access to certain personnel records of the KGB, since some career agents were listed with as many as ten different positions, covering decades of service. (It is unlikely that such biographies could have been compiled simply on the basis of other informants' testimony.) More controversially, the lists included the former agent's employer and position at the moment of disclosure. While this would appear to subject these individuals and their employers to still further exposure, the provision was defended as necessary in order to make the public (including employers) aware of where these people had once been. Moreover, since roughly 40 percent of all those individuals disclosed were listed as pensioners, the actual damage done to people's reputations was seen as limited. Nonetheless, the practice was criticized as unconstitutional by Estonia's Chancellor of Justice Allar Jõks in July 2005, when after having reviewed a complaint by two of the outed ex-KGB agents he sent a report to the Riigikogu calling on it to amend this part of the law, since in his view the provision was disproportionate to the proper aims of the law (Jõks 2005). He also viewed as disproportionate and hence unconstitutional that part of the law that required KAPO to reveal employee names even if these people were part of the technical staff of the KGB. Jõks argued that those who had worked merely as service personnel within the agency (such as office cleaners or drivers) shouldn't be subjected to this stigmatization since they never engaged in repression. On the whole, Jõks found the registration and disclosure policy to be constitutional (a fact that KAPO would later eagerly relay on its website). In relation to the two specific provisions Jõks found questionable, however, the Riigikogu never responded and Jõks never followed up with any possible appeal to the Supreme Court. As of early 2014, the registration and disclosure law had not been amended, but by the same token no agent lists had been released for four years. The process was beginning to wind itself down (Arpo, Interview, 2013).

Latvia

Latvia's desire after August 1991 not only to ban immediately all pro-Soviet organizations but also to cleanse its national parliament and local councils of all such sympathizers put the country on a lustration path, which would focus very much on preventing ex-KGB operatives from gaining access specifically to legislative office. Vetting national and local electoral candidates for former KGB ties would become the primary focus of lustration policy, essentially because the materials to do this were seemingly at hand. With some 4,500 registry cards at their fingertips, Latvian authorities were in a position to at least check whether individuals seeking political office in the new Latvian democracy had had contact with the KGB. To be sure, the cards gave no indication of the degree to which a person had collaborated with the agency. Yet it was also impossible to simply ignore the catalogue's existence. Inevitably these materials would become the main focus of lustration policy in the country. Decommunization, for example, was never considered.

The existence of the KGB materials also meant that a special state agency would be needed to oversee their use, which in turn meant that lustration policy would become institutionalized to a much greater degree than in Estonia. On March 25, 1992 the Latvian Supreme Council ordered the establishment of a Commission for the Investigation of Totalitarian Regime Crimes (*Totalitāro režīmu noziegumu izmeklēšanas komisija*, TRNIK), whose task it would be to systematize the KGB archives and prepare the groundwork for the creation of a full-scale Center for the Documentation of the Consequences of Totalitarianism (*Totalitārisma seku dokumentēšanas centrs*, TSDC) as a permanent oversight and research body (Pettai 2013a). Initially, neither of the two bodies was delegated to deal with candidate vetting. In October 1992 the Latvian Supreme Council decided that for the next parliamentary elections, due in

June 1993, all candidates would simply be required to submit to the national electoral commission an affidavit certifying that they were not currently nor had they ever been a regular employee or collaborator of the Soviet or Latvian KGB, the Soviet Defense Ministry or part of Russia's or any other foreign country's intelligence or counter-intelligence services. In addition, the affidavit had to confirm that the candidate had never been an "agent, a resident [or] a keeper of a conspiratorial flat" in any of these services (Latvijas Republikas Augstākā Padome 1992a: Art. 21). Essentially Latvia appeared set to go the Estonian way of having candidates submit an oath of conscience.

However, on March 16, 1993 the parliament tightened these provisions by saying that anyone who could not provide such a truthful statement should not run in the election. This last point particularly personalized the issue of lustration, since the amendment came to be directly associated with a single member of the Supreme Council, Juris Bojārs, the leader of the ex-communist Latvian Democratic Labor Party and a prominent critic of the Popular Front government. Bojārs had made no secret of the fact that he had been a major in the KGB. Thus, under the new legislation he had no way of running for re-election in 1993. Still, he would continue to lead his party and remain on the political scene, indeed enough so to later contest in the country's Constitutional Court the whole idea of banning ex-KGB operatives from running in parliamentary elections.

In June 1993 the Saeima elections transpired peacefully and no particular mention was made of KGB issues. The TRNIK and the TSDC had maintained discretion during the electoral campaign in terms of whether any of the candidates were mentioned in the KGB catalogue. After a meeting of the two bodies on June 17, however, the head of the TRNIK, Dainis Vanags, as well as the initial head of the TSDC, Paulis Klaviņš, could not resist making a sensational disclosure that despite the affidavit measures adopted for the recent elections, five of the newly elected MPs had KGB files, meaning that they had potentially violated the ban on former operatives standing for election. Vanags and Klaviņš would not release any additional details, citing the need for confidentiality. Yet, the fact itself that the long-awaited Saeima was already contaminated by potential KGB remnants rocked the Latvian political elite. When the Saeima met for its first session on July 7, it immediately appointed a commission to look into the accusations. This group reported back in just three weeks, saying that it had no authority to follow up on the specific allegations against the still unspecified five members. However, the commission did chastise publicly both Vanags and Klaviņš for clearly overstepping their mandate.

Still, because neither the TRNIK nor the TSDC had been institutionalized enough with a clear set of legal principles (both were still acting under provisions rules, some of which the TRNIK had established for itself), the only way to deal with the lingering accusations against the five freshly elected deputies was to conduct an investigation within the parliament itself. On September 23, 1993, the Saeima tasked its Mandate and Submissions Committee to look into the evidence prepared by the two oversight bodies. In addition, the Committee was authorized to begin expulsion procedures for these deputies, if the accusations of prior KGB involvement proved true. The Committee enlisted the help of Prosecutor General Jānis Skrastiņš and together they interviewed all five of the suspected ex-operatives as well as certified the authenticity of the KGB material against them. Through leaks and media reporting, it eventually came out that the five accused were Georgs Andrējevs, Edvīns Inkēns and Andrejs Siliņš (of the centrist Latvia's Way party), Aivars Kreituss (from the Democratic Party) and Roberts Milbergs (from the For Fatherland and Freedom party). The list was surprising for a number of reasons, not least because Andrējevs was at the time foreign minister. Likewise embarrassed was Roberts Milbergs, who had been known as a staunch anti-communist within his party. Yet it would soon become apparent that without any clear investigatory rules and procedures, even the Saeima's Mandate and Submissions Committee could not do very much. With the prosecutor general at his side, the chair of the Committee, Māris Budovskis, presented to the Saeima on April 27, 1994 a draft motion confirming the fact that KGB materials linked to the five men did exist. However, the text emphasized that the mere existence of such documents was not enough to verify conscious and secret collaboration with the former security services. Skrastiņš, for his part, stressed that his office would need clearer legal guidelines from the legislature in order to proceed further with such investigations. Thus, despite all the sensation and disbelief over the incident, the two men noted that the only lesson that could be drawn was to speed up the legislative process through which definitive lustration procedures would be enacted. In the lengthy plenary debate that followed, many deputies refused to accept this conclusion, and an amendment was put forward to supplement the parliament's declaration with a provision that the parliamentary mandates of the five accused be "suspended" until court proceedings could clarify their guilt or innocence. By a vote of 45 to 20 with eleven abstentions the amendment went through, and the five deputies were put on suspension.

For Andrējevs, the scandal would eventually cost him his government post: he resigned as foreign minister on June 7, and days later from the Saeima itself. Meanwhile in order to pursue further investigations into the remaining four MPs, the Saeima finally passed on May 19 the Law on the Preservation and Use of Documents of the Former State Security Committee and the Determination of Individuals' Collaboration with the KGB (Latvijas Republikas Saeima 1994a). On this basis, the Board of the Saeima forwarded to the Prosecutor General's Office all of the materials relating to Milbergs, Kreituss, Inkēns and Siliņš. Over the next six months, these cases all went to trial, at the conclusion of which only Edvīns Inkēns was completely exonerated. In relation to Kreituss, Milbers and Siliņš, the court found that there was no evidence of conscious and secret collaboration on their part; however, the KGB materials collected on them were deemed authentic (Budovskis 1995). Bowing therefore to these conclusions, the Saeima adopted a second resolution on March 9, 1995 reinstating the mandates of all five previously accused. Yet the entire drama surrounding these "Cheka five" had proven how precarious Latvia's lustration procedure had become.

In fact, even the newly enacted "Law on the Preservation . . ." would not prove foolproof, as the system would continue to be based on the principle that each individual should assess for him- or herself what their degree of contact with the KGB had been, and if this was in any way problematic, they should desist from running for or seeking appointment to public office. In an argument that would later be reiterated by Latvia's Constitutional Court (Latvijas Republikas Satversmes Tiesa 2005: points 23 and 24), the emerging system was seen as fair in that each individual was given the right (via the "Law on the Preservation . . .") to inquire via the TSDC whether any KGB materials existed on them. If such materials existed, the individual could review them and relay his/her opinion to the TSDC. However, in contrast to Estonia's procedures, the Latvian rules did not allow the TSDC to declare materials secret if an ex-operative came to confess. Thus, in case a person still wanted to run for elected office or be appointed to a top civil service position, the only way to resolve the controversy would be to go through the courts.

By the time the initial controversy surrounding the "Cheka five" began to subside, Latvia was headed toward new parliamentary elections set for October 1995. In this connection, the Saeima prepared a new electoral law, which this time included prohibitions on ex-KGB operatives being elected as well as a ban on any individual running for office who had been associated with certain pro-Soviet organizations after January 13, 1991 (see details above). Moreover, to this was now added an important role for the TSDC; henceforth, the Center would be required to review all electoral candidate lists and announce to the Central Electoral Commission the names of any candidates who were listed in the KGB card catalogue. In fact, the wording of the new electoral law was surprisingly vague, in that the TSDC needed merely to show that it had documents that indicated the candidate "might have cooperated" ("varētu būt sadarbojušies") with the KGB or another Soviet security agency. Whether there had been any conscious collaboration was an issue left open for the courts to decide. In any case, the Central Electoral Commission was required to report this information next to the person's name when the final electoral lists were released. A candidate could not contest this connection except to begin a frantic court investigation before an election.

Thus, the dilemma of Latvia's lustration policy became more and more apparent. On the one hand, the country had decided to create a formal agency tasked with screening candidates for elected and appointed office. Yet on the other hand, all this agency could do was raise questions about *possible* past collaboration, and not undertake any definitive investigations of its own. Instead, in cases of suspicion it had to forward its materials to the Prosecutor General's Office, which would then decide whether to pursue the case. However, here the challenges would be no easier: of around 400 cases of alleged KGB collaboration that the prosecutor would attempt to press in court over the past twenty years, only 11 would result in conviction (Kesnere 2014). Lastly, for those who would stand accused of collaboration, it would be a difficult no man's land to be in. Indeed, Aivars Kreituss would be one politician to find out. Despite having been cleared in November 1994 by a Riga district court of any active collaboration with the KGB, Kreituss saw his case actually overturned by the Latvian Supreme Court, and he was ordered to stand trial anew in 1995. For some time Kreituss was able to suspend the process by submitting a request to Russian authorities for them to provide whatever information they had on his possible KGB activities. Only after Russia responded that it had no file on Kreituss did the lower court rule conclusively that there was no evidence against Kreituss. But this was only in October 1997 – more than four years after the TSDC had first raised its suspicions (Ločmele 1997).

To avoid much of this angst, Latvian political parties slowly began to adjust their electoral strategies.[16] In 1998, a new party, the People's Party, explicitly required all of its more prominent members to present to the party leadership a certification from the TSDC that they were not in the KGB catalogue. In this way, the party could be sure that it would never have to face any embarrassing KGB questions. Anecdotal evidence indicates that other Latvian parties slowly followed suit. Nevertheless, during each subsequent parliamentary election, the TSDC would continue to identify around a half-dozen candidates (from some 1,000 candidates during each election) who had entries in the KGB files. Usually, however, these were among marginal parties, and often they were the same individuals each election.

With the first law on using KGB documents in place and the TSDC also gaining a clearer profile, the system of lustration in Latvia began to expand. In June 1994, an amendment was made to the Law on Judicial Power in which ex-KGB operatives were excluded from becoming judges. In November 1996, a ban on ex-KGB and post-January 1991 pro-Soviet activists was included in Latvia's municipal electoral law. Moreover, in this law local electoral commissions were for the first time given the power to strike entirely from an electoral list any candidate whom a court ruled had been in the KGB or a pro-Soviet activist. A year and a half later, the Latvian parliament added this procedure to the Saeima election law as well.

It was this new specification that would trip up Tatyana Ždanoka, a well-known Russian minority community organizer and also member of the Latvian Communist Party after January 1991. In March 1997 Ždanoka ran for the Riga City Council, and although everyone knew that she was liable for prosecution under the ex-Soviet activist ban, there had as yet been no court ruling against her and thus her name could not be struck from the list. When she then gained election to the Council, she prepared herself for the Saeima elections in October 1998. By this time, however, the Central Electoral Commission threatened to refuse to register her party's entire list, as a result of which she agreed to withdraw voluntarily. In the meantime, the Prosecutor General's Office initiated a court case to prove her involvement with anti-independence forces in January 1991. In December 1999, a Riga district court found Ždanoka

[16] Monika Nalepa (2009a) makes a similar observation concerning East Central Europe as a whole.

guilty of that involvement and ordered her removed from the Riga City Council. This ruling was later upheld by the Latvian Supreme Court.

With this important decision, the Latvian lustration system solidified one more practice, namely, using court rulings to bar, and where necessary remove, former regime operatives from electoral office. Just three months later, the same Riga district court ruled that a prominent leader of the Social Democratic Party and member of the Saeima, Jānis Adamsons, had been a KGB staff officer and was therefore also in violation of lustration legislation. Adamsons' case was again very poignant in that he had served in the Soviet border guard (which was subordinated to the KGB) from 1979 all the way until June 1992. Moreover, upon returning to Latvia he had enlisted in the Latvian Army and was in April 1994 appointed head of the Army's border brigade. Thereafter, Adamsons even served as interior minister from November 1994 to December 1995.

Yet, as Latvia's lustration procedures began to take on more force, Adamsons' high-level service to his native land no longer sufficed to pardon his past career. Following the court ruling against him in March 2000, Adamsons appealed the verdict. In September 2000 he was able to avoid being expelled from the Saeima after a vote to remove his parliamentary immunity failed. Yet, when he and twenty-two other deputies from the Saeima attempted to contest the electoral restrictions in Latvia's Constitutional Court, the high court rejected the case, maintaining that the lustration measures conformed to both Latvian and international law (Latvijas Republikas Satversmes Tiesa 2000). Two years later, both Adamsons and Ždanoka would try to run again for parliament and both would now be formally struck from the candidate rosters because of their prior court rulings. This would set up the final denouement in relation to these two politicians, when each of them would move to appeal their convictions before the ECtHR (see below).

In the meantime, these controversies also stirred debate over whether Latvia's lustration procedures were working. The issue was not so much whether the bans on elective office and civil service appointment for ex-regime operatives were justified, but rather the procedure of using information based on the cards found in the famous "Cheka bags." It was here that Latvia would begin to lurch toward its own version of far-reaching lustration. In late 1999 and early 2000, Latvia's Prime Minister Andris Šķēle made a suggestion that the names listed in the "Cheka bags" be simply made public, so that everyone would know who had had contact with the KGB. For many, the proposal was not a surprise, since

Šķēle had been the founder of the People's Party, the first party to make sure its ranks were clean before getting into electoral politics, and therefore it had nothing to lose. The proposition also gained some traction among other party groups in the Saeima before being shelved, not least because Šķēle himself left office in May 2000.

Nonetheless, the idea had been vented and would linger in the air until it would erupt again in a most unexpected manner. The occasion would be the need to review the 1994 "Law on the Preservation . . ." in terms of the deadline it set for how long the KGB's materials could continue to be used. Originally, this had been fixed at ten years and therefore was coming to an end in May 2004. Also on the agenda was the need to end the overlap between the TRNIK and the TSDC by finally abolishing the former. When the cabinet submitted a respective bill to parliament to amend the 1994 "Law on the Preservation . . .," it unleashed a renewed debate over whether Latvia's KGB materials should not be released in full. The Saeima's Legal Affairs Committee had kept the debate in check during its preliminary examination of the bill. Likewise, the head of the TSDC at the time, Indulis Zālīte, personally contacted all the party groups in parliament and convinced both the People's Party and the New Party to reject any publication of KGB material (Zālīte, Interview, 2013). Yet during the parliament's plenary session, deliberations suddenly went awry. First, Māris Grīnblats, a deputy from the For Fatherland and Freedom/LNNK party, succeeded in getting an amendment passed from the floor extending the usage period of the KGB files until 2014. Thereafter, the debate ran even more amok when Leopolds Ozoliņš, a populist member of the Farmers' Union and Greens coalition, forwarded a motion to open all the files to the public. After lengthy debate the amendment passed with a surprising margin of 78 to 9. Members of both the People's Party and the New Party had in the end voted in favor of the bill. They later told the horror-struck Zālīte that they had never thought the bill would pass. They had simply decided to cast an opportunistic vote in order to be able to isolate as much as possible the Russian minority party Harmony Center, whom they knew would oppose the amendment. When the bill in its entirety passed at the end of the day, Latvia was suddenly in a situation where its lustration system was about to be turned on its head.

In the ensuing disbelief over how Latvia's KGB past was about to be spewed out into the public domain, the one institution standing in the way was Latvia's President Vaira Vīķe-Freiberga. On May 21, Vīķe-Freiberga vetoed the measure and returned it to the Saeima for review.

The president cited the fact that it was inadmissible to divulge en masse all of the names contained in the KGB materials, since there would be no control over whether this information was at all accurate or truthful (Zake 2010). These arguments seemed to bring the Saeima back down to earth, and on May 27 the parliament passed a new piece of legislation merely extending the ten-year deadline for using the KGB files to twenty years, and calling on the government to review the entire lustration system by June 1, 2005 and submit respective proposals to the Saeima.[17]

Yet this did not bury the issue, especially as the country began to approach new parliamentary elections in 2006. In the spring of that year, twenty left-wing deputies from the Saeima again contested the electoral restrictions on former KGB operatives in the Constitutional Court. Moreover, they were joined this time by the already mentioned former KGB officer and one-time leader of the ex-communist Latvian Democratic Labor Party, Juris Bojārs. Once again, the Constitutional Court found that the general prohibition on ex-operatives gaining electoral office was valid (Latvijas Republikas Satversmes Tiesa 2006). However, the Court made an exception for Bojārs, since it now finally agreed that an individual's merits to the Latvian state also needed consideration. In this respect, the issue of how much time had passed since an individual's KGB service as well as what they had done since then began to weigh more and more on the Court's views toward lustration.

Meanwhile another reigning in of lustration zeal would take place that same spring, when the Farmers' Union and Greens coalition began once again to push for an opening of all KGB materials. Their pretext was the fact that in reality no one had formally dismissed the original bill that President Vīķe-Freiberga had vetoed in 2004. Instead, at the time the Saeima had resolved the issue as quickly as possible by adopting a completely new piece of legislation. Hence, the Saeima's Legal Affairs Committee was free to return to the original bill, and in May 2006 it reactivated deliberation on the legislation with only minor changes. When the bill was passed once again on June 7, 2006, President Vīķe-Freiberga reiterated her opposition with a veto. Thereafter, the Saeima riposted with only a minor change to the date after which all names listed

[17] This extension of lustration procedures based on the "Cheka bags" was later contested in the Latvian Constitutional Court by a group of twenty Saeima deputies. However, in an analogous fashion to previous cases, the Court sustained the new deadline extension, citing the fact that although the legislature had adopted a blanket decision, it had also asked the government to provide feedback, meaning the parliament was ready for changes (Latvijas Republikas Satversmes Tiesa 2005).

in the KGB catalogue would be published in the public record. But President Vīķe-Freiberga held her ground and stamped an exceptional third veto on the legislation.[18] This quieted things down for another few years.[19]

The final evolution in Latvia's lustration policy came in 2004 and 2008, when the ECtHR ruled in favor of both Tatyana Ždanoka and Jānis Adamsons and their complaints against Latvia's electoral bans. In Ždanoka's case, the Court ruled that a prohibition on elective office for members of the Latvian Communist Party and other pro-Soviet organizations after January 13, 1991 was unfair if these organizations themselves were banned only after August 1991. Moreover, while the Court

> did not exclude the possibility that the restriction in issue could have been justified and proportionate during the first years after the re-establishment of Latvia's independence . . . as time went on it was necessary to ascertain whether other factors, in particular the applicant's participation in the events concerned, continued to justify her ineligibility.
>
> (European Court of Human Rights 2004b)

Likewise in the Adamsons case, the Court struck down Latvia's unmitigated ban on ex-KGB operatives running for elective office. It pointed in particular to the fact that the Latvian parliament had in 2004 already called on the government to think through the need for a more individualized approach. Moreover, in the Court's view the case of Jānis

[18] Under Article 71 of Latvia's Constitution, the president is required to promulgate vetoed legislation if the Saeima succeeds in adopting the disputed bill a second time with absolutely no changes. However, since in this instance the Saeima changed its measure each time, the president could use her veto repeatedly (Zake 2010).

[19] In early 2014 the National Union party group in the Saeima proposed once again the release of all KGB names, this time promising that academic historians would write an explanation of the meaning of the catalogue to accompany the opening of the files. This did little to comfort the three main Latvian officials charged with dealing with the KGB materials – the new director of the TSDC, Zinta Ābola, the director of the SAB, Jānis Maizītis, and Prosecutor General Ēriks Kalnmeiers – all of whom voiced strong objections to any wholesale release of names. Nevertheless, on May 8 parliament passed a version of the nationalists' proposal, mandating that information in the Cheka bags be made public on May 31, 2018 after a period of "scientific study" to be carried out by the TSDC. The law did not elaborate on what this research should look like. But presumably it would involve providing background information. One journalist predicted that countless court cases would still ensue, since many people would seek to prove that their name was in the file by accident or that their inclusion in the KGB's database said nothing about whether they had actually ever been linked to the secret organization (Kincis 2014).

Adamsons was especially characteristic of the need to take into consideration a person's behavior since restored independence. As we will see later in Chapter 7, the Latvian government eventually appealed its loss in the Ždanoka case to the Grand Chamber of the ECtHR and actually succeeded in getting the initial ruling overturned. This represented a victory for the kind of transitional justice Latvia was pursuing against those who had actively conspired against its re-independence in 1991. However, the ECtHR's opinion on overall lustration needing to be measured remained in force.

Lithuania

Judging by the different dimensions of decommunization and lustration policy laid out in Table 4.1, Lithuania has been the most strident among the three Baltic states in going after former KGB agents and operatives. It has been so in two respects. First, it has gone through many more political debates and crises surrounding the issue than Estonia and Latvia. Second, it has ended up adopting (and not just considering) farther-reaching lustration measures – in particular the extension of self-reporting rules to the private sector. Although these have since been struck down by the ECtHR, the issue remains unresolved and may not come to a clean conclusion. This in a way also reflects the charged nature of the problem: agreeing on closure has been very difficult.

Earlier in this chapter we recounted the first political pendulum swing in Lithuanian lustration activities in terms of the Gajauskas Commission and its investigations into former KGB agents sitting in parliament. During the 1992 parliamentary election, the Commission was also given a kind of vetting function in that it could make candidates' links to the former KGB public, but only if it could be proven that this collaboration was conscious and if two-thirds of the commission members agreed to such a release. In the event, this mechanism did not prove very effective. After the ex-communist LDDP returned to power, little was undertaken to pursue lustration any farther. Instead, it would not be until the center-right Homeland Union-Lithuanian Conservatives (TS-LK) regained control of government in October 1996 that efforts to pass effective lustration legislation would surge again. These moves came in two stages, first with the adoption on July 16, 1998 of the Law on Evaluation of the USSR State Security Committee (NKVD, NKGB, MGB, KGB) and the Present Activities of Former Permanent Employees of This Organization, and later in November 1999 with the passage of the

Law on Registering, Confession, Entry into Records and Protection of the Persons Who Have Admitted to Secret Collaboration with Special Services of the Former USSR (Lietuvos Respublikos Seimas 1998c, 1998d, 1999). The gap between the two measures was caused by an appeal from a group of Seimas deputies before the Lithuanian Constitutional Court, resulting in parts of the first act being struck down and hence requiring adoption of the second.

With the first piece of legislation, Lithuania formally prohibited former employees of the KGB from working for the next ten years (i.e. from January 1, 1999 to December 31, 2008) in a range of civil service posts including the judiciary, law enforcement, diplomatic service and public oversight. In addition, however, the measure forbade such people from working:

> as lawyers or notaries, as employees of banks and other credit institutions, on strategic economic projects, in security companies (structures), in other companies (structures) providing detective services, in communications systems, in the educational system as teachers, educators or heads of institutions; nor may they perform a job requiring to carry a weapon.
>
> (Lietuvos Respublikos Seimas 1998c: Art. 2)

In this respect, Lithuania took the first step among the three Baltic states toward applying lustration procedures to the private sector, especially in those areas where ex-KGB operatives were said to have crept in the most and were becoming a threat to national economic security. The measure made an exception for all those former agents who had come over to the Lithuanian side after March 1990 and provided information to nascent Lithuanian security officials. However, such immunity still needed to be cleared by the Lithuanian Genocide and Resistance Research Center (LGGRTC) and the Lithuanian State Security Department. Moreover, the original version of the law foresaw the presidential appointment of a three-person review board to determine whether in some cases the lustration recommendations made by the LGGRTC and State Security Department might be suspended. The clear intention here was to keep open a back door, through which certain valued individuals might be spared automatic exposure or dismissal (analogous to cases such as Latvia's Jānis Adamsons).

However, the law entered a legal vacuum in January 1999, when President Valdas Adamkus refused to appoint the necessary three-person review board, citing an earlier veto he had given the law as well as the need to wait for a Constitutional Court ruling that was due to be handed down shortly. In this interim period, confusion persisted, as some private companies, wanting to make sure they complied with the possible law, drew up initial lists of former KGB agents and in some cases even moved to dismiss them (Immigration and Refugee Board of Canada 2002). The conservative government under Prime Minister Gediminas Vagnorius only added to the pressure by releasing a list of state-owned companies in which it was set to begin a dismissal policy of ex-KGB agents (Stan 2009a: 51). In all, around 300 former KGB personnel still employed in Lithuanian state service were affected (Anušauskas 2006: 199).

Amidst all this ambiguity, the Constitutional Court convened to hear an appeal from three Seimas deputies seeking to have the law dismissed entirely (Constitutional Court of the Republic of Lithuania 1999). The deputies challenged the ten-year professional ban being imposed on former KGB operatives as well as the intrusion into the private sector. In their view these restrictions amounted to criminal punishment and could therefore only be imposed by a court of law. Yet, in its decision the Court upheld the principle of lustration and of imposing restrictions on former KGB operatives. It ordered merely that the parliament find an alternative way of regulating the final decisions of the LGGRTC and State Security Department. Doing so via a presidentially appointed commission would in its view accord a kind of judicial function to the president. Likewise, the Court alleged that the original procedures did not allow individuals to contest preliminary collaboration rulings in a court of law. Legislation, however, which does not provide for adequate appeal opportunities is unconstitutional, said the Court.

This sent the more specific lustration procedure back to the drawing board, and the result was the "Law on Registering . . ." adopted on November 23, 1999. Similar to the Estonian law on recording and dealing with former KGB operatives, the new Lithuanian measure introduced the notion of registering with the State Security Department all former KGB operatives, who admitted to their past activities in order to be granted a degree of immunity. To this end, the law specified the full range of ex-Soviet security services whose members would be subject to the new procedure. Likewise, it outlined fully seven different categories of collaboration, ranging from being a full-time agent to the other well-known categories of "confidant" and "keeper of conspiratorial or rendezvous flats." Lastly, the law clarified the creation of a special Lustration Commission to review all of these applications and examine instances where collaboration had not been reported. The five-member commission would be composed of one member nominated by the Prosecutor General's Office and two each from the State Security Department and the LGGRTC. The final appointment would be made by the Director of the State Security Department with the approval of the Seimas Committee on National Security and Defense. In this respect, the commission was closely linked to the State Security Department, the same institution that oversaw the self-reporting procedure and controlled the information that came from it. The LGGRTC's role was to provide a certain degree of external expert opinion. However, the overriding focus was on managing the process from a national security perspective and not necessarily revealing collaborators now in high office.

The self-reporting period would last for six months following a decision by the Lustration Commission to start the process. In the event, this deadline would be in August 2000. Applicants would be required not only to detail the extent of their service or collaboration with the KGB, but also to hand over any materials they may still have from that era. All of this information was required to be accurate or else it would be subject to criminal sanction under perjury laws. After review by the Lustration Commission, a person's materials would be declared a state secret and locked away from further public scrutiny. Yet in contrast to Estonia, the Lithuanian law made no promises of anonymity to candidates for high elected office in the country. Hence, individuals running for parliament, the presidency or local councils as well as those appointed to cabinet office could still be disclosed even if they registered voluntarily. Moreover, if a person did not register and was later found to have collaborated with the KGB, his or her employer would be required to fire that person forthwith and without severance pay. Additionally, the same ten-year professional bans listed in the 1998 "Law on Evaluation . . ." would apply.

Despite these provisions coming more than ten years after Lithuania formally declared independence in 1990, the Lithuanian measure was a relative success in that 1,589 people registered themselves by the official deadline (Urmonas, Interview, 2013). The Lustration Commission proceeded to take up its work, focusing its attention initially on those accounts that had been given by the self-reportees and checking for inconsistencies. During its first three years of operation, the Commission therefore examined just two alleged cases of unreported collaboration. In 2005, the director of the LGGRTC, Dalia Kuodytė, was appointed chair of the Commission, and the pace of examinations picked up. By the end of 2006, the Commission had formally reviewed 120 cases of possibly unreported collaboration and issued fifty-three rulings.[20] Yet, slowly dissatisfaction with the Commission began to grow, not least among its own members. Chairwoman Kuodytė complained that the Commission had no budgetary resources at its disposal[21] and that it lacked professional legal help when its rulings were challenged in court by those accused of not having reported collaboration. Additionally, an uneasy relationship developed with the State Security Department, which had been mandated by the 1999 law to prepare materials for the Commission, but which could also withhold files from it if it said that these pertained to individuals who had self-reported and therefore were entitled to confidentiality. The Commission was clearly far weaker than the Latvian TSDC. Lithuania's lustration process was getting stuck.

A second blow to the policy came from abroad, when the ECtHR began to rule on three separate appeals from Lithuania contesting the legality of the 1998 law. The first case, *Sidabras and Džiaustas v. Lithuania*, was decided in July 2004, roughly five years into the new lustration period. In 1999, the two plaintiffs had been dismissed from their respective jobs as tax inspector and prosecutor on the basis of the 1998 "Law on Evaluation . . .," since they had worked previously for the KGB. During their hearing, the plaintiffs argued that Lithuania's blanket ban on ex-KGB officials filling certain posts disregarded the need to evaluate the specific level of purported threat that any such person posed to the Lithuanian state in order to justify such a measure. In its ruling, the ECtHR did not question the Lithuanian state's right to define what it considered the proper parameters of state security. Yet it did challenge the state's right to impose such criteria on private enterprises.

The Court reiterated that the requirement of an employee's loyalty to the state is an inherent condition of employment with state authorities responsible for protecting and securing the general interest. However, such a requirement is not inevitably the case for employment with private companies (European Court of Human Rights 2004a).

[20] See Eurasian Secret Services Daily Review (2006) and ELTA (2011). Interestingly, the form of publication of former KGB operations in Lithuania is much more circumspect than in Estonia. The standard statement issued by the lustration commission reads only that person XYZ (identified further with their date of birth) "secretly collaborated with the secret services of the former USSR – the State Security Committee under the Lithuanian SSR Council of Ministers."

[21] It was specifically written in the law that members would work without remuneration.

Moreover, the Court took issue (as had the Lithuanian Constitutional Court in 1999) with the way in which private-sector positions were defined in the "Law on Evaluation ..." These were in the opinion of the Court so vague that "it is impossible to ascertain any reasonable link between the positions concerned and the legitimate aims sought by the ban on holding those positions." Thirdly, the Court reiterated again its incredulity over whether it was sufficiently proportional to punish individuals more than a decade after their service in the KGB had ended.

In a second ECtHR ruling coming just ten months later, the Court delivered another verdict against Lithuania in favor of a pair of plaintiffs, who this time had been fired from their positions in the private sector. In particular, the Court declared that the Lithuanian state had

> failed to disprove that the applicants' inability to pursue their former professions as, respectively, a lawyer in a private telecommunications company and barrister, and their continuing inability to find private-sector employment on the basis of their "former KGB officer" status under the ["Law on Evaluation ..."], constitutes a disproportionate and thus discriminatory measure, even having regard to the legitimacy of the aims sought after.
>
> (European Court of Human Rights 2005)

Both of the plaintiffs were awarded monetary compensation. Lastly, the ECtHR was asked in April 2009 to rule on a third type of lustration where, pursuant to the "Law on Registering ...," the plaintiff had been disbarred by the Lithuanian Bar Association because of this prior KGB connection. On this point as well, the Court found in favor of the plaintiff, saying that such actions were disproportionate in relation to the aims of lustration (European Court of Human Rights 2009a).

In the wake of these different legal setbacks, the Lithuanian parliament began a renewed effort at revamping its lustration laws in late 2005. This endeavor had become all the more imperative in January of that year, when it was revealed that three key members of the Lithuanian political elite had all been reservists in the KGB. First to come clean was the country's foreign minister, Antanas Valionis, who acknowledged following some investigative media reports that he had been a captain in the KGB reserves. Shortly thereafter the Deputy Speaker of the Seimas, Alfredas Pekeliūnas, agreed to step down from that post, bowing to revelations that he, too, had been listed in the KGB reserves. Lastly, as if to add insult to injury, the entire evaluation procedure for ex-KGB agents (i.e. the Lustration Commission) was called into question by the disclosure that the head of the State Security Department (or the person authorized to appoint members of the Lustration Commission), Arvydas Pocius, had also been a KGB reservist.

The status of "reservist" had been a gap in Lithuania's earlier legislation. Such people were not required to report under the 1999 "Law on Registering . . ." Moreover, it was not always the case that individuals necessarily knew in what capacity the KGB had listed them, as ostensibly the reserves were only meant for wartime conscription. However, individuals did need to give their consent to such a listing; thus some kind of active knowledge was necessary. Moreover, now with so many high-level officials implicated in this category and some 415 KGB reservist files thought to exist in total, the carrousel of accusations, innuendo and investigation began once again. On January 20, 2005 the Seimas hastily appointed a twelve-member commission to look into how to deal with reservists. In the meantime, the media reported that the names of ten additional Lithuanian officials (ranging from municipal councilors and administrators to judges and an additional MP) had been handed over to the commission for investigation (Baltic Times 2005). Yet, two months later, the commission concluded that while the KGB reserves had been an ambiguous category, there was no indication to conclude that members on this list had consciously collaborated with the secret services, that is, carried out any repressive operations (Anušauskas 2006). The three main casualties of the scandal, Valionis, Pocius and Pekeliūnas, thus survived.

However, the controversy cast the task of revamping Lithuania's lustration procedures following the ECtHR's rulings into a new light. Despite the Lithuanian government having submitted several draft amendments to the Seimas to resolve these issues, the parliament vacillated for over a year with the proposals. Meanwhile, another KGB scandal involving an advisor to Prime Minister Algirdas Brazauskas erupted in January 2006. Vilius Kavaliauskas stood accused by the Lustration Commission of having cooperated with the KGB while working during the 1980s as a Soviet journalist stationed in the United States. Kavaliauskas challenged the accusations in court, but eventually lost his case before Lithuania's Supreme Administrative Court in October 2007.

During all this time, the Seimas therefore deliberated changes to Lithuania's lustration procedures, focusing most of all on how to integrate the new category of KGB reservists into the existing system, but also improving conditions for the Lustration Commission. When an initial bill in the Seimas to formally ban reservists from public service was vetoed by President Adamkus in May 2007 (citing *inter alia* the ECtHR's recent rulings), deputies finally settled on a system whereby such people would be given another chance to come forward and register themselves, much like the previous round in 2000. The formal legislation passed on October 11; however, President Adamkus again stamped a veto on it, this time leaving his decision unsubstantiated. Although Adamkus later clarified in separate correspondence his objections to the legislation (calling, for example, for an extended period of registration lasting until December 31, 2012), a group of Seimas deputies took his original veto letter to the Constitutional Court, claiming that such an unmotivated decision on the part of the president was unconstitutional. Yet, in its ruling on February 22, 2008, the Court found in favor of the president, thus upholding his suspension of the new lustration procedure (Baltic Times 2008). Amidst all of this upheaval, the chair of the Lustration Commission, Dalia Kuodytė, resigned along with several other members. The Commission became moribund for almost a year (Stašaitytė 2008).

Following parliamentary elections in October 2008, a new center-right majority led by the Homeland Union-Lithuanian Christian Democrats (TS-LDK) returned to power and immediately promised to "initiate the adoption of laws that regulate the lustration process so that the Lustration Commission formed on different grounds could efficiently continue and complete the lustration process" (Lietuvos Respublikos Seimas 2008: point 244). The point man for this effort would be historian Arvydas Anušauskas, who for eleven years had worked as research director at the LGGRTC, but had now been elected to the Seimas on the TS-LDK ticket. Moreover, Anušauskas was appointed chair of the National Security and Defense Committee, a position that would give him clout to move legislation. In 2009, additional impetus for fixing the lustration process came from the newly elected president, Dalia Grybauskaitė, who expressed support for making more KGB information public. Meanwhile, a highly negative impulse came from the former prime minister, Kazimiera Prunskienė, who to the dismay of many won an appeal against a Lustration Commission ruling confirming her past links with the KGB. This Prunskienė saga convinced many activists that the courts were not the venue where lustration efforts could be waged. Too many Lustration Commission findings had been reversed upon appeal by the accused ex-KGB operatives, primarily because the courts would apply (as in Latvia) a very strict legal logic to the case and rule that if the accused had not actually signed some kind of KGB document agreeing to collaborate, then definitive collaboration could not be proven.[22]

Still, the process of finding solutions to these problems was slow. It would not be until June 2010 that Anušauskas would be able to shepherd through parliament an amendment to the 1999 law streamlining the list of state positions banned for anyone whose name had been published in the state gazette as a former KGB agent. And although the ten-year ban on outed ex-KGB operatives working in certain areas of the private sector had by now expired, the requirement for employers (public or private) to sack such people immediately upon their names being published remained. A second difficulty that Anušauskas tried to fix was the status of the Lustration Commission. In April 2009, he put forward a bill trying to link the Commission more to the LGGRTC. In the meantime, Algimantas Urmonas, a university law professor who had been appointed the new chair of the Lustration Commission in 2008, echoed the continued need to increase the Commission's muscle. When Anušauskas' legislation got delayed, Urmonas threatened to resign like his predecessor Kuodytė. Although it was impossible to cut the State Security Department completely out of the process, Anušauskas was finally able to get parliament to approve a measure obliging the Department to transfer all of its remaining KGB materials to a set of specially secured rooms at the LGGRTC (Lietuvos Respublikos Seimas 2010). Urmonas, too, expressed satisfaction over having all of the files available, although the Lustration Commission's formal rules did not change. Still, work within the Commission resumed in earnest, with members clearing a backlog of over 300 cases in 2010. By the end of 2012, the Commission had reached a total of over 460 reviewed cases and had approved the publication of fifty ex-KGB names in the state gazette (Urmonas, Interview, 2013).

The final change spearheaded by Anušauskas was to open up an additional form of lustration by getting parliament to allow the LGGRTC "to examine, analyze and publish former Soviet special services documentation." This formulation was important, since it would give the Center a green light to begin posting in May 2011 a wide range of

[22] Interestingly, this was rarely the case in Estonia. Individuals called in by the Estonian Security Police Board to explain or refute material that KAPO had gathered on them could also ask a judge to adjudicate the issue. However, because KAPO generally worked on revealing only full-time employees of the KGB (and not casual collaborators), proving this employment before a judge was never very difficult.

archival materials about the KGB on a special website (www.kgbveikla.lt). On the one hand, this would help the Center to promote more public awareness about the KGB in Lithuania, since the website included analyses of how the KGB worked and what relationships it had with the Communist Party. More importantly, however, the Center was keen to use the site to publish actual names of KGB officials. To this end, it began by posting the biographies of top KGB leaders stretching back to 1940. It then expanded the list to include municipal and county KGB chiefs. Lastly, it turned to one of the most significant KGB materials that had been obtained from the State Security Department: a series of agent ledgers similar to the fifty-three books that Latvian officials had discovered. The ledgers contained the names of around 1,700 operatives, as well as 62 individual agent cards. In 2012, the Center began publishing on its special website batches of these agent names after analysts had carefully reviewed each one. For the most part, the outing action would be symbolic, since all of the operatives had been from the 1950s and the information released about them involved merely the ledger entry itself. Officials were also quick to note that if any names popped up of people who were still alive and had voluntarily confessed their activities in 2000, they would not be revealed.

Symbolic punishment of perpetrators

The Lithuanian decision to begin making public the names of certain KGB operatives moved the country toward the "indiscriminate outing" category of political-administrative measures against perpetrators (Table 4.1). The LGGRTC was taking a catalogue of old KGB contacts and publishing it on the Web without any information about how these people had been connected with the agency or what they might have done. At the same time, because all of the names were of a historical nature, this was not lustration per se. It was instead more of a symbolic-representational measure. This therefore brings us to consider how policies belonging to Boxes 3a and 3b of our analytical matrix were enacted in the Baltic states. In reality, it is often difficult to distinguish measures that would unequivocally belong to one or the other box. Clearly, the Lithuanian publication of KGB names from the 1950s falls more into the category of retrospective symbolic justice, hence within Box 3a of our matrix. The LGGRTC's campaign represents a systematic attempt to name perpetrators from the past, while at the same time knowing there is nothing more that can be done against these people except to fix their place in history as repressors.

A similar type of action was pursued by the Estonian International Commission for the Investigation of Crimes Against Humanity (IKUERK) in its final reports on the various periods of totalitarian occupation in Estonia (Hiio et al. 2005; Hiio et al. 2009). Of the three historical commissions formed in the Baltic states in 1998 and discussed further in Chapter 6, the Estonian one focused the most on detailing the types of crimes committed and naming those responsible. It thus aimed not only to recognize the past suffering of victims but also to identify the perpetrators for posterity and thereby contribute to symbolic retrospective justice. The three sets of conclusions issued by the IKUERK devoted considerable attention to outlining the "principles of responsibility" and on naming specific individuals responsible for ordering and executing crimes against humanity. As we noted in Chapter 3, the Commission's researchers also assisted the Estonian Security Police Board in identifying still living individuals suspected of having committed crimes against humanity and war crimes for possible prosecution.

Straddling the fields of retrospective and transitional justice are the numerous official declarations that the Baltic states have adopted condemning the KGB, the Soviet regime or Communism more broadly. The Lithuanian 1998 lustration law, for example, began with the damning statement, "The USSR State Security Committee . . . shall be regarded as a criminal organization which has committed war crimes, genocide, acts of repression, terror and political persecution in the Republic of Lithuania occupied by the USSR." Meanwhile, in Latvia the Saeima adopted on May 12, 2005 a three-page resolution condemning the "totalitarian, communist occupation regime of the USSR," as if to make sure that all of the crimes committed by the regime were covered (Latvijas Republikas Saeima 2005). This document ended up addressing a whole range of audiences, condemning on the one hand all those people who had participated in maintaining the regime (the direct perpetrators), but on the other calling on the Russian Federation to work toward a recognition of and compensation for these crimes, and on European governments to support an international condemnation of Soviet Communism. As we will see later in Chapter 7, such denunciations often morph into rebukes of Russia, since for the Balts the ultimate perpetrator was a foreign country, the USSR, and by extension its successor state, Russia.

Yet an Estonian declaration from June 2002 did attempt to attribute more specific blame to particular institutions, albeit in a slightly convoluted manner. Speaking out "On the Crimes of the Occupation Regime in Estonia," the Riigikogu began by denouncing the entire "communist occupation regime of the Soviet Union" for the genocide, crimes against humanity and societal-cultural ruin that it had wrought on the Estonian population. It then declared "criminal" the NKVD, the KGB and all other repressive organs of the regime. And finally, as if to finish off the pyramid, it recalled that the ultimate responsibility for this repression lay with the organizations at the top: the Communist Party of the Soviet Union and its sub-unit the Communist Party of Estonia. Nevertheless, the statement then went on to reiterate that this did not mean collective guilt for all those individuals who had been a member of these organizations. "An individual's accountability for the crimes of the regime is not determined by his belonging to the afore-mentioned institutions and organizations," said the document (Eesti Vabariigi Riigikogu 2002). In fact, this sentence had been a particularly contested part of the resolution. Nationalist deputies in parliament only put it in after center-left parties in the chamber actually succeeded in blocking the adoption of the statement in June 2001 and forced its proponents to wait a whole year before trying it again.

This kind of condemnation of communism as a perpetrator ideology has also manifested itself in a desire to ban the use of communist symbols alongside those of Nazism. A July 2008 change to the Lithuanian Civil Code forbade the public display of images of Soviet and Nazi leaders, of flags, uniforms, emblems and badges carrying insignia such as the hammer and sickle or swastika as well as the playing of the national anthem of either regime. Violation of the ban would incur a heavy fine and possible cancellation of a political organization's registration. A similar measure was passed by the Latvian Saeima in July 2013. Added as an amendment to the Public Entertainment and Special Events Security Act, the new regulation would prohibit "the use, also in stylistic form, of former USSR, Latvian SSR or Nazi flags, uniforms and anthems, the Nazi swastika, SS signs and Soviet symbols – hammer and sickle together with the five-point star" (Latvijas Republikas Saeima 2013). Calls for such a law had been voiced for many years, usually around May 9 when thousands of people, mostly Russians, would gather around the Soviet World War II victory monument in Riga. Over the years this had turned into a full-scale public festival for war veterans and their families as well as for ordinary people wanting to celebrate one of the most important days in Soviet/Russian memory. However, the waving of Soviet flags and other symbols along with public references to the liberation of Latvia from fascism had been a thorn in the flesh for most Latvians, who saw the return of the Red Army in 1944 as nothing less than the continuation of Stalinist terror and repression. Moreover, several of the previous memorial events had turned into violent street fights among young Russians and Latvians, thus raising security concerns among Latvian lawmakers (Ločmele et al. 2011). The draft law was therefore proposed in March 2013 by a group of MPs from the ruling coalition, perhaps in the hope that it would be adopted before the May celebrations that year. However, the proposal stirred considerable protest especially from the opposition Harmony Center party, which defended the remembrance day (with all its related symbols) as important and historically appropriate. Finally, after the third reading of the bill in June, the draft went to a vote in which the entire Harmony Center group abstained, while all other MPs unanimously voted in favor (LETA 2013).

A final reflection on the kinds of symbolic steps governments can take in order to identify past perpetrators involves the removal of monuments to former regime heroes. Needless to say, this practice blurs very quickly into the broader domain of memory politics, including the way in which new democracies often change street names, put up new monuments of their own, etc. It is therefore in this context that Estonia's Bronze Soldier controversy in 2007 has been most often discussed (Brüggemann and Kasekamp 2008; Petersoo and Tamm 2008; Ehala 2009; Kattago 2012). However, our aim here is to note that the Estonian government's decision in April 2007 to relocate the so-called Bronze Soldier away from downtown Tallinn represented not only a classic example of memory politics but also an effort to (re-)cast the Soviet Army as a perpetrator institution, since it re-occupied Estonia in 1944. One of the prime justifications that Prime Minister Andrus Ansip would give for moving the monument was that it was not fitting to have this symbol of a perpetrator military so centrally located in the downtown area.

Comparative summary

As we move successively through our analysis of transitional and retrospective justice in the Baltic states, we encountered in this chapter one of the more politically tumultuous realms of this process, the debate over lustration. Much more than with the criminal-legal measures we examined in the previous chapter, political-administrative policies against individuals considered to have been perpetrators under a previous regime are invariably fraught with highly controversial decisions as to who exactly should fall into this category. Should action be taken only against direct repressors in the form of those who carried out surveillance and other forms of repression? Or should the net be cast wider to include political leaders and functionaries of the old system? Moreover, should such people be excluded merely from politics or from economics as well? Should they perhaps be simply outed as previous regime collaborators, leaving it up to members of society to decide how they want to view these people?

In our examination of these issues, we noted that a kind of spectrum exists between decommunization (political and/or economic), on the one hand, and mere social ostracization, on the other. Newly democratizing countries can decide to punish former regime officials to the point of collectively (and indiscriminately) barring all such individuals from political and economic activity. Or they can decide to modulate this political-administrative punishment by targeting only certain people with only certain exclusionary rules, such as vetting prior to a political appointment or an electoral candidacy. Or the final measure might be relatively symbolic such as an oath of conscience, which may or may not be verifiable by others.

In this chapter we have tried to show that in the Baltic states almost all of these options have surfaced at one point or another and that the three countries have differed notably in terms of the temporal pace of these political debates as well as the level of their final outcome twenty years after re-independence. Whereas Estonia started off considering one of the most radical political-administrative approaches possible, decommunization, it soon cooled down substantially until it was left with a mix of largely self-enforced, declarative lustration measures. True, the policy of outing KGB agents, who had not come clean by April 1996, would eventually publicly reveal the identities of several hundred erstwhile direct repressors from the Soviet regime. However, the policy was also intended as a means of information gathering about the former Soviet security system. In this respect, there was just as much reconnaissance going on as there was retribution.

The Lithuanian debate, by contrast, appears to have merely ratcheted and ratcheted over the past two decades with an initial set of purges in the early 1990s giving way to more formalized self-reporting after 1999 and finally a series of acrimonious lustration controversies in the late 2000s. Lithuania has also reached the highest formal degree of political-administrative sanction against former direct repressors, that is, its ban on ex-KGB operatives serving not only in politics and the civil service but also in numerous areas of the private economy. Although this measure was later censured by the ECtHR, it generated enough acrimony and uncertainty to show that lustration remained a highly charged issue between the two main anti- and ex-communist political camps in the country.

In Latvia, an approach emerged that was largely driven by a kind of proverbial elephant in the room or the unique set of KGB agent cards that were recovered in August 1991. On the one hand, these materials would prove useful as a clear point of departure for instituting screening of existing officials and vetting for future officials and electoral candidates. However, the Cheka bags would also be akin to a poisoned well, since the information to be had from these files was incomplete at best, and completely fraudulent at worst. Hence, political trepidation would characterize how Latvian politicians would attempt to harness the uses and legacy of these materials, until in 2004 this tiptoeing would boil over into an outright attempt to indiscriminately out everyone in the archive. Although this outburst was eventually reined back in by a series of presidential vetoes, its shadow would remain on the horizon, probably for decades to come.

5

Righting past wrong: rehabilitation, compensation and restitution for victims

The bulletin board in front of the Resistance Participants' Rights Commission at the Lithuanian Genocide and Resistance Research Center in Vilnius stretches almost three meters as it displays all of the legal regulations and the different application forms enacted for individuals to request either for themselves or for a deceased relative the legal status of having been "a volunteer fighter," "a freedom fighter" or "a victim of the 1939–1990 occupations." In applying for one or the other status, applicants must provide detailed information about where they were repressed, for what activities, how long the repression lasted, etc. Their accounts must be validated with supporting documentation such as rehabilitation certificates, archival evidence or court rulings. The application forms, meanwhile, assist the applicant by asking indicative questions such as "By whom, when and where were you arrested? What were you convicted for? Where and how much time were you imprisoned, repressed?" In addition, the forms allude to certain specific victim categories by asking questions such as "How were you able to avoid deportation, by fleeing, going into hiding? Were you on a deportation list?" Likewise, the forms inquire, "If you were born in a prison, a concentration camp or during deportation, where were your parents held?" Lastly, the documents ask applicants "Were you denied the right to live in Lithuania? When was your property lost, confiscated or destroyed? Were you summarily dismissed from work or from studying in an educational institution?"

Lithuania's list of over forty categories of Soviet and/or Nazi victim status reads like a condensed history of totalitarian repression. It is a story not only of how historians have been able to outline in minute detail the myriad ways in which individuals suffered under these regimes, but also of how different political processes have led to the actual creation of such an extensive justice framework. As this and the next chapter will demonstrate, truth and justice measures for victims of

Soviet and Nazi repression in the Baltic states span the full spectrum of policies outlined in our matrix. In particular, the Soviet use of politically motivated criminal trials as a means of repression has meant that the legal rehabilitation of the tens of thousands of people who fell prey to these repressions would become one of the first forms of victim-oriented truth and justice to be undertaken. Soviet criminal offenses such as "counter-revolutionary activity" or "betrayal of the homeland" served as the basis for scores of arrests, trials and ultimately convictions of innocent people. While a majority of these individuals would be sentenced to prison terms, hundreds were also summarily executed. The only form of redress to be offered these people would be posthumous legal exoneration.

Yet newly democratic governments often have numerous other past injustices that need rectifying and require more political-administrative means. In this chapter we will therefore combine Boxes 4 and 5 of our analytical matrix, since the measures characterized by these categories often concern one and the same victims (e.g. instances where legal-criminal rehabilitation is followed up by additional financial compensation), or at a minimum they represent measures in which the state and victim are involved in a formal procedural activity with an administrative outcome. The process of restituting private property seized by a former regime is one such measure. Here, too, the new democratic state has a critical role to play (as well as an administrative burden to take on) in verifying and processing claims put forth by victims. There is needless to say considerably more politics involved here as well, since the return of property which may now be in the hands of someone else can easily generate charges of renewed repression among those seemingly dispossessed.

As we survey the Baltic states across these categories, we will see firstly that retrospective justice dominates transitional justice in that the three countries have concentrated mostly on righting the wrongs committed during the early years of Soviet rule. It goes without saying that the need to rehabilitate in legal-criminal terms all those thousands of people wrongfully tried, deported or killed during the Stalinist era has constituted a major part of victim-oriented justice-seeking in the Baltic states. In our analytical matrix, Box 4a thus predominates over Box 4b. Yet, a frequent corollary to this judicial level of action has been the adoption of various additional, political-administrative compensation schemes that in our matrix are represented by Boxes 5a and 5b. Given the fact that the Stalinist system ended up repressing a wide range of people for different anti-regime activities, an important aspect of these measures has been not only their scope but also their administrative consolidation around a single legal status of "repressed persons." The enactment of this kind of legislation, as well as its implementation through the issuing of special identification documents and welfare benefits, represents another indicator in terms of analyzing victim-focused justice measures.

In our comparative analysis we will note that Lithuania stands out again with a much more extensive approach to legal rehabilitation and administrative compensation. Not only has the country defined a much wider range of repressed persons from the Stalinist era, but it has also actively identified victims of the more recent Soviet era, most notably victims of the Soviet crackdown in January 1991. It has also been more intense in its implementation of rehabilitation procedures. For example, the country became embroiled in controversy following an early effort in 1990 to rehabilitate a broad swath of people repressed by the Soviets. However, once it became apparent that some of these victims had likewise committed punishable crimes (during the Nazi period), the policy would be slowed down and lessons learned. Nonetheless, Lithuania would also repeat the pattern of intensifying its justice policies (as seen already in the realms of trials and lustration), when during the period 1996–2000 the nationalist-conservative majority in power would enact a series of additional legal and compensatory measures for Soviet regime victims, all of which would generate a very intricate, though also sometimes contested system of dealing with these realms of justice.

By contrast, in Estonia and Latvia rehabilitation policies have been more subdued and managed with less fanfare. Particularly in Estonia, the process of acknowledging victims of Soviet repression as a legal category emerged only in 2003–2004, while additional attempts to declare active resisters to Soviet power as "freedom fighters" have failed. Meanwhile, in 1995 Latvia passed an all-encompassing law establishing legal status for repressed persons and followed up a year later with legislation creating a special category for "participants in the national resistance movement." But in contrast to its controversies over criminal trials or lustration, these measures have attracted little public attention.

Yet the ranking of the three countries is reversed when we examine the domain of property restitution, where Estonia and Latvia would administer much more extensive policies, and in so doing generate greater amounts of political and social controversy. By defining the circle of eligible claimants very broadly, as well as by insisting that former owners of residential housing should have as much opportunity as possible to get back their properties even if these were now inhabited by other individuals, the two states embarked on a long process of not only adjudicating conflicting claims but also dealing with the social consequences of finding housing for those forced out of restituted property. In Lithuania, we will see (as we did in the case of lustration in Chapter 4) that following an initial move toward far-reaching policy on property restitution under the nationalist *Sąjūdis* parliament in 1990–92, the return of the ex-communist Lithuanian Democratic Labor Party (LDDP) to power in 1993 would initiate a process of softening and even reversing the policy by 1996. Moreover, in contrast to the conservatives' efforts during 1997–99 to ratchet up lustration policies or elevate rehabilitation processes, the opportunity to effect a pendulum swing within the field of property restitution after defeating the ex-communists would not be possible, since a number of intervening constitutional court decisions would mean these avenues would be closed. In other words, when it came to property restitution, the Lithuanian ex-communists would begin a process of dismantling the conservatives' initial policies, which would immediately undergo challenge by the conservatives in the Constitutional Court. However, once the Court actually upheld the ex-communists' decision to soften restitution policy, the conservatives had no legal grounds to completely upend the issue once they controlled parliament again in the late 1990s.

This chapter will cover these two broad forms of establishing legal and administrative justice for victims. First, we will examine both the scope and the pace of legal-criminal rehabilitations. Although from a political point of view this measure is one of the easiest to adopt and implement, and it is relatively inexpensive in administrative and financial terms, it can still generate controversy if it is applied wholesale or indiscriminately. We will see that critical questions emerge in relation to which categories of repression are included, and what benefits (if any at all) are offered for compensating this past injustice. From an analytical perspective timing will become an important feature: when do certain frameworks get adopted and with what consequences? Secondly, we will evaluate the evolution of property restitution by examining both the politics around the initial adoption of relevant legislation and the social controversies in the following years. In what way can we assess the justice obtained through either far-reaching restitution or more limited property re-establishment?

Initial rehabilitations

It is once again a particularity of the Baltic states that in contrast to the other Central and Eastern European countries the processes of rehabilitation of victims of Stalinist-era injustice would receive their first impulse not from within the countries themselves, but rather from the broader Soviet context. As Kathleen Smith (1996) and others have pointed out, the drive to begin a re-examination of Stalinist repression in the USSR and to restore justice to its victims began at the all-Union level, where grassroots commemorative organizations first began calling for official action, and the Central Committee of the Communist Party of the Soviet Union (CPSU) eventually agreed to initiate a special review process concerning cases of mass repression.

As a consequence, the first rehabilitation Acts in the Baltic states were adopted only in late 1988, following largely the central Soviet lead. A decree passed by the Presidium of the Estonian SSR Supreme Soviet on December 7, 1988, for example, even cited the CPSU's precedents explicitly. Likewise, the degree to which the first rehabilitation documents in the three Soviet Baltic republics would resemble each other indicated that these measures were very much inspired by a Soviet-level directive.

To be sure, the Soviet Baltic authorities' attempts to address the rehabilitation issue were not due only to Moscow's example. Nationalist and democratic pressures had already begun to build in the region during late 1987 and early 1988, and critical reassessments of the Stalinist period had quickly become one of the issues seen as permissible. Moreover, part of the Baltic nationalist political mobilization during these years was linked to historically meaningful days in the calendar year, and one of those would readily become June 14, the day of the first mass Soviet deportation in 1941. (See Chapter 6.) Although these were merely commemorative events, they did build pressure on lawmakers to think up ways of rendering justice to the victims of these repressions in legal and political terms. Hence, they explain why rehabilitation had already become a policy issue for the Soviet Baltic administrations. These authorities were responding to pressures from both above and below. In this sense the Soviet Baltic authorities were riding two impulses at once.

Lithuania was the first to adopt an overall rehabilitation measure on October 21, 1988 (Lietuvos TSR Aukščiausiosios Tarybos Prezidiumas 1988). The LSSR Supreme Soviet Presidium decree was very succinct, declaring merely that all persons sent out from Lithuania on the basis of "anti-constitutional administrative decisions" were now declared rehabilitated. The document also instructed the government to work out procedures for victims to be informed of their rehabilitation as well as their rights to obtain material compensation. A similar format was followed in Estonia as part of a December 7, 1988 law on "extrajudicial mass repressions" (Eesti NSV Ülemnõukogu 1988). The law condemned these events from the 1940s and 1950s as "crimes against humanity" and proclaimed the automatic rehabilitation of all those who had been deported from Estonia. Additionally, the law tasked the government with not only preparing a compensation system but also developing a commemoration program and preserving all possible documentation connected to extra-judicial repressions from the Stalinist period. Moreover, as noted in Chapter 3 this 1988 law was the first in the Baltic states to call for criminal investigations into mass killings and crimes against humanity, and for trials against possible perpetrators. By contrast, Latvia's initial rehabilitation legislation was the most circumspect of the three. A decision by the Soviet Latvian Cabinet of Ministers on November 2, 1988 moved merely to annul two previous decrees from March 1949, in which the government at the time had authorized the "deportation of kulak families" (Latvijas PSR Ministru Padome 1988). This invalidation meant that deportees from 1949 could apply for rehabilitation. However, it was limited to a single period of repression. It would only be six months later that this measure would be supplemented by another Supreme Soviet Presidium decree that would speak broadly about individuals deported from the Latvian SSR "during the 1940s and 1950s" (Latvijas PSR Augstākās Padomes Prezidija 1989).

Although all three of the basic measures adopted in the Baltic states in late 1988 seemed to some degree perfunctory, they did generate four important after effects. First, the declarations got the wheels turning in terms of prompting administrative officials to begin working out the details for issuing rehabilitation certificates and clearing victims' legal records. Already by June 1, 1989, officials in Latvia had certified 6,274 individuals who had been illegally deported, and over 14,600 applications had been received (Indrikovs 1989). Meanwhile, over 50,000 people in Lithuania had their legal record restored as of spring 1991 (Balkelis and Davoliūtė 2009: 25). The upshot was that a clearly defined category of victims emerged, one that would be embellished later on with still further subgroups of victims.

A second administrative procedure to flow from the rehabilitation process involved calculating the period of a person's deportation as part of their employment history (in Estonia, multiplied by 3!) and not as simply lost time. This measure would make deportees eligible for better pensions and in most cases added privatization benefits, since often privatization vouchers would be issued on the basis of a person's lifetime employment history and deportees would therefore be able to count their years of suffering as part of that history. Moreover, this time period would be calculated for the entire length of that suffering, including initial detention, travel to Siberia and the duration of the deportation itself.

Thirdly, in all three Soviet republics additional guidelines were adopted for the return or compensation of property taken from deportees. In most cases, the expectation was that deportees would receive compensation for such property, as often their houses, farms and/or livestock had already been taken over by other individuals or state enterprises. However, there were some instances where deportees had returned from Siberia and re-purchased their property from individuals to whom the Soviet authorities had given it. In these cases, Estonian law, for example, allowed for these deportees to have the purchasing amount compensated by the state. Although many of these details were complicated, and often local officials or collective farm managers would drag their feet in processing claims, the decision to nevertheless implement the restitution principle vis-à-vis victims of deportation set an important precedent when it came time to consider the question of returning all property nationalized by the Soviets in 1940. The idea for enacting such a policy would no longer be foreign.[1]

Lastly, these early struggles helped to launch a fourth characteristic pattern of action that applied most of all to Lithuania. Some six months after the Lithuanian Supreme Soviet Presidium had adopted its blanket decree on rehabilitation, deputies from the full parliament began to query the implementation process. They lobbied for the adoption of a special resolution that would call on the government to intensify the rehabilitation process and to monitor local authorities in their enactment of the proper rules (Lietuvos TSR Aukščiausioji Taryba 1989). In this manner, parliamentarians became a direct part of the oversight process concerning rehabilitation. In the future, there would be many more instances where Lithuanian legislators would become frontline players in the victim compensation and acknowledgment process.

Likewise, Lithuania would be more generous in terms of compensating victims monetarily for their suffering as well as providing other social benefits. A July 1989 Lithuanian SSR government decree allocated

[1] According to Raidla (1991), a total of 12,270 restitution claims were lodged by deportees. Of these, 9,982 had been settled by January 1, 1991.

50 Soviet rubles for each month of imprisonment for any individual arrested or convicted of "state crimes" under Soviet law (Lietuvos Ministrų Taryba 1989). Moreover, in case the victim had since passed away or had been killed, this compensation was to be paid out to the victim's descendants. Deportees were also entitled to receive priority in the allocation of state housing. Although this is a principle that Estonia also adopted, Lithuania continually updated the benefit through subsequent decrees and other regulations, even after the re-establishment of independence.

Formalizing rehabilitation procedures

A new phase in the process of rehabilitating victims of Soviet repression opened up in early 1990, after each of the three Baltic states had held their first democratic parliamentary elections under Soviet rule and established pro-independence governments. Under these new authorities, the countries moved to adopt even more specific rehabilitation principles, procedures and benefits. In this phase the trendsetter was Estonia, where a more precise rehabilitation decree was actually adopted even before the March 1990 parliamentary elections or in other words by the outgoing Supreme Soviet Presidium. Although this new measure was thus adopted by a departing institution, the political atmosphere was by then so clearly pro-independence that the decision as such was not a surprise. The key novelty of the measure lay in the fact that for the first time a legal act would serve to define the specific set of criminal paragraphs to be rehabilitated as drawn from the RSFSR (Russian Soviet Federated Socialist Republic) Criminal Code that had been enacted on Estonia in 1940 and on the basis of which tens of thousands of people had been repressed, deported and killed (Eesti NSV Ülemnõukogu Presiidium 1990). This list would include some of the most notorious forms of Stalinist repression such as convicting people for "treason against the motherland" (§58–1a), support for "counter-revolutionary activity" (§58–11), "anti-Soviet and counter-revolutionary propaganda and agitation" (§58–10) and for having been part of the pre-1940 "counter-revolutionary government" (§58–13). According to the main victim organization in Estonia, the Memento Union, more than 65 percent of the roughly 50,000 political sentences handed down during the Stalinist period in Estonia involved these four paragraphs (Õispuu 1996b: D56–59). At the same time, the new decree took care to delineate some of the more particular crimes associated with the deportations, such as conviction for trying to flee one's place of deportation and trying to return home (§82). It also noted a number of economic crimes, under which wealthier farmers were declared kulaks or coerced into giving up their property.

In administrative terms, the new decree mandated two institutions to deal with the upwards of 20,000 people eventually identified as having been repressed under these specific Soviet criminal paragraphs (see Õispuu 1996b). These would be the Estonian Supreme Court in the case of those formally convicted by Soviet courts and the Estonian Prosecutor General's Office in the case of those convicted by extra-judicial authorities such as spontaneous Soviet tribunals. Of these two forms of criminal prosecution, the overwhelming majority had been carried out by Soviet tribunals.

In February 1992, the Supreme Council adopted a formal rehabilitation law (Eesti Vabariigi Ülemnõukogu 1992). On the one hand, this legislation served merely to slightly expand the list of RSFSR criminal paragraphs subject to rehabilitation; at the same time it stipulated clear guidelines for the government to carry out property restitution for those whose wealth had been confiscated as part of deportation or repression. In early 1993, this law was further amended to allow the Estonian Supreme Court to review petitions from people who wanted rehabilitation for Soviet-era convictions, which they claimed had been politically motivated. This included convictions for hooliganism and other crimes when, for example, people attempted during the Soviet era to display the Estonian national flag or yelled anti-Soviet slogans.

In Lithuania, the approach to fleshing out the rehabilitation process was much more broad-brush. On May 2, 1990 the Lithuanian Supreme Council adopted a one-page law, which declared that all those who had been "sentenced or imprisoned out of court by repressive bodies, or their freedom [had been] curtailed under the Criminal Code of the RSFSR" were "innocent before the Republic of Lithuania and all their civil rights are hereby restored" (Lietuvos Respublikos Aukščiausioji Taryba 1990). The law was very general in that it did not specify any precise paragraphs of the RSFSR Criminal Code under which people might have been convicted. As a result, it appeared as if anyone convicted by the Soviets under the Russian Criminal Code was now eligible for rehabilitation. Characteristic of Lithuania's more complicated World War II history, the Supreme Council law also declared rehabilitated those repressed by the occupying Nazi regime from 1941 to 1944. These included thousands of people deported to Germany as forced laborers by the Nazis. Lastly, the law resembled the Estonian precedent in that it tasked the Lithuanian Supreme Court and the Prosecutor General's Office with the process of issuing rehabilitation certificates. It also added the Ministry of Internal Affairs as the institution responsible for issuing rehabilitation documentation to deportees.

Latvia was the last Baltic state to adopt a more elaborate rehabilitation framework. In a pair of legal acts passed on August 3, 1990, the Latvian Supreme Council decided to mirror Estonia's practice of formally listing all of the different paragraphs of the RSFSR Criminal Code, in relation to which convicted individuals could seek rehabilitation (Latvijas Republikas Augstākā Padome 1990b, 1990c). The list was almost identical to the Estonian one. Likewise, the legislation would divide up the administrative responsibility for rehabilitation among the Prosecutor General's Office, the Latvian Supreme Court and lower courts. At the same time, the Latvian legislators added an additional category of repressed persons, namely those who had been forced into psychiatric treatment by the Soviet regime because of their political beliefs or activities. The Latvian legislation called for the creation of a special committee to examine these instances separately. As the lead author of the legislation, Linards Muciņš, would say, this category even affected a number of newly elected deputies in the parliament, who until then had not received any acknowledgment for their persecution (Muciņš 1990). At the same time, the new legislation elicited a certain amount of controversy, since many pro-Soviet deputies in the parliament claimed the process would lead to the rehabilitation of individuals who had actually committed punishable crimes, such as the murder of Soviet officials. One deputy even argued that it was incorrect to call the Soviet deportations "illegal," since according to Soviet law at the time such forced resettlement of people was entirely lawful (Šapovālovs 1990).

Thus, although the new series of rehabilitation legislation in all three Baltic states was passed without any major obstruction, some problems did linger, especially in Lithuania. Already in October 1990 the Lithuanian Supreme Council was obliged to adopt an additional resolution creating a special high-level commission to examine contested cases of rehabilitation (Lietuvos Respublikos Aukščiausiosios Tarybos Prezidiumas 1990). The commission would include MPs, but also the Prosecutor General, Artūras Paulauskas, and the head of the Lithuanian State Security Department, Mečys Laurinkus. As such, it would become another instance in Lithuania of more intense involvement on the part of legislators in the rehabilitation process. Indeed, this particular commission would become the precursor of the Resistance Participants' Rights Commission to be established just a year later.

In the meantime, the Lithuanian Supreme Council again became involved in rehabilitation controversies, when in September 1991 *The New York Times* newspaper published a report claiming that Lithuania was rehabilitating Nazi war criminals as part of its blanket-style review procedure (Kinzer 1991). In its report the newspaper cited the names of Lithuanians, who apparently had been rehabilitated, even though Jewish survivor organizations had accused them of having committed Nazi crimes. The controversy was further magnified by the Soviet news agency TASS, which disseminated an exaggerated report saying that Lithuania may have rehabilitated up to 35,000 people whom the Soviets had convicted of Nazi atrocities. Lithuanian officials such as Prosecutor General Paulauskas sought to defend the rehabilitation approach by saying that all Stalinist-era convictions (even those against Nazi war criminals) were fundamentally flawed since no real due process existed at that time. Hence, in his view it was impossible to let any of these convictions stand (Kinzer 1991). These clarifications, however, were not enough for a group of seven US senators, who wrote a letter to the chairman of the Lithuanian parliament, Vytautas Landsbergis, offering Lithuania special cooperation with the US Department of Justice in order to examine war crimes cases. Sensing that the controversy was beginning to cause damage to Lithuania's international image barely two weeks after the full restoration of independence, the Presidium of the Lithuanian Supreme Council issued a statement on September 9 admitting that some mistakes may have been made when reviewing those postwar convictions that had been based on very sketchy NKVD material (Lietuvos Respublikos Aukščiausiosios Tarybos Prezidiumas 1991b). The statement also said that officials may have been slow in examining evidence presented by Jewish groups in relation to alleged Nazi collaborators. At the same time, the statement reiterated the fact that Lithuania's legislation prohibited the rehabilitation of those convicted of genocide or the massacre of unarmed civilians, implying that this was a safeguard against indiscriminate rehabilitation. As proof, the statement noted that since the process of reviewing rehabilitation applications had begun, some 500 such requests had been rejected. The statement also said that Lithuania would gladly accept the offer to cooperate with the US Department of Justice. It equally welcomed the creation of a joint Lithuanian-Israeli parliamentary working group to monitor future problems.

Broadening rehabilitation categories

A third stage of rehabilitation politics in the Baltic states has involved the delineation of still another category of Soviet and Nazi regime victims, namely former dissidents and other individuals deemed to have participated in resistance to foreign rule, but who were never deported or criminally charged. Again, Lithuania was the pioneer of this approach, adopting a Supreme Council Presidium resolution in October 1991 that mandated the issuing of special certificates to individuals who had "actively fought for the freedom and independence of Lithuania" (Lietuvos Respublikos Aukščiausiosios Tarybos Prezidiumas 1991a). The new regulation defined resistance (*pasipriešinimas*) as participation in any activity that might bring on political repression by the occupation authorities. As an example, the resolution cited the dissemination of underground materials hostile to the regime. The measure, however, was not declarative or symbolic. Rather, the resolution authorized the rehabilitation oversight commission created in October 1990 to take on this new task of identifying and certifying "participants in the resistance." The Presidium therefore upgraded the commission's status by formally naming it the Resistance Participants' Rights Commission (*Pasipriešinimo dalyvių [rezistentų] teisių komisija*). It also ordered the allocation of funds for its work, including a salary for its chair. Thirdly, it issued the Commission a set of formal guidelines for making its rulings, including procedures for reviewing contested cases. Most importantly, the new procedure accorded an important role to the victims' rights group, the Union of Political Prisoners and Deportees (*Lietuvos politinių kalinių ir tremtinių sąjunga*). The Union was called upon to disseminate information about the new status through its nationwide network of local branches. It was also given the task of collecting all relevant documentation for applicants seeking the new certificate as well as preparing a preliminary recommendation to the Commission concerning the eligibility of the applicant. This recommendation was to be formally published in the Union's newspaper *Tremtinys* ("Deportee"), and if after two months no objections were received from the public, the Commission would make its final decision. In November 1994, the Lithuanian parliament decided to merge the Commission with the Genocide and Resistance Research Center of Lithuania (LGGRTC), and thereafter have the Center issue resistance certificates (Lietuvos Respublikos Seimas 1994b). Although this seemed a downgrading of the process, the Center actually continued to have a Resistance Participants' Rights Commission as one of its departments.

Moreover, the Commission regained stature in 1997 when the entire LGGRTC would be reorganized and the Commission would be given additional functions such as certifying the identity of armed resistance fighters against the Soviet regime.

All of this procedural and institutional effort stood in considerable contrast to what was undertaken in the other two Baltic states. In Latvia, legislators got around to adopting a law on defining participants in the "national resistance movement" (*nacionālās pretošanās kustība*) only in 1996 and after an overall repressed persons' law had been passed (see below Latvijas Republikas Saeima 1996a). The initiative was driven by MPs from the nationalist For Fatherland and Freedom (*Tēvzemei un Brīvībai*) party and quickly obtained widespread parliamentary support. Still, disagreements arose over how officials would be able to determine who qualified for the designation and who did not. One problem was that all those who had resisted the Soviet regime and had been punished for it already – either as a postwar partisan and convicted by a Soviet tribunal or as a dissident and sentenced by a Soviet court – had already been rehabilitated and therefore acknowledged by the state. Those who had perhaps helped the partisans by offering food or who had distributed samizdat materials but had never been caught could now conceivably step forward and obtain recognition. Yet, as some deputies argued during the parliamentary debate, would this kind of porous category not prompt thousands of people to seek the new benefit? Whereas government officials supporting the measure estimated the number of eligible claimants to be perhaps 200 people, opposition deputies warned that the number could reach 200,000 (Mauliņš 1996).

From the point of view of the politics of the issue, it is interesting to point out that because the Latvians undertook to institute the status of "national resistance movement participant" via a law passed in parliament, they also engendered more critical debates about how the eligibility for this category would be determined. In all, the Latvians debated the issue for some eight months counting from when an initial legislative bill was submitted in August 1995. By contrast, Lithuania passed its measure in the more delimited Presidium of the Supreme Council, where the political currents were under the control of its chairman, Vytautas Landsbergis.

The final Latvian Law on the Status of a Participant in the National Resistance Movement sought to find compromises for some of the controversies that had arisen during the debates (Latvijas Republikas Saeima 1996). One important distinction included in the law was a temporal division between resistance that occurred before and after January 1, 1961. The former was meant to refer first and foremost to the postwar partisan movement; it included, however, people who had offered "material and other assistance" to the fighters and in so doing had "risked their own freedom and life." In addition, the law acknowledged those who before 1961 had "propagated the idea of restoring the independence" of Latvia, had disseminated illegal materials or had publicly opposed the Soviet or Nazi regimes. By contrast, those who had engaged in such activities after 1961 were recognized only if they had been convicted by a Soviet court for political activities and been rehabilitated. This made the category slightly redundant. A subsequent amendment to the law would add to the post-1961 category those people who had been committed by the Soviets to psychiatric and other medical institutions for political reasons. A further specification of the law was that resistance participant status could not be given to any individual who had worked in the repressive structures of the Soviet or Nazi regimes or had participated in repressive acts under those regimes. This was a softened formulation in comparison to initial versions, which had specifically excluded anyone who had been a member of the Soviet Communist Party. Such a restriction, however, would have barred from eligibility a number of former Communists who later participated in dissident activities.

Procedurally the 1996 law would limit the ability of individuals to apply for the new status by requiring them to have relevant documentation from either the Latvian state archive, the Commission for the Investigation of Totalitarian Regime Crimes (later the Ministry of Justice) or a court that had certified the person's involvement in or conviction for resistance activities. Likewise, the law would decentralize the implementation process by having municipalities set up local review commissions that would comprise local officials, but also representatives from repressed persons' organizations. In most cases, the latter would come from the Latvian Association of Victims of Political Repression (*Latvijas politiski represēto apvienība* – LPRA). Hence, although victims' groups would be involved in Latvia, they would not have as prominent a role as in Lithuania.

In the wake of the law's original adoption, a number of controversies continued to linger. For one, deputies from different minority Russian parties in the Latvian parliament tried repeatedly to get the legislature to create a comparable legal status for individuals who had fought in the "anti-Hitler coalition" or, in other words, the Red Army during World

War II. Not one of the more than a dozen bills they submitted between 1996 and 2010 was accepted on to the parliament's agenda. Meanwhile, nationalist deputies tried from 2007 onwards to get Latvians who fought in the *Wehrmacht* to be declared part of the "national resistance movement." These proposals attempted to add some legal weight to the yearly commemorations that had been organized since the 1990s in honor of those who had been part of the Latvian Legion created in 1943 under the German Army (see Chapter 6). Initially, the nationalists' bills in parliament were all scuttled. However, when the National Alliance coalition became part of the government in 2011, they began actively pushing the issue within the cabinet. Prime Minister Valdis Dombrovskis resisted the pressure, while other coalition politicians stressed the fact that it would simply be illogical to declare individuals who had been part of a regular army participants in a national resistance movement. In late 2013, the issue receded somewhat, when Dombrovski resigned as prime minister and parliamentary elections approached in 2014. In the meantime, another initiative took hold in late 2012 when the parliament's Social Cohesion Commission introduced a bill aimed at giving legal status to all those who had been mobilized into either the Soviet or the Nazi army. The idea had come from President Andris Bērziņš, who upon entering office in July 2011 had called for cooperation among veterans from both sides. Nonetheless, deputies from the minority Russian Harmony Center party voted against the bill when it was first introduced in parliament in November 2012, saying that by virtue of its stress on mobilized veterans the bill would deny the new status to those who had served in underground or partisan Soviet forces, and therefore it remained unfair (Saskaņas centrs 2012).

By 2013, approximately 700 people had been issued the status of participant in the national resistance movement. This number did not rise much despite the fact that the Latvian government decided in January 2005 to introduce a special 50 lats per month social welfare payment for all registered national resistance movement participants. Quite evidently the addition of this benefit contributed much to the nationalist deputies' motivation as of 2007 to push for national resistance movement participant status for former members of the *Wehrmacht*; the deputies' legislative proposals called explicitly for the so-called legionnaires to receive the same monthly payment. However, the deputies themselves predicted that the new benefit would cost the state up to 360,000 lats (€512,236) per year, an amount that became particularly foreboding when the country hit its financial and economic crisis in 2008. Later when the Latvian government suspended entirely a number of support payments for repressed persons because of national austerity policies, municipalities such as Riga attempted to pay some of these benefits out of their local budgets.

In Estonia no special status has ever been established for resistors to the Soviet occupation, either armed or unarmed. Despite numerous calls for such a measure by victims' rights groups, politicians have been wary of creating a separate legal status for "freedom fighters" or *vabadusvõitlejad.* In part, this is because the phrase has become an often-used expression to refer to those who fought in the German Army during 1944 in the hopes of stemming the Soviet re-occupation of Estonia. Precisely for this reason the notion has also been seen as controversial and therefore precarious to legislate. In 2005–2006, opposition MPs from the Pro Patria Union and the Res Publica party tried to get parliament to adopt at least a statement acknowledging all those who had fought against Soviet aggression in World War II as "freedom fighters." The Reform Party-led government at the time stymied the MPs' efforts by introducing a bill of its own that declared all those people who had opposed Soviet and Nazi occupation as "freedom fighters." Although the opposition criticized the new formulation as being ridiculously diluted, the government was able to vote down the opposition's proposal and thereafter let its own proposal languish in committee. A second attempt by national-conservative politicians to push the "freedom fighter" notion came in 2011 when the Pro Patria and Res Publica Union returned to government and insisted in its coalition agreement with the Reform Party that a parliamentary resolution be passed. In the end, however, this too was watered down to a three-paragraph statement that merely acknowledged all those who had "acted in the name of the restoration" of Estonian independence during the Soviet and Nazi occupations (Eesti Vabariigi Riigikogu 2012). There was no mention of freedom fighters or special acknowledgment of those who had fought the returning Red Army.

Repressed persons' status laws

A final level of victim politics involves systematizing the various victim categories into a single legal status of repressed person. As each of the Baltic states began to sort out the different types of victims it would acknowledge, it became logical to develop an overarching legal framework for these groups, which would help organize the agencies responsible for them as well as possible benefits they might be entitled to. Latvia was in this instance the first to adopt, in May 1992, a general law On the Determination of the Status of a Politically Repressed Person (Latvijas Republikas Augstākā Padome 1992e, 1992f). Although the law was accompanied by an implementation Act, which tasked the government with adopting a more specific set of regulations and procedures, the law appears to have remained largely a dead letter. One problem, which legislators acknowledged even during debates over the law, was the fact that the measure aimed to define two separate categories of "directly" and "indirectly" politically repressed. Alongside the obvious category of formally rehabilitated (and hence directly repressed) individuals, the lawmakers attempted to at least acknowledge those victims who had never been formally charged with anything. One clear case involved those men who had been part of the partisan resistance movement immediately after the war, but who for whatever reason or luck had been able to re-enter regular life without any repercussions. Likewise, legislators aimed to encompass, for example, those people who had been prevented for political reasons from entering university or practicing a certain profession. A more complicated, and yet agreed-upon, category involved farmers in the late 1940s who had been disproportionately taxed by the Stalinist regime in order to force them into joining a collective farm. Lastly, the law even declared as indirectly repressed those people whose property had been nationalized. All of this seemed to leave the floodgates open to broad interpretation – all the more so since the law declared not only these people indirectly repressed but also any "relatives" who had suffered alongside them. However, there was a limitation in that only directly repressed people could apply for a repressed person's identity card and be eligible for concrete benefits. In parliament, deputies acknowledged the purely symbolic nature of this aspect of the law, but they insisted that public pressure required some kind of recognition of this kind of suffering.

A second controversy concerned differentiating between citizens and non-citizens, as well as between Latvians in Latvia and Latvians from Siberia. A number of MPs spoke out in favor of eligibility, for example, for Latvians who had been repressed in Siberian villages during the 1930s, but had moved back to Latvia after the war. Similarly, it was unclear whether people who had moved to Latvia after 1940 and had been repressed in Latvia might also be eligible for the new status. In the end, the law was liberal in that it declared both ethnic Latvians and all permanent residents of Latvia eligible.

The 1992 law, however, remained largely dysfunctional, since it left unclear how people were supposed to make use of this new designation or status. A government decree adopted in August established the form of a repressed person's identity card, and stated that the card may be shown wherever the bearer needs to prove eligibility for benefits. However, since the card was to be issued by local government authorities, it was also left open as to how the decision to issue such a card would be made. An applicant needed, of course, to present documents regarding their earlier rehabilitation or a claim to have been repressed. Yet in contrast to a later decision to involve victims' organizations, this initial decision-making procedure was left basically to civil servants.

When Latvia elected a new parliament in June 1993, legislators began a renewed effort to institute a repressed person's status (Latvijas Republikas Saeima 1995b). In a first move, they dropped any mention of indirectly repressed persons. Secondly, they made a very clear distinction between victims under Soviet and Nazi rule, adding the name of both regimes in the title of the law and devoting separate paragraphs to each. (See Table 5.1.) Each category of individuals also had a detailed list of documents on the basis of which legal recognition would be accorded. The same principles of eligibility as before were declared for Latvian citizens, permanent residents and Latvians from Russia. The new law continued the practice of having local authorities make the formal decisions; however, the relevant review committee now had to include representatives from repressed persons' organizations. The law reiterated a somewhat declarative and controversial point from the 1992 version, namely, that state authorities were obliged to make sure that "the aftereffects of limitations on the civil, economic and social rights" of the repressed that had been caused by the totalitarian regimes were removed; equally that any material, physical or moral damage caused by the regimes should be compensated. At the same time, the 1995 law formally stated that repressed persons would be eligible for earlier pension benefits, free medical care, reduced public transport fares and personal income tax reductions.

In future years, the law would be amended relatively little. The only major change involved shifting the entire process of reviewing applications away from local governments and onto the shoulders of the Latvian Office of Citizenship and Migration Affairs. This was welcomed by victims groups, since it would help to concentrate the decision-making process within a single authority and avoid the subjectivity that sometimes characterized local officials' decisions (Ruska 2012). At the same

Table 5.1 *Victim categories in Latvia's repressed persons' status law*

Article 2: Eligible legal categories

a. Latvian citizens
b. Permanent residents up until June 17, 1940
c. Their descendants
d. Ethnic Latvians and Livonians, who have been repressed in Latvia or outside Latvia
e. Permanent residents, who were repressed in Latvia after May 8, 1945

Individuals to be recognized as politically repressed by the communist or Nazi regime:

i. Indivuals killed or who died as a result of repression
ii. Individuals imprisoned or jailed in concentration, filtration or labor camps, ghettoes or forcibly held in institutions, where coercion of a medical nature was applied
iii. Individuals deported, resettled or relocated from their place of permanent residence or who were born during deportation or resettlement until the moment of their return to Latvia
iv. Individuals deported by the Nazi authorities to forced labor camps
v. Individuals repressed by the Nazis for their national or ethnic background
vi. All minors jailed by the Nazis in prisons or concentration camps on the territory of Latvia

Compiled from: Saeima (1995b), as amended

time, the leader of the LPRA, Gunārs Resnais, surprised many in 2009 when he publicly called on the government to stop granting any more cases of repressed person's status, claiming that too many people were beginning to abuse the system (Resnais and Pētersons 2010; Ruska 2010). Resnais argued that many people were attempting to obtain the special status because of the economic difficulties Latvia was suffering following the 2008 financial crisis. This, however, was unfair in relation to those who had actually suffered. Similarly, Resnais maintained that whoever was truly deserving of the status should have applied for it long ago. Resnais lobbied the government to suspend the given policy; when the cabinet refused to do so, he turned to the parliament's Human Rights and Public Affairs Committee, asking it to draft a formal legislative amendment. However, no immediate change emerged.

According to the LPRA, the number of people with the status of politically repressed in Latvia has slowly declined over the years due to beneficiaries passing away. In line with Resnais' grievances, however, the number of applications each year has increased. If in 2007 the number of registered repressed persons under the Soviet regime was 21,283 and under the Nazi regime 2,698, by 2012 these figures had dropped to 16,670 and 1,896. At the same time, the number of new applications continued to top 100 per year, with around half being rejected (Ruska 2012).

Efforts in Lithuania to institutionalize a repressed person's status grew out of the overall effort by the conservative Homeland Union government in 1996 to push a new agenda regarding transitional and retrospective justice. The initial laws that had been passed in 1990 and 1991 had sparked a rapid process of rehabilitating Stalinist-era victims and of identifying in particular individuals who had contributed to national resistance. At the same time, from late 1992 to late 1996, when the ex-communist LDDP was in power, little was done either to embellish these measures or to curtail them. As a Communist successor party, the LDDP had little inclination to cater to these particular groups in society, but there was equally no point in antagonizing them by rescinding their policies. As a result, the party's only change in this area was an attempt to resolve some of the lingering doubts about the propriety of some of the rehabilitations. In February 1995 President Algirdas Brazauskas decided to act by ordering the institutions involved with rehabilitation to re-examine the legality of those certificates issued to individuals suspected of crimes of genocide (Lietuvos Republikos Prezidentas 1995). He also instructed the Ministry of Justice to analyze the current rehabilitation system and to draw up a set of amendments for improvement. In September 1995, the Seimas passed a law adding a series of new points to the original rehabilitation Act, more than doubling its previous length. The most important of these instituted a formal system for revoking rehabilitation certificates when evidence arose that an individual may have been improperly accorded such status. The amendments permitted the prosecutor general to open additional investigations as well as to have the Lithuanian Supreme Court review the findings and make a final decision. Individuals who had been denied rehabilitation were also given the right to appeal those decisions in the lower courts. Lastly, family members of repressed people were also now allowed to apply for the rehabilitation of loved ones, opening up an avenue for posthumous rehabilitation (Lietuvos Respublikos Seimas 1995). Over the next year, additional small amendments would be passed that would expand eligibility for rehabilitation to individuals who had been punished for avoiding Soviet military service or for desertion.

The shift toward allowing authorities to actually rescind questionable rehabilitation certificates prompted a steady stream of procedural reviews on the part of the Prosecutor General's Office and the Supreme Court. Between 1997 and 2008, more than 225 certificates were rescinded; among these were numerous cases of individuals who had taken part in the murder of Jews during World War II, had been convicted by the Soviets for treason and then cursorily rehabilitated by the Lithuanian authorities (Generalinės Prokuratūros STS 2008).

A second measure undertaken by the LDDP during its time in power was to pass a measure gratifying an opposite segment of society: veterans of the Soviet Army. In August 1996, just before the LDDP was to go down to electoral defeat, the parliament passed a law giving legal status to all those who had fought on the side of the "anti-Hitler coalition" (Lietuvos Respublikos Seimas 1996). The measure was mostly declarative, in that it left to future legislation all decisions concerning the benefits these veterans would enjoy. Still, this did not prevent the conservative opposition from ridiculing the measure. Homeland Union MP Andrius Kubilius, for example, submitted an amendment to the bill changing its name to the law on members of the Soviet Army that had occupied Lithuania (with no mention of the anti-Hitler coalition). With regard to the plan to issue these veterans special certificates, Kubilius proposed adding to the bill an almost surreal specification that "persons holding such certificates shall be considered victims of Soviet occupation." Needless to say, the amendments were not accepted.

Still, Kubilius' audacity showed that the conservatives had not lost any of their zeal to continue dealing with victims' issues after their electoral victory in October–November. Just two days after the new conservative-majority parliament convened, an amendment was passed to the 1990 rehabilitation law elevating the status of those who had participated in the post-1945 armed resistance to that of "volunteer fighters" and according them all military ranks and titles. Two months later, the parliament adopted a resolution ordering the government to work out new laws for specially acknowledging participants in the anti-Soviet partisan struggle. Legislation passed in July 1997 finalized this effort, mandating the LGGRTC to issue special certificates to this highest category of victims (Lietuvos Respublikos Seimas 1997d). This was followed up in November by an additional law that provided one-time compensation payments between 5,600 and 14,400 litas (€1,625 and €4,170) for those who had been injured or debilitated during the partisan struggle. This was in addition to eligibility for a state pension of the first degree or roughly €400 per month. Finally, in October 1998 parliament passed still further legislation providing survivor pensions (under certain conditions) to the spouses, children and siblings of partisan fighters.

During the same period, legislators also began drawing up a complete and consolidated victim status bill. This six-page framework law, adopted on June 30, 1997, laid out for the first time the full array of victim categories to be acknowledged under Lithuanian law (Lietuvos Respublikos Seimas 1997a). In a lengthy preamble, the law began by stating that during the years 1939–90 the Soviet and Nazi regimes had carried out a "policy of physical and spiritual genocide" in Lithuania, and that up until now the different types of repressed and victimized people had yet to be defined in a clear legal manner. The measure therefore went on to delineate five different historical periods of suffering under the different occupation regimes: (1) the Nazi German occupation of Klaipėda as of March 1939, (2) the Soviet occupation of the Vilnius region as of September 1939, (3) the Soviet occupation of Lithuania between 1940 and 1941, (4) the Nazi German occupation of Lithuania between 1941 and 1944, (5) the Soviet occupation of Lithuania between 1944 and 1990. Across these periods, the law defined four types of victims: (a) political prisoners, (b) deportees, (c) other repressed persons, (d) other victims. In Table 5.2, we outline the various subcategories

Table 5.2 *Victim categories in Lithuania's repressed persons' status law*

Article 4: Political prisoners and individuals accorded equivalent status

1. Individuals convicted under Article 58 of the RSFSR Criminal Code or analogous Soviet codes
2. Individuals imprisoned by the Nazi authorities for actions in the name or defense of Lithuanian independence or its property
3. Individuals convicted or imprisoned for belonging to "counter-revolutionary" or other socially dangerous circles
4. Individuals convicted for not paying taxes or other levies imposed by the occupation regime
5. Individuals convicted for refusing to serve in or for deserting armies occupying Lithuania out of political motivations
6. Individuals imprisoned for attempting to cross the borders of the USSR
7. Individuals imprisoned for resisting occupation or being a member of the family of a state official of the Republic of Lithuania
8. Individuals subjected to forced treatment in psychiatric hospitals out of political motivations

Table 5.2 (*cont.*)

Individuals accorded equivalent status with political prisoners:

1. Individuals held in filtration camps after World War II
2. Individuals convicted or imprisoned for supporting the partisans or underground organizations
3. Individuals arrested or held in custody for at least six months and later freed as part of punitive actions or for the extraction of evidence by the occupation regime
4. Individuals born in prison, concentration camps or other places of detention if at least one of the parents was a political prisoner or person accorded equivalent status

Article 5. Deportees

1. Individuals deported or forcibly resettled from their place of residence by occupation authorities for political reasons
2. Individuals forcibly resettled from their place of residence to specific locations by occupation authorities for political reasons
3. Individuals forcibly settled in a specific location following the end of a period of imprisonment
4. Individuals prohibited from returning to their place of residence in Lithuania following the end of a period of imprisonment
5. Individuals born to parents, of whom at least one was deported or forcibly settled
6. Individuals who voluntarily joined deported family members and in relation to whom similar restrictions on movement were then applied

Individuals accorded equivalent status to deportees:

1. Family members of deportees, if at least one of the spouses was deported or resettled
2. Individuals who were on lists of persons slated for deportation, but fled or hid and were unable thereafter to live in their previous place of residence

Article 6. Other repressed persons

1. Individuals imprisoned in concentration camps or other punitive locations for their nationality, ethnicity, race, religion, political beliefs, social background or organization affiliation, or individuals born in such locations
2. Individuals arrested or held in custody for up to six months and later freed as part of punitive actions or for the extraction of evidence by the occupation regime

Article 7. Other victims of occupation

1. Individuals who during repressions or punitive actions undertaken by units of an occupying army, the repressive structures of an occupying regime, or the underground units of an occupying regime working against the state independence of Lithuania and for the benefit of another state:

Table 5.2 (*cont.*)

a. were killed, debilitated or injured
b. lost property
c. had relatives (parents, spouses or children) killed in such actions

2. Relatives of killed or deceased resistance members, political prisoners and deportees, including parents, spouses, children and siblings (if the last two categories were of minor age upon the death of the individual)
3. Individuals whose property was nationalized, confiscated or otherwise taken away or destroyed for political reasons by occupation authorities
4. Individuals who because of discrimination for political reasons or because of the loss of a home were not allowed to live and work legally in their prior place of residence in Lithuania
5. Individuals who because of discrimination for political reasons were prohibited from studying in secondary or tertiary educational institutions, from obtaining a scientific degree, from working in fields corresponding to their specialization, or [who]were dismissed from their position
6. Individuals who lost their health or who became disabled (invalids)
   a. during forcible military service or military training
   b. following forcible conscription into military units
   c. following forcible conscription into units cleaning up catastrophes or disasters
   d. while carrying out punitive labor in Lithuania or elsewhere
   e. as a result of illnesses subsequently linked to the above instances
7. Individuals obliged to leave their place of residence or Lithuania and later unable to return out of the fear of political repression
8. Individuals who:
   a. were obliged to change their family name or become a member of another family out of the fear of political repression
   b. were forcibly resettled within Lithuania or the territory controlled by the occupation regime or outside it
   c. were members of families who evaded deportation, and were able to continue living in their prior place of residence
   d. were members of families of partisans and political prisoners
   e. were forced to work as informers or join the Soviet Youth League or Communist Party and were forced to leave their job or place of study or resettle to a new place of residence
   f. were members of families of individuals named in categories b–e if they were minors at the time of repression
   g. were removed from Lithuania as part of forced labor together with their minors
   h. were victimized or pursued by occupation authorities for the rescue or care of minors targeted by the regime

Compiled from Lietuvos Respublikos Seimas (1997a)

included under each major victim type. The detail and precision, with which these groups were defined, provide a clear testimony to the importance legislators attached to mapping out and providing due recognition to all of the different dimensions of suffering experienced in the country. This array would far surpass any classification adopted in Latvia or Estonia.

An important novelty in the law was the precise reference to Article 58 of the RSFSR Criminal Code, which removed some of the ambiguity created by Lithuania's first rehabilitation law of 1990. Another essential category involved the varied forms of deportation that people suffered, including those who had decided to join loved ones already in deportation or those who had been prevented from returning to Lithuania. A third unique array of victims concerned individuals who had suffered what the Latvians had tried to call "indirect repression" or political discrimination during the Soviet period. These were often more contemporary categories, and from the perspective of our analytical framework they would qualify as a type of transitional justice, especially in instances, for example, where a person was prevented from studying at university because they were the child of a deportee or had engaged in political activities as a teenager. While these would be some of the more difficult cases to prove in terms of eligibility, they were an important signal that more discrete forms of repression would be considered as part of Lithuanian justice policy. A similarly more contemporary category of victims concerned Lithuanians sent to fight in Afghanistan during the Soviet invasion of that country or those conscripted to clean up damage from the Chernobyl nuclear power station disaster. These two categories would equally be acknowledged by Estonia and Latvia, but in some cases only via social welfare legislation and not via victim status laws.[2]

Lastly, the Lithuanian law defined a sizable number of people who would be eligible for legal status by virtue of the fact that a family member had suffered direct repression. One obvious category here comprised children born to deported or imprisoned individuals. But also included, for example, were the spouses of partisans and their children, if they were of minor age when their parent was killed or imprisoned. Many of these people would come forth only as they themselves reached pensionable age and began to inquire into the benefits they were now eligible for. An additional aspect of this link to other

[2] For a discussion of Lithuanian social security law, see Nekrosius and Petrylaitė (2010).

relatives is that thousands of Lithuanians would use the opportunity to seek posthumous recognition of the suffering of loved ones, in particular the children of partisans or deportees. Certificates issued in these cases had purely symbolic value, since the applicants themselves did not qualify for any victim category. They simply wanted to have a document issued for a deceased relative in order to honor their memory and record their victim status for posterity.

Akin to many earlier rehabilitation and victim status laws, the 1997 Lithuanian legislation ruled out legal recognition for anyone who had committed genocide, crimes against humanity or war crimes. In addition, however, the law excluded anyone who had worked in the repressive apparatus of the Soviet or Nazi regimes, either as a basic employee, agent or informer. Moreover, it rejected anyone who had been a high-ranking member of either the Nazi or Communist parties. In relation to the latter, the law laid out a series of positions that fell under this restriction, including party secretaries and department heads within the Central Committee and even party chiefs at the municipal and enterprise level. Although it is unknown how many people would be affected by these limitations, the political message was there, and to a much greater extent than the Latvians had ventured to include.

A final important procedural modification of the law was that in the future all decisions regarding victims' status would be taken by a revamped Resistance Participants' Rights Commission located within the LGGRTC (Lietuvos Respublikos Vyriausybė 1997). The Commission would include representatives from victims' organizations such as the Union of Political Prisoners and Deportees and the Union of Lithuanian Freedom Fighters, as well as from law enforcement bodies such as the Special Investigations Division of the Prosecutor General's Office, the State Security Department and the Ministry of Justice. Specifically, the Commission was given authority to subpoena all necessary archival and other documents necessary to make victim status decisions. Appeals procedures were also established as part of the new regulation. Lastly, because the Commission was henceforth located under the LGGRTC, it became a tradition for the Center to hand over all victim identity cards during special public ceremonies in the Vilnius Officers House organized several times a year.

According to data from the LGGRTC, over 83,000 different victim status cards had been issued by early 2013 (Šidlauskas, Interview, 2013). Of these, the vast majority were for the category of deportees (58,023); the second largest group involved victims of the occupation (18,724).

Political prisoners numbered 5,684, and other repressed persons 943. In addition, the Center had certified directly or posthumously 7,039 participants in the armed resistance (volunteer fighters) and 6,494 participants in unarmed resistance or supporters of the resistance. Within the framework of these last two categories, the Center had authorized some 3,500 one-time compensation payments (as mandated by the law entitled On the Certification of Participants in the Resistance). Over 2,100 applications for victim status had been denied, mostly for lack of sufficient documentation.

When comparing the three Baltic states in terms of their adoption of overall victim status laws, it is perhaps the biggest surprise that Estonia moved to adopt such a law only in 2003 or fully twelve years following the passage of any of its earlier rehabilitation or victim legislation. This intermediate dearth of activity can be explained by the fact that many of the essential social benefits and other aspects of political-administrative victim justice had been resolved via other legal acts, such as pension regulations and privatization legislation. Where necessary, the existing category of "rehabilitated person" had been incorporated into these other policies instead of aiming to establish a framework for repressed persons as such. Equally significant was the fact that the governments that were in power during this period were predominantly centrist and not linked in any particular way to victims' organizations. Symbolic measures, such as President Lennart Meri's Broken Cornflower campaign in 2001 (see Chapter 6), tended to serve as ersatz policies for more substantive political-administrative recognition.

All of this changed with the emergence of the center-right Res Publica Party in 2002. Although the party focused most of its electoral program on typical newcomer political issues such as anti-corruption and lower taxes, it also sought to develop its national-conservative credentials by developing close ties with victim groups. On the one hand, this was because some of the more prominent leaders of Res Publica had served on President Meri's staff when he conducted his 2001 remembrance campaign. At the same time, the victim groups themselves appeared interested in engaging with the upstart party. On February 22, 2003 Memento and Res Publica signed a cooperation agreement in which the party pledged to support the adoption of a repressed persons' law should it come to power. By contrast, none of the other mainstream Estonian parties (including the Pro Patria Union) expressed any interest in joining the pledge (Raude 2013).

When Res Publica won a spectacular electoral victory in March 2003 and its chair, Juhan Parts, became prime minister, the new government moved quickly to establish a special expert commission to prepare a consolidated victim status law for Estonia. The commission, which would include several victim organization representatives, drew heavily on proposals already formulated by Memento and other groups (Raude 2013). In early November a bill was introduced in parliament, and in less than four weeks the new Individuals Repressed by Occupation Regimes Act was passed with a huge majority (Eesti Vabariigi Riigikogu 2003). Akin to Lithuania's legislation, Estonia's new law determined a relatively detailed set of repressed persons' categories, some of which were drawn from existing legislation on pensions and other social benefits. (See Table 5.3.) At the same time, the final wording in the law was rather

Table 5.3 *Victim categories in Estonia's repressed persons' status law*

Article 2. Illegally repressed persons

1. Individuals who are victims of genocide, as defined by the 1948 Genocide Convention
2. Individuals who have been imprisoned, deported or placed into a special psychiatric institution for their beliefs, political views, religious confession, racial or ethnic affiliation, citizenship, origin of birth, social status or property standing
3. Individuals who have been imprisoned, deported for having failed to fulfill special duties imposed by the occupying state on its citizens (military conscription, state loyalty, compulsory worldview, proscription on leaving the country)
4. Individuals who have been imprisoned, deported for acts committed before the occupation or during transition periods, except where such acts were punishable under the laws of the Republic of Estonia
5. Individuals who have been imprisoned, deported for their origin or other human characteristics and irrespective of any individual culpability
6. Individuals who have been imprisoned, deported for participation in any protest action against the occupation regime or one stressing a right to national self-determination or attempting to exercise internationally recognized human rights or civil liberties, irrespective of the crime prescribed to it by the occupying state
7. Individuals who have been deported from their permanent place of residence either to territory of either occupying state or to some other state or who after completing their period of punishment were forcibly settled outside of Estonia
8. Individuals who were removed from Estonia in 1941 to work in forced labor battalions in the USSR or who were sent to forced labor outside Estonia during the German occupation
9. Individuals who were subjected to forced labor in the USSR after having been a prisoner of war or a repatriated person

Table 5.3 (*cont.*)

10. Individuals who have been imprisoned or deported for actions committed in self-defense while in hiding from illegal repression, except in cases where such actions would have been punishable under the laws of the Republic of Estonia
11. Individuals who were prohibited from living in Estonia
12. Individuals who were subjected to experimental doses of radiation as part of trial nuclear bomb explosions
13. Individuals who were forcibly sent to clean up areas of nuclear catastrophe
14. Children who were born while their parents were deported or imprisoned, or during the period between the parent's release and their actual opportunity to return to Estonia

Individuals accorded a status equivalent to repressed persons

1. Estonian citizens who participated as of June 16, 1940 in the armed struggle for the restoration of Estonian state independence
2. Estonian citizens who were disabled while having been mobilized or conscripted into the Soviet armed forces and did not participate in the execution of repression on Estonian territory

Compiled from Eesti Vabariigi Riigikogu (2003)

generic. The law defined Estonia's period of occupation rule as having lasted from June 16, 1940 to August 20, 1991; however, its preamble did not mention the occupying states by name, and neither did it delineate the different sub-periods of occupation, as in Lithuania. Even when defining different types of repression that were clearly specific to one occupier or the other, the law made sparse reference to either the Nazi or the Soviet regime. In many ways, therefore, the Estonian approach was a much more legal one, whereas the Lithuanian one was more historical. The Lithuanian law was written in a way that each repressed person could readily find their category among the list of victim types, and indeed the eventual victim certificates that were issued would state the precise sub-paragraph of the law on the basis of which the status was accorded. By contrast, the Estonian law required more focus, as often victims of either Nazi or Soviet repression could find themselves under the same broadly worded provision. Likewise, the Lithuanian law was particular for its differentiation across political prisoners, deportees and other repressed persons. The Estonian legislation made no such distinction.

Needless to say, the Estonian law denied repressed person's status to any individual who had themselves engaged in acts of repression.

However, again the law was more basic in its terminology as it excluded anyone who had worked in an agency that had carried out any of the repressions listed in its victim categories. The only more specific exclusion was in regard to anyone who had been a member of the Soviet Communist Party before January 1, 1954, or had been drafted into the Red Army as a Communist Party member or into the *Wehrmacht* as a NSDAP member. The law stated that all those who had been rehabilitated based on earlier legislation were automatically eligible for repressed persons' status. At the same time, it limited future victim eligibility to those who had been Estonian citizens at the time of their repression. The measure did not allow for posthumous recognition, as its primary focus was on defining those individuals who would be eligible for specific social benefits.

Equally characteristic of the Estonian approach was the fact that the law delegated the procedural aspect of the new framework completely to the government. In a separate government decree, the Parts cabinet designated the Social Insurance Board, or the main social welfare administration agency in Estonia, as the body responsible for determining applicants' eligibility for repressed persons' status. This decision mirrored Estonia's previously existing approach to dealing with the rehabilitated and their benefits, as most of their eligibility rules had up until then been incorporated into pension laws and other such legislation. One consequence of this approach, however, was that no victims' groups were engaged in the process, nor were any special ceremonies developed for awarding the new status. At the same time, alongside the formal certificate of acknowledgment handed over to a recipient, the person was also bestowed with a lapel pin of a broken cornflower, echoing President Meri's 2001 remembrance campaign. Estonia would in this respect be the only Baltic country to offer their victims a physical symbol of their status that they could wear publicly.

As noted earlier, Estonia's repressed persons' Act served in part to consolidate many of the pension and other benefits that had been previously scattered across other legislation. For example, already as of 1992 individuals who had been imprisoned as part of their repression were eligible for a pension up to five years earlier than the nominal age. In 1993, as part of housing privatization, former deportees and political prisoners of the Soviet regime were given triple the value of privatization vouchers for each year spent as a victim of repression. A similar coefficient would later be used for calculating a person's employment history as part of determining their old-age pension. Lastly, Estonia's 2003 repressed persons' law would establish a number of new benefits such as providing each certified victim a yearly payment of €160, with which they could pay for wellness or other medical treatments. Repressed persons were also allowed to visit once a year a special rehabilitation center run by the Ministry of Defense. Repressed persons could equally receive free entrance to state museums and free tickets to the national Song and Dance Festival held every five years.

Although on the whole Estonia's benefits for repressed persons were far less extensive than in Lithuania (not least because benefits would not extend to the relatives of the repressed), the enactment of the 2003 law did represent an additional yearly budgetary expense of around €2 million (alongside the extra pensions that already existed). Originally the law was expected to affect about 25,000 rehabilitated and other repressed people. Of these, some 19,000 were already pensioners, approximately 4,000 were not yet of pension age, while 1,700 were individuals born during deportation or captivity (Vaher and Pärna 2003). These numbers declined over the years, such that in 2012, for example, only 11,647 individuals applied for the yearly medical treatment benefit. In all, only 15,851 people applied for the repressed persons' certificate, two-thirds of them during the first year of the law (Raude 2013).

Transitional justice measures for later Soviet victims

Within the victim status laws outlined in the previous section, one can see that to some degree the Baltic states have also acknowledged individuals who suffered repression during later years of Soviet rule – what we have termed transitional justice victim categories or Box 5b of our matrix. Two of the more prominent victim categories concern men conscripted into the Soviet Army in order to fight in Afghanistan from 1979 to 1988, and men conscripted by the Soviets to participate in the clean-up of the Chernobyl nuclear power plant explosion in April 1986. Both Lithuania and Estonia accord official victim status to these individuals; Latvia has adopted social welfare laws for Chernobyl clean-up victims, but nothing at all for Afghanistan fighters (Kārkliņa 2011).

Additionally, Lithuania has declared as victims those who suffered injury or were killed while serving as conscripts in the Soviet Army during the entire period from 1945 to 1991. In all, 1,639 Lithuanians were killed during military service in the Soviet Army (either in Afghanistan, Chernobyl or elsewhere in the USSR) and 2,431 were injured (Balynienė and Buškevičienė 2001). In July 1994, the Seimas passed a law according special pensions to these individuals, and in instances of their death, one-time compensation payments to their families (Lietuvos Respublikos Seimas 1994a).[3] In 2004 the government revamped these regulations, and in 2012 the Seimas enacted still another category of late-Soviet victims: men who from 1990 to 1991 had suffered while trying to evade conscription in the Soviet Army after Lithuania had declared itself re-independent (Lietuvos Respublikos Seimas 2012). These individuals were also offered a one-time payment of up to 4,000 litas (€1,158).

Indeed, this focus on identifying people as Soviet victims even after Lithuania had become nominally independent is unique to the Baltic states. It was manifested even more so in January 1991, when barely three days after Soviet troops killed thirteen civilians during an assault on the Vilnius television tower, the Lithuanian Supreme Council immediately passed a law according survivors pensions and other social benefits to the family members of the deceased (Lietuvos Respublikos Aukščiausioji Taryba 1991a). Over the years, this victim category would be expanded to include over 500 people who suffered injuries and handicaps during that attack and subsequent events. For instance, many individuals would complain of hearing loss after Soviet troops set off grenades and other ammunition during the assault. In January 1992 parliament approved one-time compensation payments for these people along with other benefits such as a 50 percent reduction in housing rents and utility fees, all to be paid for by the government. Eight years later, the Seimas passed another law officially according these people repressed persons' status (Lietuvos Respublikos Seimas 2000). As we will note later in Chapter 6, January has become a month of remembrance concerning these events in Lithuania, often prompting politicians to propose still further proclamations and recognitions. In Latvia, where Soviet troops also killed civilians during an attempted crackdown, the government has merely awarded commemorative medals to those who manned the "barricades" around prominent government buildings during two weeks of tense stand-off.

Overall, the different stages and strands of rehabilitation policy in the Baltic states can be seen in Table 5.4. These dates and figures tell a story

[3] One of main promoters of this bill was a special victims organization, the Lithuanian Union of Soldiers Mothers (*Lietuvos kareivių motinų sąjunga*).

Table 5.4 *Major victim-oriented policies in the Baltic states*

	Estonia	Latvia	Lithuania
1. Adoption of initial rehabilitation legislation	December 7, 1988	June 8, 1989	October 21, 1988
2. Approximate number of initial rehabilitations	approx. 10,000	approx. 10,000	>50,000
3. Adoption of second-stage rehabilitation legislation	February 19, 1990 February 19, 1992	August 3, 1990	May 2, 1990
4. Adoption of "resistance fighter" legislation	*None*	April 25, 1996	October 16, 1991
5. Adoption of repressed persons' status legislation	December 17, 2003	May 13, 1992 April 12, 1995	June 30, 1997
6. Approximate number of certified repressed persons	15,851	16,670 *(USSR)* 1,896 *(Nazi)*	over 83,000
7. Adoption of legislation for victims of January 1991 events	*None*	April 29, 1999	January 16, 1991 January 4, 2000

Sources: Baltic legislation

of how the issue of providing legal recognition and compensation for victims of past repression emerged onto the political agenda much earlier than in the case of any other truth and justice measure. At the same time, the table indicates how these policies would undergo change, evolving from largely declarative steps in the late 1980s to more structured and administratively serviceable measures following re-independence. In large measure, these policies would reflect how importantly past suffering under the Soviet and Nazi regimes would be acknowledged. The number of victim categories (compare Tables 5.1–5.3), as well as the level of benefits accorded such individuals, serve here as a good indicator. On both counts we see that Lithuania far surpasses the other two Baltic states. As we will discuss later in the Conclusion, part of this is clearly a function of the greater historical degree of repression in Lithuania (thanks largely to the two waves of deportation in the country in 1948 and 1949, and the more extended anti-Soviet partisan struggle of the late 1940s). However, these policies also reflect political choices that have been driven sometimes by political lobbying, but mostly by electoral maneuvering by political parties. Victims groups have been present in all three countries, and they have often been included in both policy development and policy implementation. However, they have not been strong enough to shape policy on their own. The decreasing size of their membership rolls has also limited their political influence. Rather, major policy initiatives in the areas of rehabilitation and compensation appear to have taken place as a result of political parties seeking to demonstrate their commitment to victim-oriented measures more broadly. Proposals to expand victim categories or their benefits concern not only the victims themselves but also the population at large in terms of the message such initiatives send to the public about what politicians are willing to focus state resources on. That Estonia has been least active in this regard, and Lithuania most active, adds another piece to our composite picture of truth and justice policies in the Baltic states.

Property restitution

Property restitution, or the return of real estate and other property nationalized or confiscated by a previous regime to its original owners or their descendants, is frequently overlooked by scholars as an integral part of transitional or retrospective justice. On the one hand, the loss of mere material possessions often pales in comparison with the terror, murder or other repression experienced as part of the past. As a result, justice is seen as more incumbent in terms of punishing the specific perpetrators of repression and acknowledging their immediate victims, whereas more indirect injustices such as the loss of a home, livestock or land during the course of that repression can be dealt with in a second instance.[4] Additionally, in the post-communist context, property restitution has often been treated within the framework of housing privatization or in other words merely as a part of the overall restructuring of housing after the collapse of socialism (Fisher and Jaffe 2000; Tsenkova

[4] For a broader discussion of how socio-economic issues are nonetheless becoming more and more a formal part of transitional justice, see Waldorf (2012).

and Turner 2004). Here, the analytical focus has been on how property restitution hinders or facilitates the establishment of a vibrant and free property market. Lastly, there have been examinations of the property restitution from the standpoint of international law, especially where restitution issues have reached European courts or have involved foreign nationals (Karadjova 2004; Koleva 2007).

However, when we take as our perspective the politics of the past, we see that property restitution is often an important field of contention for victims, politicians and state institutions (Offe 1997). It involves not only a formal righting of wrongs for those from whom property was taken but also a challenging battleground for politicians to navigate in terms of public opinion. Moreover, of all the political-administrative dimensions of transitional or retrospective justice, property restitution represents for state institutions the most complicated and resource-demanding of policy domains, since it requires years of administrative processing, frequent adjudication of disputes and long-term monitoring of social consequences.

There are two interrelated facets of property restitution that make it a very particular dimension of transitional or retrospective justice. First, the category of perpetrator is not as clear as with physical repression. There is no single individual who can be identified (much less put on trial) for having issued a nationalization decree or for having carried out an order to confiscate a person's property. Without this half of the perpetrator–victim pair, the impulse for justice is less strong. Secondly, property restitution is a domain that can often create new injustice, in cases where property has in the meantime been handed over to others and those individuals have come to rely on that property for their housing or livelihood. Where this property is then handed back to its original owners, large-scale social consequences may ensue that need further rectification or smoothing out. In other words, property restitution can engender its own class of victims, which confounds still further the notion of justice and its proper implementation.

In contrast to authoritarianism or post-authoritarianism, communism and post-communism are especially likely to exhibit dilemmas of property restitution, since communism was a socio-economic ideology that aimed to even out wealth in society and therefore had a special proclivity to resort to widespread nationalization or property redistribution. This does not make property restitution a foregone conclusion since, as mentioned, the very fact that property has been redistributed means that it must be taken away from the person to whom it has been bestowed; and depending on how long that individual has had it, the complications of property restitution and the likelihood that new suffering will be inflicted will grow. This is precisely why, however, the variety of outcomes that we see in terms of possible property restitution in post-communist Central and Eastern Europe has proved intriguing to many scholars (Blacksell and Born 2002; Kuti 2009).

The Baltic states represented a seemingly easy case of dealing with property restitution, since the act of property nationalization – as carried out by the newly installed Soviet authorities in the summer and autumn of 1940 – was clear-cut and reasonably well documented, in contrast to, say, the Czech Republic or Hungary, where more uneven or multiple rounds of property redistribution were enacted (Fisher and Jaffe 2000; Blacksell and Born 2002; Stan 2006; Nalepa 2009b). A much more vexing aspect of this issue was that the time span since this communist nationalization had occurred was longer than in most of the Central and East European states. Moreover, war had not only ravaged part of this property but also displaced many of its owners, in some cases into exile in the West. Lastly, a new wave of property confiscation and loss occurred with the large-scale deportations of the late 1940s, an added layer of complexity that we have already touched upon in this chapter under the rubric of rehabilitation.

Against the backdrop of these overall circumstances, it is therefore striking to note the significant differences across the three Baltic states in terms of how they have approached the notion of property restitution. In contrast to the trend we see in other domains of our transitional and retrospective justice matrix, Lithuania emerges as a surprisingly mild case of property restitution, especially in terms of the amount of residential housing restituted to owners. Moreover, the Lithuanian state has taken on a major role in resolving problems arising from restitution, most importantly the dilemma of what to do with individuals living in restituted apartment buildings, often called "forced renters." Estonia and Latvia, by contrast, have taken a much more vigorous stance in terms of returning residential property. Likewise, they have adopted fewer alleviating measures for forced renters.

Table 5.5 summarizes the main policies and outcomes of property restitution in the Baltic states. In addition to basic information on legislative provisions, we present data on the number of restitution claims filed, the number of final government decisions made, the number of properties returned and the amount of compensation paid out. Data for all three countries across all of the indicators is not always

Table 5.5 *Property restitution provisions and outcomes in the Baltic states*

	Estonia	Latvia	Lithuania
1. Date of adoption of major property restitution legislation	December 19, 1990	October 30, 1991	1st round: June 18, 1991/July 16, 1991 2nd round: July 1, 1997
2. Claimants' eligibility rules	Former owners and immediate heirs; civil society and religious organizations	Former owners and immediate heirs; legal persons Later expanded under land restitution to include all relatives, privileging first-order relatives	Former owners and immediate heirs Originally, claimant needed to be citizen of Lithuania and permanent resident; later limited to just citizenship
3. Deadlines for claims	December 31, 1991	June 1, 1994 for houses; continually extended for land claims	March 31, 1992, later December 31, 2001
4. Number of individuals who submitted claims (claimants)	*c.* 240,000	Residential properties: *c.* 23,000 Land: Data not available	Residential properties: 9,631 Land: 835,360
5. Number of claimants declared valid	233,237	Residential properties: 14,151 Land: Data not available	Residential properties: 6,817 Land: 803,436
6. Number of property objects claimed (cases)	132,398	Residential properties: 22,152 Land: Data not available	Residential properties: 3,000 (est.) Land: 866,657
7. Number of positive decisions (restitution and/or compensation)	129,422 (97.7%)	15,138 (69.9%) Land: Data not available	Residential properties: Data not available Land: 833,240 (%?)
8. Number of buildings claimed	43,512	Residential properties: 11,850 Land: Data not available	Residential properties: 2,849
9. Number of apartment buildings and apartments returned	*c.* 6,000 Apartments : *c.* 25,000	10,321 Apartments: 78,046	*c.* 1,200 Apartments: *c.* 7,150
10. Percentage of dwelling stock affected by restitution	2.6%	7%	0.7%

Table 5.5 (*cont.*)

	Estonia		Latvia	Lithuania	
11. Amount of land returned or compensated, ha	Returned: Resid. plots: 3,148 Land, forest: 1,428,133	Compensated: Resid. plots: 11,205 Land: 1,139,470	Data not available	Returned: Urban land: 7,210 Rural land: 3,342,652	Compensated: Urban land: 22,805 Rural land: 647,807
12. Percentage of land area involved in restitution	57.1%		Data not available	62.3%	
13. Number of 'forced renters'	*c.* 75,000		*c.* 230,000	*c.* 30,000	
14. Provisions that rule out restitution of property in kind	If property rebuilt or changed by more than 75%		If property rebuilt or changed by more than 65%	If residential dwelling was rebuilt or changed by more than 50%, commercial property by 60%; if residential dwelling rebuilt into a new institution (e.g. kindergarten); if land is under infrastructural project, a military establishment, public facility, gardeners' society, state park, state agricultural firm, or has been sold to *bona fide* owner. No more than 150 ha of land may be restituted in kind.	
15. Forms of compensation	Privatization certificates that could be later sold on the stock market		Privatization certificates that could be later sold on the stock market	A replacement piece of land or property; a new plot of land for home construction; canceling other debts to the state; privatization securities; cash.	
16. Amount of compensation paid out	€8,251,995 in privatization certificates		Data not available	Budget allocations for eviction of tenant families LTL thousand, 4,362,428 Lt (€1,264, 472)	

Table 5.5 (*cont.*)

	Estonia	Latvia	Lithuania
17. Eviction limitations	8 years	7 years Owners cannot evict the disabled, pensioners or repressed persons unless alternative housing is found.	1991 law: 10 years 1997: Owner must sign rental agreement with municipality, which then sublets apartments to existing renters; rent is paid by the local government and compensated by the state.
18. Rent control	Until December 2004	Until January 1, 2007	No legal specification in law
19. Forced renters' rights	Forced renters can apply for social housing in their local government, housing credits from the state. If the restituted dwelling is sold on, tenants shall have right to buy first. Renters can apply for privatization of vacant dwellings by a right of pre-emption.	Forced renters can apply for social housing in their local government. From 2006–2009 forced renters could apply for state and local government aid to make a down payment for alternative housing.	Forced renters can apply for: alternative housing in their local government; a free plot of land to build a new home; joining a housing construction cooperative; housing credit. If the restituted dwelling is sold on, tenants shall have right to buy first.
20. Other status quo restrictions		If property is a medical facility or cultural establishment, owner must allow it to continue to operate.	Owner must keep agricultural land or forests in use.

Sources: Estonia: Strauss (2013), Lux et al. (2012); Latvia: Bogdanova (2007), Latvijas Republikas Centrālā statistikas pārvalde (2013), Tsenkova (2000); Lithuania: Lietuvos statistikos departamentas (2013), Nacionalinė žemės tarnyba (2013a, 2013b), Andruškevičiūtė (2008); and relevant restitution legislation.

possible to obtain. For example, Latvia has no aggregated statistics about its process of land restitution.[5] As a result, information about the number of claims and the amount of compensation issued is incomplete. At the same time, since much of the social aspect of property restitution has involved the return of apartment houses and the emergence of forced renters, statistics about this dimension of the process have been more thorough.

Examining Table 5.5 more closely, it would appear at first glance that the overall picture is rather mixed. For example, property restitution in Lithuania ended up involving an astounding 62.3% of the country's territory, which was 5% more than in Estonia. Similarly, whereas some 24% of the population in Lithuania submitted a claim for restitution, only 17.5% did so in Estonia. At the same time, Estonia and Latvia differed considerably from Lithuania in terms of the restitution of residential housing. The number of restituted apartment buildings and apartments in these two countries was several times that in Lithuania. Moreover, when one renders these amounts as a percentage of the national dwelling stock in 1995[6] (making the three countries directly comparable), one sees that not even 1% of Lithuanian housing was affected by residential property restitution, whereas in Estonia this figure was roughly 2.6% and in Latvia some 7%. Moreover, in large cities this percentage was dramatically higher, particularly in Latvia. According to the Latvian Central Statistical Bureau, the proportion of dwelling stock affected by residential property restitution in larger cities was 12.3%, and in Riga the figure was nearly 16%. Indeed, in the Latvian capital the more affluent downtown area was especially affected, with fully 56.7% of the dwelling stock being subject to restitution (Latvijas Republikas Centrālā statistikas pārvalde 2003: 10). Correspondingly, the number of "victims" of restitution, that is, forced renters or individuals threatened by eviction by restituted owners, has been much greater in Estonia and Latvia. Based on the number of apartments restituted or the number of households

5 Personal communication, Judīte Mierkalne, State Land Service of the Republic of Latvia, January 7, 2014.

6 This year is chosen since it reflected the high point of when restitution claims were submitted as well as the size of the dwelling stock at that moment. Other sources (Latvijas Republikas Centrālā statistikas pārvalde 2003) measure the magnitude of residential property restitution as a percentage of the dwelling stock for later years, e.g. 2003. However, this underestimates the actual context in which restitution played itself out, since by the mid-2000s lots of new private residential housing had been built (thus distorting the baseline comparison).

reported in official statistics to be affected by restitution, we estimate the number of forced renters in Estonia, Latvia and Lithuania to be 75,000, 230,000 and 30,000, respectively. These figures, again, range from just 1% of the population in Lithuania to nearly 10% in Latvia.

To explain some of these divergences, we can see already in Table 5.5 that Lithuania stemmed the consequences of restitution by restricting the eligibility of claimants initially to only those individuals who were citizens of Lithuania and also permanent residents. This meant that a majority of émigré Lithuanians (who had fled the country during World War II and abandoned property nationalized already in 1940 or seized by the Nazis) would be prevented from participating in the first wave of restitution policy in the early 1990s. Only after the adoption of a new restitution framework in 1997 would this situation ease, as the permanent residency requirement was dropped. To gauge the significance of this particular provision, it is worth noting applicable statistics from Latvia and Estonia, where no citizenship or residency restrictions applied. According to official figures, only 73.3% of restituted residential property owners in Latvia lived in the country at the moment of restitution, and they controlled only 67.6% of the returned properties. Fully 11% of owners lived in the United States and some 3% each in Australia, Israel and Canada (Latvijas Republikas Centrālā statistikas pārvalde 2003: 9–10). Likewise in Estonia, 5.8% of those eventually declared legitimate claimants had non-Estonian citizenship (Strauss 2013: 14). Hence, it is likely that a sizable number of former owners in Lithuania were deterred from restitution by the special legal requirements.

Additionally, Lithuania established from the very beginning many more stringent ground rules for approving the actual return of former property. First, the Lithuanian parliament established a wide range of property categories, which could not be restituted in kind; these included land used by state agricultural firms as well as land under public facilities. Second, certain types of property could be restituted only if the restituted owner agreed to maintain the property in its current function. Hence, for example, agricultural land had to be kept in use, as did forests. Third, if owners received back a residential property and they wanted to take up an apartment within that building, they were required to relinquish whatever state apartment they happened to be renting at that moment, and as a consequence they would not be able to privatize that state apartment (and add it to their restituted property) once large-scale housing privatization began. Instead, the two types of property were implicitly seen as linked; the return of state property was seen as a *quid pro quo* for the restitution of nationalized property. No such provisions ever existed in Estonia or Latvia. Fourth, the Lithuanian state inserted itself as an active participant in the process of residential property restitution. Under the country's second restitution law, from 1997, it was established that if an owner were given back a dwelling house with existing tenants, he or she would conclude a rental agreement with the local municipality, and the municipality would sublet the dwelling's apartments free of charge to their current occupants (Lietuvos Respublikos Seimas 1997e). In this way, the state placed itself in-between the restituted owner and the forced renters instead of leaving them to work out their relations in a private context. Needless to say, this was meant to protect the rights of renters better than simply establishing eviction restrictions or rent control provisions as in Estonia and Latvia. However, it would also put an administrative burden on municipalities and a financial burden on the state, as the law said that the state would pay the rent of forced renters for an initial period following restitution. Lastly, Lithuania developed a broader set of forms of compensation, which may have proved more attractive to many claimants than the physical return of erstwhile property. Namely, lawful claimants could choose to apply instead for an alternative piece of land on which to build a house or engage in other activities. They could also use their claim to cancel any debts they had with the state.

In a word, the Lithuanian approach to property restitution involved seeing this property as just one part of the larger re-shuffle that was about to take place with privatization. Where possible, the difficulties of restitution could be resolved using more fungible resources from the rest of property reform. By extension, property restitution was not seen as a principle in itself, but rather as a right that would be accorded to the extent that other circumstances and considerations permitted. By contrast, Estonia and Latvia viewed restitution as a fundamental point of departure, and only after this injustice had been cleared could the rest of property reform be carried out. This did not mean that privatization would be delayed until all restitution claims were processed. However, it did mean that where former property was claimed, these applications would be processed with a view to restoring that property in kind, especially in the case of residential houses.

The general stringency with which Estonia and Latvia carried out property restitution has been explained with reference to the countries' strong sense of nationalism toward the end of the Soviet era (Grūtups and Krastiņš 1995; Andersen 1997; Feldman 1999; Lux et al. 2012). The desire to right the Soviet wrongs would therefore seem to have been stronger in these countries if restitution had such far-reaching consequences. Yet, as we have seen elsewhere in this book, Lithuania actually comes out as stronger across almost all of the other justice categories we identify. Hence, why didn't this fervor carry over to the realm of property restitution? The answers lie on both sides of the equation, meaning that certain factors goaded the Estonians and Latvians to follow a stricter path, whereas other circumstances also curbed restorationist sentiment in Lithuania.

On the one hand, all three Baltic countries have professed to be sovereign states that have continued to exist since 1920, but had simply a prolonged period of illegal foreign occupation from 1940 to 1990. This stance, known as the doctrine of legal continuity, was widely followed during the re-independence struggle, and it became the basis for a further doctrine of legal restorationism that aimed to achieve a maximum degree of restoring the *status quo ante* in each country from before the Soviet takeover. This principle was seen as a bulwark against any attempt to pull the countries back into the Soviet or Russian orbit or to make them susceptible in any way to the legacies of the USSR. In this vein, all three Baltic countries formally declared a *restoration* of their independence in 1990 and rejected any views that they were creating new states or even French-style Second or Third republics. However, the difference between Estonia and Latvia, on the one hand, and Lithuania, on the other, is that in the first two countries broad-scale political movements existed that militated for these doctrines much more than was ever the case in Lithuania. The Citizens Committees in both Estonia and Latvia never became as dominant as the more moderate Popular Fronts would. However, from the standpoint of imbuing a more pronounced adherence to the principle of legal continuity and restorationism, the Estonian and Latvian Citizens Committees would give the respective nationalist sentiment in their countries a very special hue that would go on to have an important effect in terms of prompting politicians to implement strident restorationism also in relation to nationalized property.

Meanwhile, in Lithuania the restitutionist sentiment was tempered by the different kind of cleavage that existed in that country's political realm. Instead of having moderate and radical nationalist forces, the key dividing line was between anti-communists and ex-communists. Needless to say, at some point the former could have triumphed over the latter and then carried out more strident restitution. Indeed, this is what Vytautas Landsbergis aimed to do across so many areas of transitional and retrospective justice while in power from 1990 to 1992. Hence, the first property restitution law passed in 1991 did seek to sanctify a principle of restoration. However, even within this law a number of provisions were not as stringent as those in Estonia and Latvia. Moreover, this initial framework would be considerably softened from 1993 to 1996, when the ex-communist LDDP would be in power and would adopt a number of amendments in favor of forced renters and other affected groups. For example, after just a few months in office the LDDP-dominated parliament changed the restitution law to say that apartment buildings could be returned to former owners only if existing tenants "consent[ed] to move, at their own will, by settling on a dwelling unit allotted to them" (Lietuvos Respublikos Seimas 1993a). The decision was meant to toughen the pre-existing provision in the law that said that tenants needed merely to be informed of their rights to seek alternative housing if their apartment was being restituted. As a result of the ex-communists' amendment, the entire restitution process now seemed to be at the behest of the tenants. This prompted the first in a series of Constitutional Court challenges launched by Andrius Kubilius, a leader of the Homeland Union-Lithuanian Conservatives (TS-LK), seeking to keep restitution going.

In June 1994 the Court agreed with Kubilius, saying that allowing tenants such a degree of discretion would violate the constitutional principle of private property. At the same time, the Court stressed that the right to property was not absolute, especially when it involved housing. "Tenants must not bear the obligation assumed by the state with regard to the former owners," said the Court, hinting that lawmakers needed to find another solution (Constitutional Court of the Republic of Lithuania 1994). In a later ruling from 1995, the Court intoned, "When solving the ownership right restoration problems, one should pursue the provision of the preamble of the Constitution which states that the Lithuanian nation strives for an open, just, and harmonious civil society and law-governed State'" (Constitutional Court of the Republic of Lithuania 1995). The Court therefore acknowledged the state's right to modify restitution procedures in the name of broader equity. It also stressed in several rulings that what the state was providing through restitution was merely the restoration of abstract property rights. The form in which that property would actually be restored remained at the discretion of lawmakers. Hence, if certain former owners were required by the state to accept compensation (and were denied the in kind restitution of their property), this could not be viewed as a violation of their property rights, since technically that property as worth has been returned. The Court used this same logic to uphold a set of June 1993 amendments to the restitution law, which required individuals getting back agricultural land to provide for its continued agricultural use either by farming it themselves or renting it out to a certified farmer.

When in late 1996 the center-right TS-LK returned to power, an effort was undertaken to revamp the country's restitution legislation given the fact that successive LDDP amendments as well as nearly a dozen Constitutional Court rulings had left the procedure looking like Swiss cheese. In their final version of the legislation, the conservatives acknowledged the many different Constitutional Court rulings that had set parameters for revisiting the policy. As a way of resolving the most serious conundrum between residential property owners and their forced renters, the law mandated (as mentioned earlier) that municipalities would sublet from owners any apartments occupied by existing tenants until such time as the municipality would be able to provide these renters with alternative housing. The law also rewrote the entire way in which the state would buy out land, forests, water bodies, commercial property and residential buildings as part of compensation. Lastly, in line with the conservatives' other new policy of exalting certain victim categories (already covered in this chapter), the law established special provisions for the restitution of homesteads and farms to former participants in the armed resistance movement and their descendants.

Two important historical parameters also bear mention when comparing the Baltic states across property restitution policy. First, because Lithuania's borders were variously shifted during 1939–40 (both via the seizure of Memel-Klaipėda by the Nazis in 1939 and via the return of Vilnius and the Vilnius region to Lithuania from Poland after the Soviet annexation), an important part of the property nationalization carried out by the Soviets in 1940 would concern German, Jewish or Polish owners, the majority of whom would disappear from the country during World War II. After Lithuanian national independence was restored in 1991, property restitution for these groups would become politically sensitive. Citizenship and residency requirements were one way of getting around these claimants. At the same time, Jewish groups continued to seek the return of their religious or community property, a settlement for which was finally reached in 2012. In Estonia and Latvia, the question of whether to allow some of the Baltic Germans, who had left these countries in 1939–40 in advance of the Soviet takeover, to claim back properties they had relinquished in haste arose on occasion. But no real political debate ensued.

Second, the impression that one gets from Table 5.5 that Latvia was more strident than Estonia in returning nationalized residential housing (for example, as a percentage of its national housing stock) masks the fact that a significant share of Estonia's housing was destroyed during World War II and therefore this property could only be compensated, not restituted. Particularly in cities like Tartu, Pärnu and Narva (as well as part of Tallinn), entire neighborhoods were lost to either Soviet or Nazi bombing and shelling. Had these properties remained, the number of restituted houses as well as forced renters would have undoubtedly been higher.

Comparative summary

The broader literature on transitional justice has often pointed to the fact that democratic politicians have an easier time passing and administering measures aimed at redressing the suffering of victims of a past regime than they do in identifying and punishing perpetrators from such regimes (Grodsky 2011). The Baltic cases profiled here underscore this overall conclusion, especially as concerns the vast array of victim categories enumerated in many of the rehabilitation and other laws adopted in Estonia, Latvia and Lithuania. As we outlined in Chapter 2, the Baltic states have a particular historical landscape, in which Stalinist terror involved not only political repression but also wholesale deportations of tens of thousands of people to far-off Siberian camps and resettlement areas. In this respect, the political impulse to acknowledge and compensate this suffering was only to be expected. Yet, we have also seen stark differences in the way in which Estonia, Latvia and Lithuania have resolved this impulse. Quite remarkable has been the way in which in Estonia not only has there been little political mobilization around the issue of repressed persons, but also the administrative procedures adopted in order to carry out repressed persons' policy have been relatively technocratic and closely linked to general social welfare policy. To put it starkly, it would seem that repressed people in Estonia are just one more welfare group among all others. There has been little in terms of imbuing victims with a more substantive political-administrative status. By the time a move in this direction was undertaken (in 2003), the effect was limited, since more than ten years had passed since the last rehabilitation legislation had been enacted. Inevitably, victim numbers had greatly declined by then.

By contrast, victim issues have been a recurrent political theme in Lithuania, in part because of controversies involving the rehabilitation of people who may have actually committed repressive acts, but also because of clear political engagement on the part of both right- and left-wing political parties that has caused both victim categories and benefits to be continually expanded. All of these measures are also distinctly more institutionalized through the work of special government bodies as well as the involvement of victim groups. Latvia, in this respect, has equally sought to work together with victims groups by appointing their representatives to the review boards that certify the status of victims. However, the decentralized nature of this policy (up until 2011) has meant that the overall level of state involvement has been modest. Moreover, while Latvia was the first of the three Baltic states to adopt a comprehensive victim status law (already in 1992), this pioneer status also showed in the fact that its legislation would be the sketchiest.

By contrast, both Estonia and Latvia have devoted considerable political attention and government resources to the policy of property restitution. Very institutionalized procedures were adopted in Estonia already in the early 1990s, and these were largely completed by the mid-2000s. Latvia has seen many more fits and starts, especially in terms of synchronizing restitution with the parallel process of housing and land privatization. Still, in both countries the policy has been about not only recompensing victims of Soviet nationalization but also cleaning away the socialist past. Restitution had a strong symbolic value in terms of helping to exalt the return of private property as a part of "normal" society. Although what was one person's return to normality was often another's pitch into uncertainty (as a forced renter), these consequences were somehow weathered politically. Major reversals such as in Lithuania did not result. Moreover, it is worthwhile noting that one reason why property restitution did not gain much traction in Lithuania is that although the fault lines on this issue were again archetypically drawn between ex-communists and anti-communists, this time the Constitutional Court sided more or less with the ex-communists (in contrast to its stance on, say, lustration issues). Therefore, even when the center-right returned to power in Lithuania in 1996, it was not able to carry out a large-scale reversal in this area of justice, as it would in many others.

6

Official recognition of victims: non-judicial truth-seeking and commemoration

On the occasion of the sixtieth anniversary of the June 1941 deportation, Estonia's President Lennart Meri launched a campaign, during which he would travel the country and personally hand over "symbolic mourning tokens" in the form of a broken cornflower (the Estonian national flower) to individuals who had been repressed by the Soviet regime. Over the course of two weeks, Meri visited each of the fifteen counties of Estonia to share in local commemorative ceremonies, shake hands with former deportees and call on people to remember and unite. This highly symbolic gesture of recognition by a state representative (in fact, the head of state) sent a strong message to the victims of Stalinist repression that their experiences would not be forgotten. Moreover, it encouraged them to share their memories with a society that seemed increasingly uninterested in the stories of former deportees, political prisoners and other victims of Stalinism (Anepaio 2002). In turn, the president opened a competition for young people to interview and collect stories from people who had suffered under the Soviet regime. The contest was supported by a €30,000 grant from the Estonian government and received widespread media coverage (Marmei 2001). By the end of his campaign, President Meri had personally bestowed broken cornflower pins on 6,660 people. Another 3,000 people applied for the pin, but were unable to attend their regional ceremony and were presented with their honor later by the county governor. Two years later the emblem was made into the official token for certifying a person's special "victim status" following a revamping of Estonia's victim status laws (see Chapter 5).

In turning to the last box of our analytical matrix, this chapter will discuss the politics of truth and justice involving state-led policies that aim at providing official, yet largely symbolic and non-material recognition to victims of past regime repression. Recognition campaigns like the one launched by President Meri in Estonia as well as other state-sponsored acts of remembrance and truth-seeking can be powerful signals to a society with a history of mass atrocities and state abuse, conveying that the wrongdoings of the previous regime have not been forgotten, and neither have their immediate victims. Indeed, the essence of this analytical category is that it deals with "the lingering political, social, moral and psychological after-effects" of mass crimes (Nollendorfs 2010: 1). Where material compensation for victims is limited and retributive justice against former wrongdoers is difficult to achieve due to legal limitations, political wranglings or lack of resources, symbolic measures of recognition directed at the victims can still contribute to restoring a sense of justice and to fostering public trust in the moral standing of the new government. Such a wish was certainly reflected in Meri's 2001 campaign when he insisted that this was not so much about mourning the past, but about a sense of citizenship in the future. Through remembering, Estonians should learn to appreciate their rights but also their obligations toward each other as citizens and the "Broken Cornflower should first and foremost reunite [Estonians]" (Meri 2001).

The campaign of 2001 exemplifies several important features of Baltic symbolic truth and justice processes as they evolved over the past two decades. First, it shows how state policies directed at individual victims can strongly overlap with state measures that aim at the nation at large. As we discussed earlier with regard to measures falling within our conceptual matrix in Boxes 6a and 6b, the analytical distinction between victim-targeted symbolic truth and justice policies and the broader politics of memory that fosters national identity and unity in a post-repression state context is often difficult to make. Indeed, while the Broken Cornflower campaign was about giving recognition to individuals quite literally by pinning a token to their chests, it simultaneously aimed at a much broader audience, the Estonian nation, and at remembering its victimization under foreign rule and occupation. To be sure, Meri's personal approach to the campaign was yet more differentiated as he reminded people of the fact that many Estonians had been among those who had assisted in the deportations, benefited from a neighbor's expropriation or simply turned a blind eye to fellow citizens' fates (Meri 2001). Still, as we will show in this chapter, Baltic policies of truth establishment and remembrance have often been concerned less with revealing complexity or with reconstructing the fate of individuals than with assessing and remembering the aggregate suffering of the entire nation under Soviet occupation. The latter, in turn, can serve broader political purposes, such as to reject allegations of co-responsibility, demand international recognition or make claims for reparation, as we will see in Chapter 7.

We will therefore try to keep issues of transitional and retrospective truth and justice separate from those involving the politics of collective remembering and national identity construction. To give an example, legislation and policies that promote investigations into past mass atrocities and human rights violations by a previous regime always involve a degree of recognition of those whose lives were destroyed and/or rights violated. Therefore, they belong within our analytical category of symbolic truth and justice. However, measures that prohibit the denial or trivialization of past regime crimes or governmental acts that intervene in public remembrance by dismantling monuments or renaming streets that carry names of the previous abusive regime's leaders constitute cases of memory politics. They are legislating how the nation is supposed to remember. Admittedly, such a sharp distinction is not always possible to draw; thus, our chapter will inevitably include measures that imply a collective target and shape public remembrance, when, for example, they help foster an image of a victim-nation or they speak of the nation's heroism in resistance. However, they are also always victim measures, with specific individuals behind them.

A second core feature of Baltic symbolic truth and justice processes that is embodied by the Meri campaign of 2001 is its highlighting of the predominantly retrospective character of state policies aimed at truth-seeking and remembrance. The main targets of the campaign were the remaining former victims of Stalin-era mass repression (mostly former deportees), not those individuals who had suffered for their political convictions in later decades of Soviet rule. Within our analytical matrix we thus see a clear preference by Baltic policy-makers and social actors to focus more on the distant Stalinist period of mass crimes (Box 6a) than on the later years of Soviet rule (Box 6b).

Finally, the fact that the Broken Cornflower campaign was initiated ten years after independence had been restored and became the instigator of a new wave of recognition policies that involved not only new laws but also considerable expenditures for the Estonian state in the realm of special victim pensions (see Chapter 5) shows that matters of retrospective truth and justice remained politically important long after regime transition. This is true for all three Baltic states, but especially for Lithuania. Overall, issues of historical justice and public remembering remain an important point on the political agenda in both domestic and international politics.

The chapter will begin with a discussion of state symbolic policies of truth-revelation and acknowledgment directed at the victims of more recent regime abuses, in other words issues of *transitional* symbolic justice. The focus here will be in particular on state-sponsored truth-telling mechanisms. In a next step we will look at the Baltic states' politics of public remembrance through an examination of official holidays and state declarations that demonstrate a commitment to honoring the memory of the victims of Soviet Communism. This comparative discussion will include both acts of remembrance directed at victims of recent regime abuses and those remembering more distant mass crimes during Stalinism. The bulk of the chapter, however, will be dedicated to closely examining the various state institutions and policies established since 1990 to acknowledge the victims of Stalin-era mass deportations, terror and other forms of repression, that is, measures of *retrospective* justice. This will include an examination of state institutions aimed at establishing the truth about past atrocities and identifying their targets as well as of state-sponsored programs and activities that foster remembering. As we will see, many of these institutions and programs came into being or could be realized only due to the impact of non-governmental actors, mostly victim organizations. For that reason a brief overview of the main actors involved here will precede the later analysis of measures.

This chapter engages with perhaps the most diverse and complex area of truth and justice outlined in our conceptual model. Its aim is to determine the scope and intensity of state-led truth and remembrance policies in each state and to give a sense of the degree of their institutionalization. As we will show, the three countries diverge quite a lot in this domain, too, as policy-makers pursued rather different strategies in achieving truth and remembering victims. Divergences occur not only in the meaning that is given to specific historical events, such as the deportations or the postwar partisan struggles, but also in the degree of state involvement, in both legislative and budgetary terms.

As one might guess by now in this book, Lithuania displays by far the most well-established, publicly funded and sustained infrastructure of research and remembrance relating to the Soviet period. Estonia, by contrast, exhibits the least firmly institutionalized process of truth-seeking and remembrance, leaving much of the work to non-governmental organizations (NGOs) or institutions that engage in victim-centered research and remembrance. Latvia falls somewhere in between: on the one hand, state actors are more inclined to get involved in public remembering by way of legislating official remembrance days for victims or sponsoring institutions of truth-revelation and victim-centered memory work. On the other hand, with regard to building and sustaining an infrastructure of remembrance and truth-seeking, in both institutional and political terms Latvian state actors have shown less commitment than their Lithuanian counterparts, and state support in this realm has further declined during the years of the economic crisis.

Transitional truth-telling: acknowledging the victims of recent regime repression

After their re-emergence from Communism, none of the states of Central and Eastern Europe chose to initiate a broad process of truth-revelation that would engage victims and perpetrators together with the population in the same way as, for example, the Truth and Reconciliation Commission would around the same time in South Africa. Instead, truth-revelation was pursued via political-administrative procedures such as screening state employees and vetting candidates running for public office for their previous involvement with the repressive state apparatus (Chapter 4). True, the numerous scandals that revealed past collaboration with state security agencies among high-ranking politicians did contribute somewhat to involving a broader public in this truth process. However, not only was the public confined to an observer position, but also the political scandals surrounding former secret agents and informants contributed little to providing recognition for those whose rights had been violated by the regime. In other words, truth-revelation was geared toward the perpetrators of past transgressions rather than to their targets. Secret police files about surveillance and other operations – where they could be saved from destruction – are to this day kept mostly closed to the broader public.

In the Baltic states, access to personal files for former regime opponents and victims of rights abuses has been possible, yet strictly regulated. In all three states individuals are free to submit requests to the Special Archives in Lithuania, to the State Archive in Estonia or to the Center for the Documentation of the Consequences of Totalitarianism (TSDC) in Latvia in order to gain information about their personal stories of deprivation or coercion. However, the overall state approach to confronting forms of recent regime repression and to start public discussions on what those who worked with the repressive system did to their fellow citizens remains rather ambiguous. One reason for this is certainly the highly incomplete and often questionable character of the files that were left over by the KGB, as we discussed in Chapter 4. As the most prominent researcher of KGB files in Latvia has explained, many of the reports by secret agents that could be recovered contain coded information or information that cannot be verified due to missing data. Thus the "truth" gained from these documents often remains incomplete or misrepresented, and thus constitutes a danger in itself of being misunderstood and causing new injustice (Zālīte, Interview, 2013).

Why then, if the records of the former oppressors were so unreliable did none of the post-communist states establish truth commissions that might have brought more direct evidence to light? We understand the concept of truth commissions as institutions tasked with establishing the facts concerning recent gross human rights violations and acknowledging the victims by engaging with the subjective truth of both victims and witnesses (as well as sometimes victimizers) and to do so in a rather public manner (Hayner 2002; Brahm 2009). As Timothy Garton Ash (2002: 276) observes, truth commissions contain a "strong element of political theatre," whether by holding public hearings where victims can tell their personal stories or by otherwise seeking out the stories and evidence from victims and victimizers in order to establish truth. In the post-communist context, Garton Ash maintains, this would have been particularly useful given the fact that the communist regimes had been "kept in place less by direct coercion than by the everyday clay tissue of lies."

Explanations for why such public forums of truth-telling and *Aufarbeitung* did not materialize are manifold. Some have argued that instead of truth commissions post-communist countries had roundtable talks or other forms of negotiation that allowed officials of the Communist regime to re-integrate into society without having to fear too harsh sanctions (Mink 2013: 162). Another explanation may have more to do with the ambiguities involved in determining right and wrong in relation to late socialist methods of coercion, subtle control and abuse. Indeed, not every report filed to the KGB necessarily caused damage to those on whom they reported; not every person who reported did so voluntarily or because he or she wholeheartedly supported the repressive state system. Finally, not every employee of the KGB actually did wrong, as the state security agencies were also responsible for fighting corruption, illegal trafficking or other violations of the law. Whether or not these ambiguities would have found an appropriate place in a rather open public deliberation led by a truth commission may be questionable. To be sure, some ad hoc official truth bodies concerned with regime rights violations after Stalin's death were set up in the immediate post-communist period across the region. However, they were mostly single-issue commissions of inquiry concerned with concrete incidents of regime violence such as the 1956 Hungarian uprising, the 1968

Prague Spring or the 1981 imposition of martial law in Poland. None of these investigations, except the German Enquete Commission established by the Bundestag in 1992, ever reached beyond these singular events and engaged in broader-scale fact-finding and deliberation of the erstwhile regime.[1]

In the Baltic states as well, we see a number of investigative commissions being created during and after regaining independence, yet as we will discuss in a later section of this chapter, these were concerned most of all with the more distant historical crimes committed by the Stalinist regime in the 1940s and 1950s, that is, with issues of retrospective truth-seeking. Apart from this, the Baltic states (and especially Lithuania and Latvia) went the way of most other Central European states by establishing institutions tasked with researching and evaluating the material available from leftover KGB files and state archives, not least for vetting purposes. They thus created an institutional infrastructure to investigate both historical crimes and more recent human rights violations. This truth-revelation has been carried out mostly by the TSDC in Latvia and the Research Department at the Lithuanian Genocide and Resistance Research Center (LGGRTC). The Estonian Institute of Historical Memory (*Mälu Instituut*) is a much more recent player on the scene, and its investigations into late-Soviet violations of human rights comes alongside a number of NGOs doing the same work.

In Latvia, the TSDC in particular played a central role in the process of state-led truth-revelation. Endowed with powers to obtain information from both individuals and institutions, the Center's team of researchers has aimed at revealing the mechanisms of past regime repression. It did so with a rather broad understanding of recent regime victims. According to the law that regulates the TSDC's activities, "all persons who were politically repressed during the entire period of Soviet occupation, but also persons . . . about whom the KGB collected information"

[1] The German Bundestag Commissions of 1992 and 1995 have, indeed, been discussed as truth commissions in the literature. The 1992 commission, in particular, engaged extensively in hearing hundreds of witnesses, both former victims of the SED regime and Stasi agents, and in organizing encounters and expert reports as well as securing a wide coverage of these activities in the media. However, even here it has been noted that the bulk of the investigative work nevertheless relied on archival research and the aim of the Commission markedly shifted over the years from seeking out subjective truths and acknowledging victims to establishing a historical narrative of the SED regime that revolved around the early years of Communist takeover and around questions of regime legitimacy (Beattie 2008). Within our understanding, it thus shifted from being a measure belonging into Box 6b to one exhibiting more of the characteristics of a Box 6a measure.

were classified as "victims" (*cietušie*) (Latvijas Republikas Ministru Kabinets 1995). While this definition of victims had no bearing on legal or administrative procedures regarding their status and related social benefits, the formulation had great symbolic meaning for those whose lives had been impaired by the Soviet security police and who wished to know the truth. Moreover, in order to complement the limited number of regime files left in Latvia after 1991, the TSDC often contacted these people directly when they found their names in the electronic database of KGB reports. The discussions not only revealed the identity of secret agents and informers, but also brought to light additional victims of rights abuses and helped individuals to make sense of what had happened to them (Zālīte, Interview, 2013).

Part of the information gathered from these interviews as well as the questioning of former KGB operatives was used for the vetting of candidates for public and elected office (see Chapter 4). Other information about more harmful experiences of those targeted by the KGB, such as temporary arrests, brutal interrogations and legal convictions, served as the basis for rehabilitation procedures and the verification of claims for special status as discussed in Chapter 5. Yet, the bulk of the stories and testimonies collected by TSDC staff have been recorded and systematized for use by future researchers or journalists as a number of publications confirm (Zālīte 1997, 1998; Rimšāns 2006; Jansons 2007).[2]

In Lithuania, research into the KGB operations of later decades and their targets has been carried out on a project basis by researchers of the Special Research Department of the LGGRTC as well as by the Museum of Genocide Victims under the same roof (Jakubčionis 2007; Burinskaitė and Okuličiūtė 2010). Within the framework of preparing exhibitions about resistance in Soviet Lithuania, the museum, for example, has cooperated with former political convicts in collecting relevant material such as samizdat literature, magazines and leaflets produced by the Catholic Church or by members of the "creative intelligentsia" (Ruzgas 2010). Moreover, researchers have worked with former political prisoners and deportees to preserve pictures, diaries and other memorabilia brought to the museum by former victims themselves. Although most of

[2] See also several articles in volume 20 of the Symposium of the Commission of Historians of Latvia series presenting the proceedings of an international conference held in Riga in October 2006 called "Latvia and Eastern Europe in the 1960–1980." Several studies presented there deal with issues of oral history in the reconstruction of everyday life in the Soviet Union, with manifestations of Latvian youth resistance and repressive policies toward religious minorities in Soviet Latvia.

this material concerns suffering during incarceration and forced labor in the Gulag of the 1940s and 1950s, some of the material has shed light on more recent experiences of repression against different dissident groups or the church.[3]

As said, Estonia has not institutionalized research into recent Soviet repression the same way its southern neighbors have. As we will see later on, a state commission created in 1992 nominally to investigate the entire period between 1940 and 1991 paid little attention to the post-Stalinist era. Only in 2008 did President Toomas Hendrik Ilves create the *Mälu Instituut*, tasked with carrying out research into human rights violations committed after 1956. However, the new institution was a direct successor to the Estonian International Commission for the Investigation of Crimes Against Humanity (IKUERK), and since the latter had started a tradition of pure fact-finding with a heavy focus on archival material, the new institute would continue in this vein. According to its mission statement, the Institute of Historical Memory aims to "intensify the collection of individual memories in order to determine precisely and without ideological bias how, and to what extent, the human rights of the people of Estonia were violated."[4] To begin this work, Ilves secured roughly €150,000 from the 2009 state budget that would be used mainly to fund individual research grants for historians preparing studies for the Institute. However, the work has gone rather slowly. As of early 2014, six individual studies had been produced, mostly by young Estonian historians on diverse issues ranging from the issuing of internal passports, to late Stalinist education and the working of Soviet government institutions such as the Supreme Soviet of the ESSR.

To sum up, while in all three countries limited truth-seeking has been carried out with regard to human rights violations of the late Soviet regime, in particular in relation to the KGB, this has remained rather limited. The truth that has been revealed in this process has certainly contributed to providing some symbolic recognition to those individuals, who experienced pressures and rights violations by the regime. However, with regard to broader public recognition these initiatives have been rather narrow since "the truth" is usually filtered by academics and other experts before being presented to society as a whole. Neither the newly created Institute of Historical Memory in Estonia nor the

[3] See the official website of the museum at: www.genocid.lt/muziejus/en/395/a/). See also Streikus (2012).

[4] See the official website of the *Mälu Instituut* at www.mnemosyne.ee/.

already longer-established research institutions in Latvia and Lithuania see themselves as providing a public forum for broader societal debates on the subjective truths and often ambiguous stories of those who suffered under or worked for the repressive system. This lack of engagement underscores what we have already noted as a predilection in the Baltics to deal more with the distant experiences of regime abuse during the Stalinist years.

Legislating the national memory of victims: official declarations and remembrance days

Days of remembrance are not only markers of the official historical narrative of a given state, they are also important occasions for state officials to engage with a wider audience in what has been referred to as national memory (Assmann 2004). Remembrance days provide the possibility for state representatives to give speeches and frame the "lessons" of the past in a way that molds public perceptions about the present. They are thus central tools in the politics of memory of every state. However, official remembrance days are also important ways for the victims of past crimes and abuses to come together, to remember their lost family and friends and to receive personal acknowledgment through increased media and political attention. In order to place both truth-seeking and remembrance campaigns and activities in the broader picture of state commemoration policies, we will therefore start with a review of official remembrance days in each state, focusing on their public meanings and politics. The discussion will also include solemn declarations passed by national parliaments on the occasion of a remembrance day or shortly before that, providing an insight into the "official reading" of the past by the re-independent Baltic states. While there are clearly similarities across the three cases, it is the divergences in the way issues of past victimization and heroism are addressed as well as the politics surrounding some of the remembrance days added later that are most interesting.

Already in the late 1980s when in the context of *glasnost* and *perestroika* nascent opposition groups emerged in all three Baltic republics, the historical dates of Stalinist mass crimes, especially relating to the mass deportations in 1941 and 1949 prompted people to gather in remembrance. The "calendar demonstrations," as Anatol Lieven (1994) would term them, started around 1987 with commemorative acts carried out by human rights organizations and other anti-Soviet activists reminding people of the deportations of June 14, 1941 and March 25, 1949 as well as about the Hitler–Stalin Pact of August 23, 1939. Increasingly over the years, these were the dates when thousands of people assembled to condemn Soviet rule and demand the return of national self-determination. Thus, it was not only after regaining independence that these particular dates would gain national significance as occasions when official state ceremonies would take place to mourn the victims of Stalinist crimes. Yet while all three states would go on to observe June 14 as a national memorial day, only in Latvia was March 25 also added in an official capacity together with regular state ceremonies. In Lithuania and Estonia, politicians merely attend commemorative gatherings otherwise organized by victims groups. In addition, Lithuania and Latvia have decided to institute June 15 and June 17, respectively, as remembrance days for the occupation of the independent republics by Soviet troops in 1940.

Interestingly, August 23 – the day of the Baltic Way in 1989 that united the populations of the Soviet Baltic republics in reminding the world of the Hitler–Stalin Pact sixty years earlier – was initially instituted only in Lithuania as an official remembrance day. Listed as the "Black Ribbon and Baltic Chain day," the day was supposed to remind people of the loss of state independence and of the victimization of the population this entailed (Lietuvos Respublikos Seimas 1997b). For more than a decade, Lithuania remained the only Baltic state recognizing this day in its memorial calendar and attributing great meaning to its annual observation. Moreover, in 2004 Lithuanian members of the European Parliament were among the leaders of a joint push to institute August 23 as a pan-European remembrance day for the victims of totalitarian regimes. In September 2008 this initiative was successful, and the European Parliament signed the declaration proclaiming August 23 as a European Day of Remembrance for Victims of Stalinism and Nazism (European Parliament 2008). Only then did Estonian and Latvian legislators, together with several others in European member states, formally institute this date as a state-observed remembrance day (Eesti Vabariigi Valitsus 2009; Latvijas Republikas Saeima 2009b). In a small act of opposition to the European Parliament's careful phrasing of this remembrance day, Estonian legislators chose to replace the word *Stalinism* with *Communism*, stressing once again the understanding of communism itself as a criminal regime – a notion that is strongly rejected among left-wing parliamentarians in the EU (see Chapter 7).

Apart from these core days that the three states have in common, legislators in each individual country have chosen to add other dates to the memorial calendar or have changed the title of existing remembrance days by legislative amendment. These moves have involved a certain degree of politics and showmanship, since politicians are always eager to use "discursive and institutional opportunities to reshape or re-negotiate the recent past" (Matonyte 2013: 116). In what follows we will thus focus on the politics involved with introducing particular remembrance days or changing existing names in each state separately. Table 6.1 provides a combined overview of the official remembrance days relating to the totalitarian past as observed by each state today.

As Table 6.1 shows, Lithuania far surpasses Estonia and Latvia in terms of the days designated as serving to remember the totalitarian past. Of the fourteen national remembrance days concerned with the Communist and Nazi regimes and stipulated over the years, eleven are directly dedicated to the memory of victims of mass crime and repression, including genocide and deportations as well as civil and armed resistance against the Soviets. Six of the days were already included in the first comprehensive legislative Act on Remembrance Days in 1997. Among these were June 14 as the Day of Mourning and Hope, September 23 as Holocaust Remembrance Day and August 23 as Black Ribbon Day. In 1998 the day of June 15 was added as the official Day of Occupation and Genocide marking the Soviet military occupation in 1940. Over the years four more days have been added in relation to Soviet repressions and the national resistance. On the occasion of the sixtieth anniversary of the end of World War II, the Seimas designated May 8 as a remembrance day, and in 2006 another "Genocide remembrance day" was added paying tribute to the mass killings and deportation between 1944 and 1947 that extinguished almost the entire ethnic Lithuanian population of what is referred to as "Lithuania Minor" or the current Kaliningrad and Klaipeda region.

Among the five days of the calendar dedicated to those who died in resistance to Soviet rule, two could be qualified as acts of transitional truth and justice, while the remaining three are retrospective. On May 14, 1972, a young Lithuanian, Romas Kalanta, carried out an act of self-immolation in downtown Kaunas in order to protest the Soviet occupation of his country. Kalanta's death has become a leading symbol of civil resistance to Soviet rule, and therefore this date was proclaimed an official remembrance day in 1997.[5] Equally important in the history of

[5] This did not, however, come without controversy, as more orthodox Catholics among the political elites expressed disapproval over "celebrating" a suicide in this form.

Table 6.1 *State remembrance days for victims of Stalinism and Nazism*

Date	Estonia	Latvia	Lithuania
January 13 / January 20 (1991)		1991 Defenders of the Barikades Day (1997)	Defenders of Freedom Day (1991)*
January 27 (1945)	International Holocaust Remembrance Day (2003) (not stipulated in law)		
March 16		Latvian Soldier's Remembrance Day (1998, removed 2000)	
March 25 (1949)		Remembrance Day to the Victims of Communist Genocide (1990, renamed 1998)	
May 8 (1945)	International Day of Remembrance for the Victims of WWII (not stipulated in law)	Remembrance Day for the Defeat of Nazism and the Victims of WWII (1990, date switched 1995)	WWII Remembrance Day (2005)*
May 14 (1972)			Civil Resistance Day (2002)
3rd Sun in May			Day of Commemoration of Partisans and Unity of the Army and Society (1997)
June 14 (1941)	Day of Mourning (1998)	Remembrance Day to the Victims of Communist Genocide (1990, renamed 1998)	Day of Mourning and Hope (1997)*

Table 6.1 (*cont.*)

Date	Estonia	Latvia	Lithuania
June 15 / June 17 (1940)		Day of the Occupation of the Latvian Republic (2000)	Day of Occupation and Genocide (1998)*
June 23 (1941)			Day of the June Uprising (1997)
July 4 (1941)		Jewish Genocide Remembrance Day (1990)	
August 23 (1939)	Day of Remembrance for Victims of Communism and Nazism (2009)	Remembrance Day for the Victims of Stalinism and Nazism (2009)	Black Ribbon Day and the Baltic Chain (1997)*
September 22 (1944)	Day of Remembrance for the Resistance (2010)		
September 23 (1943)			Lithuanian Jewish Holocaust Remembrance Day (1997)
September 28 (1944)			Day of Commemoration for the Victims of Tuskulėnai (2006)
October 16 (1944)			Day of Commemoration for the Victims of the Genocide in Lithuania Minor (2006)
1st Sun December (1937–38)		Victims of Genocide Against the Latvian People by the Totalitarian Communist Regime (1998)	

Note: In Lithuania, not all state-declared remembrance days have equal importance. The law actually differentiates between "flag days," which require public buildings to put out the national flag, and simple "remembrance days." In this table, "flag days" are denoted with an asterisk.

citizen opposition to Soviet rule is the date of January 13, which marked the day in 1991 when thousands of people sought to defend the country against an attempted Soviet crackdown; thirteen people died as Soviet tanks attempted to take over the Vilnius TV tower, and the date was immediately declared the Defenders of Freedom Day (Lietuvos Respublikos Aukščiausiosios Tarybos Prezidiumas 1991). Moreover, a special medal was instituted to honor those who demonstrated "courage and self-sacrifice in defense of the freedom and independence of Lithuania," as stated in one of numerous decrees issued by the Presidium of the Supreme Council (Lietuvos Respublikos Aukščiausiosios Tarybos Prezidiumas 1992). Over the next twenty years, several thousand Lithuanians would receive this token of acknowledgment (along with many qualifying for special victims benefits). The date of January 13 also became a regular occasion for center-right and populist politicians to demand justice from Russia in terms of getting Moscow to hand over for trial those ex-Soviet troops who actually killed the protesters on that day.

The remaining three Lithuanian resistance days concern the more distant past, and are dedicated to the armed fight against Soviet rule in the 1940s and 1950s. None of them requires the hoisting of the flag, like most of the victim-related memorial days, but they are still an important part of the public remembrance culture. Thus, every third Sunday in May is dedicated to the memory of the armed fight against Soviet occupation especially in the postwar years, while June 23 marks the day when a proclamation of national independence was made during an uprising that took place right before the invasion of Lithuania by the *Wehrmacht*. Lastly, in 2006 the Seimas adopted an amendment to stipulate September 28 as the day to remember those people who were tortured and killed by the Soviet NKGB during 1945–47.

The last two remembrance days have stirred particular controversy, as they epitomize the difficult historical entanglement between anti-Soviet resistance in Lithuania and the widespread collaboration of Lithuanians in realizing the Nazi mass murder of Jews. The June 23 memorial day was first discussed in the framework of adopting the 1997 Act on Remembrance Days. The day had been informally observed ever since the regaining of independence, mostly by national-conservative politicians and veterans of the anti-Soviet armed resistance. However, its introduction as a state commemoration day met with protests both from other parliamentarians and the Jewish community. The latter pointed to the more controversial historical aspects involving the uprising and its leading organization, the Lithuanian Activist Front (*Lietuvos aktyvistų frontas* – LAF) in promoting anti-Jewish acts and paving the way for an easy takeover of the country by Nazi Germany. Indeed, the deeply anti-Semitic propaganda of the LAF and the later involvement of former members of the June Uprising in anti-Jewish pogroms and arrests infallibly link the date to the Holocaust in Lithuania (Arad 2004b). During the parliamentary debate, Emanuelis Zingeris, one of the signatories of the independence declaration of 1990 and member of the Lithuanian Jewish community, urged his fellow parliamentarians to show more sensitivity for the fate of their fellow Jewish countrymen, many of whom were killed literally during the same week the uprising took place. His and other commentators' interventions caused an intense public debate about the significance of the June Uprising and the anti-Semitism among those who participated in it (Budrytė 2004: 90). In the end, however, none of the objections could deter the majority of the Seimas members from including the day among Lithuania's state remembrance days, albeit not as an official "flag day."

The suggestion to officially remember those killed by the NKGB during 1945–47 and buried in a park close to the center of Vilnius was put forward in 2006 by national-conservative MPs. Their motion came in the wake of a controversy following the discovery of human bones in 1994 and the subsequent idea to erect a memorial for the martyrs of the Lithuanian national resistance fight at the burial site. Again, as we will show in later sections, the debates involved members of the Jewish community, but also historians, who rejected the notion of a memorial for victims, noting the fact that among the people killed had been former Nazi collaborators and mass murderers. The impossibility of clearly identifying those buried in the Tuskulėnai park and thus the danger of possibly honoring a different set of perpetrators was seen as too high. Parliament nonetheless passed the motion and September 28 became Tuskulėnai Remembrance Day.

Equally in the category of official Lithuanian martyrology belongs a parliamentary initiative launched on the sixtieth anniversary of the founding of the Lithuanian Freedom Fighters Movement in 1949. Again national-conservative MPs proposed a law that was subsequently adopted by the right-wing dominated Seimas in March 2009 that declared Jonas Žemaitis, the last leader of the Lithuanian national partisan movement, the *de jure* fourth president of Lithuania (Lietuvos Respublikos Seimas 2009). To be sure, this type of truth and justice measure has little to do with victims as such; rather, it is again a form of legislating national memory and of fostering the heroic narrative of resistance. However, we mention it here because it sets the tone for other commemorative activities, and it contributes to institutionalizing the overall collective image of a victim and fighter nation (Matonyte 2013).[6]

Similar to Lithuania, we see also in Latvia considerable changes of the remembrance calendar and related political controversies. From the very beginning, the Latvian state calendar adopted by the Supreme Council in 1990 contained four days of national remembering dedicated to the victims of the totalitarian regimes. Besides June 14 and March 25 as well as May 8, Latvian law stipulated July 4 as the day to officially remember the "Jewish Genocide in Latvia" (Latvijas Republikas Augstākā Padome 1990d).[7] Both June 14 and March 25 are observed with a military ceremony and public speeches by high state officials. At the same time, Latvia does not have a remembrance day for the postwar anti-Soviet partisan movement. The only "resistance"-related remembrance day in the Latvian calendar concerns the events of January 1991 when barricades were erected in Riga to prevent Soviet forces from taking over the TV tower and parliament. As in Lithuania, yet only as of 1997, these events are officially marked by a new remembrance day on January 20, called the 1991 Defenders of the Barricades Day (Latvijas Republikas Saeima 1997). At the same time, memorial signs were placed in several locations around downtown Riga to remember the five individuals who had been killed during the January 1991 events. Moreover, further paralleling Lithuania's policies, the state ordered the development of a special medal, the "Barricades participants' remembrance sign" (*Barikāžu dalībnieka piemiņas zīmi*), eventually bestowed to thousands of individuals over the course of the following years. Yet as Table 6.1 shows, all other remembrance days for victims in Latvia relate to the more distant past. Here Latvian lawmakers have instituted a number of

[6] It was also clearly meant as a signal toward Russia and the EU, since around the same time Lithuanian MEPs were actively lobbying the European Parliament for the adoption of pan-European legislation condemning the crimes of Communism. See Chapter 7.

[7] Among the three Baltic states, Latvia was thus the first to introduce a national Holocaust memorial day, even before state independence was fully established. Like its Lithuanian counterpart, the Latvian Supreme Council also adopted a resolution already in September 1990 On the Condemnation and Impermissability of Genocide and Anti-Semitism in Latvia, acknowledging the involvement of Latvian citizens in the mass murder of Latvian Jews, pledging to remember the victims and condemning any form of anti-Semitism (Latvijas Republikas Augstākā Padome 1990a).

new remembrance days since 1990 and have amended their law more than a dozen times, often changing the titles of existing days, or in one case abolishing the day altogether. In many cases these changes were borne out of broader public debates or international political developments that merit further discussion.

The very first amendment to Latvia's calendar law took place in 1995 and concerned a seemingly small, and yet significant switch of dates. Thus, in the original law of 1990 Latvia still observed the end of World War II as May 9, just as during the Soviet period to mark the end of the Great Patriotic War. In 1995 Latvian legislators changed the date to May 8, thus symbolically underpinning the country's political reorientation to the West and the Western historical discourse (Latvijas Republikas Saeima 1995a). Feeling somewhat alienated by this new calendar, however, many Russians in the country continued to observe May 9. As a result, in subsequent years the day became an unofficial but highly significant remembrance day for many of these people. To this day veterans of the Red Army, Soviet nostalgics and people who identify with Russia (among them an increasing number of younger Russians) gather at the Soviet-era victory monument in Riga to celebrate and remember the defeat over fascism on May 9 (Ločmele et al. 2011: 125).

Another interesting switch involved the title for the June 14 deportation remembrance day. In 1998 an amendment was passed changing the name from "Remembrance Day for the Victims of Communist Terror" to the day of the "Victims of Communist Genocide." In the same amendment the Saeima introduced yet another genocide remembrance day on every first Sunday in December – the Memorial Day for the Victims of Genocide Against the Latvian People by the Totalitarian Communist Regime. The date marks the period when approximately 70,000 ethnic Latvian inhabitants of Soviet Russia fell victim to the Stalinist purges of 1937–38 (Latvijas Republikas Saeima 1998b, see also Riekstiņš 2009). Proposed by an organization called the Society of Eastern Latvians (*Austrumu latviešu biedrība*) and supported by national-conservative MPs, neither of these two amendments caused much controversy within the Saeima despite the rather bold introduction of the term "genocide" (Kaprāns et al. 2012: 44).

Indeed, this radicalization of terminology did not come as a surprise, as the mass deportations had already been classified as genocide in official documents and legal Acts. In the Declaration on the Occupation of Latvia adopted on August 22, 1996, the Saeima had stated that

> [t]hroughout the occupation, the Soviet Union conducted a targeted genocide against the Latvian people, in breach of the Convention on the Prevention and Punishment of the Crime of Genocide of 9 December 1948. The occupation regime killed innocent people, carried out several mass deportations and other repressive policies, cruelly punished those, who with or without arms fought for the restoration of Latvian independence, and unlawfully expropriated Latvian citizens without compensation and suppressed freedom of expression.
>
> (Latvijas Republikas Saeima 1996b)

The initiative to change the wording of the June 14 memorial day can thus be seen as the logical continuation of this narrative development. It can also be interpreted as a response by nationally minded Latvian lawmakers to increasing criticism from outside the country regarding Latvia's official remembrance culture in relation to Nazi-era veterans and collaborators (Latvijas Republikas Saeima 1998c). At the center of these controversies – that brought Latvia "to the brink of international isolation" as the newspaper *Diena* put it – was yet another remembrance day, March 16.

Ever since the early 1990s, this had been the day when veterans of the two battalions of Latvian *Waffen-SS* (the so-called Latvian Legion), established by the Nazis in 1943 to fight the approaching Red Army, remembered their fallen comrades with a church service in the Riga Dome Cathedral and a march through the Old Town to lay down flowers at the Freedom monument. Though this was not a state-sanctioned day of remembrance, until March 1998 the event was attended by high-ranking representatives of the state, including President Guntis Ulmanis, who honored the legionnaires as "national heroes" and "fighters against the Bolsheviks." Officials and media in Russia, however, took the day as a welcome occasion to tar Latvia internationally, denouncing the remembrance ceremonies as a sign of the re-emergence of a "fascist state" and calling for economic sanctions. Western media also criticized Latvia's unreflective honoring of former German servicemen, thereby showing a similar tendency to associate the legion *tout court* with war crimes and crimes against humanity (Onken 2003: 196; Rislakki 2008: 127–42). In 1998 the furor around the March day became especially intense, and Latvia's Prime Minister Vilis Krištopāns announced that "taking into account domestic and foreign policy considerations, the Cabinet of Ministers agreed that no minister shall participate in these public activities. The same decision was taken regarding military personnel of the National Armed Forces" (Cabinet of Ministers of the Republic of Latvia 1998).

A few months later the Saeima tried again to quell allegations that Latvia was honoring Nazi collaborators by instituting March 16 as merely an official Remembrance Day for Latvian Soldiers. This formulation very much constituted a compromise between those nationalist MPs of the For Fatherland and Freedom Party/LNNK who proposed to establish March 16 as a "remembrance day for the Latvian Legion" and those more cautious voices who warned against the consequences this would have for the international reputation of Latvia (Latvijas Republikas Saeima 1998c). The new interpretation, therefore, was that the day would honor all Latvians who had been involuntarily and against international legal conventions drafted into foreign armies during World War II. Moreover, the Saeima followed this up a few months later with the Declaration on the Latvian Legionnaires in World War II, but this was able to pass only after heated debates lasting over several plenary sessions. Legislators in favor of the document stressed that the drafting of these men into the German Army had violated the Hague Convention of 1907 that prohibits the recruitment of locals into the army of an occupying power. Moreover, the final resolution proclaimed that just as those who had fought on the Soviet side should not be associated with Stalinist mass crimes, so too those drafted into the *Wehrmacht* should not be seen as supporting the murderous Nazi regime (Latvijas Republikas Saeima 1998a).

Yet neither the effort to link the March 16 date to the memory of victim-soldiers, nor the quiet removal of the controversial Soldiers Day from the list of official remembrance days hardly two years after its institution, in February 2000, would end the controversy. Just as the annual gatherings of veterans continued, so did the international headlines accusing Latvia of honoring Nazi collaborators. In fact, since 2000 the day has been increasingly linked by the media to May 9, the day that is still celebrated by many Russian speakers in Latvia as Victory Day. Commentators have seen these two dates as opposing markers of Latvian public memory culture – all the more dangerous since they overlap with ethnic divides and have on occasion resulted in street fights between Latvian and Russian extremists (Rozenšteine et al. 2011).

Compared to Lithuania, Latvia uses the notion of genocide somewhat more expressly in its official remembrance calendar, having in total three days dedicated to remembering the "Communist genocide" against the Latvian people. This may be somewhat surprising given the fact that Lithuania employs the notion much more widely in other domains, such as the very name of its main remembrance institution, the Lithuanian

Genocide and Resistance Research Center. Yet, as we have seen, the Latvian insistence on this approach has been prompted in part by external pressure and the perceived need to counter this pressure with a clear statement of conviction that Soviet rule meant genocide. In later years, this stance appears to have softened. In 2005 the Saeima adopted a Declaration on the Condemnation of the Totalitarian Communist Occupation Regime Implemented in Latvia by the USSR which no longer used the term "genocide" in describing the mass crimes of the Soviet regime, although it was addressed as much to Western European politicians as to Russia (Latvijas Republikas Saeima 2005), as we discuss in Chapter 7.

Returning one last time to Table 6.1, we can see that Estonia appears relatively moderate when it comes to the naming of national remembrance days (*riiklikud tähtpäevad*) in honor of past victims. The original Holidays and Remembrance Days Act of 1998 only dedicated one day to the memory of victims – the Day of Mourning on June 14 (Eesti Vabariigi Riigikogu 1998). Since then only two more remembrance days have been stipulated by law, while some others are officially observed, though not legally instituted. As noted above, August 23 was officially dedicated as a commemorative day by the Riigikogu only in 2009. Meanwhile, an initiative dating back to 2006 to dedicate a day for remembering the anti-Soviet resistance was finally realized only in 2010. Lastly, both May 8 and the International Holocaust Remembrance Day on January 27 have been declared commemorative days by the government and are observed by way of public speeches and educational measures in schools, yet they have never been formally consecrated by a legislative Act. It was in particular this later remembrance day that was steeped in controversy.

As can be seen from Table 6.1, in contrast to Latvia and Lithuania, Estonia does not officially mark a national Holocaust memorial day. In 2002, US Ambassador to Estonia, Joseph DeThomas, tried to prod the Estonian government into acknowledging the need for at least an educational program in Estonian schools to be carried out on January 27. He was met, however, with disdain by Estonian politicians and the media, who argued that since Estonia had been affected by the Holocaust relatively little, the few commemorative forms that were in the country (a few monuments left over from the Soviet era and others erected afterwards with foreign funds) were enough (see also Weiss-Wendt 2008). In fact, it was not until 2005 that a high-ranking Estonian state leader would make an official Holocaust apology "for the fact that Estonian citizens could be found among those who participated in the murdering of people or assisted in the perpetration of these crimes" (Ansip 2005). This was followed two days later by a full cabinet statement expressing "regret" that Estonian citizens were among the perpetrators of the Holocaust (Eesti Vabariigi Valitsus 2005). In 2006, the Estonian Ministry of Education issued a directive to Estonian schools "to explain to students the tragic events of the last century" and mark the International Holocaust Remembrance Day on January 27, and Estonian politicians have taken part in ceremonies on that day (Stevick 2007: 229).[8] However, no discussion has been given to incorporating the day into law.

In 2006 yet a new twist was given to public remembering, when conservative MPs from the Pro Patria and Res Publica Union began to push for the establishment of a day of remembrance for the anti-Soviet resistance that was linked to the day when a group of Estonian politicians desperately tried to form a free Estonian government just as the Soviets re-occupied Tallinn on September 22, 1944. In an explanatory text, the sponsors of the bill noted that on that day a makeshift Estonian cabinet headed by Otto Tief had hoisted the Estonian flag atop the Tall Hermann tower in Tallinn in an attempt to show that the Soviets were actually re-occupying a sovereign Estonia. While this was historically true, the deputies' proposal also carried with it a clear political motive, since the initiative came exactly as tensions were brewing around the issue of the Bronze Soldier in Tallinn. Since the Bronze Soldier had been erected to commemorate the Soviet "liberation" of Tallinn in September 1944, the nationalist deputies' desire to counter this narrative with a rival commemorative day was evident. Initially, however, their proposal was delayed after protests over the Estonian government's plan to remove the statue turned violent in April 2007. It was reactivated only in 2010 when September 22 was stipulated as the official Remembrance Day for the Resistance by legislative amendment (Eesti Vabariigi Riigikogu 2010).

Non-state actors and their role in historical truth-seeking and victim recognition

In all three Baltic Soviet republics the search for historical truth about the mass crimes of the Stalinist years as well as the public remembering of

[8] Other, more historically related, dates had been suggested not least by the Simon Wiesenthal Center's representative, Efraim Zuroff, for example, January 20 – the day of the Wannsee Conference in 1942 at which Estonia had been declared "Judenfrei" (Zuroff 2002).

the victims was an essential part of the growing anti-Soviet opposition during the late 1980s. Pushed by former deportees and political prisoners who had returned to the Baltic shores in the 1950s–1970s and taken up by human rights and independence activists, grassroots-level investigations were carried out to determine the numbers, identities and fate of those who perished during the period of mass terror. This was an important outlet for political discontent during the early years of *glasnost* and *perestroika*, since these people were real, they had suffered and they had a right to talk openly about what had been done to them. Collecting these testimonies or revealing the truth about the extent of Stalinist repressions, however, produced a corollary effect of wanting to gather information about other damages caused by Soviet rule. In all three countries activists grappled to establish an estimate of the overall demographic, economic, cultural and environmental costs of what they increasingly declared to have been an illegal occupation by the Soviet Union. This was done not least with a view to having ammunition for possibly demanding reparations from the Soviet Union or the Russian Federation, as we will see in Chapter 7.

In this way, efforts at individual-level truth-seeking slowly grew into becoming a broader political endeavor and vehicle for demanding a full-fledged restoration of independence. In July 1988, just a few days after its founding, the Lithuanian popular movement *Sąjūdis* reacted to these demands by creating a Commission for Investigation of Stalinist Crimes (the so-called *Sąjūdis* Commission) to research and record the names of those who had been deported during the various waves of terror and to educate society about those crimes. The Commission did so mainly by sending out questionnaires and calling on people to submit their own testimonials (Budrytė 2013b: 137). The creation of victim organizations for former political prisoners and deportees in all three countries over the course of 1988–89 further enhanced the mass engagement with the memory of Stalinist repressions. In both Estonia and Latvia lists of those deported in 1940 compiled by the emerging victim organizations appeared in newspapers, and former deportees related their stories in the public realm (Rahi 2003b: 19–20). While the initial aim of this was very much focused on revealing the truth and recovering information about the identity and fate of victims, these organizations increasingly became advocates for defending their members' interests vis-à-vis the emerging national state authorities. They assisted in collecting data and representing individuals in the judicial process of rehabilitations. In many instances, they were even actively recruited by state authorities to help them implement these policies. But more than anything, these organizations were important for providing symbolic recognition for thousands of previously voiceless and faceless victims of Soviet mass repression and for making them a part of national remembrance culture. They did so mainly by reconstructing countless individual stories of those perished and by giving a public voice to those who survived in the new national discourse over the shared past. By entertaining close links to political parties and working with research institutions, archives and museums, these organizations were instrumental in the evolution of state-led policies of truth establishment and dissemination.

The Lithuanian Club of the Exiled (*Tremtinio klubas*) was founded in July 1988, and within a year had emerged into a broad organization with fifty-eight local branches and some 28,000 members. Alongside the broader *Sąjūdis* movement, mass rallies were organized around particular historical anniversaries and other remembrance rituals. Thus, for example, in 1989 several pilgrimages to Siberian and other faraway grave sites where Lithuanians had been buried were carried out. Moreover, several thousand bodies of former deportees were brought home to be reburied in Lithuanian soil (Budrytė 2004: 86). With the declaration of state independence in spring 1990, the Club of the Exiled renamed itself the Lithuanian Union of Political Prisoners and Deportees (*Lietuvos politinių kalinių ir tremtinių sąjunga* – LPKTS). A political branch of this organization ran in the 1990 elections and soon constituted an influential center-right political force within the Lithuanian party system.[9] The wider organization, however, remained an important non-state actor proclaiming its aim to contribute to "the liquidation of the consequences of the Communist genocide of the Lithuanian nation and the reconstitution of the historical truth about the resistance to occupations" (Lietuvos Politinių Kalinių ir Tremtinių Sąjunga 2013). In its statutes the organization lists educational activities, remembrance work as well as advocacy and rights protection for its members among its main activities. Thus, a considerable portion of the LPKTS' endeavors continue to be concerned with recording and disseminating historical research and memories of former victims, among them both partisans and deportees. The organization is also active in raising awareness among younger generations of Lithuanians through educational

[9] Later, in October 2004, the LPKTS merged with the conservative Homeland Union–Lithuanian Conservatives and remains an influential force within the party.

materials and the organization of remembrance and cultural events and exhibitions.[10]

Similar to Lithuania, former deportees and political prisoners also started to organize in Latvia and Estonia as early as 1988. However, neither the Latvian Association of the Politically Repressed (*Latvijas politiski represēto apvienība* – LPRA) nor the Estonian Memento Union (*Eesti Memento liit*) ever turned into a political party the way parts of the LPKTS did. Several of its members took up public office for one or more legislative periods, among them the current head of the LPRA, Gunārs Resnais, and the former leader of the Estonian Memento Union, Enn Tarto. Both organizations were deeply concerned with "gathering evidence and memories of [past state] terror from those who suffered under it and disseminate it" (Eesti Memento Liit no date). Moreover, they saw themselves as political advocacy organizations, regularly calling on government institutions and representatives to support the material well-being of their members and to honor their memory. In recent years, moreover, the LPRA leadership began actively lobbying politicians to demand compensation for victims of Soviet repressions from Russia as the legal heir to the Soviet Union (Bigg 2006). Yet the two organizations differ in the degree to which they engage in these two realms, truth-seeking and advocacy work. While the Memento Union has put most of its resources and efforts into documenting the identity and fates of former repressed people, the LPRA is more active in political debates over social benefits and other state policies of recognition.

Since 2006 the Memento Union has published eleven volumes not only listing the names of the repressed and an account of repressive acts, but also producing statistical analyses of the data.[11] Most of this painstaking work has been carried out by the Estonian Repressed Persons' Records Bureau (*Eesti represseeritute registri büroo* – ERPRB), a Memento-affiliated commemorative group based in Tallinn. Using mainly volunteers, the Bureau has combed through leftover Soviet archives and other sources to compile a total tally of 87,035 repressed residents of Estonia. These results have been published from 1996 to 2007 in seven volumes identified as R1–R7. In 2012 an additional volume was released, adding the names of another 8,873 persons previously not included. Since many of the individuals had been arrested or sentenced

[10] For a full list of publications by the LPKTS, see its official website at www.lpkts.lt/.

[11] All of the Union's materials, including its statutes and publications, are available via an extensive (albeit Estonian-language) website at www.memento.ee/index.php.

several times (e.g. deported both in 1941 and 1949), entries can appear several times in the dataset. In total the ERPRB database contains 319,204 personal entries of "repressed persons" as of December 2010 (Õispuu 2010: 14).

The LPRA has devoted much of its efforts to providing legal advice for members as well as to serving on municipal committees tasked with determining individuals' eligibility for repressed persons' status (see Chapter 5). The association has also worked with municipal authorities in setting up monuments and memorial signs to those deported and killed by the Soviets as well as organizing public events during important historical anniversaries and official remembrance days. Although the LRPA has helped researchers and archives compile data about the repressed, much of this work has ultimately been done by the State Archive. In two books dedicated to the victims of mass deportation, the lists of repressed persons' names and other related stories were compiled by Latvian historians (Pelkaus 2001; Šķinķe 2007). Carried out as distinctly victim-centered remembrance projects about the deportees (*aizvestie*), these two volumes aimed at combining memory with professional historical scholarship; alongside the sometimes patchy and non-chronological memories of victims, the research sought to add factual verification and contextualization (Šķinķe, quoted in Kaprāns et al. 2012: 44).[12]

In legal terms all three of the main victim associations in the Baltic states are NGOs. However, they all receive substantial state support, which makes them indirect state actors. The degree to which each Baltic government financially supports these organizations can be taken as an indicator of the political importance that is placed on victim remembrance and advocacy (alongside the social benefits that are accorded victims and were covered in Chapter 5). This funding also varies in form. In both Estonia and Lithuania, formal state foundations have been established for supporting victims' activities and remembrance. In July 1994, the Lithuanian

[12] Since 1997 the LPRA administers more or less regularly an internet website on which it publishes official documents, media reports, information about public events, academic studies and other material compiled by the various state and non-governmental institutions concerned with Soviet-era crimes against humanity and human rights violations in Latvia. Among them are the LPRA itself, but also the TSDC, the Latvian Occupation Museum and the State Archive (see http://lpra.vip.lv/). Though rather eclectic, incomplete and not always sufficiently referenced, the information posted here provides a most valuable insight not only into the historical findings and debates, but also into Latvia's truth and justice process over the years more broadly.

Seimas mandated the creation of the Lithuanian Support Fund for Genocide and Resistance Victims (*Lietuvos gyventojų genocido ir rezistencijos aukų rėmimo fondas*).[13] During the 1990s, the fund received around 400,000 litas (around €115,845) per year; this amount rose to nearly a million litas in 2008 before being curtailed during the economic crisis. Although no direct allocations were paid to groups like the LPKTS (except during 2001–2004 when special subventions were provided for), it was from this overall fund that organizations could apply for regular project money.[14] In Estonia, one of the reforms of the 2003 Individuals Repressed by the Occupation Regimes Act was to create a Repressed Persons Assistance Fund (*Eesti represseeritute abistamise fond*). Each year the Estonian government concluded agreements with the fund to distribute around €230,000, including directly to organizations like Memento. In Latvia, the LPRA received rather meager funding from the state, around 10,000 lats (about €15,000) per year, which it then tried to bolster with private donations, although these largely dried up after the recession of 2009 (Kaprāns et al. 2012: 122–23).

Since the late 1990s Baltic victim organizations have increasingly joined forces and organized pan-Baltic meetings and conferences to exchange information and experiences. Perhaps the biggest event to be jointly organized was the 2000 International Vilnius Tribunal on the Crimes of Communism. The idea behind this public proceeding was to review the dimensions of Soviet and more broadly communist crimes and to symbolically adjudicate them. The Tribunal would last several months and was kicked off with an International Anti-Communist Congress in July 2000. For three full days the Congress heard from witnesses and victims of political repression as well as historical, political and legal experts from twenty-three countries, including Russia, who gave testimony and provided evidence about the mass crimes and dimensions of crimes and repression under Communism (International Congress on the Evaluation of the Crimes of Communism 2000). More witness and victims testimonies and expert evaluations were collected in subsequent months. The Tribunal was presided over by Vytautas Zabiela, a Lithuanian lawyer. In

13 The fund was renamed slightly in 1998 to include the word "research": The Lithuanian Fund for Genocide and Resistance Research, Victim Support and Commemoration (*Lietuvos gyventojų genocido ir rezistencijos tyrimo, aukų rėmimo ir atminimo įamžinimo fondas*).

14 Budget figures based on a review of Lithuanian state budgets 1993–2013 by the authors. Also, interview with Elžbieta Jūratė Marcinkevičienė, former managing director of the LPKTS.

its final judgment, announced in October 2000 and published in English, the Tribunal once again determined that the core responsibility for most of the mass crimes of Communism lay with the criminal organization of the Soviet Communist Party and its local branches. The Tribunal also called for bringing to justice those who committed these crimes. The reading of the verdict took four hours and the accusations were mammoth: Communism was charged with having caused the death of at least 100 million people worldwide, and the crimes of communists were declared to have been "on a bigger scale than Nazi crimes" (Tracevskis 2000b).

Though this was in no way a state-sanctioned initiative, several MPs from the Baltic states attended the International Anti-Communist Congress and public hearings, and some rather prominent political figures, among them former Polish president Lech Wałęsa, former dissident and later Russian MP Sergey Kovalev and Lithuanian parliament chair Vytautas Landsbergis took part in either the June Congress or attended the Tribunal. In subsequent years this first attempt at a public tribunal in the post-communist region further branched out to form strong international networks of victim organizations, government agencies for research and remembrance as well as NGOs to lobby and campaign Europe-wide for an International Tribunal on Communism in the spirit of the Nuremberg trials (see also Chapter 7).

State policies of establishing truth and victim recognition

The tremendous efforts undertaken by victims groups during the early 1990s to gather and preserve the memory of those who suffered under Soviet repression bear witness to the degree that civil society in the Baltics has aimed to deal with the tasks of symbolic truth and justice. Since in this book our focus is more on state measures regarding these matters, our attention turns now to government-financed remembrance institutions, of which, unsurprisingly, there have been many in the Baltic states. At the same time, the breadth of this state commitment and involvement varies; either the state takes a very active role in planning and executing programs for preserving and promoting memory (as in Lithuania), or it becomes only marginally involved through certain targeted endeavors (as in Estonia).

When in 1990 the first free elections were held in the Baltic states and pro-independence governments were swept into office, a series of legislative initiatives were undertaken to create an institutional infrastructure for the more systematic investigation of past repression as well as the establishment of commemorative practices. This was most evident in Lithuania, where during the first years of Vytautas Landsbergis' chairmanship of the Supreme Council a plethora of legislative Acts and decisions was passed creating several institutions of research and remembrance. First to be formed (in late 1992) was the Research Center for the Study of Repressions in Lithuania (*Represijų Lietuvoje tyrimo centras*) within the Institute of Philosophy, Sociology and Law. The aim of this center was to continue the work of the earlier *Sąjūdis* Commission by expanding and systematizing the material collected by the Commission's campaigns from the late 1980s. Likewise, the Museum of Genocide Victims was founded in October 1992 with the task of collecting and exhibiting pictures, personal belongings and other artifacts of the recent history of victimization. Finally, also in October 1992, a Genocide Center of Lithuania (or forerunner to the LGGRTC) was founded by a parliamentary resolution and tasked with both research about former deportees and partisans and the preservation and evaluation of leftover KGB material (Lietuvos Respublikos Aukščiausioji Taryba 1992). This latter aspect, the investigation into former KGB activities, was curbed, however, after the return of the former communists to power. Under President Algirdas Brazauskas the Genocide Research Center was renamed the Genocide and Resistance Research Center, and its task was laid out as primarily focused on the victims of genocide and on the history of national resistance (Lietuvos Respublikos Seimas 1993b; Budrytė 2013c: 138).

Over the course of the 1990s, several similar national and municipal museums were established across Lithuania, often initiated by former victims and dissidents and many of them carrying the words freedom fight, resistance, partisans or deportations in their titles. Moreover, in 1995 a specially drafted government program helped to launch a country-wide campaign aimed at designing and setting up "commemorative signs, symbols and monuments to the victims of genocide and those repressed for resisting the occupation regimes." The main priority of the four-year program was in fact the final category of resistance. Monuments to the postwar guerilla movement were to be erected in all nine of the "partisan districts" that the movement had had across Lithuania (Lietuvos Respublikos Vyriausybė 1995a).

This government program was notable also because it was approved under the center-left (LDDP) government of Adolfas Šleževičius. This showed that at least on this symbolic issue the ex-communists were willing to engage in truth and justice. However, as we have noted already repeatedly in this book, the return to power of the Homeland Union-Lithuanian Conservatives (TS-LK) in late 1996 marked a significant watershed in government approaches and policies. Within the realm of state-sponsored memory institutions, it was perhaps not all that surprising that the new government would undertake an effort to consolidate the many small institutions that had emerged dealing with truth-seeking and commemoration. Indeed, one of the conservatives' critiques while in opposition was that such large-scale government programs to remember the past (as Šleževičius had implemented) could not be carried out effectively unless they were more centrally coordinated. Nevertheless, the extent to which these existing strands in Lithuania would now be put under one roof was impressive. Both the Research Center for the Study of Repressions in Lithuania and the Museum of Genocide Victims were now placed under the meanwhile renamed Genocide and Resistance Research Center of Lithuania (LGGRTC). Moreover, in 1998 the Lithuanian Support Fund for Genocide and Resistance Victims was moved under the auspices of the LGGRTC and given the name Lithuanian Foundation for Genocide and Resistance Research and for Victims Support and Remembrance. Its main purpose was to manage the yearly state budgetary allocations to support victims of repression and participants in the resistance movement as well as to fund special remembrance programs. The different materials compiled hitherto by the three institutions were joined in a Special Archive, part of the State Archive, but located at one of the main buildings of the Center. Moreover, under the newly appointed director of the Center, Dalia Kuodytė, the Memorial Department was extended not only to further refine and implement commemorative programs but also to start new initiatives in the area of oral history and life-story research.[15] Thus, work with surviving victims and witnesses of the deportations, as well as of the postwar partisan struggle was intensified as the Center's staff was specially trained to seek out and record special testimonials[16] (Juodvalkytė 2004). The result of this activity was a quantitative and qualitative leap in the national

[15] Programs currently run or concluded by the LGGRTC Memorial Department include the "Registry of Memorial Places and Buildings", a project involving "Live Memory"; research into the "psychological consequences of Soviet and Nazi repressions"; a campaign to get young people to research the past called "post-war history for the young people"; research and activities relating to the Holocaust and more recent-era Lithuanian dissidents movements (see the LGGRTC's website at www.genocid.lt/centras/en/479/a/).

[16] Kuodytė travelled personally to the United States to visit and learn from museums and organizations doing precisely this kind of work (Kuodytė, Interview, 2013).

collection of documentation about Soviet repression. According to Kuodytė, who was personally behind many of the oral history and storytelling projects, this memory work had an enormous psychological effect on those who participated and relayed their stories – especially if they had never spoken openly about these experiences before (Kuodytė, Interview, 2013).

The LGGRTC's Memorial Department also supervises the work of the Museum of Genocide Victims. Located in the former headquarters of the KGB in Vilnius, the museum hosts a permanent exhibition displaying, as formulated in its official brochure, the various "forms of physical and spiritual genocide against the Lithuanian people."[17] In addition the museum's staff organizes traveling exhibitions, seminars and film screenings as well as youth meetings with contemporary witnesses, former deportees, political prisoners and partisans.[18] Lastly, the LGGRTC runs a publication department responsible for publishing and disseminating the results of the Center's research[19] as well as personal memoirs, compilations of life stories and documents, fiction and film documentaries about Lithuania's recent past. It is within this sub-unit that several volumes containing the names and basic information of people deported and/or killed by the Soviets have been published, akin to what the Estonian ERPRB or the Latvian State Archive have done.

Summing up the ambitions of the new LGGRTC, former director Kuodytė said in an interview, "we wanted to create a structure like Yad Vashem [the Holocaust memorial institution in Israel] with a museum, research, work with victims, books and education. I think our results are not bad" (Kuodytė, Interview, 2013). This success was reflected in ever-increasing budgetary allocations to the Center. Already in 1995, the Center was granted over 4.2 million litas (€1,220,000) in funding. After the revamping of the Center in 1997, this amount grew slightly to an average of 4.8 million litas, before climbing sharply to over 6 million (or €1.7 million) after 2008. Moreover, this funding level was maintained throughout the economic crisis and continued through 2013.[20]

17 See Genocide and Resistance Research Center in Lithuania (n.d.).

18 In late 1998, the Seimas declared 1999 a "Year of Remembering the Struggle for Freedom." Among the activities that took place was a campaign by researchers to have schoolteachers, students and community activists collect first-hand memories of the Soviet past among victims and resistance fighters.

19 Via, for example, the scholarly journal *Genocide and Resistance*, issued biennially since 1997.

20 Authors' review of Lithuanian state budget laws 1993–2013.

All of this money reinforced still more state activities in the area of historical research and public remembrance. In 2002 a second government program on monuments and commemorative sites was adopted to continue the previous one from 1997. Over several pages the government detailed which monuments in memory of which former partisans (and in some cases even naming individual fighters) were to be created and what educational sites and programs (including their titles) were to be developed for teachers and students in order to "contribute to the patriotic education of the youth" (Lietuvos Respublikos Vyriausybė 2002a). Clearly the government's decree had been prepared with help from the LGGRTC, which was charged with carrying out the initiatives. However, it was notable that the measure was adopted by the full cabinet, demonstrating the state's engagement with matters of remembrance at the highest levels.

This involvement, however, would also force the government to deal with historical controversy when it arose. A clear example was the dispute over the Tuskulėnai burial site. The mass grave at Tuskulėnai (barely 5 kilometers from Vilnius city center) had been discovered in 1994. Exhumations eventually revealed the remains of over 700 bodies (reported numbers differ), most of them carrying marks of torture and brutal killing. It soon turned out that these had been individuals killed by the Soviet security forces (NKGB at the time) in the years between 1945 and 1947 for their actual or alleged involvement in anti-Soviet resistance. It was known that the anti-Soviet partisan war had been particularly fierce around Vilnius at the time of the killings. This was therefore the prevailing assumption. A subsequent presidential decree ordered further forensic analysis as well as special research into the activities of the NKGB in those years. Meanwhile, nationalist politicians were quick to propose that Tuskulėnai park be turned into a memorial site for the martyrs of the Lithuanian resistance movement. In February 1998 the Vagnorius government issued a decree creating a Commission for Immortalization of the Memory of the Tuskulėnai Victims and tasked it with making plans for a memorial to be set up at the site (Lietuvos Respublikos Vyriausybė 1998). Yet over the next few years, research by historians at the LGGRTC and forensic experts revealed that only some of the victims killed at Tuskulėnai had indeed been anti-Soviet partisans; many others had been other types of "Soviet enemies" or indeed criminals. Among these people were Polish members of the Home Army (*Armia Krajowa*), Lithuanian members of the 1941 uprising, some Catholic priests, Red Army deserters and German members of Nazi death squads as well as a more sizable number of Lithuanians who had collaborated with the Nazis and most likely taken part in the murder of Jews. Although the remains of only forty-nine persons could ever be identified without a doubt, the fact that historical records showed that all kinds of killing took place at Tuskulėnai and that separating murderers from victims would become impossible prompted the government to demur in its grand plans. Several prominent members of the Jewish community spoke out against a one-sided commemorative monument, stressing that this would represent a provocation to their people. Again, it was Emanuelis Zingeris, director of the Gaon Jewish Museum in Vilnius at the time, who best summarized the dilemma. "It is as if the NKVD made this 'cocktail' and jigsaw for our generation with the intention of puzzling us . . . Completely innocent people and fighters for an independent and democratic Lithuania are mixed up with those who participated in the Holocaust" (cited in Tracevskis 2003). Critique would also come from people like Dalia Kuodytė, now an MP for the Liberal party, who warned about the international repercussions of such a project (Chersonski 2012).

Nonetheless, in 2002 the Brazauskas government decided to go ahead with creating a memorial site and "a proper ossuary for those 706 persons who had been shot and buried in that area between 1944 and 1947" (Lietuvos Respublikos Vyriausybė 2002b). In 2007, the government revamped this program by adding further detail about the programmatic content of the complex, as well as delegating administrative responsibility for the site to the LGGRTC and the Ministry of Culture (Lietuvos Respublikos Vyriausybė 2007). Meanwhile controversy also ensued over whether to create a "Tuskulėnai remembrance day," as discussed above. However, the Seimas continued to support the commemorative site as such. Finally, in September 2011 the Memorial Complex of the Tuskulėnai Peace Park (*Tuskulėnų memorialinis kompleksas*) was opened to the public.

For visitors, the Memorial Complex presents a rather indiscriminate picture of those whose remains have been found at the location. The actual burial site for the victims is very solemn with each set of remains being accorded an individual interment box. In turn, the boxes are stacked in the form of a circular wall, all built underground. Those who have been identified are marked with names. However, no other differentiation is made among the interred. In the adjacent Museum of Martyrs, no mention is made of the controversies and concerns that have surrounded the evolution of the site. Members of the Jewish community have seen in the entire controversy yet again a reflection of the broader tendency among Lithuanian politicians to indiscriminately classify persons targeted by Soviet security services as victims, thus ignoring or openly neglecting historical facts such as the involvement of many Lithuanians in the Nazi-led murder of Jews, or the anti-Semitic attitudes and at times criminal behaviour of national resistance fighters against (Lithuanian) civilians (Chersonski 2012).

Turning to Latvia, we see that the establishment of a more institutionalized truth-seeking body as well as a national framework for remembrance were influenced (as in Lithuania) by the initial surge of victim commemoration during the late 1980s. However, one of the specific catalysts for creating an official truth-seeking body, the TSDC, was to deal with two particular tasks: first, to collect information on individuals who might be suspected of having committed crimes against humanity as part of Stalinist terror in the 1940s, and second, to preserve and analyze the unique and complete card catalogue of former agent names recovered from the Soviet KGB in August 1991. Both of these issues have been discussed in Chapters 3 and 4, respectively. However, the important thing to note is how these tasks helped the TSDC to become a key institution of truth-seeking in Latvia, even though how it got there was slightly different from the LGGRTC in Lithuania.

As noted in Chapter 4, the TSDC was originally established in tandem with the Commission for the Investigation of Totalitarian Regime Crimes (TRNIK). Consisting of nineteen members from among both elected politicians and representatives of the Lutheran Church and victim organizations, the Commission was tasked with organizing and carrying out investigations into the crimes of totalitarian regimes and to submit the collected material to the courts. In turn, the Commission was empowered to create the TSDC in order to store and further analyze its collected material. Both truth bodies were to be financed from the state budget, and local municipalities were required to cooperate actively with them (Latvijas Republikas Augstākā Padome 1992c).

The key importance of the TRNIK and TSDC in terms of symbolic-representational justice is that the TSDC, in particular, followed up its specific investigations into crimes against humanity with broader studies of repression and suffering among victims. The TSDC's director, Indulis Zālīte, took an active part in these studies, having been a pro-independence activist during the late-1980s and having already started back then to collect information about the deportations. Researchers working at the Center carried out numerous interviews with victims and witnesses of Stalinist-era repressions, thus contributing considerably to overall truth about these crimes. Admittedly, most of these testimonials were gathered in connection with pre-trial investigations against former KGB agents whom prosecutors were thinking of indicting, and thus they were not part of any sociological-anthropological process of truth-seeking and recognition (as with the LGGRTC). However, by engaging with victims perhaps more than their mere criminal investigations would have required, researchers at the TSDC were able to contribute to truth-telling in a more durable sense.

More victim-centered efforts at storytelling and life-story collection in Latvia have been carried out by the Latvian Occupation Museum (*Latvijas Okupācijas muzejs*, LOM). This research and remembrance institution was initiated originally by émigré Latvians as early as 1993. Under the leadership of historian Paulis Lazda and with support from the Latvian Ministry of Culture, a private foundation was set up to run the museum. As with the Museum of Genocide Victims in Vilnius, the LOM also found a highly poignant location for its endeavor: the former Soviet-era Museum of the Latvian Red Riflemen situated in the Old Town of Riga. We include the LOM in our overview of symbolic truth and justice measures, for although the museum describes itself as a non-state entity and is politically independent, it does have an official law sanctioning and governing its activities (Latvijas Republikas Saeima 2006). This law, of course, reiterates the fact that the museum is a "private institution." However, the law also requires the state to finance part of the museum's budget (on average around 20%, the rest coming from private donations), and it acknowledges the LOM's collection as "a special and important component of Latvian cultural heritage." The LOM, for its part, acknowledges its role as a national caretaker in its mission statement, "to inform and educate the people of Latvia and other nations about the history and consequences of the occupation period *in order to strengthen the Latvian state and its place among the free and democratic nations* of the world" (emphasis added). Another indicator of the LOM's semi-official position is that for any foreign head of state or government leader visiting Riga, a de rigueur stop on the tour is the LOM. Hence, the museum is also indirectly a part of Latvia's public diplomacy.

At the same time, this semi-public, semi-private status may also have given LOM more leeway to deal with some of the problematic parts of recent Latvian history and thereby contribute more to *Aufarbeitung* (or dealing with that past) than was the case, for example, in Lithuania's Tuskulėnai controversy. For many years the LOM has cooperated actively with the Jewish Museum and Documentation Center in Riga to revise and improve those parts of its permanent exhibition that tell the story of the mass murder of Jews in Latvia. In 2012, the two institutions prepared a temporary exhibition showcasing one of the single most horrible mass killings of Jews that took place in the forest of Rumbula during the winter of 1941–42. The account did not shy away from also detailing the involvement of local Latvian collaborators in this mass crime. Moreover, with scholarly articles from its own as well as other researchers dealing with often most controversial aspects of Latvia's totalitarian past and published in the LOM's yearbooks, the museum positioned itself strongly within the Latvian and international academic discourse.[21]

In terms of directly working with victims on the level of symbolic truth and justice, the LOM is important because of its aim to "collect and record narratives of persons whose lives were dramatically influenced by the Soviet and Nazi occupation policies," as the museum puts it on its website. Alongside its permanent exhibition displaying artifacts, pictures and descriptions of people who were deported or perished under both Nazi and Soviet occupation, museum researchers have carried out since the late 1990s life-story interviews and recorded victim testimonials from those who survived their ordeal. According to one of the main collectors in this area at the museum, Lelde Neimane, by 2012 the LOM had collected some 2,000 videotaped testimonies (all together about 3,550 hours of material); moreover 2,370 video films (or 452 hours) have been put together. Nine full-scale documentaries have been produced for public viewing and can be purchased in the museum shop. Finally, the museum's "Audio-Visual Archive" contains countless other visual material, photos, diaries, paintings and drawings as well as other memorabilia from people who had been repressed by the Soviet regime. Among the LOM's 2,000 recorded testimonies, a large share (or 722) tell the story of the two mass deportations of 1941 and 1949 as well as of the subsequent hardship in Siberian exile. In some cases stories are related by the children of the deportees who were born in forced exile. Another 374 testimonies were collected from Latvians who had been part of various military and police units under Nazi occupation. Moreover,

[21] For a full list of these yearbooks and their contents, see the LOM's website at http://okupacijasmuzejs.lv/izzinai/publikacijas.

roughly 200 testimonies were recorded from people who had fled to the West (Sweden and Germany) in 1944–45 and either remained in Western exile or returned to Soviet Latvia. The rest of the audiovisual materials categorized by historical themes reflect the complexity of the Latvian totalitarian experience. They include stories of anti-Soviet partisans (forest brethren) and their supporters, of political convicts and various resistance groups as well as of Nazi-period forced laborers and repressed individuals (Neimane 2012). The museum researchers coded all of these testimonies for research purposes and thus created a unique database of oral material concerning often undocumented historical events to be included in documentaries, teaching materials and other representations of the past. But as Neimane confirmed from her own experiences of meeting with former victims and taking hundreds of interviews, these recordings have also a deeply personal effect on those who agree to give testimony and relate their often painful and intimate stories of suffering and subjugation. In this sense and on a very individual level, the truth-telling and dissemination efforts undertaken by the LOM have been a most direct form of recognition for the victims of repression.

The Estonian configuration of state institutions dealing with truth-seeking and truth-telling has been much more low-key, so much so that one could almost say there have been no such state institutions. True, the popular demand for historical research during 1988–90 did give rise to at least three national commissions charged with examining different aspects of the Soviet past. However, each of these was eventually concluded, and no formal state institution like the LGGRTC or the TSDC was created. The Institute of Historical Memory, as we have mentioned already, is definitely an important successor to the Estonian International Commission for the Investigation of Crimes Against Humanity (to be discussed below). However, because the Institute is located under the auspices of the president, it is not as grounded as a long-term state institution as its counterparts in Latvia and Lithuania.

Instead of permanent institutions, Estonia has seen a succession of temporal historical commissions, each of which has ended up examining different dimensions of the truth about Soviet rule in the country. The first such commission was formed back in June 1989 to examine the events surrounding the Soviet takeover of Estonia in 1940. Although it was composed of members of the Estonian Academy of Sciences, it was a rather politically driven body, because it was convened by the Presidium of the Estonian SSR Supreme Soviet and with the specific task of determining whether Estonia had joined the USSR voluntarily or not. In November of that year, the commission delivered its findings before a session of the Supreme Soviet, following which the parliament adopted a resolution nullifying the Acts by which Estonia had putatively joined the USSR. The commission in this respect played an explicit role in Estonia's overall independence struggle by laying down one of the markers on the basis of which Estonia would argue its right to restore its statehood. However, this was still an important milestone in national truth-telling.

Moreover, the experience of this first commission seemed to appeal to Estonian lawmakers, who shortly thereafter appointed another body of experts to analyze and calculate damages to Estonia as a result of Soviet occupation. Known as the Kahk commission (after its chair, the social historian and academician Juhan Kahk), this new body labored for three months before submitting its thirty-page report in January 1990. The report, which we will discuss in further detail in Chapter 7, presented a first comprehensive calculation of damages caused by Soviet rule in Estonia on the overall population numbers, the economy, nature, culture and language. Its main purpose (alongside contributing to historical truth), however, was to provide the Estonian side with a bargaining chip with Moscow in negotiations over independence.

Needless to say, the fact that both of these early commissions concluded their work so quickly said something about how much official truth-telling about Soviet and Nazi rule remained to be done. To this end, and once Estonia had become independent again in August 1991, the Presidium of the Estonian Supreme Council deemed the moment appropriate to form a third commission, this time to be named the State Commission for the Examination of Repressive Policies Carried out During the Occupations (*Okupatsioonide repressiivpoliitika uurimise riiklik komsijon* – ORURK) (Eesti Vabariigi Ülemnõukogu Presiidium 1992). The Commission's task was to examine policies of repression and genocide against Estonian citizens under the two totalitarian occupations, and to provide an overall assessment of the occupations. However, the Presidium did not provide the Commission with a clear set of guidelines as to how to fulfill this enormous task. Nor did it work out any practical details like financing. Rather, it was left largely to the appointed chair of ORURK, the distinguished novelist Jaan Kross, to figure out both the composition and operative details of this new state-sanctioned truth body. Eventually Kross recruited twenty-eight commission members, among them economists, historians, lawyers, psychologists and medical scientists. Also included were two representatives from victim organizations (among them the Memento Union) and members of the Lutheran Church. There was no non-Estonian or representative of an ethnic minority on the Commission; the only female member was a Virve Kask, a university professor.

The Commission came together for its first meeting on July 6, 1992. However, its momentum would be short-lived, since already in October the Supreme Council was succeeded by the restored Riigikogu, and with that the Commission no longer had a sponsor to report to nor funding to draw on.[22] After several months of uncertainty, Jaan Kross, now a member of the Riigikogu himself, eventually convinced the new parliament to re-confirm the mandate and composition of the Commission. A resolution adopted in June 1993 also reaffirmed the Commission's state financing and obliged it to report back to the Riigikogu twice a year.[23] Added to ORURK's pre-existing mandate was now a task to "evaluate the degree of economic damage inflicted on the Estonian people by the occupations." The final goal was to produce a "White Book" tallying the total damages suffered by Estonia's inhabitants since 1940. Overall, the Commission was given two years to complete its work (Eesti Vabariigi Riigikogu 1993b).

In comparative terms we can now see that ORURK had some of the same elements that the TRNIK had in Latvia. Both were composed of prominent individuals and tasked with examining the occupation period as a whole. In fact, the Riigikogu's 1993 resolution said that ORURK had the right to cooperate with comparable commissions formed in Latvia and Lithuania and with victims groups in the Russian Federation. The key difference would be that ORURK would remain on the level of a blue-ribbon panel with none of its members meant to actually devote themselves full-time to this endeavor.[24] Moreover, nothing like the Latvian TSDC was created alongside ORURK. True, ORURK would eventually have enough money to pay for archival research. However, none of this evolved into a real institution. Lastly, the Riigikogu's 1993 resolution stipulated that while commission members would be issued

22 The Riigikogu would no longer have a Presidium the way the Supreme Council did. Its presiding authority was a simple three-member board, whose main responsibility was to organize parliamentary business, not oversee political initiatives.

23 Moreover, in an interesting combination of transitional justice measures, the Riigikogu resolution also required that members of the reaffirmed commission submit to its chairman (Kross) a signed oath of conscience that they had not collaborated with the KGB or any other secret security agency.

24 Indeed, the voluntary basis on which commission members were to work was stated explicitly in the Riigikogu resolution.

identification cards, could gain access to all archives and could interview all individuals relevant for its research, they were required at the same time to hand over to the Prosecutor General's Office any material that might pertain to possible crimes against humanity. In this sense, ORURK's investigatory prerogatives were also much more circumspect than that of the TSDC, which worked closely with Latvian prosecutorial authorities. During debates before the Riigikogu, Jaan Kross admitted that many had wanted the Commission to serve as a preliminary investigatory committee for a possible Nuremburg-type trial of occupation officials. However, he defended the final format of the Commission, saying that in his opinion the most important task was to determine the extent of repression and suffering during the two occupations (Pettai 2013b).

As might have been expected given the parameters of the Commission, ORURK's *White Book* was not completed by 1995. Jaan Kross stepped down as chair in January 1996 (mainly for personal reasons), and his duties were taken up by the émigré Estonian Catholic priest and historian, Vello Salo. Over the next several years, Salo was able to push for substantially increased funding. Yearly allocations directly from the Estonian state budget went from less than €2,000 in 1994 to over €36,000 by 2000. This allowed the Commission to begin issuing individual reports and monographs, mostly on specific repressive policies and their targets, for example, about the fate of doctors during the occupations or children during the 1941 deportations as well as about artistic life under the regimes (Tamm 2013: 10). Many of these early studies were about victims; presenting lists of those deported and killed during the years of Soviet occupation (Hiio 2005). Yet, as the years dragged on, the Commission began to lose its political relevance and investigative purpose. Indeed, by the time ORURK released in 2005 its long-awaited *White Book: Losses Inflicted on the Estonian Nation by Occupation Regimes, 1940–1991* (Salo 2005), the Riigikogu had actually already ended the body's official status a year earlier. Moreover, both historical research and public discourse had evolved so much by then that the 175 pages of the *White Book* ultimately revealed little new in terms of conclusions.[25]

It is important to note in this regard that whatever weakness ORURK had, this did not mean that truth-telling did not take place in Estonia. On

[25] It is still worth noting that the *White Book* (2005) declared the June 14, 1941 deportation "a timeless genocide crime of the Soviet government with the aim of destroying the Estonian nation" (p. 14). Likewise, operation "Priboi" in March 1949 was classified as a "genocide crime" (p. 20).

the contrary, NGOs like the S-Keskus (affiliated with the State Archive) as well as the Estonian Occupation Museum (created by the private Kistler-Ritso Foundation) engaged very much in examining the Soviet past. However, from the perspective of identifying state-led truth-telling processes (as an indicator of truth and justice policies overall), Estonia was a quite limited example. As noted, Estonia even has an occupation museum that is comparable to that of Latvia. However, the museum was never a state-involved project. Rather, it has been financed and run since its inception by a private endowment donated by a wealthy émigré Estonian.

Against this backdrop of relative non-engagement by the state, it is no surprise to observe that efforts to symbolically recognize victims on a government level have also been limited. The most prominent example here remains President Meri's Broken Cornflower campaign from 2001. His was the only effort not only to offer individual victims recognition through his own persona but also to use the campaign as a way of raising societal awareness and overcoming many Estonians' seeming disinterest in the experiences endured by the older generation of fellow citizens during and after the war (Anepaio 2002). What is more, we can see a kind of correlation between this perceived indifference and the fact that Estonia has far fewer remembrance days during which public attention might be drawn to these issues. Overall there is practically no state-level involvement with "memory work." The only program that comes close to providing some form of individual-level recognition to victims through storytelling is carried out by mostly literary scholars and ethnologists under the roof of the Literary Museum and the Estonian National Museum in Tartu. Since 1996 these scholars have organized several public campaigns calling on people to write down their life stories and send them to the museums.[26] Moreover, more targeted campaigns were launched to collect individuals' recollections of repressions or of activities in the anti-Soviet resistance after the war. This has therefore been an invaluable effort at securing and preserving the subjective memories of people who lived and suffered during the worst periods of recent Estonian history. However, it cannot be considered a state-led policy of truth and justice aimed at recognizing victims. Its main effect

[26] Similar activities have been carried out by the Institute of Philosophy and Sociology at the Latvian Academy of Science, now University of Latvia since 1992. Over 2000 audio-recorded life stories have been collected over the years, preserved and stored for research in the archive (see Zirnite 2006; Bela-Krumina 2004).

may be personal-level catharsis for those who decide to participate, while its public consumption remains limited. As Terje Anepaio (2002: 56) observes, "the memories of repressions are nothing special anymore and have become a part of routinely collected memoirs."

The international historical commissions

In the previous sections of this chapter, we have analyzed a number of conventional ways in which states go about offering symbolic recognition to victims and thereby also aim to mold societal understandings and attitudes about the importance of the past. As a rule, these initiatives are domestic, and they emerge as an attempt by the nation to understand its own recent history. In the Baltic cases, however, an additional form of such inquiry has been present, and it is one that has had a prominent international dimension to it.

During a summit in the spring of 1998, the three Baltic presidents, Lennart Meri, Guntis Ulmanis and Valdas Adamkus, agreed to establish in each of their countries an international historical commission in order to organize research and carry out an evaluation of crimes against humanity committed under the Stalinist and Nazi occupation regimes from 1940 to 1956. This simultaneity, although conceivably a sign of Baltic affinity, was actually prompted by an external impulse, in relation to which the three presidents then decided to act jointly. As we noted earlier, since the early 1990s international Jewish organizations like the Simon Wiesenthal Center and the American Jewish Committee as well as representatives from the US State Department had been calling on the Baltic governments to undertake steps to legally and morally confront the history of their countries during Nazi occupation. Both in meetings behind closed doors and through media comments, the Baltic publics and political elites were reminded of the fact that in order to be fully allowed entry into the "Western community of values" a full examination of the historical truth surrounding the Nazi period was needed. Moreover, Efraim Zuroff from the Wiesenthal Center demanded that Baltic prosecutors finally start to look into cases of local Nazi collaborators involved with the mass murder of Jews and still living, whether in the Baltic states or abroad (see also Chapter 3). These, at times, rather vigorous allegations coming from both Holocaust survivors and those who spoke in their name were further enhanced by the scandals and controversies surrounding the Lithuanian rehabilitation of former Nazi collaborators in the early 1990s (see Chapter 5) or the Latvian honoring of former *Waffen-SS* legionnaires (discussed above).[27]

It was thus in response to these international voices that the Baltic presidents decided to create commissions that would include international members, historians, civic activists and public figures. The aims of these commissions (declared either by the presidents via speeches or via founding documents) were not only to establish factual knowledge about a rather insufficiently researched period but also to foster dialogue between the proponents of sometimes rather opposing views about past responsibilities and motivations.

Hence, these internationally precipitated and very much Holocaust-motivated historical commissions would seem to make them unrelated to our focus on post-communist truth and justice measures. Moreover, in Chapter 7 we will be discussing international reverberations to Baltic truth and justice policies, and there too we will address the commissions in that context. However, here we lay out a lot of what the commissions did or have done for two reasons. First, all three presidents decided in 1998 to task the commissions not just with undertaking Holocaust research but also with evaluating crimes against humanity committed on Baltic territory during the Stalinist period. Secondly, the results of the commissions' evaluative work, especially in Lithuania and Latvia, ended up having as a goal to influence not only an international audience but also "[the country's] official position on the historical questions which are the most painful, stereotyped and still uncovered," as the Lithuanian commission would proclaim on its website. Thus, these commissions became part of the politics of state-sanctioned truth and justice. Furthermore, the amount of archival material (mostly in the local languages) that was gathered and presented in the commissions' publications would be impressive and form a basis for further domestic and international scholarly research.

Yet, despite their shared origins and basic historical focus, the three Baltic historical commissions also exhibited striking differences in terms

[27] Estonia remained relatively untouched by the international media hype surrounding Baltic commemorative practices during the 1990s. It was only in the early 2000s when the Wiesenthal Center geared up its "Operation Last Chance" and in 2004 when the local government in the small town of Lihula set up a controversial monument in honor of Estonians who fought on the German side against the Soviets in World War II that Estonia also attracted wider international criticism of its handling of World War II commemoration. By that time, however, the Commission had already concluded its investigation into the Nazi period, thus refuting accusations that Estonia lacked the will to confront the historical truth. See also Pettai (2011b).

of their composition, organization and investigative mandates. In this respect we will see that if we take these variations to their logical conclusion, we could even conceptualize each of them differently within our broad analytical framework of truth and justice.

The International Commission for the Evaluation of the Crimes of the Soviet and Nazi Occupation Regimes in Lithuania (*Tarptautinė komisija nacių ir sovietinio okupacinių režimų nusikaltimams Lietuvoje įvertinti* – TKNSORNLI) was established by presidential decree on September 7, 1998 (Lietuvos Respublikos Prezidentas 1998). From the beginning, the Commission consisted of a more or less equal number of Lithuanian and international members, among them the émigré Lithuanian historian Saulius Sužiedėlis from the United States, German historians Joachim Tauber and Christoph Dieckmann, Israeli historian Yitzak Arad and two representatives of the American Jewish Committee, Nicholas Lane and Andrew Baker. As the first chair of the Commission, President Adamkus appointed Emanuelis Zingeris, then a member of the Seimas (affiliated with the Homeland Union-Lithuanian Conservatives).

After its very first meeting in November 1998, the Commission decided to form two parallel sub-commissions, separating research on the Soviet regime (1940–41 and 1944–53) from that of the Nazi occupation period (1941–45). With one exception, all the international members of the TKNSORNLI chose to serve on the Nazi-era sub-commission. Meanwhile, the research under the Soviet-era sub-commission would largely parallel work being carried out by the LGGRTC not only in terms of topics, but also in terms of authors, as many historians employed by the Center would end up writing the mostly English-language reports commissioned by the TKNSORNLI. However, given their different purpose as intermediate reports for an international commission, these writings did not just duplicate research done by the LGGRTC. Instead, most of them provided a thorough overview of existing archival knowledge about a particular event or historical issue in question, then detailed complementary findings or corrected previous conclusions. Moreover, the TKNSORNLI's rather detailed procedural regulations required each interim report to be reviewed by one or two other experts in the field before being scrutinized and approved by the full commission. Admittedly, most reports on the Soviet period were not submitted to *international* review but, rather, were evaluated by other Lithuanian scholars. Nonetheless, the requirement that all working texts be peer-reviewed allowed outside readers of these reports and their reviews to gain a more diverse picture of past events and of their historical evaluation.[28] Arguably, the more controversial studies that have been released are those concerning crimes committed during the early months of the Nazi occupation starting in late June 1941. For example, one study entitled "Holocaust in the Lithuanian Province 1941" by Lithuanian historian Arūnas Bubnys (2003) was ultimately not approved by the full plenum, since three different reviewers (including the Israeli commission member Yitzak Arad) challenged a number of the facts cited and sources referenced in the study. That notwithstanding, both the original text and the three reviews were published on the Commission's website in the interests of transparency and discussion.

From the outset the TKNSORNLI was viewed with much suspicion, among both Lithuanians and Jewish observers (Suziedelis 2007). While Lithuanians at home as well as among the émigré community saw the Commission as a foreign imposition and an attempt to paint Lithuania as a Holocaust perpetrator, Jewish commentators castigated the dual mandate of the body, calling it a "Red-Brown Commission" and reproaching it as an effort by Lithuanians to equalize the crimes of the Soviets with those of the Nazis and their local henchmen (Katz 2009). In the early years Emanuelis Zingeris tried to gain acceptance among Lithuanian politicians for the Commission's activities by organizing joint receptions during the annual meetings of the TKNSORNLI. Yet these efforts showed little effect, as hostilities against the Commission continued to be voiced in the media (Lane, Interview, 2011).

In 2007 the situation reached a climax, when the Israeli commission member Yitzak Arad, who happened to be a survivor of the Lithuanian Holocaust himself, was summoned by the Lithuanian Prosecutor General's Office to give witness testimony in an investigation into the killing of Lithuanian civilians by Soviet partisans in the Lithuanian countryside in 1944. As a 16-year-old escapee from the Vilnius Ghetto, Arad had joined a group of anti-Nazi partisans, and in his later memoirs Arad even described the killing in question (Arad 1979). Although the Prosecutor's Office took pains to emphasize that no criminal charges were being considered against Arad, the mere fact that a Holocaust survivor was being questioned in connection with a war crimes investigation caused an international outcry and led to the resignation not only of Arad but also of several other commission members and to a paralyzing of the Commission's entire research activities (Pettai 2011a).

[28] All of the Commission's texts have been made available on its website under "research works database."

In the wake of this turmoil, the TKNSORNLI was never formally dissolved; however, it did not meet again after 2007, and only a few reports were still published through 2009, all of them about Soviet regime crimes. Attention therefore shifted toward the educational aims of the Commission. Since Lithuania had joined the International Task Force for Holocaust Research and Education (now the International Holocaust Research Alliance, IHRA) in 2003, the Commission was given the additional task to oversee the establishment of "civic education centers" in museums, schools and other public institutions that would facilitate teaching about the country's totalitarian past (Budrytė 2013b). Engaging in teacher training and tolerance education, these centers work rather autonomously, each of them determining the direction and form of its own educational activities. In August 2012 President Dalia Grybauskaitė revived the Commission by issuing a new decree that outlined a new composition of international members, now encompassing renowned US historians of Soviet crimes like Timothy Snyder and Norman Naimark as well as again historians from Germany, Israel and elsewhere (President of the Republic of Lithuania 2012). Still, the new committee would not formally gather until a year later, pledging at the time to continue research especially on the Nazi period, picking up where previous investigations left off.

Similar to Lithuania, the establishment of the Estonian International Commission for the Investigation of Crimes Against Humanity (*Inimsusevastaste kuritegude uurimise Eesti rahvusvaheline komisjon* – IKUERK) constituted a duplication of already existing truth-seeking endeavors such as ORURK. Indeed, for several years Estonia maintained two parallel state commissions of inquiry into past regimes crimes. Yet while ORURK had been called into being by parliament and its research and publications were aimed mainly at a domestic audience, the IKUERK remained a purely presidential creation and had from the very beginning a distinctly international orientation. Moreover, President Meri went about forming his commission in a way that particularly enhanced its somewhat alien character within the Estonian political and societal context. Rather than entrusting established Estonian historians with the task of evaluating the historical crimes, Meri opted to form the commission of exclusively non-Estonians and mostly individuals he knew personally.[29] Moreover, among the seven members of the IKUERK

[29] According to commission member Nicholas Lane, Meri once voiced in a private conversation that he would not appoint any Estonian to the Commission, "because the

not a single one was a practicing historian, though some of the members had taken degrees in history. Thus the chair of the Commission, Max Jakobson, was a senior Finnish diplomat; other members included former Danish foreign minister, Uffe Ellemann-Jensen and German MP Wolfgang Freiherr von Stetten, the American Soviet affairs analyst, Paul Goble, a representative of the American Jewish Committee, Nicholas Lane, the Russian human rights activist, Arseny Roginsky, and the British political scientist Peter Reddaway. As in Lithuania, there were again no women among the commission members and no representative of any domestic constituency, except for the presidential advisee and point person for the Commission, Toomas Hiio, who coordinated the research teams of historians and PhD candidates who carried out the archival research.

During its first meeting in January 1999, IKUERK decided to structure its research work along the three main historical periods under scrutiny (1940–41, 1941–44 and 1944–53) and to start with the second one. This initial focus on the Nazi period was not a surprise given the background to the Commission's creation. In terms of its practical operation, the Commission convened (at least in its first years) twice a year to review the reports prepared by the Estonian researchers. Hiio would present the reports, followed by questions from the Commission and deliberations. Eventually the Commission would draw up joint "final conclusions" about each of the three historical periods.

The first of the "final conclusions" about the Nazi period was released in 2001 in English and later translated into Estonian and Russian. Over ten pages, the Commission outlined a "definition of terms" clarifying the use of legal terms such as "crimes against humanity," "genocide" and "war crimes." Firmly basing its use of these terms on international legal standards such as the Rome Statute of the International Criminal Court, the Commission ended up diverging somewhat from how Estonian criminal law, for example, had defined these crimes (especially genocide). In a second step the conclusion provided a brief overview of the "historical background," which included a listing of the criminal events during the period under investigation. The Commission provided a detailed assessment of the responsibility for these crimes, including naming individual perpetrators as well as organizations and institutions as part of its final summary. Both of the other "conclusions" that followed in 2004 (for the year 1940–41) and 2008 (for the period 1944/

moment he did, there would be political concerns, and this was something he wanted to avoid" (Lane, e-mail correspondence, June 2, 2011).

45–1953) were structured in a similar vein (Pettai 2013b). As a further product of the Commission's work, in 2006 Toomas Hiio (together with other Estonian historians) published the full collection of the individual research reports (along with the two first conclusions available at the time) in a monumental 1,300-page volume (Hiio et al. 2005). A second, more limited, volume of reports followed in 2009 covering the remaining period of the late Stalinist years (Hiio et al. 2009).

Again in contrast to its Lithuanian counterpart, the IKUERK approached its task to reveal and evaluate the facts about past mass atrocities and gross human rights violations from a viewpoint that can be described as technical rather than discursive or aimed at revealing complexities and ambiguities. The main sources used by the researchers for preparing their reports were official documents or other written sources. Research was carried out outside the public realm, and none of the individual reports was ever critically scrutinized by anyone other than the seven commission members. Thus, the results of the Estonian commission are important above all in terms of their academic value. They are useful as reference works that give a thorough insight into the activities of the different occupation authorities as documented in various archives. In our context, the results were also useful as a source for perpetrator-oriented judicial and symbolic truth and justice. Indeed, the Estonian commission's findings were consulted by the European Court of Human Rights in its 2006 ruling on *Kolk and Kislyiy v. Estonia* (see Chapter 7). However, as a source for engaging with survivors or for initiating policies that would honor the victims, the Commission's outcome was much more circumspect.

After the release of its final set of conclusions in 2008, the Estonian commission was officially dissolved. Hence, from among the original three Baltic commissions, only the Estonian one had been formally concluded as of 2014. Indeed, as is, the Estonian commission seemed to drag on a bit longer than originally expected. One reason for this was practical. When President Meri stepped down in August 2001, Toomas Hiio was put in charge of other tasks, leaving the Commission in a state of organizational ambiguity for several years. In addition, however, although Meri's successor, Arnold Rüütel, had nothing against the work of the Commission and even succeeded in increasing funding for it,[30] nothing was done to speed up the actual investigative process (Lane,

[30] The Commission started off with around €65,000 in annual funding under Lennart Meri. This rose to €130,000 under Rüütel before ending with a huge injection of €325,000 in 2008 to complete the Commission's final publications.

Interview, 2011). After Rüütel was replaced by Toomas Hendrik Ilves in 2006, the Commission had just completed its mammoth 1,300-page volume. This indicated that an end to the Commission was on the horizon. Under Ilves, administrative assistance for the Commission also improved, so much so that a final push was made in 2008 to release the final set of conclusions. Thereafter, Ilves pivoted toward the creation of the Institute of Historical Memory, as noted earlier.

The context for Latvia's creation of a history commission was again different from that of Estonia and Lithuania in that the Commission of the Historians of Latvia (*Latvijas vēsturnieku komisija* – LVK) convened by Guntis Ulmanis in the fall of 1998 actually represented the first state-sponsored truth-seeking forum that had a sole focus on the Nazi and Stalinist-era periods. To be sure, the TSDC had also been mandated to research the 1940s and 1950s, and as we showed earlier, it had already done a lot in this area. However, the rather small team of historians under Indulis Zālīte had to divide its attention among a vast number of tasks, including the complementing of material about more recent KGB activities, the verification of rehabilitation and victim status requests and carrying out pre-trial investigation for the Prosecutor General's Office. Additional historical research into Stalinist-era crimes remained beyond its immediate capacities.

What also marks the LVK off from its two Baltic equivalents (especially the Estonian one) is the fact that it was in the first instance a Latvian commission and only secondarily involved with international historians and other experts. This was reflected not only in the Commission's name (in that it did not have the word "international" in it) but also in its official mandate outlined in the Decree on the Commission of Historians adopted by the Cabinet of Ministers in 1999 (Latvijas Republikas Ministru Kabinets 1999). The regulations stated that the Commission shall (a) contribute to the analysis and assessment of crimes against humanity committed in Latvia by two totalitarian occupation regimes; (b) explain the research results to the Latvian population and the international community; and (c) encourage the involvement of younger scholars to research twentieth-century Latvian history. Thus, even though the "international community" was mentioned, the primary aim of the LVK's activities was domestically focused. This was further indicated by the fact that local membership of the Commission consisted of most of the well-established academic historians of Latvia as well as a few other experts such as the vice-director of the Latvian Occupation Museum, Valters Nollendorfs, and the Holocaust survivor, historian and long-time director of the Jewish Museum and

Documentation Center Marģers Vestermānis (Pettai 2011a). The Commission's research activities were subdivided into initially four research units headed by Latvian historians, one on the first year of Soviet occupation 1940–41, one on the Nazi occupation period 1941–44, one specifically on the Holocaust and the last one on the second Stalinist occupation 1944–56. Later, a fifth subunit was added to research Soviet rule in Latvia after 1956. During the first decade, the full commission met about once or twice annually to review and discuss the research activities of the various subunits as well as to organize international academic conferences on problems of researching particular aspects of the country's history. Yet, not only was a large part of the research carried out by Latvian historians, but also the results were published as individual studies in successive volumes mostly in Latvian. This meant that they were actually inaccessible to most of the non-Latvian-speaking commission members, not to mention an international audience. All of these factors indicate that the Latvian commission was the least internationally oriented of the three presidential commissions.

Moreover, from the perspective of domestic truth-seeking aimed at giving recognition to the victims of past regime repressions, the outcome was also rather mixed. To be sure, many of the individual academic studies published in the LVK's proceedings sought to reconstruct different concrete repressive acts against Latvians and other inhabitants of the country. They thus not only provided insight into the motives and actions of perpetrators but also acknowledged the victims of these acts (Onken 2007b). However, this was done in a rather unsystematic form and only to the extent that any conventional historical scholarship would involve the identification or mentioning of victims. This brings us to the second main difference between the LVK and the other two Baltic commissions, namely the way in which research results were presented to the public. Both the Estonian and Lithuanian commissions contracted historians to write reports on single historical issues determined by the commission. In turn, these were published in a systematic, mostly chronological and thematic fashion. By contrast, the LVK merely functioned as a publisher of rather eclectic conference papers, individual studies, bibliographical reviews, primary documents and reflections on theoretical and methodological aspects of researching the totalitarian past. Ordered roughly under rather general historical themes, these were published in a series of volumes called the "Symposium of the Commission of Historians of Latvia." By 2013, twenty-seven volumes in this series had appeared, published in both printed and online form.

This form of "truth dissemination," as well as the fact that there has never been any kind of joint commission report or concise summary of conclusions about the events and actions under investigation (or at least joint statements on individual research findings as done by the Lithuanian commission), further underlines the more academic rather than political character of this commission. Put perhaps more strongly, one could say that the LVK was little more than a state-sponsored academic history department, or a state-funded "clearing house for distributing research money, organizing conferences and publishing conference proceedings and research results," as one of its members described it (Nollendorfs, email correspondence, 2009).

Indeed, by the late 2000s the LVK had become the central institution for determining much of what was going on in contemporary historical scholarship in Latvia. In 2011, when President Jānis Bērziņš re-confirmed the Commission without giving any indication as to the time frame for completing its investigative tasks, it became even clearer that this was no longer (and perhaps never had been) the kind of ad hoc, temporary truth measure usually associated with a historically oriented official truth body. The re-confirmation took place after a period of several years in which funding for the Commission had completely dried up as a consequence of the 2008–2009 economic crisis. It also led to a *de facto* restructuring of the LVK in the sense that it was no longer composed of an equal number of local and international members. Despite a few names remaining listed among the "international members," no formal meetings with these members had been convened since 2008, and the LVK became a clearly domestic, long-term council of historical research.

To sum up this discussion of the Baltic international historical commissions, we may note that the commissions differed not only in their structural and operative forms but also in their goals over time, and the outcome of their investigative endeavors radically diverged. From a comparative perspective, it seems that the Estonian commission was the outlier. First, it was the only one that was composed exclusively of outsiders, i.e. non-Estonians. Secondly, as said before, the IKUERK remained the only one to conclude its ten-year operation, while the Latvian commission turned into a semi-permanent body of historical research and the Lithuanian commission had to interrupt and restart its work after a period of political controversy and organizational limbo. Thirdly, and related to the previous point, only the IKUERK managed to issue a final report and joint conclusions about its historical findings.

The other two commissions either never aimed at a final report, or limited themselves to joint statements on singular historical issues. Fourthly, and perhaps most interestingly, when analyzing the outcome of the three commissions we see that the joint conclusions drawn up by the IKUERK were primarily concerned with determining responsibilities for crimes against humanity that had been committed during both occupations of Estonia. Thus, as a non-judicial and mostly symbolic truth measure, the Estonian commission actually focused more on perpetrators than victims. It spent most of its time naming individuals responsible for specific crimes, detailing the structures of command and assessing the individual scope of freedom to refuse orders. By contrast, both the Lithuanian and the Latvian commissions concentrated on determining the extent to which the populations of their countries had been victimized by the two foreign powers. To be sure, we are talking here about the dominant investigative purpose and, of course, especially with regard to the Nazi period all three commissions aimed to detail the degree of local involvement in mass crimes. Nevertheless, when it comes to the Soviet past, the divergences in focus are evident. If we strictly followed our own conceptualization of state truth and justice measures, the Estonian commission would thus belong mainly to the category of symbolic-representational measures directed at perpetrators, thus Box 3a of our matrix. We do discuss the IKUERK briefly in that chapter; however, for the sake of comparative clarity and because truth-seeking is usually associated primarily with victims, the Estonian commission also has relevance here.

Finally, the Latvian commission stands out among the three commissions in that it featured very few of the key components usually associated with ad hoc state bodies aimed at truth-revelation for victims. In contrast to its Baltic counterparts, the LVK never systematically commissioned reports and drew up joint conclusions presented to the public in a concise and focused form. The fact that we still consider it a state policy of truth establishment arises mainly due to the fact that its creation in 1998 was based on a presidential decree and confirmed by the government, and that much of the research it subsequently sponsored aimed at revealing hitherto unknown facts about the suffering inflicted on Latvia's population by the Soviet regime.[31]

[31] In lieu of a final report, volume 14 of the series Symposium of the Historians of Latvia, edited by two members of the Commission, Valters Nollendorfs and Erwin Oberländer (2005), can

Comparative summary

This comparative look at truth and justice policies meant to provide symbolic-representational recognition for victims (categorized as Box 6 of our matrix model) has revealed considerable divergences across the cases with regard to the role of the state in this process of truth and remembrance, especially between Lithuania and Estonia. Once again, the patterns evident in some of our other areas of truth and justice recur. At one end of the spectrum, we have Lithuania taking a rather state-dominated approach to issues of remembering and historical truth by firmly institutionalizing these domains within government structures. At the other end we have Estonia exhibiting relatively little state engagement and regulatory ambitions in this area. As is so often the case, Latvia features a more varied picture, falling somewhere in between. While in the first decade after re-independence Latvia showed considerable determination in shaping public remembrance through legislative Acts and state-sponsored historical truth-seeking, during its second decade political support for sustaining this infrastructure and for sponsoring additional programs diminished.

These contrasts point to another comparative conclusion, which is that the divergence in approaches tends to increase over time. Whereas state funding for research institutions and regulatory enthusiasm among the legislators fade in both Latvia and Estonia, these actually increase in Lithuania. To put this in numbers, while funding in Latvia for the presidential commission and for research activities at the TSDC almost completely evaporated during 2008–10, the Lithuanian state budgetary allocation for the LGGRTC was in 2009 its highest on record, exceeding 7.5 million litas (€2.1 million). In Estonia, there are admittedly some later symbolic policies, such as the Broken Cornflower campaign of 2001 and the establishment of the *Mälu Instituut* in 2008. However, the fact that both were initiated by state presidents, whose powers are otherwise limited, is somewhat indicative of the overall lack of enthusiasm on the side of Estonian legislators concerning matters of public remembrance and truth-seeking.

With its firm institutionalization and centralization of symbolic truth and justice in the form of the LGGRTC, Lithuania clearly stands out

be considered the most comprehensive and yet thorough summary of the LVK's investigative work and outcomes until 2004. However, there is no indication in the book whether the claims and conclusions drawn by the various authors of this volume may be seen as any kind of formal and official conclusions by the entire commission.

among the three Baltic states. At its best time during the late 1990s, the Latvian TSDC came close to resembling the LGGRTC, as both institutions' activities stretched across most domains of judicial, administrative and symbolic truth and justice as outlined in our conceptual model. However, with the ending of criminal investigations after 2000 and considerable budget cutbacks after 2008, the TSDC no longer played such an active role in Latvia's truth and justice politics. Today, neither the recently established Estonian *Mälu Instituut* nor any Latvian institution comes even close to the kind of omnipotence the LGGRTC exhibits in the realm of truth and justice (as well as memory politics). If anything, the LGGRTC can be compared to a number of "national memory institutes" (NMIs), as George Mink (2013) calls them, in Central Europe, especially the Polish Institute of National Remembrance (*Instytut pamięci narodowej* – IPN), established in 1998 and funded by specific legislation. With the IPN the Lithuanian Center shares not only the characteristic of being in charge of procedures that stretch the entire scope of truth and justice measures toward both victims and perpetrators, but also the high degree of politicization of its investigative and commemorative work.[32] But also in other countries of Central Europe, NMIs have increasingly assumed the role of central agents of national memory deeply imbued in the politics of truth and justice after Communism.

Although the Baltic states therefore do have differences, they also have similarities in that all three states assigned considerable political and social meaning to revealing "the truth" and publicly remembering the Stalinist-era mass crimes. Though this did not necessarily show in the institutional set-ups or their funding, public references to the totalitarian past and to issues of historical justice have been a strong component of symbolic politics throughout the past two decades. All three Baltic societies share a historical understanding of their nations' recent past as that of collective victimization by two totalitarian powers. This is most pronounced in Lithuania, although it also evident in Latvia and Estonia. The countries also share an image of themselves as having engaged in collective resistance to Soviet rule – if not in armed form, then at least in

[32] In terms of sheer size, the IPN probably beats all other NMIs across the region; in 2009 it had over 2,100 employees, several local branches across the country and a budget of over €50 million. However, given Lithuania's smaller population and considerably more limited access to material from the KGB, the over 130 employees of the LGGRTC and its annual budget of over €1.5 million are still noteworthy.

moral and cultural terms. While this is important for national unity, the "fighting and suffering" paradigm (Budryte 2014) leaves little room for divergences or even an acknowledgment of the complexity of past experiences and current meaning-making processes. This is just as true for Latvia and Estonia as it is for Lithuania. Since alternative stories always emerge, this exclusivist paradigm has repeatedly become an issue of political contention, involving to various degrees domestic and international claimants.

These alternative historical experiences and narratives concern first of all the events of World War II and here in particular the involvement of local Estonians, Latvians and Lithuanians in Nazi mass crimes against Jews. This has certainly been one of the most politically charged issues in relation to Baltic retrospective truth and justice processes over the past two decades. As we have seen in this chapter, the contrasting views in relation not only to the historical circumstances, but also to how these should be addressed today has often involved high politics and, indeed, triggered the implementation of several state measures such as international historical commissions or the introduction or removal of remembrance days. When reviewing the political controversies around remembrance days or commissions that have emerged over the past years, it seems fair to say that this issue has been by far more relevant for Lithuanian truth and justice processes than for those in Latvia and Estonia. Moreover, when comparing political reactions to outside and domestic criticism, it is striking how much less willing Lithuanian legislators have been to compromise or at least acknowledge the fact that the recent past holds many truths, some of them less comfortable. Whereas, for example, Latvian legislators finally removed the controversial remembrance day for the Latvian Legion, Lithuanian MPs pressed ahead with much more contentious memorial days such as the Day for the Victims of Tuskulėnai.

The collective "others" in terms of symbolic truth and justice have also been different across the three states. Whereas Lithuanian policies have been greatly determined by the Jewish-Lithuanian conundrum, Latvian and Estonian official acts have often been influenced by lingering mistrust vis-à-vis Russians. As we saw also in Chapter 3 concerning criminal-judicial measures, the "Russia factor" often drives political contention. Thus, the Latvian Legion controversy in 1998 was aggravated not least by the fact that Russia launched considerable critique at the country, and to this day it is mostly young local Russians who protest during the unofficial remembrance ceremonies on March 16. Meanwhile in Estonia, the Bronze Soldier riots of 2007 merely underscore this point. The refusal among Estonian officials to acknowledge the importance of this monument to local Russian historical memory ended up causing considerable public and political turmoil.

Yet apart from these two particular alternative views on Estonian, Latvian and Lithuanian recent history, it is worth noting that the state-endorsed national "fighting and suffering" paradigm also could stand one day to be complemented by other, perhaps even more painful, stories of collaboration and victimization. These recount anti-Soviet resistance fighters terrorizing the population in the Lithuanian countryside and the individual stories of survival in a most violently polarized context; they talk also about Estonian, Latvian and Lithuanian Communists who actively helped to denounce and deport their neighbors or benefited from the disappearance of these fellow citizens. While some historians and social scientists have begun moving toward revealing these previously blank pages of the national past,[33] the victims from these wrongdoings will probably remain for some time without commensurate recognition for their suffering.

[33] See, for example, the study by Strods and Kott (2002) on the "operation Priboi" in 1949 where they state how "striking . . . is the shattering of the perception that these forces [of the MGB] bear the sole responsibility for forcing Balts from their homes from 25 to 29 March 1949. The level of local complicity and participation (over 60%) in the operation is truly shocking, and will undoubtedly prompt some soul-searching among peoples usually accustomed to thinking of themselves as largely blameless victims" (p. 30). Moreover, it is often the inquiries into subjective memories done by oral history and social memory researchers in all three Baltic states that reveal alternative victim-stories. This is in particular true where inquiries go into individual motivations and actions in the violent context of postwar partisan battles. Here oral history research has revealed many undocumented stories of victimization that appear to stand in conflict with dominant master narratives about the heroic fight against suppression in the public realm. See Petersen (2001), especially ch. 6; Pušinskytė (2008); Davoliūtė (2014).

7

External reverberations: the international dimension of Baltic truth and justice

Since April 2007 the visitor's area of the European Parliament's Strasbourg building has been endowed with a memorial plaque that reads "Commemorating the victims of Soviet Totalitarian Communism, 65 years after the first mass deportations 14.06.1941 – 14.06.2006 Estonia, Latvia, Lithuania." The idea to open such a site had been initiated less than a year earlier by a group of mostly Baltic MEPs from the European People's Party (EPP-ED), among them Tunne Kelam from Estonia, Vytautas Landsbergis from Lithuania and Aldis Kušķis from Latvia. Since its unveiling, the plaque reminds members and visitors to the European Parliament of one of the worst mass crimes committed against the Baltic peoples by the Soviet regime. In March 2008 Estonia's President Toomas Hendrik Ilves together with Hans-Gert Pöttering, then president of the European Parliament, laid flowers at the memorial, and in 2011 the Parliament held a special plenary session commemorating the seventieth anniversary of the June 14 deportations. During this session Tunne Kelam, speaking on behalf of the EPP-ED group, impressed upon the legislators that "full knowledge of these massive crimes against humanity should become an integral part of the common European history, because only in this way can United Europe send a message of 'Never Again' to tens of thousands of victims and their descendants" (Reconciliation of European Histories Group 2011).

Since becoming full members of the European Union (EU) in May 2004, representatives from the three Baltic states have been at the forefront of what has been called a "European battlefield" of memory (Leggewie 2009). From the Eastern European and Baltic perspective, this was a struggle not only to change historical perceptions to include the memories of two totalitarian regimes in a broader European historical narrative but also to put issues of retrospective justice, victim recognition and criminal adjudication onto a European political agenda. So far this book has dealt with national political contexts as this is the primary arena in which the search for truth and justice (both retributive and restorative) takes place. Political and social actors aim to bring forth or to hinder the adoption of particular measures as part of a domestic political struggle over the past. However, often, and not just in the European context, these efforts will flow beyond a single country's borders. Actors will attempt to promote their campaign vis-à-vis other countries, international actors or international publics. Cath Collins (2010) has demonstrated vividly in the case of Latin American countries how transitional justice advocates have attempted to draw on international human rights norms in order to find new allies in their domestic political struggles. In cases of post-conflict transitional justice, the international community plays an even more direct role.

In this chapter we will lay out the external reverberations of the Baltic states' struggles for transitional and retrospective justice. Three such dimensions will be examined. We will begin with a brief recapitulation of the different transitional and retrospective justice issues that have streamed beyond the formal national jurisdictions of the Baltic states and have found adjudication in international institutions like the European Court of Human Rights (ECtHR). What bears additional examination here is the combined or overall impact that institutions such as the ECtHR have acquired in relation to settling transitional and retrospective justice claims. Can we say that European judicial bodies have developed a role in setting norms for such issues because truth and justice actors from different member states have decided to appeal to them for relief or adjudication? Have such institutions been dragged into such disputes against their will or have they taken up this new domain and sought to find equitable solutions? We will see that the Baltic states have helped to develop this phenomenon quite distinctively within the two realms of criminal trials against perpetrators of recognized international crimes as well as lustration, with some landmark precedents being set.

The remaining two dimensions of external reverberation involve efforts to bring truth and justice issues to the attention of other countries or international organizations. Within the context of post-communist transitional and retrospective justice, the two main target groups have been European-level arenas and Russia.

To start with the latter, it is indeed rarely the case anywhere in post-communist Central and Eastern Europe that truth and justice issues would be dealt with without any kind of external reverberation vis-à-vis the Russian Federation. To the extent that Russia has been considered the successor state of the Soviet Union in international legal terms, many political groups and even state actors in Central and Eastern Europe have sought to incorporate Russia into their truth and justice endeavors. Moreover, over the past two decades Russia has itself actively sought this heritage, not just by taking over the USSR chair in the UN Security Council and other international bodies, but also through reintroducing the tune of the Soviet anthem or celebrating certain Soviet holidays. At the same time, the state has continuously refused to take legal responsibility for the criminal legacy of the Soviet regime, both within its own state borders and beyond. Unsurprisingly, the Baltic states as former Soviet republics have sought from the beginning of their regained statehood to link Russia directly to possible compensation for damages caused by Soviet rule. The Balts' entire political doctrine concerning the illegal Soviet occupation and annexation of their countries has prompted many politicians to develop a formal approach toward demanding justice in the form of reparations from Russia as the next-best source of accountability. To what extent any of these efforts have been consequential will be examined in a second part of this chapter.

Already during the early years of negotiations with the Soviet Union over economic and political independence, Baltic leaders sought to rally international support behind their cause, not least by reminding the world of the illegal character of their countries' 1940 annexation, now classified as an aggression, and the policy of non-recognition pursued by many Western states throughout the Cold War period. While they were relatively successful in this respect during the independence struggle, the subsequent years of democratic state-building and international integration revealed deep divergences with regard to the historical-legal interpretations of the Soviet-communist legacy as struggles over citizenship legislation and minority rights in Estonia and Latvia as well as controversies over World War II commemorations revealed. The issue of contrasting memories not only came to define Baltic–Russian relations, it posed also serious challenges to the nascent democracies' Western foreign relations. After gaining full membership in the EU in 2004, Baltic "mnemonical recognition-seeking" (Mälksoo 2014: 95) reached a new level. Now Baltic political representatives could forge new alliances and make use of European legislative instruments to further push their claim for a pan-European political and judicial response to the crimes of Communism.

To be sure, almost all of the countries of Central and Eastern Europe have in one way or another been involved in campaigns to get the EU, the Council of Europe (CoE) and other European institutions to denounce the Communist regime crimes and to acknowledge the enormous suffering Communism inflicted on their nations. Often they have done so by linking the recognition of the victims of Communism and of Nazism, in particular the Jews, demanding equal treatment and thus implicitly, sometimes explicitly, equalizing the totalitarian regimes' mass crimes. While these attempts have been fraught with controversy and mostly counterproductive with regard to any form of dialogue, such campaigns have been a logical consequence of the burgeoning of truth and justice issues within and beyond the confines of individual post-communist countries. Baltic politicians have been particularly active in these campaigns, initiating several resolutions and sponsoring remembrance programs and activities. The last section of this chapter will therefore examine these efforts in more detail and note in turn three subtypes of this struggle. The first pertains to formal institutional campaigns within European institutional arenas such as the European Parliament (EP) or the Parliamentary Assembly of the Council of Europe (PACE). As we will see, the activities of Baltic politicians in lobbying for the condemnation and remembrance of Communism in different institutional settings has yielded a rather mixed outcome. On the one hand, the EU as such continues to unequivocally reject a pan-European judicial approach to the legacies of Communism and declares this a domain of national legislation and jurisdiction. On the other hand, the EP and the European Commission (EC) have shifted over the past decade toward greater recognition of Stalinist crimes and active support for the memory of victims. The latter aspect becomes particularly evident when examining the various parliamentary resolutions and declarations adopted since EU enlargement in 2004 on the memory of totalitarianism in Europe. Equally telling are developments toward further strengthening of EU financial instruments to support grassroots remembrance projects relating to both the Nazi and Stalinist-era crimes (Prutsch 2013).

Besides "working the EU institutions," another subtype of promoting post-communist truth and justice in Europe involves individual politicians addressing public audiences and forums. Needless to say, the debate over evaluating the historical meaning of Communism in Europe takes place at many levels in society, and the aim of this book is not to cover all of them.[1] However, we do want to highlight the way in

[1] A vivid example of how the historical meaning of communism has been altered at the cultural level in Europe involves the critical acclaim and popularity enjoyed by the novels written by the young contemporary Finnish writer Sofi Oksanen (2010). Her most famous work, *Purge*, is set in the Estonian countryside and tells the story of two women of different generations forced to confront their own dark pasts of collaboration and resistance, of rape and sexual slavery set against the backdrop of the Soviet occupation of Estonia.

which political actors from the Baltic states have attempted to take their justice message directly to Western publics as an extension of their own domestic truth and justice efforts.

A third form of Western-oriented justice communication involves a combination of the previous two subtypes, when we describe efforts by Baltic presidents to promote their perspective on the communist past by convening high-profile international commissions or by addressing international summits and other diplomatic events. While the former may contribute mostly to the promotion of a more knowledge-based international debate among experts and "memory agents," the latter becomes important because it can actually generate considerable international media coverage, thereby also reaching wider publics. Our discussion will hence return briefly to the three presidential historical commissions already discussed in Chapter 6 as well as touch upon the ways in which the three Baltic presidents decided to deal with Russia's invitation to mark the sixtieth anniversary of the Soviet victory over fascism on May 9, 2005 in Moscow.

Baltic cases adjudicated by the European Court of Human Rights

As part of their accession to the CoE during the early 1990s, Estonia, Latvia and Lithuania all ratified the European Convention on Human Rights (ECHR). This accord allowed residents of these countries to appeal domestic court judgments to the ECtHR if such rulings violated fundamental rights as defined by the ECHR. In terms of retrospective and transitional justice, this had considerable importance since several individuals who had been sentenced or otherwise sanctioned by domestic courts for their past involvement with the repressive Soviet state apparatus did in fact lodge appeals with the ECtHR. As we will show in the following, where these cases involve *retrospective* justice (i.e. convictions relating to the mass crimes of the 1940s), the ECtHR mostly found in favor of national judgments. The few cases where European judges voiced concern about domestic legal interpretations pertained to certain convictions of ex-KGB operatives for genocide. Yet these rulings had little impact on subsequent prosecutorial activities, nor did they directly affect domestic criminal proceedings or legislation. The issue was quite different, however, with regard to *transitional* justice cases, where political restrictions or professional bans had been imposed on individuals who had been previously involved with the Soviet KGB or with anti-state activities after 1990. Here the ECtHR has considerably reined in domestic jurisdiction, by revoking national judgments and/or demanding monetary compensation for the appellants.

Of the roughly three dozen individuals who have been sentenced by Baltic courts for crimes against humanity, genocide or war crimes discussed in Chapter 3, eight have sought to appeal their convictions with the ECtHR in Strasbourg. Three have been from Estonia (Kolk, Kislyiy and Penart), four from Latvia (Farbtuhs, Kononov, Larionovs and Tess) and one from Lithuania (Vasiliauskas). The essence of the appellants' claim has been that their conviction violated Article 7 of the ECHR or the prohibition on trying individuals for acts not deemed criminal at the moment of their commission. In all of these instances, however, the Baltic states were vindicated: their conviction of former Soviet KGB (NKVD, MGB) agents for involvement in deportations and other acts of severe repression was deemed in accord with international human rights law. In a few instances, cases were communicated back to the responsible governments for further consideration, as is done in cases where the European judges were not in a position to admit the application, but did see a potential violation of the ECHR. Some of these cases as well as one particularly controversial war crimes case, that of *Kononov v. Latvia*, deserve a closer look in this chapter, as they reveal surprising ambiguity among the international judges with regard to the legal assessment of crimes committed by the Stalinist regime in the Baltics during and after World War II.[2]

As we showed in Chapter 3, the Fourth Section of the ECtHR fully confirmed in 2006 Estonia's judicial rulings against August Kolk and Petr Kislyiy, stressing the applicability of international norms that define deportations as crimes against humanity at the time of the two defendants' involvement with the 1949 deportations in the country. The judges thus found no violation of Article 7 of the ECHR and rejected admission of the case due to the "manifestly ill-founded" arguments of the applicant (European Court of Human Rights 2006a). Moreover, the chamber concurred with the Estonian courts' reasoning that retroactive prosecution and punishment were admissible even for acts that were not considered a crime in national or international law at the time, yet were "criminal according to the general principles of law recognised by civilised nations." In taking this view, the Court drew expressly on the

[2] For a comprehensive, albeit mainly legal analysis of the ECtHR's rulings on cases of retrospective criminal justice from Latvia, see Švarca (2014).

second part of Article 7 of the ECHR, which states that retroactivity is permitted in cases where crimes are of such extensive proportions.

Two years later the Third Section of the ECtHR ruled on a very similar case from Latvia against Nikolajs Larionovs, who had been convicted for crimes against humanity and genocide by the Latvian courts for his ordering of the deportation of over 500 people in 1949. Here, however, the European judges did see a potential violation of Article 7 to the extent that the conviction was for genocide, and they decided to communicate the case back to the Latvian government. In fact, in contrast to their colleagues in the *Kolk and Kislyiy v. Estonia* case, the judges in this instance did not further consider the historical circumstances through which Latvia had come under Soviet rule, nor did they consider the previous arguments pertaining to Article 7.2 of the ECHR. Instead, the judges declared themselves not in a position to rule on the admissibility of the complaint and deferred a decision on the matter to a later point (European Court of Human Rights 2008c).

One of the reasons for the divergent conclusions in these two cases (despite the fact that both concerned individuals actively involved in the 1949 deportations) could well be the fact that while the Estonian courts had convicted Kolk and Kislyiy for crimes against humanity, Larionovs' conviction included the crime of genocide pursuant to Article 68.1 of the Latvian Criminal Code. The broad definition of genocide in this law allowed Latvian courts to classify the deportations of 1949 as genocide, even though this treatment diverges from conventional international understandings of this crime in legal terms. This interpretive divergence might have been behind the European judges' decision in the Larionovs ruling not to even consider Article 7.2. Instead, the chamber took a rather narrow and domestically focused view on the issues of legality and foreseeability, taking the Soviet law at the time as their point of departure. While it is not in the ECtHR's competence to rule on national legal interpretations of international norms and principles, the post-ponement of a decision in this as well as in one other Latvian case indicates a certain uneasiness among European judges with the genocide concept in the Latvian law. Similar conclusions were reached a year later in the only Lithuanian case so far brought to the Court, that of *Vasiliauskas v. Lithuania*, which involved a genocide conviction for the killing of anti-Soviet partisans (Žilinskas 2009: 334).

The two decisions on admissibility discussed here reveal, however, also deeper differences that cannot be explained merely by acknowl-edging diverging interpretations of international legal norms. Rather, the way in which the two sections of the ECtHR elaborated on the history and relevant legal norms in these cases as well as their treatment of the national courts' rulings hints at more fundamental ambiguities with regard to the crimes of the Soviet regime in the Baltics and their legal-judicial assessment. Thus, in *Kolk and Kislyiy v. Estonia* the judges left no doubt about the illegal nature of the occupation and annexation of Estonia by the Soviet Union in 1940, and hence irrespective of whatever Soviet law may have been in force at the time, the deportations of 1949 took place under an illegal regime.[3] By contrast, the ECtHR decision in the Larionovs case presented the historical and judicial context in a way that suggested no illegal interruption of Latvian sovereignty. Instead, the 1940 introduction of the Soviet Criminal Code in Latvia was treated as if it were done by a fully sovereign entity, the Latvian SSR. The ruling bore no mention of the Hitler–Stalin Pact, the forced military takeover of the country or of the liquidation of independent statehood. In this light, the retroactive conviction of Larionovs did seem like a violation of the ECHR. In this respect, the Court had yet to fully synchronize its understanding of the Soviet period in the Baltic states.

This same lack of consensus became evident in another case brought to the ECtHR from the Baltic states that was admitted around the same time and concerned the former Red Army veteran and war crimes convict Vassily Kononov. As we showed in Chapter 3, this case had already quite fatigued the Latvian court system with contradictory judgments being reached by various level courts. After the final judgment of the Latvian Supreme Court in 2004 that upheld the conviction for war crimes, Kononov filed a complaint to the ECtHR with the declared intention of obtaining full acquittal. He claimed (as had others) a violation of Article 7 of the ECHR, since his actions during World War II in the village of Mazi Batie could not be considered a war crime according to the laws of war recognized at the time.[4] A first judgment reached in 2008 by the (Former) Third Section of the ECtHR (the same that had ruled on the other Latvian cases) found the applicant's allegation confirmed, thus promulgating that Latvia had violated Article 7.1 of the ECHR. Latvia subsequently appealed this judgment to the Court's Grand Chamber and thereafter received a complete vindication of its arguments.

[3] Indeed, tellingly from the perspective of this book, the Court also relied heavily on the findings of the Estonian international historical commission when drafting its historical overview.

[4] The historical details of this case are discussed in Chapter 3.

Specifically, three key issues came to define the ECtHR's contradictory rulings. These involved, first, the question of whether or not the villagers killed in Mazie Bati could be classified as "combatants" or as "civilians." Secondly, it was necessary to clarify which laws of war applied in this particular case and, thirdly, whether or not Latvia at the time was occupied by one or two foreign powers. For the first two questions, a precise re-examination of the gruesome events of May 27, 1944 was essential and indeed would become central to the second judgment of the Grand Chamber. However, the issue of whether or not Latvia was a doubly occupied state in 1944 was pivotal to the first judgment of 2008. Both judgments demonstrate the extent to which European institutions are still grappling with the criminal legacy of Soviet Communism and how little consensus there is about the ways in which the Baltic states have adjudicated these crimes after 1991.

In the 2008 judgment that found in favor of Kononov, a narrow majority of ECtHR judges concluded that Kononov had "legitimate grounds for considering the male villagers [in Mazie Bati] to be collaborators with the German forces," and hence the killing of the villagers was a justifiable measure protected by relevant laws at the time, including the 1907 Hague Convention. On the basis of this assessment, the judges ruled that Kononov's conviction for war crimes was insufficiently grounded (European Court of Human Rights 2008a; see also Mälksoo and Laaring 2011: 103).

As we saw earlier with the Larionovs case, the ECtHR judges in this instance also did not consider whether the second part of Article 7 might apply. Moreover, the final ruling's assessment of the events in 1944 revealed a striking ignorance of the historical circumstances under which Latvia had come under Soviet control and found itself in a situation of "double occupation" as the Latvian side insisted. To be sure, the judges were deeply divided, as confirmed by the fact that several of them felt the need to add their personal opinions to the ruling – something rather unusual for the ECtHR. In a "concurring opinion" added to the judgment, Dutch judge Egbert Myer explained his vote in favor of Kononov by noting a personal uneasiness with seeing a former member of the anti-Hitler Allies retroactively punished for war crimes. Kononov's prosecution over fifty years after the alleged offenses seemed to him like a "flagrant injustice" that would be only justifiable if there had been immediate, yet failed efforts right after the war to criminally adjudicate the case. This, however, had not been the case, as he observed. Rather, Kononov had been decorated as a war hero even though the events of that day in May 1944 were well known (para 2). Judge Myer refused to formally comment on the "'double occupation' viewpoint of the Latvian government." Rather, he did so implicitly by equalizing the situation of Latvia under Nazi occupation with that of the Netherlands, his home country. Even though he admitted to the possibility that Latvia's situation might have been more complicated, he ultimately came to the conclusion that, similar to the Netherlands, "there was no justification for a pro-Nazi attitude or active collaboration with the Nazis in Latvia" (para 10). With its final ruling the Court thus ultimately ignored a whole wealth of legal and historical research accumulated on the issue over the previous two decades. It also missed a chance to overcome the "discriminatory standard for war crimes in the context of World War II" as established by the postwar legal settlements exempting former members of the Allied powers from charges of war crimes (Mälksoo and Laaring 2011: 105).

This was somewhat revised by the second judgment on the case, this time by the Grand Chamber of the ECtHR (European Court of Human Rights 2010). As said, the Latvian government appealed the first judgment thus forcing another decision on the case. This time, the Latvian government's position was strengthened not only by having a renowned international legal scholar, William Schabas, on the official governmental delegation to the proceedings but also by the Lithuanian government which made its own written submissions in the case, just as Russia continued to serve as a third party in support of Kononov. In May 2010 the Grand Chamber of the Court reversed the previous judgment and confirmed that Latvia's conviction of Kononov for war crimes did not violate Article 7 of the ECHR. Addressing the issue of defining the villagers as combatants or civilians, the Court now took a wholly different approach. Rather than arguing purely in legalistic terms (i.e. what constituted a "combatant" or what type of law existed at the time) or morally (i.e. judging the villagers for their Nazi sympathies), the full Chamber now pointed to the horrible details of the committed offense, namely the burning alive of a pregnant woman. Moreover, the judges declared that

> even if the deceased villagers were considered combatants or civilians who had participated in hostilities, *jus in bello* in 1944 considered the circumstances of their murder and ill-treatment a war crime since those acts violated a fundamental rule of the laws and customs of war protecting an enemy rendered hors de combat [outside the fight]."
>
> (European Court of Human Rights 2010: para 216, 67)

The brutal and violent way in which the villagers had been killed was thus considered a crime falling under Article 7.2 of the Convention, which states that certain acts are punishable regardless of the will or wording of current law. As several commentators have pointed out, this second judgment by the ECtHR wrote legal history, as it applied for the first time a universalist concept of war crimes to crimes committed by an Allied power during World War II (Mälksoo and Laaring 2011; Volzhskaya 2011; Žilinskas 2011).

Not surprisingly, Russia reacted strongly to this judgment, calling it a "dangerous precedent," an attempt to revise the Nuremberg trials and to legitimize Baltic efforts to rewrite history (RIA Novosti 2010; Pravda.ru 2010). Indeed, the contrasting arguments and claims made in the two Strasbourg court proceedings against Kononov very much mirrored the divergences in historical and political interpretations that define current relations between the Baltic states and the Russian Federation, as we will further explore in the next section. The ECtHR's ruling on Baltic retrospective criminal justice cases ultimately therefore stand in a broader context of pan-European processes of reassessing the legacies of the two totalitarian regimes of the twentieth century, both in historiographical and legal-political terms. Whether the Kononov judgment of 2010 represents, indeed, "a major victory for the broader politics of seeking recognition for the distinct East European experiences with twentieth-century totalitarian regimes and the legal treatment of communist crimes on par with the crimes of the Nazis," as Maria Mälksoo asserts (2014: 93), may be debated. It certainly did not mean a general confirmation of Baltic rulings with regard to Stalinist-era crimes, as an ECtHR judgment on one of the Baltic (most likely Lithuanian) "genocide cases" has yet to occur.

As already pointed out, none of the ECtHR rulings of war crimes and crimes against humanity cases had much effect on national prosecutorial processes. In Latvia, where the Court's Larionovs ruling might have prompted prosecutors and judges to formulate their legal argumentation more carefully, the impact was only hypothetical, since the prosecution of former NKVD operatives had by then largely tapered off. The 2009 adoption of an amendment to the criminal law that finally instituted a separate codification of crimes against humanity (and not just war crimes or genocide) might have been partially influenced by the ECtHR, yet it would not result in any new court cases. In Estonia, the confirmation of national jurisdiction in both the Kolk/Kislyiy and the Penart cases was met with great satisfaction by the law enforcement agencies. As one of the persons in charge of these criminal cases within the Estonian Security Police Board, Martin Arpo, wrote:

> For Estonia, these cases were more than just disputes about maintaining human rights during a criminal proceeding. They were actually disputes about the universal validity of international humanitarian law. The result was an important landmark for our law enforcement authorities and courts.
>
> (2012: 104)

While the cases discussed so far pertained to retrospective criminal justice cases, namely, cases concerned with relatively distant crimes, we may now shift attention to cases of transitional criminal justice that have been appealed to the ECtHR. Here advocates of criminal-legal measures against erstwhile perpetrators had a similarly victorious moment in 2008 when the Court ruled against a joint appeal lodged by Juozas Kuolelis, Leonas Bartoševičius and Mykolas Burokevičius – the three one-time leaders of the Lithuanian Communist Party who had been convicted of treason for having conspired against the re-establishment of Lithuanian independence in 1990–91. Once again, the appellants sought recourse to Article 7, saying that because Lithuania had been in flux during those years, it had been impossible to know what would happen and that their activities in defense of a certain vision for Lithuania could not be criminalized *post hoc*.

In this instance, however, the ECtHR had little problem dismissing the case, since Lithuania had adopted in November 1990 a series of changes to its legal code criminalizing precisely the kinds of militancy that the three defendants had engaged in. In other words, the three men had been responsible for "publicly urging the forceful overthrow of the sovereignty of the state" and creating "anti-state organizations" after the criminal code had been amended. Therefore, they had been convicted in full conformity with the ECHR. The Court also expressed its belief that given the free and fair nature of the February 1990 elections that had created the Lithuanian parliament at the time, the legislature was fully legitimate to pass and enforce specific legislation concerning treason (European Court of Human Rights 2008b).

A second domain of justice, where the ECtHR would develop a certain degree of case law in the realm of transitional justice, involved assessing the merits of political-administrative measures adopted (or Box 2b in our matrix). However, here the outcome for the Baltic states would be mixed. Whereas Latvia would find vindication in its efforts to prevent erstwhile pro-Soviet activists from being able to stand for public office, Lithuania would be rebuffed in its lustration policy.

The facts concerning these cases were outlined already in Chapter 4. Namely, the Latvian politician Tatyana Ždanoka had appealed to overturn Latvian legislation barring her from running as a candidate in national and local elections because she had been active in a pro-Soviet organization that had attempted a coup against the Latvian government in January 1991. In June 2004 Ždanoka appeared to obtain victory, when a chamber of the ECtHR found in her favor. At the time, the judges stressed the issue that limiting a person's passive electoral rights because of actions carried out before such restrictions were imposed went too far. However, the Latvian government appealed this initial finding to the Court's Grand Chamber, where in March 2006 a group of thirteen judges ruled (9 to 4) in Latvia's favor.

Indeed, as we observed already with the Kononov case, a key factor explaining the ECtHR's readiness to reverse its initial judgments has involved the degree to which the Baltic states have been able to get judges to consider the broader historical circumstances surrounding Estonia, Latvia and Lithuania. In the case of Ždanoka, the Latvian government presented within the Grand Chamber an extensive overview of how Latvia became an occupied Soviet republic (referring all the way back to the Hitler–Stalin Pact) in order to show that the Latvian state had a legitimate right to defend its democracy against anti-independence forces. These arguments largely prevailed among the judges and therefore served to cement further an acceptance of the Baltic view that Soviet occupation justified the use of criminal-judicial justice measures for both retrospective and transitional purposes. That said, considerable dissent within the ECtHR remained. For example, one judge, Boštjan M. Zupančič, complained bitterly in his opposing opinion on the Ždanoka case that "Even international law does not have the power to wipe away a historical period of some fifty years. Consequently, if [Ždanoka's] activity were to be a priori declared illegitimate or illegal, much of what had been happening in the Soviet Union ought to have been a posteriori declared illegitimate or illegal" (European Court of Human Rights 2006b). This was something Judge Zupančič was loath to do. Posing the question point-blank, the judge would ask, "Are we here to correct the historical wrongs?" In the Baltic states' opinion, the answer was yes.

Yet, when the issue of contention would turn to lustration legislation, Baltic zeal would be curbed by the ECtHR, just as the Court has done with many other post-communist countries (Horne 2009a). In the case of Latvian MP Jānis Ādamsons the Court found that his prevention from running for parliament (because of his one-time service in the Soviet border guards and hence as a part of the KGB) was unjustified to the extent that Latvian courts had no opportunity under Latvian legislation to consider extenuating circumstances (such as a person's other merits or services to the state). Likewise the Court rejected major tenets of Lithuania's 1999 lustration legislation, when it overturned provisions imposing lustration on the private sector as well as bans on outed ex-KGB agents working in certain professional spheres (see Chapter 4). In other words, the Court has developed a clear willingness to speak out on how far lustration should go, touching on issues of due process rights when seeking transitional justice against perpetrators on a political-administrative level. As years have gone by, the Court has taken a more restrictive approach. When reverberations concerning these justice policies have reached Strasbourg, the Court has ruled against the Baltic states. These rulings should, however, not be interpreted as a sign that the ECtHR found lustration to be "intrinsically incompatible with due process safeguards" and thus against the rule of law. As Horne (2009a: 727) shows, most rulings of the Court on domestic lustration laws in Central European states revolved "around 'the way' the laws were applied, not on the legality of the laws themselves." In the Lithuanian case however, this conclusion was less clear, since ECtHR decisions like those in the case of *Rainys and Gasparavičius v. Lithuania* in 2005 plainly rejected Lithuania's extension of lustration to the private sector. In this sense it rejected, at least in part, the very legality of this measure.

External reverberations of Baltic truth and justice processes toward Russia

Given the overriding focus that Baltic truth and justice processes have had on righting the wrongs of the Soviet era, it is not surprising that another geographic direction in which these practices have reverberated has been toward the East. Here the Baltic objective has been to prompt Russia into accepting its responsibility for the damages wrought by Soviet occupation based on Moscow's own self-proclaimed status as successor state to the USSR. If the USSR was guilty of illegal state annexation, mass human rights violations and decades-long repression in the Baltic states, then Russia as the heir to that regime should acknowledge its proper obligations at least in terms of recognizing that broadscale injustice, if not to mention possible compensation or reparation.

Needless to say, Baltic success in achieving these aims has so far been scant. The deadlock between the two sides begins already with the question of whether there was ever any illegal occupation in the Baltic states. From there the dispute ranges (as we saw in Chapter 3) to whether in Russia's view individuals involved in the Stalinist deportations or other repressions should be brought to justice or whether they were simply operating under the laws existing at the time. Ultimately, the dispute pertains to whether Russia owes the Baltic states reparations for the human and material damage suffered during the Soviet period or, on the contrary, whether the Baltics owe Russia for the infrastructure and economic development fostered by the Soviet regime.

This subsection of the chapter will not attempt to outline Baltic–Russian relations in their entirety.[5] Rather, our focus will be on the extent to which Baltic politics concerning truth and justice issues have at times spilled over into formulating formal demands toward Russia, and how Russia has reacted to these moves. As hinted above, these demands have stretched from getting Moscow to simply acknowledge its historical responsibility for Soviet wrongdoing all the way to presenting Russia with an actual bill for damages caused by Soviet rule.

On the level of historical acknowledgment, Russia's attitude toward the Baltic states has shifted from an initial acceptance of the Soviet breakup (particularly during the early presidency of Boris Yeltsin) to an openly antagonistic critique of alleged Baltic "falsifications of history." This has led in turn to an effort by Russia to mount its own historical counter-narrative, and thus the Baltic–Russian chasm has only grown. Whereas Mikhail Gorbachev had been the one to admit in 1989 to the existence of the secret protocols of the Hitler–Stalin Pact and thus to a certain degree had acknowledged the narrative of illegal annexation of the Baltics, this stance changed considerably during the 1990s when the notion of illegal occupation became a red flag for Russian officials, who instead aimed to implicate Baltic truth and justice efforts with the alleged discrimination of Russian minority residents. As we saw in Chapter 3, Russian state representatives in both Estonia and especially Latvia took an avid interest in the

[5] For a good discussion of these relations in light of the common past addressing issues of memory, identity politics, security and justice, see Ehin and Berg (2009) as well as Muižnieks (2011).

criminal procedures against Russian citizens accused of having committed crimes against humanity. In Chapters 4 and 6 we also touched upon incidents where Russian media, ignited not least by official statements, launched considerable campaigns against the Baltic states for "falsifying" the history and memory of World War II. Thus, when it comes to Baltic truth and justice processes, Russia has very much assumed the role of outside defender of what it sees as the "true history" of World War II and of those it views as the victims of new Baltic injustice.

Ideally for the Baltic states, had this effort to get Russia to acknowledge its historical responsibility toward Soviet wrongdoings been successful, the next logical step would have been to move toward a bilateral discussion of possible compensation and reparation. To the extent that this first process has not materialized, the second has also clearly been impaired. However, this has not deterred the Baltic states from working on such compensation claims nonetheless. Indeed, as we shall see, these processes need not at all be linked, since domestic pressures often go quite far in prompting work to be undertaken on such demands even when the probability of them ever being acted upon is quite faint. In this sense, these reverberations from Baltic truth and justice politics have, indeed, been focused on the East. But because Russia has staunchly rejected any consideration of these demands, the reverberations themselves have been left to ricochet largely among the Balts themselves.

Estonia was the first Baltic republic to officially commission a calculation of Soviet occupation damages. The initiative was contained in a November 1989 Supreme Soviet resolution that officially renounced Estonia's coerced decision to join the USSR in 1940. Specifically, the resolution mandated the creation of a commission tasked with "evaluating the economic, political and social consequences of the Soviet annexation of Estonia in 1940" (Eesti NSV Ülemnõukogu 1989).[6] The commission would work under the aegis of the Estonian Academy of Sciences and would be led by the well-known social historian Juhan Kahk. Somewhat surprisingly (given the seemingly monumental nature of this task), the commission produced its official "damages report" within just two months. A year later (in January 1991) the report was translated into English and then published as a small book

[6] In fact, the commission was established as a continuation of an earlier one, appointed in August 1989 to evaluate the events of 1940 from a historical and legal perspective. The conclusions of this commission – that Soviet rule in the republic had been a product of coercion and aggression in 1940 – would serve as the basis for the November 1989 resolution declaring Estonia's accession to the USSR null and void.

(Kahk 1991). Hence, in a rather interesting manner the legacy of the Kahk report would be shaped very much by the fact that its prime outlet would be in the English language. The report has been cited by various observers as illustrative of Estonia's initial quest to tally Soviet damages. And yet its place in domestic debates over reparations has been scant.

Across roughly sixty pages of text and thirty pages of original documents, the Kahk report presented an estimate of the human losses suffered during Stalinist terror; it also calculated the environmental damage caused by the Soviet system as well as its cost in terms of natural resources and economic stagnation. Lastly, the report looked into losses in terms of quality of life, culture and the Estonian language. The data for these calculations came from already published material as well as from archives and state statistical offices. In several places, the Kahk report acknowledged the rather preliminary character of the estimates, as huge amounts of yet unknown material remained unexplored in various state archives, especially with regard to the number of people deported and repressed.[7] Still, the report did draw some conclusions as to who should be held responsible for these damages, thus hinting at potential compensation claims to be made by Estonia vis-à-vis the Soviet Union (Mälksoo 2003b: 66).

When Estonia did finally break free from the Soviet Union, the Kahk report might have served as an initial starting point for resolving relations with Moscow. However, as we saw in Chapter 6, Estonia took a different path when in March 1992 it created the State Commission for the Examination of Repressive Policies Carried Out During the Occupations (ORURK). Moreover, because this commission would end up working for more than twelve years, it would soon become evident that even if the Commission's final *White Book* would be wide-ranging and multifaceted, it would not become *the* damages report that would lay the basis for a concerted reparations campaign vis-à-vis Russia. On the contrary, Estonia would actually never take up any notable effort to extract compensation from the Russian Federation. Had Estonian politicians wanted to do this, they might have pressured ORURK to complete its work faster. Instead, they largely ignored the Commission and financed it only marginally. All of this contributed to a situation where of the three Baltic states Estonia's truth and justice processes have reverberated the least toward the East.

[7] One later observer (Hiio 2005) nevertheless noted that the Kahk commission had presented important and "completely adequate results."

Slightly more palpable has been the eastward resonance of Latvia's search for truth and justice. Just two months after the release of the Kahk report in Estonia, the Latvian government decided in March 1990 to commission a similar study to be compiled by a group of experts led by Modris Šmulders, an economist and statistician. One of the main objectives for the Latvian government in commissioning such a damage report was not so much to make compensation claims but, rather, to refute the proposition often voiced by Soviet officials that the Baltic states actually owed the Soviet Union for the latter's investments in the republics during the past decades (Ijabs 2011: 179). The Economics Reform Commission was thus tasked with assessing the mutual economic accounts between Latvia and the USSR. Over the course of (again just) three months Šmulders compiled a report that demonstrated that the overall losses suffered by Latvia, both in economic and demographic terms, far outnumbered whatever investments had been done during the fifty years of Soviet rule. The calculations covered a wide range of areas of "mutual accounts," including data on property nationalized in the 1940s, exchanged goods and services during the postwar years, human losses due to Stalinist terror and deportation and a (rather speculative) comparative calculation of where Latvia would have been without the annexation, based on data from Finland since 1940 (Prikulis 2011). The report lacked a degree of clarity in terms of sources and methods and, like its Estonian counterpart, could not include much of the material still undiscovered in the archives. Still, as Ijabs (2011: 79) has pointed out, the Šmulders report did serve an important function when in later years Moscow would attempt to put forward compensation claims of its own (for the cost of Soviet-era economic subsidies), and Latvia would be able to quickly riposte by pulling out the Šmulders report. Indeed, Šmulders' calculations would remain for some time the only clear numerical assessment of Soviet damages in Latvia and would therefore be frequently cited in both scholarly works and political debates.

In this respect, it is worth noting that neither the Estonian nor the Latvian reports from these early years were drawn up specifically with the intention of making formal reparation claims toward Moscow. Instead, they had been commissioned purely for testimonial reasons. Indeed, politicians at the time understood that any demand for reparations would be unrealistic. All three Baltic states had to tread carefully, since former Soviet troops were still stationed on Baltic territory, and Moscow was most reluctant to allow its influence in the region to diminish. Only in Lithuania, therefore, were damage calculations started that would actually be tied to future compensation claims. In fact, even before the advent of full re-independence in August 1991, the Lithuanian Supreme Council passed a resolution called On Compensation for the Damage Inflicted by the USSR on the Republic of Lithuania and its Citizens. In it the legislature called on the government to draw up a tally of damages to use in the negotiations with Moscow and for making compensation claims (Lietuvos Respublikos Aukščiausioji Taryba 1991b). When these negotiations formally began in 1992, the Lithuanian delegation presented to Moscow estimations of over $80 billion (US) in damages incurred by the Soviet military alone on the people, economy, nature and agriculture of Lithuania (Stankevičius 1996). In an important move to mobilize domestic support for these talks, Lithuanian legislators also embedded the issue of compensation within a special referendum organized in June 1992. Alongside the main question of whether Lithuanians wanted the immediate and unconditional removal of ex-Soviet troops from their country, legislators added a phrase also calling for "reparations for damages done to Lithuania" (Lietuvos Respublikos Seimas 1992a). Unsurprisingly the final result was 90.6 percent in favor. Even though this was widely perceived as a mandate to pursue further reparations claims (and would be indeed frequently invoked in later years), during the immediate negotiations over Russian troop withdrawal Lithuanian negotiators decided to drop the compensation issue. The ex-Soviet troops left the country in August 1993 without any talk of reparations.

Compensation was a bigger issue in Russia's talks over the withdrawal of the military with both Estonia and Latvia. For example, in August 1992, Russian Foreign Minister Andrei Kozyrev presented his Baltic counterparts with a formal set of conditions under which Russia would agree to remove the ex-Soviet troops. These terms consisted of a demand for the Baltic states to relinquish any territorial claims they might have on Russia as a result of border shifts enacted by Stalin in 1945; to waive any future claims of compensation for damages caused during Soviet rule; to allow for continued Russian military presence on Baltic territory and to grant "equal rights and dignity" to Soviet-era settlers (Spohr Readman 2004: 157; Ijabs 2011: 181). This final condition alluded, of course, to citizenship legislation in Estonia and Latvia, which was one reason the complete withdrawal of ex-Soviet troops from these two countries took a year longer to conclude than in Lithuania. Estonia and Latvia also haggled with Russia over compensation issues. Russia demanded that the two states pay for the value of leftover military assets and the actual transfer of troops. Hence, this was a reverse reverberation of Baltic claims for justice. However, the matter was ultimately resolved with the help of the United States, which pledged its own money to pay for the withdrawal in order to get Russia's demands off the table.

Formally speaking, therefore, Russia's compensation claims were removed, but the Balts never officially rescinded theirs. If anything, these demands became accentuated as Baltic officials began analyzing how much further damage in terms of the environment had been done on these previously inaccessible Soviet military territories. Lithuania, in particular, continued to stress its right to claim compensation from Russia for the damage inflicted by the Soviet Union on its people, nature and economy.[8] However, over the next few years, the Baltic states tended to act together on this issue and in particular via multilateral forums such as the Council of Europe or the Baltic Assembly (the inter-parliamentary organ of the three Baltic states). In May 1994, they issued their first joint appeal via the Baltic Assembly, urging Moscow to recognize that "as the Russian Federation is the successor state of the Soviet Union it is also responsible for compensation of the damage and loss caused by the Soviet Union to Estonia, Latvia and Lithuania during the Years of occupation" (Baltic Assembly 1994). Within the CoE, the Baltic states hoped to further increase their leverage after Russia presented its application to join the organization, while Estonia, Latvia and Lithuania had already been admitted. In January 1996 the three states managed to get the CoE's Parliamentary Assembly to formulate certain conditions (albeit non-binding) on Russia's future accession. In the Assembly's Opinion No. 193 "on Russia's request for membership of the Council of Europe," the Assembly took note of Russia's willingness "to assist persons formerly deported from the occupied Baltic states or the descendants of deportees to return home according to special repatriation and compensation programs which must be worked out" (Parliamentary Assembly 1996). The document was remarkable not only because it clearly stated the fact of Soviet occupation of the Baltic states, but also because it became the only official document in which Russia would ever agree to engage in at least some form of compensation – if only for the repatriation of illegally displaced people. Needless to say, this declaration would remain entirely on paper, since Russia has so far not developed any policies for assisting

8 According to one of the Lithuanian negotiators at the time, Česlovas Stankevičius, a joint investigation by Baltic and international experts carried out in 1993–94 estimated that the cleaning of military facilities, of contaminated waters, soil and forests in the three republics would take up to twenty years and cost some $20 billion (US) (Stankevičius 1996).

former deportees. Still, it was another salvo in trying to push justice claims farther East.

During the later 1990s the compensation issue continued to linger here and there in Baltic politics. For example, from time to time, national-conservative members of parliament in Estonia or Latvia would request information from their governments about what was being done to claim compensation from Russia. However, the governments' priority at the time was clearly focused on EU and NATO accession. Likewise, both countries were deadlocked with Russia over how to conclude former border treaties. Thus, since these talks were at a standstill, there was no point in provoking Moscow by repeating unilateral claims for reparations. Moreover, as Ijabs suggests in the case of Latvia, the government was careful not to draw reverse attention to their own problems with citizenship and stateless persons, which the international community (for its part) was monitoring with concern. Thus, the goal of pushing truth and justice issues vis-à-vis Russia had its limits, especially when these claims would lead to other issues (such as citizenship) being brought into the debate and thereby blurring the picture.

These dilemmas were much less severe in Lithuania, and therefore we also see a much more resolute stance on compensation issues coming from Vilnius throughout the 1990s. For example, in December 1995 a cabinet commission was formed under the leadership of the former economics minister, Vincas Babilius, to look more specifically into the damages caused by the Soviet military, during both 1940–91 and 1991–93 (Lietuvos Respublikos Vyriausybė 1995b). Not quite a year later the government adopted a formal working program for the commission that would list the full spectrum of damages incurred by Soviet rule in Lithuania to be included in the calculations. On several pages attached to the resolution, these damages were enumerated in considerable detail, including human losses as a result of Soviet repressive policies as well as property confiscation, nationalization, forced labor and other violent offenses (Lietuvos Respublikos Vyriausybė 1996). In 1997 the commission presented an absolute total of Soviet damage said to have been committed in Lithuania. That figure was a staggering $667.7 billion (US) (Tracevskis 2000a). The Lithuanian government was clearly gearing up for a settling of accounts with Russia. However, for several years to come these numbers would be kept secret from the wider public, since each successive government would decide that the time was not ripe for presenting the formal claims.

It was only during a parliamentary election campaign in 2000 that the results of the commission would suddenly be taken up by national-conservative politicians. Vytautas Landsbergis, then parliamentary chairman of the Seimas and head of the Homeland Union-Lithuanian Conservatives (TS-LK), proposed a law that would require any future Lithuanian government to request compensation from Russia based on the 1997 commission calculations. The proposal reminded the parliament of the 1992 referendum in which an overwhelming majority of Lithuanians had supported compensation claims toward Moscow, yet nothing had been done since. While some MPs from the center-left agreed that Lithuania had an obligation to make reparation claims based on the one-time referendum (even if they could not exactly say when this should be done), other politicians immediately rejected Landsbergis' call as a pre-election stunt in order to keep the conservatives in power (Tracevskis 2000a). Ultimately, a Law on the Compensation of Damages was passed in July 2000 that obliged the government to prepare a written estimate of damages to be formally presented to Russia at the latest by November that same year. However, the fact that yet another expert group was charged with making calculations showed that the previous ones were considered too high and rather unrealistic. Nevertheless, the law made reference to the earlier calculations by distinguishing between damages inflicted between 1940 and 1991 and those between 1991 and 1993, the latter being considered a period of continued aggression. Moreover, the law stipulated the establishment of a Fund for the Return to the Homeland of the Persons Deported by the USSR, thereby reminding Russia of its obligation taken as part of the 1996 PACE declaration. In October 2000, a governmental committee presented its revised estimate, now totaling only some $20 billion (US). Included in these calculations were "costs for property lost by destruction or seizure, and the persecution of individuals and groups" (Satkauskas 2003: 92). Still, even though the new estimate was considerably lower than the one from 1997, this adjustment did not prompt new movement on the issue. Though subsequent Lithuanian governments have not really pushed the issue with Moscow, Lithuania's position remains the same – as does Moscow's. On a comment by Russian Ambassador to Lithuania, Vladimir Chikvadze, in May 2013 that Russia considers the issue of compensation for Soviet-inflicted damages to be resolved, Lithuanian parliamentarians promptly noted that Lithuania does not intend to withdraw its claim (Commons 2013).

In Latvia, the Lithuanians' 2000 law elicited widespread media attention, prompting both journalists and members of parliament to call for similar steps to be taken. At the same time, enthusiasm was tempered by those who said that Latvia's relations with Moscow were too delicate to undertake such an action, especially given growing Russian resistance to acknowledging the wrongdoings of the Soviet past (Ločmele 2000; Sizova 2000). This, however, did not prevent eleven representatives of the nationalist party For Fatherland and Freedom/LNNK to submit a draft law "on the compensation for damage caused by the Soviet occupation" in October of that same year. Their initiative mirrored that of Lithuania in almost all respects, including a fund to help former deportees return to Latvia (Tēvzemei un Brīvībai/LNNK 2000). However, the bill was rejected in plenary by a wide margin, with only a few more MPs than the original set of sponsors supporting the measure. An overwhelming majority of deputies simply abstained during the vote, despite the fact that the bill came from one of the ruling coalition partners. According to Ijabs (2011), this showed not only the half-hearted nature of the nationalists' initiative but also a broader feeling within the Latvian political elite that the issue of compensation claims vis-à-vis Russia were perhaps counterproductive or pointless at that time. Indeed, with Lithuanian politics shifting again toward the center-left after the 2000 elections and Estonian politicians showing no interest whatsoever in the issue, the Latvian nationalists' fervor equally waned. In fact, in December 2000 a draft declaration submitted to the Baltic Assembly – calling once again on Russia to acknowledge its state responsibility with regard to compensating the Baltic states – actually failed to find sufficient support from the delegates.

The compensation issue therefore remained dormant until 2004–2005 when, in contrast to previous incidents, it would be the Russian Federation that turned on the heat. The occasion was a relatively quixotic legislative bill submitted once again by Latvian nationalists in parliament, who proposed that Latvia not only demand compensation for Soviet-era crimes but also begin a process of repatriation of Soviet-era settlers back to Russia (a policy touted as "decolonization"). Even though the proposal had no chance of ever being passed, the Russian Foreign Ministry reacted strongly. Not only did the Russian authorities reject any notion of compensation as unfounded, but they also issued a counter-report claiming that it was in fact the Balts who owed Russia for left-behind Soviet property and for the Baltic share of Soviet-era international debt which the Balts had renounced (Schetnaya palata Rossiiskoi Federatsiya 2004). Russia's fierce reaction continued throughout the fall of 2004 with a Duma resolution that reminded the Baltic states of their liberation from fascism by the Soviet Army and accused them anew of discriminating against local Russians. This seeming overreaction finally roused the ire of Latvia's President Vaira Vīķe-Freiberga, who previously had been a rather cautious voice in debates over compensation but now felt the need to call on Latvian victims of deportations and repression to claim individual compensation from Moscow (Fridrihsone 2004). Estonian parliament speaker Ene Ergma also deplored the Duma resolution, saying it showed "the Russian parliament's unwillingness to objectively evaluate the history of its own country and that of the world" (Ergma 2004). Finally, the Baltic Assembly reacted to the Russian incitement by adopting in December 2004 its own resolution where it again reminded Russia of the fact that "liberation" in 1944–45 meant the "entrenchment of occupation and the continuation of genocide, which considerably changed the ethnic composition of the population of these countries" (Baltic Assembly 2004b). Moreover, in a second resolution the Baltic Assembly called on their national governments "to initiate negotiations with Russia and Germany on compensating damage caused by the occupations" (Baltic Assembly 2004a).

With the sixtieth anniversary of the end of World War II in sight as well as Vladimir Putin's planned celebration of Victory Day with an international gathering of heads of state, Baltic political leaders clearly felt the need to stand up to Russian revisionism. Even though all three Baltic governments at the time declared compensation claims toward Russia not to be a priority in their bilateral dealings, legislators in Latvia started working on a legislative response to Moscow's victory celebration and its liberation narrative. In May 2005 the Latvian Saeima adopted a Declaration on the Condemnation of the Totalitarian Communist Occupation Regime Established in Latvia by the USSR in which the historical cornerstones of the country's legal restorationist claim were repeated, as were the accusations that Russia had done "nothing to repair the consequences of the occupation" (Latvijas Republikas Saeima 2005). Initiated by thirteen MPs, the Declaration was meant primarily as a signal to both Western partners and Russia that not enough had been done to properly acknowledge and redress the legacy of Communism in the countries of Central and Eastern Europe (Delfi.lv 2005). Yet the Declaration not only reiterated the criminal character of the Soviet regime, it also made direct claims regarding reparations toward Russia. Specifically, the Latvian MPs called on Russia to:

> declare that the Russian Federation as the legal and political successor of the USSR is morally, legally and financially responsible for the crimes

> against humanity committed in Latvia and for the losses inflicted on the Latvian state and its citizens during the occupation, and to fulfill its obligations in accordance with the principles of international law to compensate Latvia and its people for the unlawful actions and losses.
>
> (Latvijas Republikas Saeima 2005)

The Saeima further requested that the government seek agreement with the Russian Federation on repatriating displaced Latvians to their historical homeland and for returning archival material that had been taken out of Latvia (including material of the Latvian KGB). Finally, the government was called upon to submit formal reparation claims to Russia. Although several MPs warned of the near hopeless nature of such claims, the proclamation was nevertheless reinforced with the creation of a new damages assessment commission duly named the Commission for Determining the Number of Victims and Locations of Mass Graves of the USSR Totalitarian Communist Occupation Regime, for Collecting Information about Repressions and Mass Deportations and for Calculating the Damage Inflicted on the Latvian State and Its Inhabitants.[9] The new group was subsequently composed of nineteen members, mostly ministerial officials, but also some lawyers and historians. It was put under the chairmanship of Edmunds Stankevičs, a legal advisor to the State Chancellery (Latvijas Republikas Ministru Kabinets 2005). According to Ijabs (2011), the creation of the Stankevičs commission was motivated at least partly by a feeling among Latvian politicians that compared to Estonia with its *White Book* (from ORURK) and Lithuania with its 2000 law on compensation, Latvia had so far failed to take any decisive steps toward demanding compensation. Indeed, presidential advisor Antonijs Zunda was quoted as saying that "the commission's establishment was a political decision, a solidarity move with Estonia and Lithuania who had already started the process. We needed to do something in order to not fall behind" (Sprūde 2009b).

Over the next three and a half years, the Stankevičs commission oversaw the preparation of some two dozen background papers and studies, all looking into the amount of damage done by the Soviets to the Latvian economy, population and environment. As a vast improvement on the Šmulders report hastily compiled in 1990, the researchers

9 "Komisija PSRS totalitārā komunistiskā okupācijas režīma upuru skaita un masu kapu vietu noteikšanai, informācijas par represijām un masveida deportācijām apkopošanai un Latvijas valstij un tās iedzīvotājiem nodarīto zaudējumu aprēķināšanai."

involved in this commission spent a considerable amount of time resolving important methodological issues and on developing a new database for their calculations. In 2009 the commission presented its preliminary conclusions, estimating the total monetary loss for Latvia from the Soviet occupation at 123 billion lats (or €176 billion). As with other such commissions from earlier periods, the Stankevičs commission had relied on making hypothetical comparisons with Finland and the latter's eventual level of development. In addition, the commission claimed that Latvia had lost at least 21 million man-years of labor due to its population losses and had also suffered environmental damage to the tune of 365 million lats (about €522 million) (Latvijas Republikas Ministru Kabinets 2009).

When in 2009 the world economic crisis hit Latvia and the Latvian government imposed draconian spending cuts, state funding for the Stankevičs commission was suspended. Admittedly, this state support had never been particularly high, just 150,000 lats (or around €214,000) per year. But still, without any official funding the only option remaining for Stankevičs and his colleagues was to create an NGO, the Society for the Research of Latvia's Occupation (*Latvijas Okupācijas izpētes biedrība*), which would operate on the basis of private donations (Delfi.lv 2009). Using these funds as well as high-level support not least from Latvian MEPs, the association was able to organize an international conference on reparation issues as well as publish a volume of the conference materials (Latvijas Okupācijas izpētes biedrība 2012). In November 2013, the Latvian Ministry of Finance renewed state funding for the commission, and the group found new office space in the Europe House in downtown Riga (TVnet 2013a).

Meanwhile in Lithuania, the compensation issue remained locked in a conundrum, since Lithuanian law continued to oblige the government to deal with reparation prospects, but at the same time no government ever dared to raise the issue with Russia.[10] Thus, several governmental committees did work on preparing official memos and other materials, but all of these documents remained classified in order to avoid generating any public pressure. In May 2012, Prime Minister Andrius Kubilius (from

[10] For example, further pressure was put on the Lithuanian government by a Seimas resolution in January 2010 that called on the cabinet to "officially apply to the Government of the Russian Federation concerning compensation payments to the victims of the USSR aggression perpetrated during and after 11–13 January 1991 and to their families" (Seimas of the Republic of Lithuania 2010).

the TS-LDK) tried to break out of this black hole by creating an ad hoc governmental committee, whose task this time would be "to prepare our negotiation position for talks with Russia" (quoted in 15min.lt 2012a). With this, the government claimed that it had finally fulfilled its legal obligation before parliament. Yet others saw this as once again a pre-election campaign ploy aimed at boosting the conservatives' nationalist credentials.

The expert panel, headed by the director of the Lithuanian Genocide and Resistance Research Center (LGGRTC), Teresė Birutė Burauskaitė, consisted of representatives from all of the major state institutions for historical research, several state ministries as well as victim organizations and émigré Lithuanians. Charged with looking into possible ways for individuals to seek direct compensation from Moscow as well as with employing foreign experts in order to clarify Lithuania's international rights to compensation from Russia, the committee was supposed to submit its proposals and action plan in June. According to Burauskaitė, the committee had no illusions about Russia's position on the matter; yet her goal with the committee was to "professionally prepare all of the documents, in a competent way and based on the international law" (quoted in 15min.lt 2012b). In a subsequent turn of events, Prime Minister Kubilius also called on the EU to include the issue of Russian compensation on the agenda for EU–Russia talks (15min.lt 2012b). Russia's reaction to these renewed claims was immediate and unchanged, as the Foreign Ministry dismissed any possible grounds for compensation and declared the issue to be closed (RIA Novosti 2012).

Working European institutions: Baltic campaigns for the recognition of communist crimes

If in the early 1990s Baltic politicians attempted to use European institutions in order to find allies for putting pressure on Russia to resolve post-Soviet security dilemmas (such as the removal of Russian troops from the region), as of the mid-2000s this approach began to change. With all three states acceding to the EU and NATO in 2004, many of the Balts' existential worries seemed resolved. As a result, the way in which Baltic truth and justice processes would now reverberate (or be projected) within EU governing bodies would also shift to one of influencing how these institutions perceived Soviet Communism as a historical crime and how to make them act on this new viewpoint, even if this meant challenging existing European memory regimes. One of these existing regimes was, needless to say, the unquestioned singularity of the Holocaust as the crime against humanity and founding myth of the European project. When Baltic and other East European politicians attempted to raise Soviet Communism to a comparable level of commemoration and condemnation (by sponsoring among other things the kind of memorial plaques described at the beginning of this chapter), fierce opposition would erupt from both Jewish groups and the West European left. In this section we will turn to these developments and profile them across two specific dimensions: judicial efforts to ban the denial of communist atrocities in Europe, and parliamentary resolutions and commemorative programs that aimed directly at transforming European memory structures.

One of the first attempts by Baltic MEPs to get involved in European memory debates with their own agenda took place in 2005 within the framework of the EU's Council of Ministers of Justice and Home Affairs (JHA Council). Already for several years, European governments had been negotiating a piece of framework legislation combating forms and expressions of racism and xenophobia by means of criminal law. These negotiations had stalled in 2001 due to concerns among some member states that the criminalization of Holocaust denial or of gross trivialization of crimes committed on the basis of a group's racial, ethnic or religious belonging (i.e. genocide) would curb the fundamental right to freedom of speech.

In 2005 the Luxembourg presidency of the EU decided to restart these negotiations in part with a view to the important anniversary of the end of World War II. Yet the preparations for a JHA Council meeting in February again threatened to fail when the German Minister of Justice as well as several MEPs requested to include within the framework decision a ban on Nazi symbols following a scandal that involved Britain's Prince Harry wearing a Nazi uniform with a swastika during a costume party. To this was then added an initiative by a group of new member state MEPs (led by EPP-ED deputies Joszef Szájer from Hungary and Vytautas Landsbergis from Lithuania) that proposed a similar ban on communist symbols. In a letter to the EU's Commissioner for Justice and Home Affairs, Franco Frattini, the MEPs stressed "that communist dictatorships in Europe were responsible for at least as many deaths as the Nazis" (Europolitics 2005), hence the justification for a ban on both Nazi and communist symbols.

After initially expressing a readiness to consider the issue, Commissioner Frattini soon backpedaled after protest erupted from the political left and the upcoming JHA Council meeting threatened to fail. In the end, Frattini decided that it was inappropriate to include a ban of the hammer and sickle in an EU law on racism, although he urged Europeans to engage in a wider debate on the legacies of both totalitarian regimes in Europe. Moreover, the EU member states themselves eventually postponed the issue of adopting a framework decision citing continuing concerns about freedom of speech (Lungescu 2005). No action was taken again until 2007 when the German presidency reopened negotiations and managed to negotiate a compromise agreement in which neither Nazi nor communist symbols would be brought into the directive (Littoz-Monnet 2013: 499). Moreover, at the behest of pro-free speech member states like Great Britain and the Scandinavian countries, the number of historical incidents to be covered by the denial ban would be limited. The final legislation recognized only genocides defined by international law and conventions such as the Rome statutes, thus excluding most of the mass crimes committed by the Stalinist Soviet Union. Moreover, the "public condoning, denying or grossly trivialising" of these crimes are punishable only "when the conduct [was] carried out in a manner likely to incite violence or hatred" against protected individuals or groups (Council of the European Union 2008). In this respect, the final compromise constituted a complete rejection of Eastern European attempts to criminalize the Nazi and Stalinist regimes on equal grounds. In its press release following a JHA Council meeting in April 2007, the Council stressed explicitly that "the Framework Decision is limited to crimes committed on the grounds of race, colour, religion, descent or national or ethnic origin. It does not cover crimes committed on other grounds, e.g. by totalitarian regimes" (Council of the European Union 2007).

Still, any EU legislation ultimately depends on member states transposing its provisions. This has allowed some Central and Eastern European countries a degree of leeway in still pushing their agenda. Both Latvia and Lithuania, for example, have included (either implicitly or explicitly) the crimes of Nazism and Stalinism in their bans on denial.[11] In the Latvian case legislators inserted a new Article 74.1 into the country's Criminal Code stating that "the public denial and justification of genocide, crimes against humanity, crimes against peace and war crimes are punishable by a

[11] Besides Lithuania also Poland, the Czech Republic and Hungary passed amendments to their criminal codes that define the denial, trivialization or justification of "communist crimes" as a criminal offense; see the report by the European Commission 2010. Moreover, as we showed in Chapter 4, all three Baltic states would proceed to adopt amendments to their national laws that would prohibit the displaying of Soviet symbols in public.

prison term of up to five years" (Latvijas Republikas Saeima 2009a). With this formulation the law left out the qualification by EU ministers that declared the denial of these crimes an offense only if it incited hatred against certain groups in society defined by race, color, religion, descent or national or ethnic origin. As a result, the amendment was used in May 2013 to open an investigation by the Security Police into the case of one prominent individual – the former treason convict and now MEP Alfreds Rubiks. A complaint had been lodged against Rubiks for having publicly denied the fact that Latvia had been forced to join the USSR. Moreover, Rubiks later claimed in a telephone interview that not only were the Stalinist "repressions" in conformity with Soviet law at the time, but that "many of those repressed deserved [such treatment] as they had collaborated with the fascists" (cited in TVnet 2013b).[12]

Meanwhile, Lithuania was even more explicit in its legislation. In June 2010, the Seimas amended Article 170.2 of the Lithuanian Criminal Code to state that a person who publicly condones, denies or grossly trivializes "aggression against the Republic of Lithuania, genocide, war crimes or crimes against humanity *committed by the USSR and Nazi Germany or atrocities against the Republic of Lithuania in the period 1990–1991*" (emphasis added) may be punishable by a fine or a prison term of up to two years (Žilinskas 2012). Here, the Lithuanians clearly went much beyond what the EU had envisioned. Finally, Estonia has curiously avoided taking any action. No amendments to Estonian criminal law in compliance with the EU directive had been passed as of early 2014.

Thus, while attempts to find a pan-European legal answer to the crimes of Communism had clearly failed with the Framework Decision, the debates surrounding its adoption raised the awareness among Western politicians of the need to address the crimes committed during and after World War II in the communist region. Thus, already in the statement accompanying the Framework Decision, the JHA Council called on the EC to organize a European public hearing on the crimes of the totalitarian regimes in order to find out "whether an additional instrument

[12] The subsequent decision by the Security Police and Prosecutor General's Office to dismiss the case eight months later raised harsh criticism from the LPRA, who accused the Security Police of "not working in the state's interest." Again the parallel to cases of Holocaust denial was drawn in the official press release, stating that "persons from European states who show similar attempts at justifying the Holocaust receive heavy penalties." (TVnet, 2014.) The criminal allegation against Rubiks was, indeed, resubmitted to the Prosecutor General's Office and another investigation into the case is still ongoing.

is needed, to cover publicly condoning, denying or grossly trivialising crimes of genocide, crimes against humanity and war crimes directed against a group of persons defined by other criteria."[13]

This was, indeed, realized by the Slovenian presidency in spring 2008 with a public hearing to which experts and representatives from the post-communist region were invited, among them many MEPs, civic activists, legal scholars and historians from the Baltic states. The aim of the hearing was to discuss "the crimes committed by the totalitarian regimes" and how member states have dealt with their legacies (Jambrek 2008). This was followed up by the Directorate-General for Justice and Home Affairs commissioning and financing an independent study to provide a factual overview of the methods used in member states to deal with issues relating to the memory of crimes committed by totalitarian regimes.[14] However, while all of these Council and Commission-led attempts have certainly contributed to raising awareness among Europeans, none of them has so far led to any concrete proposals for a pan-European juridical response to the criminal legacy of Communism in Europe, as many Eastern Europeans have hoped.

However, apart from seeking European legislation on the criminal legacy of Communism, Baltic and other new member state efforts have also focused on achieving non-judicial recognition for their nation's victimization by the Communist regimes. In so doing they struck up new alliances with other center-right politicians within both the EP and PACE in order to promote a pan-European condemnation of Communism. Within the latter this has resulted in one of the most poignant condemnations of totalitarian Communism so far adopted on a pan-European institutional level. In January 2006 the Political Affairs Committee of the PACE proposed a resolution, Need for International Condemnation of Crimes of Totalitarian Communist Regimes (Parliamentary Assembly 2006). In the preceding plenary debate, the initiators and supporters of this resolution argued for the need to morally assess and unambiguously condemn the

[13] In 2011, on the basis of several public hearings, conferences and official reports contracted by the EC, the Council issued its "draft conclusions on the memory of the crimes committed during the totalitarian regimes" in which it merely states that it "takes note of the Commission's intentions ... to keep under review the conditions for an additional legal instrument ... under Article 10(2) of Framework Decision 2008/913/JHA."

[14] "Study on how the memory of crimes committed by totalitarian regimes in Europe is dealt with in the Member States," submitted by Professor Dr. Carlos Closa Montero, Institute for Public Goods and Policy, Centre of Human and Social Sciences (CSIC), Madrid 2010. Available at www.ipp.csic.es/sites/default/files/IPP/proyectos/pdf/STUDY.pdf (accessed November 2013).

crimes committed by the totalitarian Communist regimes in Central and Eastern Europe. This, they maintained, would help to raise public awareness about this common legacy of the European past and provide moral redress to the victims. Though opposed by many Russian delegates and other members of the Group of Unified European Left, the resolution was adopted.

The path toward achieving a shift of existing historical narratives and memory regimes within the EU, at least on a symbolic level, was also marked by several official resolutions that contributed in particular to raising awareness through further institutionalizing a pan-European memory that would include the communist experience. The EP resolution that arguably marked the first time that "the suffering endured by Eastern nations under Communism entered the EU's agenda" (Littoz-Monnet 2012: 1190) was adopted on the occasion of the sixtieth anniversary of the end of World War II, in May 2005. The EP resolution The Future of Europe Sixty Years after the Second World War was primarily meant as an official reminder of the shared European legacy of World War II and of the duty to remember its victims. In this context the resolution not only acknowledged the sacrifices of the Allied powers in the fight against fascism, but also recognized "that for some nations the end of World War II meant renewed tyranny inflicted by the Stalinist Soviet Union" (European Parliament 2005). During the preceding plenary debate on the draft resolution on May 11, 2005, Jean-Claude Juncker, head of the Luxemburg Council presidency at the time, specifically acknowledged the historical experience of the Baltic states and proclaimed that "those people and nations that underwent one misfortune after another suffered more than other Europeans." Such an official gesture of recognition was well received among Baltic deputies. The resolution received a majority that consisted of both new and old member states as well as conservatives and liberals; meanwhile some on the European left criticized this discourse of continued suffering among Eastern Europeans after World War II as revisionist (Littoz-Monnet 2013: 495).[15]

In subsequent years the campaign by Baltic and other MEPs for additional gestures of acknowledgment became visibly more coordinated

[15] The Latvian MEP and former pro-Soviet activist Tatjana Ždanoka also criticized the resolution espoused by her fellow Baltic parliamentarians. She took objection to the term "Soviet occupation," saying that such a formulation would have "dangerous consequences for the more than half a million people who settled [in Latvia and Estonia] during those decades," as it would encourage local nationalists to draft discriminatory legislation (EP plenary debate, May 11, 2005). In the end, however, the wording remained.

as Baltic MEPs initiated several public hearings and events that drew attention to the historical legacies of their countries. Particularly active here were three members of the EPP-DP group, Vytautas Landsbergis from Lithuania, Sandra Kalniete from Latvia and Tunne Kelam from Estonia.[16] All three came with a biographical background of having been central figures in their respective countries' anti-Soviet independence movements. Kalniete brought an additional experience by having been the child of former deportees. For these three mnemonic actors, their personal profiles provided much symbolic capital, as we will discuss later in relation to Kalniete in particular. In June 2006 they organized a hearing on the "Re-unification of European History" involving EC officials and historians to discuss the totalitarian crimes of the Soviet Union. At the conclusion of that event, the politicians also unveiled the memorial plaque mentioned at the start of this chapter. Two years later Baltic politicians participated actively in a conference entitled "European Conscience and Communism" organized by the Czech government. The concluding document from that event, the Prague Declaration on European Conscience and Communism, called for a Europe-wide condemnation of communism as well as for improving efforts to educate people about the crimes of Communist regimes. It was signed by many high-ranking politicians and civil society figures, including former dissidents, deportees and political prisoners. Among them were Vaclav Havel, Joachim Gauck, Vytautas Landsbergis, Tunne Kelam, Emanuelis Zingeris and many others. The document was much criticized for its alleged attempt to relativize the Holocaust by equating it to communist crimes (Katz 2009), yet this did not diminish its highly symbolic meaning. The concerted efforts by former Communist new member states culminated in the adoption of an EP declaration in August 2008 that would proclaim August 23 a European Day of Remembrance for Victims of Stalinism and Nazism (European Parliament 2008). Though only a few member states have so far adopted this European remembrance day within their national remembrance calendars, the official observation of this day on the European level clearly marks a new degree of institutionalization of remembrance that recognizes the specific meaning of this day for Eastern Europe and specifically the Baltic states. Indeed, holding international conferences or public hearings on the crimes of Communism on this day has become something like a

[16] Both Landsbergis and Kelam had already served as representatives of their countries in PACE during the 1990s. They had therefore accumulated considerable experience on the transnational stage before becoming MEPs after 2004.

tradition ever since, especially when the day falls in the time when a new member state holds the European presidency. The particularly strong role of Baltic MEPs in all of these awareness-raising initiatives was publically confirmed in 2009, when then EP president Hans Gert Pöttering thanked in particular the "new colleagues from Estonia, Lithuania and Latvia ... [for having] given the Western part of Europe knowledge about the totalitarianism of the Soviet Union" (BNS 2009).

Another initiative to stem from these activities (and specifically from the "Prague Declaration") involved the creation of a "Platform of European Memory and Conscience." This network would bring together a great number of governmental and non-governmental institutions across mostly Eastern Europe that were active in research, documentation, awareness-raising and education about European totalitarianism. The Platform would end up serving as an important support structure for launching political initiatives within European institutions, since it provided much-needed expertise and material for public hearings and conferences. Several Baltic institutions, including the Estonian Institute of Historical Memory, the Occupation Museum of Latvia and the Genocide and Resistance Research Center of Lithuania, are among the Platform's member institutions and have taken part in different conferences, commemorative events and hearings organized by successive EU presidencies.[17] Driven by an agenda that calls for legal redress for the victims of Communism on a trans-national European level, the Platform has worked closely with conservative groups within the European Parliament and in particular with an informal parliamentary group called Reconciliation of European Histories founded in 2010 under the leadership of Latvian MEP Sandra Kalniete and consisting mostly of members of the EPP-ED group. Under her initiative the lobbying of national governments and European institutions "to adopt effective legal norms that will allow just punishment of communist criminals and abolition of all benefits they still enjoy" has continued (Platform of European Memory and Conscience 2012).

The most recent milestone for the Baltic states in terms of pushing their truth and justice agenda in Europe arrived during the second half of 2013, when Lithuania became the first of the three Baltic countries to actually hold the presidency of the European Union. Within the context of this premier occasion to promote a particular policy area, one might

[17] See the Platform's website at: www.memoryandconscience.eu/2012/05/03/declaration-2012/ (accessed November 2013).

have expected Lithuania to place the memory issue front and center. In the event, however, Vilnius did relatively little as more urgent issues such as signing an association agreement with Ukraine took precedence. Nevertheless, Lithuania continued the tradition of marking August 23 by organizing (via the Museum of Genocide under the LGGRTC) a youth conference to commemorate the European Day of Remembrance of the Victims of Totalitarianism. It also organized a meeting of Justice and Home Affairs ministers precisely on this day, thereby alluding to the past debates over Holocaust and Stalinism denial. However, no formal initiatives to enact new legislation or other policies were put forward.

Lastly, it is important to note that the lobbying done by Baltic and other Eastern European politicians has also prompted the EC to open up a special activity domain (or "action") within its Europe for Citizens program entitled "Active European Remembrance" (Gledhill 2011: 492). Under this subheading the EC has earmarked money for a wide range of remembrance projects, including those "associated with deportations as well as the commemorating of victims of Nazism and Stalinism" (European Commission 2007). Although the total sum allocated for this action amounted to just 4 percent of the overall spending for the Europe for Citizens program, the fact that a separate action was added that explicitly included remembrance of Stalinism meant that the EU recognized memory as an important policy area for fostering greater participation and identification. Moreover, in the new round of the Europe for Citizens program 2014–2020, the promotion of a common European remembrance space has been given greater significance judging by the considerably increased funds earmarked for remembrance activities (Prutsch 2013: 6).

Since the formal opening of the first "Active European Remembrance" action in 2008, Eastern European civil society organizations – and among them many Baltic ones – have actively applied for these EU funds in order to carry out or develop remembrance projects with a focus on communist-era crimes. Indeed, the degree to which local NGOs and government agencies have been able to win these monies serves as another indicator of both the level of organizational capacity among local civil society actors engaged in remembrance and the degree to which EU administrative measures could be harnessed to raise awareness both domestically and internationally about the crimes of totalitarian Communism. From this perspective, it is striking to note, once again, the difference between the three Baltic countries, as Lithuanian organizations and institutions have been far more active and successful in obtaining these funds than their

Estonian and Latvian counterparts. Between 2007 and 2013 nineteen Lithuanian projects were funded amounting to a total of €692,256, while only eight Latvian and three Estonian remembrance projects (amounting to a total of €365,547 and €104,922 respectively) received financial support through the EU program. The various projects that were funded over the years predominantly focused on the memory of Stalinist crimes, on documenting and commemorating the fate of deported people, on organizing intergenerational storytelling, as well as developing museum exhibitions, documentaries and memorial sites. Among the recipient institutions were both well-established, state-sponsored institutions such as the LGGRTC and the Occupation Museum of Latvia and many smaller non-profit groups (such as victim organizations, local museums, schools, youth groups or memorial organizations).

Achieving recognition and reaching audiences outside European institutional settings

Baltic politicians have made active use of the new opportunities and institutional settings provided through EU membership to push their anti-communist cause and to achieve official and institutional recognition for their countries' historical suffering. Convincing European elected officials and civil servants about the need to recognize the memory of Stalinism as a common European heritage and find appropriate legal and administrative responses to the crimes committed under Communist regimes in Eastern Europe has been and still is an important item on the Baltic agenda. At the same time, individual Baltic political actors have also made use of other channels and occasions outside Europe's institutional settings in order to reach a broader European public audience and raise awareness about the totalitarianisms experienced by post-communist countries that are now joined in one political union.

There have been at least two modes by which Baltic politicians have taken their message about post-communist truth and justice beyond their states' borders. The first one involves individual actors who have spoken out at various public forums or who have published books that tell the "Baltic story" to Western audiences.[18] What these efforts have in

[18] A good example for the latter is the book by Vytautas Landsbergis, *Lithuania: Independent Again*, which gives a rather subjective account of Lithuania's re-independence struggle, but also includes descriptions of the country's previous subjugation and victimization under Soviet rule.

common is that they seek to reach wider European and international audiences than is possible simply through institutional lobbying. A notable example here is the Latvian MEP Sandra Kalniete, who in addition to working within European institutions has also become famous by appearing regularly at other European venues. One such occasion that elicited considerable media attention occurred in 2004 during the Leipzig book fair. Kalniete was invited to give the opening address during this prominent German publishing event. She did so not only as Latvian foreign minister and transitional EU commissioner at the time, but also as an acclaimed author of several books, including one entitled *With Dance Shoes in Siberian Snows*.[19] In it Kalniete tells the story of her family, which was deported to Siberia in 1941, where both her grandfathers died in prison camps and where she herself was born in 1952. During her speech in Leipzig, Kalniete called the Nazi and Stalinist totalitarianisms "equally criminal," and she expressed the view that "there must never be a gradation between these philosophies just because one of them participated in the victory over the other" (cited in (Browning 2005: 37). These words so infuriated the representative of the German Jewish Community, Salomon Korn, who was present in the audience, that he left the room in protest. In the German press Korn was quoted as saying that he found Kalniete's attempt at equalizing the Nazi crimes with those of Stalin "unbearable" to listen to (Spiegel online 2004). The incident prompted so much discussion that some German media were prompted to ask whether a new *Historikerstreit* was about to start and what this post-communist reading of Europe's totalitarian past would mean for the newly enlarged European Union (Semler 2004; Arend 2004). The controversy was prolonged after Kalniete went on to repeat her statements at other forums, not least while promoting a German translation of her book a year later. One scholar has even taken to talking about a "Kalniete effect" when examining how alternative readings of World War II and totalitarian regime crimes have affected Western public discourses (Troebst 2011: 61).

The second mode by which national political leaders have sought to reach out to wider audiences is through public events, which have not

[19] The book was published in Latvian in 2001 and has since been translated into eleven different languages, including English, German, French, Russian, Finnish and even Arabic. The title of the book refers to Kalniete's mother, who as a 14-year-old was taken straight from a dancing night at school in June 1941, still in her dancing shoes, to the cattle trains that would take her and her family to Siberian forced exile.

been part of formal institutions, but which have still attracted considerable attention or media coverage. Although in Chapter 6 we covered the work of the three presidential history commissions created in 1998 as symbolic truth-seeking bodies, it is worth pointing out in the context of this chapter that these *international* commissions also had a conscious role to play in communicating a Baltic perspective on Soviet totalitarianism to an external audience. By appointing non-Baltic historians and other experts to work with local historians on reconstructing and evaluating the two periods of totalitarian occupation, the Baltic presidents pursued a dual goal – one of historical truth-seeking, and another of awareness-raising among Western audiences. Moreover, it bears remembering that the commissions were partly set up because of international reverberations from the Baltic states' truth and justice policies, namely the perception among many in the West that the Balts had not done enough to work through their Holocaust past. Hence, while responding to these external concerns by setting up the history commissions, the Baltic presidents also spun the bottle in the opposite direction by endowing the commissions with the task of researching both totalitarian occupation regimes.

This second, external-diplomatic function of a history commission was perhaps best understood by Estonia's President Lennart Meri, who chose to appoint only non-Estonians to his commission. As discussed in Chapter 6, over the course of ten years the commission compiled a wealth of archival material as well as drew up joint conclusions about the character of the occupation regimes and the main lines of responsibility for their crimes that were all eventually published in English. In its extremely straightforward and purely factual rendering, these reports served the effective purpose of becoming a reference book for Western political and legal analysts, as we saw in the ECtHR case of Kolk and Kislyiy. Neither the Lithuanian nor the Latvian presidential commission managed to achieve the same level of international visibility, nor have they in fact concluded their work to date.

Apart from taking the lead in creating these history commissions, the Baltic presidents have also sought other ways to promote awareness of their countries' historical legacy abroad. In particular, Latvia's President Vaira Vīķe-Freiberga became a very proactive communicator of Latvian (and Baltic) historical memory to Western audiences during her term in office from 1999 to 2007 (Mälksoo 2007). Probably the most effective of her numerous international appearances in this regard was her decision to accept Vladimir Putin's 2005 invitation to attend commemorative ceremonies marking the sixtieth anniversary of Soviet victory day in World War II. Understandably, Putin's invitation to honor on Red Square a day that for many Balts did not represent liberation but rather a re-occupation of their countries was a diplomatic minefield. Both the Lithuanian and the Estonian presidents at the time, Valdas Adamkus and Arnold Rüütel, weighed their response to the invitation for some time before finally deciding not to go. Vīķe-Freiberga, by contrast, announced early her intention to attend the events, and thereafter launched a massive diplomatic campaign to inform her Western colleagues about the difficulty of her decision and about the particular Baltic perspective on the end of World War II. This proactive approach resulted in several Western leaders sending personal letters to Vīķe-Freiberga expressing their admiration for her decision and acknowledging Latvia's historical suffering. In the end both Vīķe-Freiberga's campaign and Adamkus' and Rüütel's absence during the victory celebrations in Moscow attracted considerable international media attention throughout the spring of 2005, thus notably raising public awareness about the specific predicament of the three Baltic states with regard to one of the most important events in recent European history (Onken 2007a). Not only did the whole episode serve Baltic efforts to achieve a pan-European condemnation of communist crimes, it also strengthened the Baltic cause vis-à-vis Russia as it drew international attention once again to the Hitler–Stalin Pact of 1939 and to the historical fact of Soviet occupation in the Baltic states at a time when Moscow was doing everything to rehabilitate its glorious historical role as the defeater of fascism.

Comparative summary

Over the past twenty years, Baltic efforts to come to terms with the crimes and abuses of the Soviet regime have had considerable external reverberations. Indeed, Baltic and other Eastern European actors' efforts to take the issues of truth and justice beyond their state borders and into various fora of pan-European political discourse have become a subject of increasing scholarly interest (Leggewie 2009; Müller 2010; Troebst 2010; Littoz-Monnet 2012). As Maria Mälksoo (2014: 84–85) has argued, the attempts by Eastern European activists to achieve a legal and moral condemnation of Communism can be theorized in two ways. On the one hand, these activists' repeated juxtaposition of their own political-historical claims with those of the Holocaust reveals just how much the latter has become a template for European memory construction and a signifier of a truly transnational memory (Levy and Sznaider 2010). At the same time, Eastern Europeans' crusade for recognition is also not without a degree of deeper resentment or grievance over what many perceive as an unwillingness or failure by the West to assess the crimes of Communism against universalist legal norms and principles and to draw "universal lessons" from this criminal legacy for defining the common European memory space today. Needless to say, our aim in this chapter was not to open up debates on Europe's "memory battles," but rather to shed light on where and how the Baltic domestic truth and justice processes have streamed beyond their national borders to resonate in bilateral or multi-lateral contexts. In this sense, the chapter can be seen as providing further empirical evidence for what Mälksoo has called a "transnational remembrance in the making," as well as for the increasingly recognized importance of memory in international relations (Mälksoo 2014: 84; see also Langenbacher and Shain 2010).

As an extension of our debate over domestic truth and justice processes, this chapter demonstrated how issues of historical justice have come to very much define Baltic–Russian relations ever since the breakup of the Soviet Union. When it comes to the shared history of Communism, no agreement has been reached and both sides seem to be in an irreconcilable deadlock over issues of responsibility, acknowledgment and redress for past crimes. The chapter also demonstrated how Baltic truth and justice processes reverberated toward Europe, whether within the institutional framework of the European Court of Human Rights, the Council of Europe, different EU governing bodies or in other international contexts. Looked at from a maximalist perspective of those Baltic activists and politicians whose goal it has been to start a Europe-wide process of criminal-judicial reckoning with communist-era crimes, the effects of these reverberations have been limited. Neither in the ECtHR, where individual criminal cases from the Baltic states were reviewed, nor on the level of European legislation has there been an immediate consensus on whether or how to legally address the legacy of mass crimes committed by Communist regimes. To be sure, most of the relatively few cases of crimes against humanity judgments appealed to the ECtHR have been fully confirmed. However, our discussion of some of the Court's rulings demonstrated anything but unanimity among European judges, and indeed considerable disagreement on the criminal character of the entire Soviet regime in the Baltics. Moreover, in some of the cases a tangible uneasiness can be observed with some of the historical and legal conceptions in Baltic criminal law regarding the historical events of World War II. Likewise, European legislators are far from reaching agreement on the need to institute legislation that punishes the denial or trivialization of communist-era mass crimes, the way this issue is being legislated with regard to Holocaust denial.

However, looked at from a less judicially focused and perhaps more realist angle, Baltic attempts at taking their truth and justice processes beyond their national borders and achieving if not judicial, then at least political and symbolic recognition for their historical experiences, have been quite effective. Indeed, the memory of Communism can be said to have clearly entered a wider public historical consciousness, as European legislators have officially addressed the issue and allocated funds to support remembrance for creating a greater sense of European solidarity. In this sense we may agree with Claus Leggewie (2008) that the legacy of communist crimes together with, though not exactly equal to, the legacy of the Holocaust by now form the core of what has come to be called an emerging "pan-European memory."

Conclusion

In our concluding remarks we would like to return to the conceptual matrix model that we developed at the outset and see how the various analytical categories mapped out there can now be filled on the basis of our empirical analysis. We defined six different areas in which the politics of truth and justice play themselves out in a post-communist state and which we have covered in Chapters 3–6. The basic distinctions along which we organized the various state policies of truth and justice were between perpetrator- and victim-targeted measures on the one (horizontal) dimension, and between criminal-judicial, political-administrative and symbolic-representational levels on the other (vertical) dimension of a two-by-three matrix. Finally, we distinguished further between two temporal dimensions of state-led truth and justice processes: first, between transitional and retrospective, and then between transitional and post-transitional. Even though the transitional-vs-retrospective dimension further expands the number of analytical categories to be explored, it is useful in order to identify and evaluate the political dynamics and strategies involved in each of these areas more clearly. We thus made the argument that the resulting twelve-box matrix provides a most nuanced and yet holistic analytical tool for identifying *patterns of truth and justice politics* that include a broad spectrum of policies and measures aimed at reckoning with a past communist regime.

We then structured each of our empirical chapters to examine the actual policies followed by the Baltic states in different boxes of the matrix. We first determined the extent to which each state pursued policies concerned with more distant as opposed to more recent crimes and abuses. Secondly, we delineated the processes and timing of policy debates, new legislative initiatives and changes made to existing policies. The outcome of this analysis revealed certain overarching, matrix-wide regularities that combine into specific patterns for each country case. As we shall demonstrate in the following summarizing discussion, these patterns can be located along a scale that ranges between ideal-typical cases of extreme state involvement, or "etatism," on the one hand, and no involvement at all, i.e. an inactive state, on the other.

By etatism, we mean cases in which the processes of truth and justice across the various vertical categories of our matrix are regulated by state authority in a far-reaching manner through government institutions, laws and other official means. Moreover, the etatist state yields its maximum legislative and regulative power and invests considerable political and financial resources in order to determine and shape the various ways in which society comes to terms with and redresses past wrongdoing. Very little is left for non-governmental actors to do in this realm. In the post-communist region we do not really find such a case – not least because economic conditions and institutional instability have not allowed for such a comprehensive state-centered approach to the past. The one case that perhaps comes closest to a full-scale etatist approach would be the former East Germany with its relatively high number of criminal prosecutions and administrative as well as symbolic sanctions directed at former Communist leaders and Stasi operatives as well as lower-rank officials and informants. Moreover, post-unification Germany engaged actively in administrative and symbolic policies of compensation, restitution and truth-telling targeted at victims of the GDR regime (McAdams 2001; Offe and Poppe 2005). At the same time, one could argue that this high degree of regulative power and political determination by the state to pursue truth and justice was only possible due to the West German legal and administrative capacities available after 1990. Therefore, we might also look for an empirical anchor that is closer to post-communist normality, as it were. That case could well be the Czech Republic, because of its extensive lustration policies, criminal trials, compensation programs and institutions of research and remembrance.

At the other end of the scale, we would have a state that exhibits no political will or policy initiative in any of the boxes of our analytical matrix and could thus be categorized as an inactive state. Post-communist cases that come closest to this type can certainly be found among many of the former Soviet republics. However, since we focus on democratic countries, these states fall outside our matrix in any case. Among post-communist democracies Slovenia could be considered an inactive state. Since its breakaway from Yugoslavia in 1992, Slovenian leaders have pursued no criminal trials against perpetrators nor have they implemented any administrative sanctions against former communist leaders or security police agents, though such measures were frequently discussed among political parties. Likewise limited were the measures directed at victims of communist repressions, the only exception here being the relatively far-reaching restitution of previously nationalized property. Not irrelevant in the Slovenian case is also the fact, as pointed out by Tamara Kotar, that "the dearth of [truth and justice] measures has been matched by a lack of sustained societal interest in enacting transitional justice initiatives" (2013: 439). States that fall in between these two extremes display various degrees of state engagement across the matrix.

It is important to stress again that these various "types" of state approach relate to the entire matrix, and not just individual categories (or boxes of our matrix). Thus, in determining the position of a country on our scale we do not look for an uneven degree of activity among the various boxes, but rather for some kind of composite picture. Moreover, our empirical analysis seems to suggest that the boxes of our matrix hang together or correlate. Where states engage in one realm of truth and justice, they are likely to pursue (at least to some degree) the same objective in other realms. Having a country that has enacted policies only on, say, the victim side of our matrix (and across all three levels), but has failed to enact any measures against perpetrators, would, of course, be an anomalous case. (It would be difficult to then judge whether it is an etatist or an inactive state.) However, on the basis of our knowledge about truth and justice processes in Central and Eastern Europe, no such country appears to exist. We suspect there may be a reason for that.

A second scale that emerges from our matrix is closely related to this basic typological scale. As we pointed out in Chapter 1 (drawing on Grodsky), each of the various measures available to states involves risk-taking or at least the investment of political capital to be enacted and implemented at particular points in time. Indeed, looking at our conceptual matrix we can identify three specific dimensions across the matrix in which cost-benefit calculations play themselves out to different degrees and might thus determine emerging patterns of truth and justice. First, we may assume that victim-centered measures generally involve less risk-taking than those directed at perpetrators. In other words, to seek respect and redress for victims of past wrongdoing is more likely to appeal to the electorate and is less likely to encounter political opposition than it would be to go after wrongdoers, who may be highly respected by parts of society or still influential in the political or social life of the country. Second, lower levels of moral and political capital are usually required to enact policies of retrospective as opposed to transitional justice. Thus, it tends to be easier and more rewarding for leaders of nascent democracies to pursue adjudication and redress for historical crimes than to address much less clearly delineated wrongdoers and victims of more immediate past repressions. In the Baltic context this would mean that it "pays off" politically to condemn Stalinist-era actions as genocide and crimes against humanity and to push for legislation that helps to bring the remaining few perpetrators of these deplorable crimes to justice than it does to define and sanction wrongdoers of the recent past, who may be members of one's own party or otherwise active members of society. Finally, we see a gradual decrease in risk-taking and political capital involved as we move down the vertical dimension of the matrix from Box 1 to 3 and from Box 4 to 6. Whether victim- or perpetrator-centered, retrospective or transitional, it is always more cost intensive to implement legal-criminal provisions and administrative procedures in order to assess perpetrators and redress victims than it is to sponsor truth-seeking mechanisms, publish the names of former wrongdoers or officially commemorate their victims. Transferring this cost/risk-dimension to our continuum of state approaches to truth and justice (Figure 8.1), we conclude that a state that is characterized by a strong state-centered (or etatist) approach usually involves also a high degree of risk-taking among the political elites, while commensurately the inactive state is characterized by an elite that is unwilling to invest any political capital in pushing for truth and justice.

As we will show in the following discussion of the specific patterns that emerge in the politics of truth and justice in Estonia, Latvia and Lithuania, each case can be placed on a different position along the proposed typological continuum. Thus, whereas Lithuania with its far-reaching and sustained state involvement in issues of truth and justice can be located toward the left-hand side of this scale, Estonia exhibits a clearly less state-centered (though not entirely inactive) approach and can thus be placed further toward the right of the scale. Latvia falls somewhere in between, exhibiting on the one hand a tendency toward strong institutionalization of truth and justice policies (i.e. state

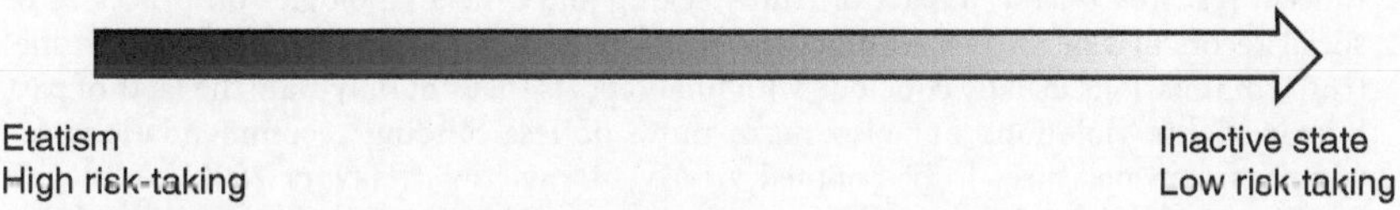

Figure 8.1 Scale of state involvement in truth and justice

involvement), yet at the same time very limited commitment in terms of investing political and economic capital in sustaining these structures and policies.

So far we have discussed how our analytical matrix enables us to identify typological patterns across the matrix. However, it is conceivable to use this analytical tool also to establish patterns of interaction within the matrix, thus determining whether there are limiting, foreclosing, enhancing or spillover effects between measures. The small number of cases discussed in this study do not allow us to make conclusive inferences in this regard. However, by speculating on a more informed basis, we may hypothesize that Boxes 1 and 4 are mutually enhancing in that a strong and effective investigative and judicial infrastructure to process rehabilitations may facilitate effective criminal investigations as well. Likewise, one may expect that a decrease (or lack of activity) in Boxes 1/4 and 2/5 – i.e. in criminal-judicial and political-administrative measures toward both perpetrators and victims – is usually compensated by increased state activity at the symbolic-representational level (Boxes 3 and 6) in the form of official declarations, apologies, the institution of national remembrance days, memory work with victims or the public disclosure of perpetrator names. Turning this relationship around, one might also speculate whether growth in the activities of Box 6 may impact on Box 5, or, in other words, the more truth-seeking and remembrance work that is done with regard to victims, the higher the pressure for policy-makers to eventually implement more substantive policies of recognition such as awarding special pensions or other forms of compensation.[1]

While more intricate relationships between the various measures and their politics would certainly come out with a larger set of cases, the matrix-wide regularities we have pointed to here emerge also in our small-n comparative study. For the purposes of this concluding discussion, we therefore stick to these outcomes and formulate the simple yet intriguing hypothesis that if a country shows significant determination and

[1] Indeed, research on the impact of truth-seeking and official apologies on processes of social reconciliation in post-conflict societies does suggest such conclusions. For one, truth commissions usually conclude with final reports that not only state the facts of past human rights violations but also make more or less binding recommendations for compensation measures to be adopted vis-à-vis the victims (Hayner 2002). Apologies for historical injustice have also been shown to yield greater effects in promoting reconciliation if they are followed up by more concrete policies of redress (Murphy 2011).

investment in one measure, it is likely to do so in others. In other words, if political leaders decide to take a radical and broad approach toward victim categorization and redress policies, it is likely that they will also pursue most radical and far-reaching approaches toward identifying, prosecuting or otherwise sanctioning perpetrators. This would equally need to be verified against a larger number of cases across the region, yet the three Baltic cases examined here clearly hint at the fact that states' approaches to issues of truth and justice are often rather holistic with regard to the different categories. This, in turn, hints at the possibility of system-wide explanatory variables that cover society in an equal manner.

After outlining the emerging patterns of truth and justice for the three states analyzed here, we will, therefore, proceed in later parts of the chapter to engage in a brief comparative discussion of possible explanations for the variation that appears to exist across Estonia, Latvia and Lithuania. As one may suspect, this will include a discussion of macro-historical arguments and historical legacies. At the same time, we cannot discount more proximate factors such as previous regime legitimacy and relative power factors during the transition that point to more actor-oriented explanations. Precisely because the Baltic states are so often treated as one with regard to both historical trajectories as well as modes of transition and post-transition politics, one of our aims here is to correct some of the existing misperceptions and conclusions. In addition, however, our findings enable us to show how even seemingly minor differences in, for example, the degree of legitimacy of the local Communist elite or particular decisions taken by the different popular movements and independence activists during the independence struggle influenced emerging attitudes and paths toward transitional and retrospective truth and justice.

Finally, by turning the issue around and taking our patterns of truth and justice as the independent variable, we will engage in a discussion about how the particular pattern that a state develops toward issues of transitional and retrospective justice can impact on other areas of state policy. Here too, the possible effects of a certain national approach to truth and justice on other policy areas certainly merit further consideration than can be done in these concluding remarks. Thus, although we did not set out in this book to make definitive causal inferences about the causes or effects of patterns of transitional and retrospective justice, we do acknowledge that the conceptual matrix that we advance here does prompt the next question, which is precisely to examine causal chains. These reflections will conclude the chapter.

Baltic patterns of truth and justice

Readers of the preceding five empirical chapters will surely have noticed many of the aggregate patterns we will now aim to synthesize in this comparative section. Although our analytical matrix already encompasses twelve different cells, we will present our empirical conclusion with an additional view to showing changes in these different categories across time. Thus, each box in the matrix will include a temporal scale that begins on the left side with 1990 and ends on the right with 2013 in order to illustrate evolution in the intensity of each category over two decades. In theory, an alternative way of visualizing this additional dimension would be to draw the matrix in a three-dimensional fashion with the third axis denoting time and each particular category of truth and justice measures would have a line passing into the third dimensional space to indicate ups and downs in the intensity of that measure. Because this would be too complicated, we have decided to illustrate temporal variations in the intensity of truth and justice measures by coloring the contents of each box in different vertical shades of gray (see Figures 8.2–8.4). Darker shades indicate moments where new policies were introduced, expanded or radicalized, lighter shades indicate moments where measures were considerably curbed or ended. The shades of gray range from white (indicating that nothing was done) to very dark gray (indicating measures were radical in legal or administrative terms, broad in scope and/or involved considerable state regulation and budgetary expense). Note also that in Box 5a, we have split the cell into two in order to reflect the two broad subcategories treated here: compensation benefits for victims (on the left) and property restitution (on the right). To our mind, these measures are sufficiently different that they deserve separate reflection in the matrix, although they are both political-administrative policies aimed at redressing victim suffering.

We acknowledge that using shades of gray is not a very formalized operationalization of measurement. Ideally, a quantified (or at least ordinal) scale could be developed. Such examples clearly exist in political science, such as Shugart and Carey's (1992) scale of presidentialism, but also Horne's (2009c) ranking of lustration policy implementation. At the same time, such a scale would inexorably be arbitrary, since not only would relative differences between qualitative policy measures be difficult to determine with precision, it would also be very much a judgment call as to which measures would constitute a maximum value within any given box in the matrix. For example, with regard to criminal trials against perpetrators, would one count as the highest value the mere fact that such proceedings were actually conducted or would one count the number of trials or the number of investigations opened or something still more qualitative such as the severity of crimes defined by prosecutors? It is for this reason that we have opted instead to give merely an indicative sense of the fluctuations in truth and justice policies. For on the one hand, our aim is to conceptualize *patterns* of truth and justice. This is our composite study variable. Therefore, we are not aiming to provide a single numerical summation or aggregate country score. By the same token, we are more than conscious of the fact that across a time span of twenty years, a country's pattern of truth and justice policies might itself change, as the intensity of one or more individual measures changes. Hence, not only does the intensity of initial measures implemented in the three states differ, but also the degree to which the policies change over time is notable; whether or not individual measures were ended or extended, whether existing measures are expanded or not and whether at some point entirely new policies are introduced that completely challenge the status quo. Here variation abounds across the three cases, and this provides an insight into more intricate forms of politics behind truth and justice. We arrive at certain landscapes of truth and justice politics, which are characteristic of each country and therefore provide the starting point for further comparative analysis and causal inferences.[2]

The hands-on state: Lithuania's politics of truth and justice

Since the restoration of independence in 1991, Lithuania has clearly shown the most ardent determination among the three Baltic states to reckon with and redress the crimes and rights abuses committed under the Soviet regime in all of the various domains we have outlined in our matrix. As Anatol Lieven (1994: 16) observed already during the early re-independence period, Lithuanian political leaders seem to "operate

[2] Astute readers will recognize that there is a degree of affinity between the approach to operationalization and measurement that we take here and some of the same challenges faced by Almond and Verba (1964) in their pioneering study on political culture. Almond and Verba were much criticized for the relatively vague aggregation mechanisms they used in tallying different components of political culture in order to come up with their assessments of parochial, subject and participant political culture. The manner in which they then designated certain patterns of such political behavior as "civic" likewise remained opaque (Pettai 2006). Still, we empathize with Almond and Verba's methodological predicament from five decades ago and maintain that quantification and arithmetic aggregation would not necessarily be the way to go with a phenomenon of this nature. Designating broad patterns falls more within the range of our own epistemological approach to political science.

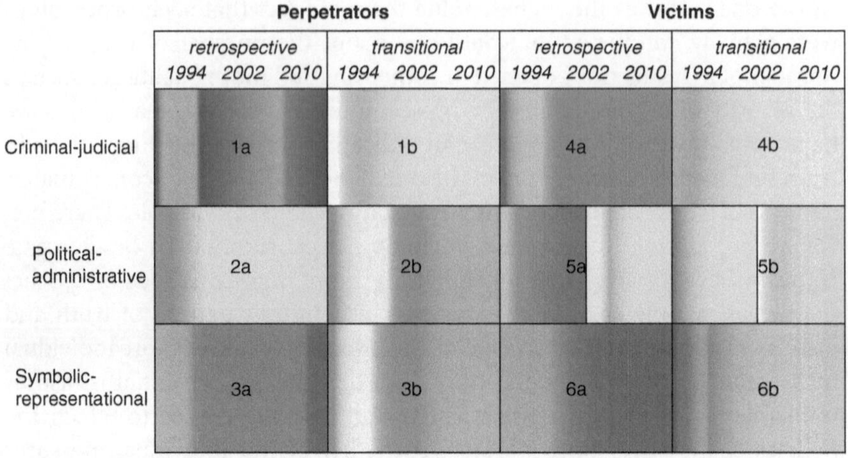

Figure 8.2 Lithuania's landscape of the politics of truth and justice

just partly in the present." Our analysis shows that this mindset appears to have continued in later years, with numerous past-oriented policies either being strengthened or newly introduced in the country. Figure 8.2 provides an illustration of this.

Lithuania's steadfastness concerning truth and justice issues shows not only in the overall number of state laws, decrees and resolutions addressing the repression committed during the Soviet and Nazi regimes, but also, for example, in the ardent investigation of Stalinist-era crimes that were later prosecuted as cases of genocide. Lithuania's particular approach is also evident in the broad scope of laws that define an ever-increasing range of victims of the Soviet regime; lastly it shows in the degree to which processes of public remembrance and victim recognition have been institutionalized through a high-powered and omnipresent state institution responsible not just for truth-revelation and remembrance, but also for policy implementation and judicial assistance. The Lithuanian landscape of truth and justice policies is therefore darker in terms of its amount of gray, but also for the way in which this has intensified over time.

What is equally striking about Figure 8.2 is that the more radical attitude and higher risk-taking among Lithuanian policy-makers also extends to various categories of *transitional* justice. Thus, as we will see later on, compared to Latvia or Estonia, Lithuania also shows considerable will to adjudicate recent state abuses and recognize their victims. Several trials took place already in the early 1990s against individuals accused of having been involved in the attempted crackdown on the Lithuanian independence movement in January 1991. Truth-revelation and remembrance with regard to more recent repressions against dissidents and other regime opponents have taken place on both more public and more institutionalized levels. Finally, the lustration laws that Lithuania adopted in 1998 and 1999 went further in scope and quality than those in Latvia and Estonia. Yet, it is notable that especially with regard to sanctioning former KGB operatives and recognizing the victims of recent communist repressions, laws and policies have come with considerable delay, thus hinting at the need for temporal explanations.

Indeed, if we look more closely into the individual boxes of the matrix we notice a sharp increase in state activity taking place around 1996–97. The suddenly darker shades indicate a major overhaul of existing truth and justice policies described in our empirical chapters that occurred right after the center-right returned to government in the 1996 elections. Through the matrix we see in a concise and visual manner how the legislative and institutional changes introduced at this moment affected almost all of our analytical categories and in at least one of them (Box 2b) completely revised pre-existing policies. Prosecutorial activities vis-à-vis perpetrators intensified around 1998 due to amendments in the criminal code that provided a broad definition of "genocide" on the basis of which a much greater number of individuals could be prosecuted for their involvement in Stalin-era mass deportations and anti-partisan repressions. Moreover, the now formalized cooperation between the Prosecutor General's Office and historical investigators at the Lithuania Genocide and Resistance Research Center (LGGRTC) further enhanced the legal muscle of the state's activities.

With regard to rehabilitation and compensation, Lithuania had adopted rather far-reaching legislative measures already in the early 1990s. As a result, we see a slight decrease of intensity in 1992, which was when the first rehabilitation wave was partially revised due to various incidents in which former Nazi collaborators had been rehabilitated. However, between 1997 and 1998 several new laws were passed that not only expanded existing victim categories to include various types of postwar resistance fighters but also stipulated a one-time compensation payment to former partisan fighters and their children. Moreover, institutional capacities and procedures were strengthened by extending the powers of the LGGRTC to issue the official victim status certificates. In 1998 and 1999 the center-right majority in the Seimas went on to adopt an unprecedented lustration law that stipulated summary dismissal from state employment and some sections of the private sector for those revealed to have worked for or cooperated with the KGB. Finally, the merging of several previously separate institutions of research and remembrance under the roof of the LGGRTC in 1997 resulted in a considerable intensification of both perpetrator- and victim-oriented research, truth-telling and remembrance work. This activity was also amplified by the creation of an international commission of historians, which although it was analogous to the ones created in Estonia and Latvia, still played the role of bolstering state-sponsored historical truth-seeking.

We are prompted to ask, therefore, against the backdrop of our conceptual framework in Chapter 1, whether the period of 1996–99 in Lithuania qualifies as an instance of post-transitional justice. Recalling our conceptualization, we defined post-transitional justice as a large-scale alteration of truth and justice measures that significantly transforms an historical narrative and/or past political agreements about which truth and justice policies are to be adopted. We also noted that temporally such alterations constitute "post-"transitional justice because they take place after the basic tenets of democracy and the rule of law have been established (and not necessarily only when democracy has been consolidated). Viewed from this angle, we argue that Lithuania does exhibit an instance of post-transitional justice, since its overall pattern of truth and justice politics did become demonstrably more etatist after 1996. In part, we draw this conclusion from two elements of our analytical matrix that clearly represent significant shifts, if not full-scale revisions, of truth and justice politics. The first is the passage of lustration laws in 1998–99. These were entirely new in the Lithuanian political system, and they also generated much acrimony. Secondly, the center-right conservative majority after 1996 dramatically reframed the policy of victim recognition in Lithuania by not only passing a new victim status law, but also elevating some of these categories to higher state recognition. (For example, the according of full military ranks to postwar anti-Soviet partisans and declaring their commander the fourth President of Lithuania.) In addition, however, we see an intensification of almost all of the other domains of truth and justice. Hence, the aggregate shift is there.[3]

[3] Moreover, many of these changes were foreshadowed (or promised) by the Homeland Union's 1996 electoral program. In it, the party pledged to deal with all of the dimensions of our matrix: criminal prosecutions, lustration, deportees' rights, property restitution, Soviet occupation damages, commemorative activities and strengthening institutions like the LGGRTC (Tevynes sajunga – Lietuvos Konservatoriu 1996).

Indeed, most of the legislative changes, new institutions and policies that were introduced in Lithuania under the national-conservative government of the late 1990s remain in force today. In fact, rather than expiring or being formally ended, successive parliaments and governments have either kept things unchanged or even increased activities by way of passing new laws and resolutions, raising budgetary spending or launching new programs that have allowed key actors in the truth and justice process – the Prosecutor General's Office and the LGGRTC – to augment their activities. The degree to which truth-seeking and remembrance in Lithuania continue to be steered or monitored by the highest levels of legislative and executive authority shows how central these issues remain in the country's politics.

The hands-off state: Estonia's politics of truth and justice

If we have placed Lithuania's approach to transitional and retrospective truth and justice somewhere toward the far left of our typological scale, then Estonia would be situated somewhere toward the right. To be sure, Estonia would not be an inactive state, but it could well be characterized as a "hands-off state," where the state provides some legal and administrative frameworks to facilitate truth and justice processes, but it declines to use its more robust regulatory power and resources for implementing laws and policies, instead leaving much of the struggle for truth and justice to non-state actors. Indeed, compared to Lithuania, Estonia's matrix of truth and justice politics, depicted in Figure 8.3, has a much lighter shade of gray across all of the analytical categories. This not only indicates lesser state involvement in judicial, political and symbolic dealings with the totalitarian past, but also points to a lower degree of risk-taking when measures are being implemented. Moreover, Estonian political leaders have shown a readiness to declare certain measures closed, thereby actually dissolving truth-seeking bodies or setting clear deadlines for lustration procedures and letting them indeed expire. This Estonian tendency toward closure is unique among the three Baltic states.

What we see here, more than in the Lithuanian case, is a state that instead of using its administrative and legislative power to shape policies of truth and justice with regard to the past chooses not to do so. While not rejecting such measures on principle (as a completely inactive state would do), legislators and policy-makers do take a less cost-intensive path, in terms of both political risk and economic expense. Thus, while

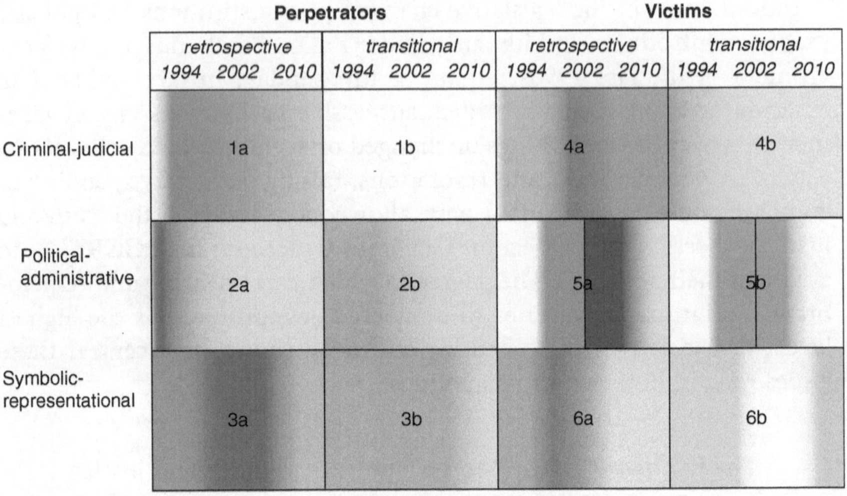

Figure 8.3 Estonia's landscape of the politics of truth and justice

Estonia established a number of truth-seeking commissions in the 1990s that were charged with assessing the damages (human and material) inflicted on the country by the Soviet regime as well as determining individual and institutional responsibility for these crimes, the overall funding and political attention paid to these commissions was limited. As we showed in Chapter 6, Estonia never considered the creation of a more omnibus institution for truth and justice policy on a par with the TSDC in Latvia or the LGGRTC in Lithuania.

On the criminal-judicial level, the tendency toward more limited involvement was also apparent. Estonian legislators did provide (albeit slightly later than their colleagues in Latvia and Lithuania) a legal framework for rehabilitating specific groups of former repressed individuals. They also enacted rather stern legislation seeking to prosecute surviving KGB (NKVD, MGB) operatives involved in the mass deportations of the 1940s and anti-partisan killings. However, the number of actual convictions was continuously lower than in Lithuania. Moreover, the legal strategy of the Prosecutor General's Office and the Security Police Board was generally more cautious in terms of its politics and criminal charges. For example, even though the legal provisions installed in 1994 (and later in 2002) provided a broad definition of genocide, Estonian authorities rarely made use of this opportunity. With the exception of the 2007 Arnold Meri case (and two others), which never reached conclusion, involvement in mass deportations on various levels was interpreted as an offense belonging essentially to the conventional category of crimes against humanity and in accordance with customary international law. This is not to say that such a way of punishing people who may have simply implemented a deportation order coming from higher up was not radical in terms of its view on justice. However, it still represents a qualitative difference, especially if we look at how the same offenses were interpreted as participation in genocide by both Latvian and Lithuanian prosecutors and judges. These various observations together thus account for a certain degree of lighter shade in Box 1a in the Estonian case.

Staying within the perpetrator dimension, the same low-risk, hands-off approach of Estonia continues within the sphere of lustration. While the oath of conscience requirement for all elected officials and public employees seemed like a bold and innovative provision of early transitional justice (enshrined as it was in the 1992 Constitution), in practice it turned out to be rather inconsequential, as individual oaths were rarely verified and even then the controversies surrounding certain public figures never resulted in resignations or court cases as they would in Latvia. Moreover, this non-judicial procedure expired in December 2000 and such measures were not extended in the way that they were in other Central European countries such as the Czech Republic. Thirdly, Estonia's other main lustration policy – volunteer self-reporting – involved again low administrative cost and by the mid-2000s was likewise coming to a *de facto* end. Although the initiative did reveal the identities of over 600 people as former KGB operatives who had not reported themselves, Estonian officials have themselves admitted that the measure was designed more as a way to obtain information about past KGB activities than as a means to extract retribution. We therefore placed this measure in Box 3b, among the symbolic policies of truth and justice.

One of the biggest time-lags that we see in Baltic truth and justice policies is Estonia's slowness in adopting a more systematized victim status law before 2003 or fully twelve years after re-independence. This delay points to a curious fact that it would not be until that time that a tangible political interest would develop in order to push such legislation and establish a commensurate administrative framework. It would take the rise of a new political party (Res Publica) and a complete circumvention of existing center-right parties in order to generate the necessary momentum for passing a repressed persons' Act. The final 2003 law not only expanded the scope of those eligible for state recognition but also increased certain benefits. At the same time, these allowances remained modest and did not extend to the descendants of the repressed; nor were they issued posthumously as in, for example, Lithuania. Moreover, Estonian lawmakers ultimately shied away from classifying those who resisted Soviet rule (including former members of the German army) as "freedom fighters," at least on a legal level.

To a certain degree this introduction of a legal status for former repressed people a good decade after the end of regime transition might be considered another case of post-transitional justice. However, we are cautious here, since the mere institutionalization of a victim status for individuals, among whom many had already been declared victims in previous (social welfare) legislation did not really constitute a new direction in policy, nor did it alter the narrative of communist repression or of transitional settlements. This is further underpinned by the fact that other than in Lithuania the 2003 law did not significantly extend the existing victim categories and thus potentially offer a new reading of the past regime's repressive scope. For example, it did not designate special status for people who might have been dismissed from work or university because of dissident activities.

The only area in which Estonia has shown considerably more state engagement and high political risk-taking has been that of property restitution (the right-hand side of Box 5a). Because the country's rather far-reaching policy on returning Soviet nationalized property has concerned so many people, it has generated considerable amounts of controversy as well as administrative expense. At the same time, the policy has remained largely unchanged since the mid-1990s and has by now been largely completed. Thus, although rather far-reaching in its consequences, Estonia's property restitution has still followed the path of the country's oath of conscience or other justice measures in that eventually it was brought to a conclusion.

The ambivalent state: Latvia's politics of truth and justice

If Lithuania and Estonia can be nicely categorized in a mirror-like fashion as cases of hands-on and hands-off truth and justice, Latvia is much more difficult to place on our comparative scale. An initial look at Figure 8.4 suggests a placement that is closer to Estonia than Lithuania. There are clearly many more patches of white and lighter shades of gray that allude to the fact that Latvia has pursued less politically strident measures and has demonstrated a weaker commitment to state agencies tasked with pursuing justice or supporting truth-seeking and remembrance. However,

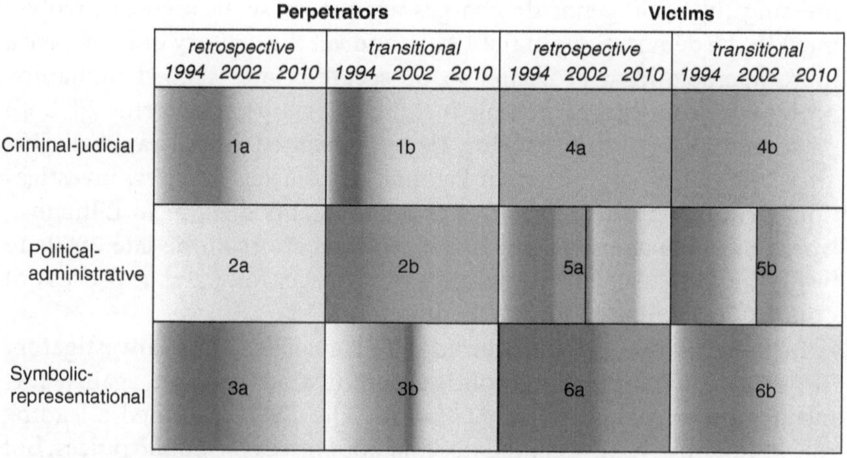

Figure 8.4 Latvia's landscape of the politics of truth and justice

at the same time we see that many boxes in the table are darker toward the left, indicating that initial acts and policies were vigorous and substantive. This fading out of the boxes over time is explained by a lack of commitment to sustain these principles or to supply established institutions with sufficient resources to carry out their work.

This ambivalent state approach, as we shall call it, is visible in almost all areas covered by our analytical matrix. On the criminal-judicial level, we see an early and radical legal framing of Stalin-era crimes as genocide and crimes against humanity, an interpretation that continued with a rather ardent prosecutorial strategy to bring both high- and low-ranking former officials responsible for deportation to justice. We also see an early and rather comprehensive rehabilitation law that included not only the criminally repressed but also psychiatric patients and other politically persecuted people. Moreover, Latvia's 1995 law on rehabilitation introduced a special legal status for repressed persons, which institutionalized very early the way in which the state would acknowledge and support these people with social benefits. These prosecutorial and rehabilitation efforts would be further undergirded by the establishment of new institutions of historical expertise and investigation in the form of the Center for the Documentation of the Consequences of Totalitarianism (TSDC) and the Commission for the Investigation of Totalitarian Regime Crimes in 1992.

The sudden decline in prosecutorial activities around 2000 (Box 1a) was caused mainly by changes within the Prosecutor General's Office, when a new prosecutor general was named who was more wary of pressing full-scale genocide charges against those accused of involvement in the deportations of the 1940s, and yet the country did not have a more operable legal provision to prosecute crimes against humanity. Moreover, a feeling of getting insufficient support in terms of both personnel and political backing also contributed to the rapid decline after 2000. Thus, other than in Estonia, where trials and new investigations petered out due to the fact that defendants died, or in Lithuania, where the state actually launched a renewed effort in the late 2000s to bring the last surviving perpetrators to justice, the Latvian process of criminal justice ended more abruptly.

In Box 2b we see the beginnings of a firm legal and investigatory infrastructure for pursuing political-administrative justice against former regime perpetrators, i.e. lustration. The TSDC assumed a leading role in not only vetting candidates and appointees for public offices, but also in investigating the structure of command and the operations of the former security police apparatus and thus identifying many more individuals associated with the previous regime's wrongdoings than could readily be discerned from the modest amount of materials left over by the Soviet KGB. In the end, however, these proceedings remained clearly more limited than those in Lithuania and only slightly harsher than those in Estonia. To be sure, the automatic vetting of candidates running for elected office and the publication of their names in cases where they appeared in the KGB files did constitute an important element of sanction. It would throw into turmoil the political careers of a number of prominent politicians. However, over time these cases of outing became limited to just a handful of marginal candidates. Self-reporting mechanisms as in Estonia or Lithuania were never put in place.

In recent years lustration controversies have centered mainly on the question of whether or not to open the "Cheka bags" or the collection of secret files left behind by the KGB in 1991 and subsequently used by the TSDC to perform its designated lustration functions. Although the possible wholesale disclosure of names is ultimately classified in our matrix as a symbolic measure (since it would not take any rights away from individuals), such a policy would still be largely indiscriminate and would therefore entail considerable political and societal fallout. The demand for adopting such a policy has increasingly become a political tool for national-conservative parties, who see electoral gain from pushing such an issue. Their attempt in 2004 (indicated by the dark gray line in Box 3b) to finally open the bags to the public got as far as being adopted by a parliamentary majority. It failed to stand as law only thanks to repeated presidential vetoes. The political dynamics that emerged in this context were particularly telling since some of the more centrist parties that had previously decided to vote against the indiscriminate disclosure of names suddenly changed their minds and felt compelled to let the measure pass. The reason suggested by observers and discussed in Chapter 4 was that they never thought the bill would go through, and they saw this as a good opportunity to discredit the Russian minority party (Harmony Center), who would thus be the only one voting against "revealing the truth." Thus, for the sake of short-term gains, these politicians took a considerable political risk that could have shifted Latvia's policy of transitional justice toward a much harsher approach. In May 2014, the Latvian parliament repeated this scenario, voting again to open the files, albeit this time only after 2018. Although this plan may still be changed before the deadline, it does appear, therefore, that the country is moving toward more openness about its KGB past.

These particular controversies hint at an important issue specific to Latvia's politics of truth and justice. In contrast to Estonia or Lithuania, the political dynamics surrounding these questions in Latvia involve an ethnic factor. By this we mean that they are more directly determined by the fact that a large part of the population does not share the core tenets of Latvia's truth and justice policies – the narrative of legal continuity and Soviet aggression during World War II. Whether it is the issue of revealing former KGB agents, trials against former NKVD operatives or the public remembrance of Latvian war veterans as victims, Russian-speaking residents have been much more vocal in rejecting these policies. Moreover, because Russian minority parties have significant political representation in the national parliament (in contrast to Estonia) and in several local governments (including the Riga City Council), this opposition has been much better organized and steady. Not only has this resulted in a more confrontational political culture within the walls of parliament and in the media, it has also led to protest actions taking place at monuments or demonstrations being organized in support of those under prosecution by the courts. This has in turn brought in the Russian Federation as a more active player in truth and justice processes in Latvia, again across many of the categories of our matrix. All of this has created a different kind of political environment and higher political costs, both internally and externally, for Latvian policy-makers to consider before adopting various measures. This might thus be one reason for the more ambivalent or at least more cautious attitudes adopted by many members of the political and judicial elite toward issues of truth and justice.

On the victim dimension as well, we see a gradual shift from an initial willingness to commit state resources to the investigation of historical truth and to the creation of recognition policies for victims, to a slow withdrawal of these resources and increasing disengagement. Initial laws on public remembrance and various state-sponsored institutions for victim-centered research embodied a relatively high degree of state involvement during the 1990s. After the mid-2000s, however, and especially after the 2008–2009 economic crisis, we see a noticeable decline in state activity especially in the symbolic-representational categories, as shown by the much lighter shade of gray in several of the matrix boxes. Moreover, this disengagement was not due to a deliberate closure of specific measures as in Estonia, but owed more to economic factors and a decline in interest among the political patrons of these institutions. Fiscal austerity, for example, led to the curbing of the TSDC's historical investigations, a temporary halt in funding for the Commission of Historians of Latvia and a further reduction in the already meager state support for public remembrance events and institutions. Political withdrawal was also symbolized by the much more limited interest Latvian presidents such as Valdis Zatlers and Andris Bērziņš took in the work of the Commission of Historians operating under their auspices.

Explaining Baltic truth and justice patterns

The previous discussion of our individual cases already hinted at a number of explanations for the overall patterns of truth and justice politics as well as for their fluctuations over time. Rather than adding to the extensive literature on individual measure explanations, our aim here is to identify some of the core factors that impact on a country's overall approach to both victim- and perpetrator-targeted truth and justice. A first comparative glance at our matrix-wide patterns reveals a clear prevalence of policies and measures relating to the more distant past, thus privileging retrospective over transitional truth and justice. This assessment remains when we look at legislative and policy developments over time: even in the mid-2000s parliamentary resolutions, amendments to social welfare laws or new directives for improving prosecutorial capacities were concerned predominantly with the crimes of the Stalinist period, not with state abuse and human rights violations from the later decades of Soviet rule. Not surprisingly, the only area in which transitional justice dominates in all three states is that concerning political-administrative measures meant to identify and sanction former operatives of the KGB. The main explanation for this preponderance of retrospective over transitional measures – a pattern that might indeed be unique within the broader Central European context – is that the specific Soviet history of these three states was much more severe, involving illegal annexation and large-scale deportation beyond the territory of these countries. The historical circumstances of the Baltic states as former Soviet republics were thus not only more traumatic in terms of sheer human suffering, but also devastating politically as independence was annihilated and a repressive regime imposed from outside. (See Chapter 2.) Exposing the crimes of those years, going after at least some of those who had executed that repression and acknowledging those whose lives had been shattered by these acts became a key political duty of the restored states, albeit to different degrees.

Going somewhat further with this distal analysis, we see that while the historical parameters of the three states have been broadly the same, there are still substantive differences across many of the details, which in turn appear to also explain variation across patterns of retrospective and transitional justice. Looking at the region both during and after World War II, it becomes apparent that the scope and intensity of state-induced violence, terror and trauma inflicted by the Nazi and Soviet regimes through occupation, mass-scale forced resettlement, indiscriminate killing and exploitation as well as extended guerilla warfare were both broader and stronger in Lithuania than they were in Latvia and Estonia. This pertains to both the Stalinist and the Nazi periods. With regard to the latter regime, the additional element of what we may call culpability further enhances the degree of intensity on this historical variable. In other words, the preoccupation with past injustice in Lithuania is definitely amplified by the scope of local complicity in the mass murder of Jews and other civilians. The radical approach taken by Lithuanian leaders toward righting past wrongs and framing Soviet-era crimes (including the killing of armed partisans) as no less than an attempted genocide against the Lithuanian nation can be seen as not only a response to an enormous loss of human life due to Stalinism but also a reaction to outside accusations that portrayed Lithuanians as willing participants in the genocide of another nation. To be sure, the genocide debate regarding Stalinist mass crimes, and with it debates over relativizing the Holocaust and local collaboration, is not limited to Lithuania alone. Indeed, Latvia has seen very similar controversies throughout the 1990s. However, the genocide controversy did not evolve into such high-level political confrontation in Latvia, and even less so in Estonia, and neither of these two states demonstrated the same degree of determination to firmly institutionalize the "Soviet genocide" narrative through state legislation, government programs, institutions and judicial proceedings.

Thus, the scope and intensity of historical conflict and injustice with regard to the Holocaust, though not the subject of detailed scrutiny in this book, has clearly impacted on how radically the crimes of communism have been addressed in these three states. Another variation on the historical variable that has arguably a more direct impact on post-communist truth and justice is the scope and degree of guerilla warfare and other violence after World War II. While Lithuania experienced a decade of anti-Soviet guerilla fighting that had a war-like character in its level of partisan organization and combat structure, resulting in thousands of deaths among both the combatants and the civilians, the partisan struggles of neither Estonia nor Latvia came anywhere close to these dimensions. Today, it is the criminal investigation of anti-partisan repression by the Soviet security organs as well as the administrative and symbolic recognition of former partisans that constitutes a considerable portion of the more extended truth and justice policies that we have seen in Lithuania.

Yet Estonia and Latvia suffered a different kind of injustice in the decades following the return of the Soviets, namely the state-sponsored settlement of hundreds of thousands of Russian speakers into these two countries. Though non-violent in character, the Soviet population policy threatened the core fabric of both nations by drastically reducing the proportion of ethnic Latvians and Estonians in each country and by limiting the official use of the native languages. Perceived as a colonial policy and as a grave injustice by most Estonians and Latvians, the issue of Russification became one of the cornerstones of the anti-Soviet independence movement. Moreover, after the restoration of independence and in a clear move to right this past wrong, both states passed citizenship laws that would deny automatic citizenship to Soviet-era settlers and their descendants, although they did accord them permanent residency. In this sense, as we already discussed in Chapter 4, the citizenship legislation of both Estonia and Latvia can be seen as a rather radical measure of transitional justice, albeit not of lustration as some authors have suggested (Jaskovska and Moran 2006).

This distal factor, that is, the impact of Soviet-era population shifts, helps us transition to some of the more proximate factors that explain the variation in country patterns of truth and justice across Estonia, Latvia and Lithuania. It is precisely this legacy of Soviet demographic engineering – or its lack thereof in the case of Lithuania – that produces additional explanatory variables. To wit, it was the successful limitation of mass immigration from the Soviet Union into Lithuania that earned the local Communist Party a certain degree of credibility among Lithuanians. Moreover, it allowed the party to "nativize" and thus further expand its legitimacy and support in the local population. Such processes never took place in Estonia or Latvia, as the higher ranks of the Communist Party as well as other key positions in the state and security apparatus were with few exceptions occupied by either Slavs or Russian-born Latvians and Estonians. (See Chapter 2.) All of this allowed the Lithuanian Communist Party not only to successfully reconfigure itself during the transition but also to return to power (with an absolute parliamentary majority) already after the elections of 1992. The party system after these elections thus became deeply divided along a strong and rather resilient ex-/anti-communist cleavage, more akin to cleavage patterns emerging in neighboring Poland than to those in the other two Baltic states. In the two decades following independence, the increasing polarization of both party politics and public debates explains some of the extreme fluctuation in policy approaches that we see in the Lithuanian matrix of truth and justice, where new policy initiatives or considerable changes to existing measures recur in the 1990s and 2000s.

A comparable prospect of success for the former Communist parties in Estonia and Latvia was unthinkable. These parties had lost all of their legitimacy (if they ever had any) given their failure to prevent Russification and later their resistance to burgeoning democracy in 1987–88. At best, some of the native Latvians or Estonians in these parties would shift toward moderate positions as soon as Mikhail Gorbachev's reforms took hold, and after 1991 they would try and join different centrist parties to continue their revamped political careers. They did not stick together, however, as a group; hence, no ex-/anti-communist cleavage ever emerged.

Yet the legacy of Soviet settlement and Russification policy still had an impact on political cleavage formation (and hence on truth and justice politics) to the extent that Russian-minority parties were able to constitute a political force after 1991. This was most pronounced in Latvia, but on a certain level also present in Estonia. As was already noted, both states broadly excised their Russian-speaking minorities from politics via restorationist citizenship laws, thus keeping them from potentially opposing particular truth and justice policies. Had this opposition been greater, either of the countries could have ended up becoming "inactive states." In Latvia a sizable number of Russians in the country were descendants of the pre-war national minority and thus received Latvian citizenship. At the same time, most of these people were culturally and linguistically as poorly integrated and increasingly alienated by the nationalizing state as were the Soviet-era settlers. Given that these individuals could still organize politically and stand for office, this (albeit limited) share of the minority population could at least make its voice heard concerning the course of truth and justice politics. Although it would take some time for many of the early Russian parties to unify and form a single political force, they would eventually constitute a vocal opposition to many Latvian-supported state policies of retribution or redress for Soviet-era crimes and abuses. As this resistance grew, Latvian legislators would in turn feel challenged to propose more radical measures; they would also feel obliged to reckon with more intense parliamentary debates, public protests and sometimes foreign policy fallouts. In the end, the political dynamics resulting from these constellations among political actors and electorates accounted to a large extent for the greater ambivalence we saw in Latvia's approach to truth and justice over time.

To be sure, in Estonia the same deep ethnopolitical and memory-based divisions have existed, and the riots surrounding the relocation of the Bronze Soldier monument in 2007 were clear evidence of this. However, due to the fact that there was only a tiny pre-war Russian minority in Estonia (while the bulk of Russian speakers came after 1945), the country's 1992 citizenship law effectively prevented the *de facto* ethno-political cleavage from defining the country's subsequent party system. Thus, it is the absence of such party political cleavages in Estonia that explains the relative ease with which state leaders passed truth and justice legislation. Likewise, it is this relative homogeneity of political cleavages that explains why Estonians were ready to allow those measures that they did enact to expire or fade out over time. And it is this lesser degree of tension within the party system as a whole that explains why there was no ratcheting effect that might have led to more severe truth and justice policies. In sum, we see that in the Estonian case it was the combination of historical circumstantial factors – in terms of both the lower scope of injustice and the course of ethno-demography – along with the coincidence of enacted restrictive citizenship legislation that prompted Estonian leaders to tend toward a more detached approach to transitional and retrospective truth and justice.

The effects of truth and justice patterns

Let us turn, finally, to the possible impact that the Baltic countries' different patterns of truth and justice may have had on other policy areas or on their broader political development. This is arguably the most speculative issue to address, yet it bears at least some reflection. On the one hand, it is difficult to say anything, since if we stick to the more holistic model of truth and justice politics that we have put forward here, there are clearly no other comparative studies on which we could now draw. As we noted in our Introduction, almost all of the studies of transitional justice politics during the 1990s have focused on single policy areas and on identifying the causes of these phenomena. Only in the 2000s have scholars turned to studying the impact of different transitional justice measures on democratizing societies and institutions. Recent studies have looked into the effects of administrative purges and vetting procedures on, for example, building popular trust in government or norms of accountability (Horne and Levi 2004; David 2011). Others have tried to analyze the role of official truth-seeking mechanisms on processes of reconciliation and human rights accountability (Rushton 2006; Wiebelhaus-Brahm 2010; Bakiner 2014). In the end, however, even these studies find that such policies have "either a moderately beneficial impact on transitional societies and judicial procedures or no measurable impact at all. Some even find a negative impact on peace, democratization and reconciliation" (Ambos 2013: 175; see also Van Der Merwe et al. 2009).

Even more questionable to our mind are those studies that attempt to compile large-N datasets in order to test the impact of truth and justice policies (either as single measures or composites) on a country's degree of democratic consolidation, its respect for rule of law and human rights or its success at conflict resolution (Horne 2009c; Olsen et al. 2010a; Olsen et al. 2010b; Binningsbø et al. 2012). Such studies may be problematic for several reasons. First, they are often forced to dilute the measurement of complex phenomena in order to be able to cover as many cases or country-years as possible. For example, the Transitional Justice Database (compiled by Leigh A. Payne, Tricia D. Olsen and Andrew G. Reiter) does code five different types of truth and justice measures (trials, truth commissions, amnesties, reparations, lustration), including instances where a country adopts more than one measure at once. This allows the authors of the database to arrive at certain claims regarding what a proper "justice balance" might be for newly democratic countries – something that our patterns of truth and justice might also reveal. However, the Database treats all five of its measures as binary categories, which clearly masks much of the variation that may be embedded within each of these measures. Meanwhile, Cynthia Horne attempts to measure lustration policies based on a three-point scale. However, she looks at the effects of just this one truth and justice measure. Thirdly, global datasets inevitably run the risk of being incomplete or inaccurate. Although the Baltic states are just three small countries in the entire set of nations that have adopted truth and justice policies, it is telling for us that in the Transitional Justice Database (as of June 2014) the lustration policies of Estonia and Lithuania are not at all mentioned and that Latvia is absent entirely. Lastly, there is always the causal endogeneity problem, meaning that it might be democratization that is causing truth and justice measures to be adopted, not the other way around (see also Riffler 2010). Hence, while different comparative datasets appear to advance our knowledge by generating positive correlation coefficients and other statistical results, these may also be entirely spurious if the cases were to be coded in a more nuanced manner. Already the numerous qualifications or caveats we have had to make in this study in order to generate composite assessments of truth and justice patterns in the Baltic states make us cautious about how far we can push the quantification of such phenomena.

We are left, therefore, with only one set of bearings on this issue. Our analysis of patterns of truth and justice politics in the Baltics led at the beginning of this chapter to a typological distinction between etatist and inactive states. In theory, this could serve as our independent variable in attempting to see whether a country's inclination toward one or the other direction might be correlated with some other phenomenon. In the event, of course, we know that our three Baltic cases do seem to vary on this variable. Whereas Lithuania appears closer to an etatist model, Estonia leans toward an inactive state and Latvia falls in between (in terms of both its measures and its evolution over time). Does this distribution match any other phenomena we might consider important?

Our first task here is to avoid positing mutually causal relationships. One obvious example would be to claim that a strong ex- vs. anti-communist political cleavage causes more etatist patterns of truth and justice politics, which in turn reinforces that same ex- and anti-communist political cleavage. On the surface, of course, this would appear to be true in the case of Lithuania. However, it does not take us further in terms of identifying independent effects of truth and justice patterns. Hence, another candidate would be to look at levels of popular trust in government or satisfaction with democracy. Over the last several years, numerous studies have confirmed that of the three Baltic countries Estonia appears to have had a consistently higher level on these variables than Latvia or Lithuania (Horne 2009c; Pettai et al. 2010; Norkus 2013). On the face of it, therefore, we might hypothesize that the more a country leans toward an etatist mode of truth and justice politics, the lower might be its level of satisfaction with democracy. The causal logic would be that heavy state involvement in truth and justice politics hints at polarization on this issue, which in turn alienates people from politics over time. The state has become increasingly enmeshed in these domains because certain political forces have sought to capture the powers of the state in order to impose their truth and justice agenda. This means that dealing with the past never really reaches closure, since either new measures are constantly introduced or existing measures are suddenly enforced with new zeal. The result is that people become tired of this recurring acrimony or state-imposed solemnity; their interest in politics wanes. Clearly we cannot argue that variation across patterns of truth and justice politics in the Baltics explains wholly the varying levels of satisfaction with democracy or interest in politics. However, reflecting on this apparent co-variation does help us think more deeply about how truth and justice politics might not always lead to the kind of societal reconciliation or democratic *Vergangenheitsbewältigung* that it is supposed to.

By the same token, it is unclear whether an inactive or hands-off state achieves more or better "truth and justice." The essence of many truth and justice processes is that there be clear discussion in society about how such measures may or may not help to alter understandings about the past as well as change perceptions about the current and future legacies of this past. In this respect, countries that bring quick closure to dealing with past oppression may do a disservice to the process of developing a vibrant democratic culture, since they forgo an opportunity to have rigorous debate about a normatively contentious issue. This appears to be particularly the case in Estonia, where truth and justice across almost all of our boxes was dealt with in relatively dispassionate terms. Be it the limited number of criminal trials, the internationalizing of truth-seeking via a historical commission comprised uniquely of foreigners, or the very staid enactment of a mere oath of conscience, Estonia seems to be a model example of taking some policy measures, and yet not getting bogged down in recurrent politics – to the point that some of these measures were even concluded. The only issue that truly divided (ethnic) Estonian society was property restitution, where a very principled decision in favor of extensive restitution was made, leading to lengthy and weighty debates about where justice truly lay on this score. This experience without a doubt dominated Estonian understandings of what was important to rectify from the Soviet past. Many other issues, however, were demonstrably less deliberated.

One is left, therefore, wondering whether Latvia might not hold the most virtue thanks to its numerous debates about lustration, property restitution, historical truth and criminal prosecution. On each of these issues, controversy has pitched back and forth, yet without leading to any fateful polarization. This is all the more remarkable since many of these contestations have been waged across ethnic lines, such as the trials against former NKVD agents or efforts to clarify Latvian history during World War II. To be sure, important ethnic divides and inequalities remain in Latvia. However, many aspects of the Soviet past that Latvians and Russians have had to work through equally as part of a re-independent Latvia have been confronted bit by bit through repeated interaction and exchange.

In the end it may be that transitional and retrospective justice cannot easily be generalized across any set of countries, since each case is invariably embedded in a singular context of past repression. Even when three countries like the Baltic states share so much in terms of a common Soviet past, we have seen in this book that it is in no way guaranteed that they will confront this past analogously. Diverse social or political sub-factors may still change either the way in which these challenges are perceived or the political terrain on which these struggles are waged. As a result, it may even seem like each country is pursuing an entirely different set of objectives or effects when it engages with these issues. If this fact is true, then our aspirations to generalize across processes of truth and justice would appear to be even more quixotic. Still, in this book we have put forward at least one new tool, which is the notion of *patterns* of transitional and retrospective justice, and we have sought to demonstrate its usefulness in terms of opening up the complexities of truth and justice in the Baltic states. Through further comparative research we might be able to flesh out other cases along the scale of etatism or inactive states. Certainly, among post-communist states this would help us to establish a more holistic view of how the past has been dealt with – if only because that past itself was so long in duration and manifold in its forms of repression.

REFERENCES

15min.lt 2012a. "Lithuanian government sets up panel to prepare for Soviet damage compensation talks," *15min.lt*, May 23.

15min.lt 2012b. "Lithuanian Prime Minister thinks Soviet occupation compensation should be included in EU-Russian dialogue," *15min.lt*, July 17.

15min.lt 2013. "Lithuanian prosecutors draft suspicions against 81 people in January 13 coup case," *15min.lt*, January 11.

Ābola, Zinta 2014. Testimony Before the Judicial Affairs Committee, Latvijas Republikas Saeima, January 15.

Aguilar, Paloma 2008. "Transitional or post-transitional justice? Recent developments in the Spanish Case," *South European Society and Politics*, 13: 4, 417–33.

Almond, Gabriel and Verba, Sidney 1964. *The Civic Culture*. Boston: Little, Brown and Co.

Ambos, Kai 2013. "Efficiency of transitional justice," in Stan and Nedelsky (eds.), II, pp. 175–80.

Andersen, Erik André 1997. "The legal status of Russians in Estonian privatisation legislation 1989–1995," *Europe-Asia Studies*, 49: 2, 303–16.

Andruškevičiūtė, Agnė 2008. "Nuosavybės teisių į miestų žemę atkūrimas Lietuvoje," unpublished PhD thesis, Vilniaus Universitetas Vilnius.

Anepaio, Terje 2002. "Reception of the topic of repression in Estonian society," *Pro Ethnologia*, 14: 47–66.

Ansip, Andrus 2005. "Address by Prime Minister Andrus Ansip in Klooga," press release, May 8.

Antonevičs, Māris 2000. "Vai tiesneši ir spaidīti?" *Lauku Avize*, April 29.

Anušauskas, Arvydas 1996. *Lietuvių tautos sovietinis naikinimas, 1940–1958 metais*. Vilnius: Mintis.

2003a. *Arrests and Other Forms of Coercion 1940–1941*. Report commissioned by the International Commission for the Evaluation of the Crimes of the Soviet and Nazi Occupation Regimes in Lithuania.

2003b. *Murder of Military and Civilian Population by the Soviets*. Report commissioned by the International Commission for the Evaluation of the Crimes of the Soviet and Nazi Regimes in Lithuania.

2005. *Deportations of the Population in 1944–1953*. Report commissioned by the International Commission for the Evaluation of the Crimes of the Soviet and Nazi Occupation Regimes in Lithuania.

2006. "The solution to the problem of KGB Reserve and/or national security interests," in R. Lopata, J. Novagrockiene and G. Vitkus (eds.), *Lithuanian Annual Strategic Review 2005*. Vilnius: Lithuanian Military Academy, pp. 195–226.

Appel, Hilary 2005. "Anti-communist justice and founding the post-communist order: lustration and restitution in Central Europe," *East European Politics & Societies*, 19: 3, 379–405.

Arad, Yitzak 1979. *The Partisan: From the Valley of Death to Mt Zion*. New York: Holocaust Library.

Arad, Yitzak 2004. "The Murder of the Jews in German-Occupied Lithuania (1941–1944)," in A. Nikžentaitis, S. Schreiner and D. Staliūnas (eds.), *The Vanished World of Lithuanian Jews*. Amsterdam: Rodopi, pp. 175–204.

Arend, Ingo 2004. "Schwundstufe. Leipzig 2004 war die Buchmesse der schiefen Vergleiche," *Der Freitag*, April 2.

Arpo, Martin 2012. "The Martens Clause and international crimes in Estonia," *ENDC Proceedings*, 15: 101–106.

Arter, David 1996. *Parties and Democracy in the Post-Soviet Republics: the Case of Estonia*. Brookfield: Dartmouth Publishing.

Assmann, Aleida 2004. "Four formats of memory: from individual to collective constructions of the past," in C. Emden and D. Midgley (eds.), *Cultural Memory and Historical Consciousness in the German-Speaking World since 1500*. Berlin: Peter Lang, pp. 19–37.

Bakiner, Onur 2014. "Truth commission impact: an assessment of how commissions influence politics and society," *International Journal of Transitional Justice*, 8: 1, 6–30.

Balkelis, Tomas and Davoliūtė, Violeta 2009. *National Report on Lithuania*. Commissioned by the European Commission, Direction D: Fundamental Rights and Citizenship of the Directorate-General for Justice, Freedom and Security for the project "How the Memory of Crimes Committed by Totalitarian and/or Other Repressive Regimes in Europe Is Dealt With."

Baltic Assembly 1994. "Resolution on relations with Russia." May 15, 4th Session.

2004a. "Resolution on the need to assess the damage inflicted on the Baltic states by the occupation." December 19, 23rd Session.

2004b. "Resolution regarding accusations by the State Duma of the Russian Federation." December 19, 23rd Session.

Baltic Times 2005. "Commission receives list of 10 more KGB reservists," January 26.

2008. "Slow progress on lustration law," February 27.

Balynienė, Rūta and Buškevičienė, Angelė 2001. "Lietuviai prievartinėje karinėje tarnyboje SSRS kariuomenėje 1945–1991 metais," *XXI amžius*, no. 12 (1019).

Barahona De Brito, Alexandra, Gonzalez Enriquez, Carmen, and Aguilar, Paloma, eds. 2001. *The Politics of Memory and Democratization: Transitional Justice in Democratizing Societies*. Oxford University Press.

Barkham, Patrick 2001. "Konrad Kalejs: Latvian Nazi lieutenant who resisted all efforts to bring him to justice," *The Guardian*, November 12.

Beattie, Andrew 2008. *Playing Politics with History: The Bundestag Inquiries into East Germany*. Oxford: Berghahn Books.

Bela-Krūmiņa, Baiba 2004. "Narrated memories: the past in the present," paper presented at the Thirteenth International Oral History Conference "Memory and Globalization," Rome, June 23–26.

Berg, Manfred and Schaefer, Bernd eds. 2009. *Historical Justice in International Perspective: How Societies Are Trying to Right the Wrongs of the Past*. Cambridge University Press.

Bergmanis, Aldis, Jansons, Ritvars, and Zālīte, Indulis 2005. "The activities and the main repressive tasks of Latvian SSR agencies of national security 1944–1956," in Nollendorfs and Oberländer (eds.), pp. 271–85.

Bigg, Claire 2006. "Latvia: still haunted by Soviet past," *Radio Free Europe/Radio Liberty*, August 16.

Binningsbø, Helga Malmin, Loyle, Cyanne E., Gates, Scott, and Elster, Jon 2012. "Armed conflict and post-conflict justice, 1946–2006: a dataset," *Journal of Peace Research*, 49: 5, 731–40.

Birn, Ruth 2001. "Collaboration with Nazi Germany in Eastern Europe: the case of the Estonian Security Police," *Contemporary European History*, 10: 2, 181–98.

Bisset, Alison 2012. *Truth Commissions and Criminal Courts*. Cambridge University Press.

Blacksell, Mark and Born, Karl Martin 2002. "Private property restitution: the geographical consequences of official government policies in Central and Eastern Europe," *Geographical Journal*, 168: 2, 178–90.

BNS 2009. "Baltic states opened Western Europe's eyes on Soviet Union totalitarianism – EP chairman in Vilnius," *Baltic News Service*, April 28.

Boesenecker, Aaron P. and Vinjamuri, Leslie 2011. "Lost in translation? Civil society, faith-based organizations and the negotiation of international norms," *International Journal of Transitional Justice*, 5: 3, 345–65.

Bogdanova, Ksenija 2007. "Denacionalizācijas procesa sociāli ekonomiskā puse Latvijā," unpublished PhD thesis, Latvijas Universitāte.

Brahm, Eric 2009. "What is a truth commission and what does it matter?," *Peace and Conflict Review*, 3: 2, 1–14.

Brinkman, Koit 2007. "Tundmatu Eesti esindaja – kas teadlane või petis?" *Äripäev*, November 1.

Browning, Christopher S. 2005. *Remaking Europe in the Margins: Northern Europe after the Enlargements*. Farnham: Ashgate.

Bruce, Garry 2009. "East Germany," in Stan (ed.), II, pp. 15–36.

Bruun, Lori Lyman 1993. "Beyond the 1948 Convention: emerging principles of genocide in customary international law," *Maryland Journal of International Law and Trade*, 17, 193–226.

Brüggemann, Karsten and Kasekamp, Andres 2008. "The politics of history and the 'War of Monuments' in Estonia," *Nationalities Papers*, 36: 3, 425–48.

Bubnys, Arūnas 1998. *Vokiečių okupuota Lietuva, 1941–1944*. Vilnius: Lietuvos gyventojų genocido ir rezistencijos tyrimo centras.

2003. *Holocaust in Lithuanian Province in 1941*. Report commissioned by the International Commission for the Evaluation of the Crimes of the Soviet and Nazi Occupation Regimes in Lithuania.

2004. "The Holocaust in Lithuania: an outline of the major stages and their results," in A. Nikžentaitis, S. Schreiner and D. Staliūnas (eds.), *The Vanished World of Lithuanian Jews*. Amsterdam: Rodopi, pp. 205–22.

Budovskis, Māris 1995. Plenary Session of the Saeima of the Republic of Latvia, 5. Saeimas sēžu stenogrammas, March 9.

Budrytė, Dovile 2004. "'We call it genocide': Soviet deportations and repressions in the memory of Lithuanians," in R. S. Frey (ed.), *The Genocidal Temptation: Auschwitz, Hiroshima, Rwanda and Beyond*. Dallas/Lanham, MD: University Press of America, pp. 79–100.

2013a. "Lithuania," in Stan and Nedelsky (eds.), II, pp. 286–93.

2013b. "International Commission for the Evaluation of the Crimes of the Soviet and Nazi Occupation Regimes in Lithuania," in Stan and Nedelsky (eds.), III, pp. 218–22.

2013c. "Genocide and Resistance Research Center of Lithuania," in Stan and Nedelsky (eds.), III, pp. 137–42.

2014. "Travelling trauma: Lithuanian transnational memory after World War II," in E. Resende and D. Budryte (eds.), *Memory and Trauma in International Relations: Theories, Cases and Debates*. London: Routledge, pp. 168–81.

Bukovskis, Igors 1994. Ziņojums. Parlamentārās izmeklēšanas komisija, lai noskaidrotu valsts budžeta izlietojumu, ārvalstu kredītu un humānās palīdzības izmantošanu, valsts īpašumu pārvaldīšanu un privatizācijas gatu, okupācijas armijas, PSKP un VDK īpašumu pārņemšanu, valsts augstāko amatpersonu rīcību. Latvijas Republikas, 5. Saeimas sēžu stenogramma, September 8.

Burinskaitė, Kristina 2011. "The ideological and political aspects of the Lithuanian SSR KGB activities in 1954–1990," unpublished PhD thesis, Vilnius University.

Burinskaitė, Kristina and Okuličiūtė, Lina 2010. *KGB in Lithuania in 1954–1991*. Vilnius: Genocide and Resistance Research Center of Lithuania.

Calhoun, Noel 2004. *Dilemmas of Justice in Eastern Europe's Democratic Transitions*. New York: Palgrave Macmillan.

Cassese, Antonio 2006. "Balancing the prosecution of crimes against humanity and non-retroactivity of criminal law: the Kolk and Kislyiy v. Estonia case before the ECHR," *Journal of International Criminal Justice*, 4: 2, 410–18.

Cassese, Antonio, Acquaviva, Guido, Fan, Mary, and Whiting, Alex, 2011. *International Criminal Law: Cases and Commentary*. Oxford University Press.

Cesarini, Paola 2009. "Transitional justice," in T. Landman and N. Robinson (eds.), *The Sage Handbook of Comparative Politics*. London: Sage Publications, pp. 497–521.

Chersonski, Milan 2012. "It's not just about the new Tuskulėnai 'Peace Park' in Vilnius. Op-ed," *DefendingHistory.com*, August 20.

Cīrulis, Ervīns 2007. "Pārbaudīs eksčekista veselības stāvokli," *Latvijas Avīze*, February 8.

2008. "Eksčekists vainu noliedz," *Latvijas Avīze*, February 28.

Collins, Cath 2010. *Post-Transitional Justice: Human Rights Trials in Chile and El Salvador*. University Park, PA: Penn State University Press.

Commons, Sarah 2013. "Lithuania continues to seek compensation from Russia for damage caused by Soviet occupation," *The Baltic Review*, May 4.

Constitutional Court of the Republic of Lithuania 1994. "On the compliance of item 4, Part 2, item 2 of the Law of the Republic of Lithuania 'On Amending the Law on the Procedure and Conditions of the Restoration of the Rights of Ownership to the Existing Real Property.'" June 15.

1995. "On the compliance of item 4 of Part 2 of Article 8 and the norm of Part 4 of the Law 'On the Procedure and Conditions of the Restoration of the Rights of Ownership to the Existing Real Property' with the Constitution of the Republic of Lithuania." December 22.

1999. "On the compliance of Articles 1 and 2, Part 2 of Article 3 of the Republic of Lithuania Law 'On the Assessment of the USSR Committee of State Security (NKVD, NKGB, MGB, KGB) and Present Activities of the Regular Employees of This Organisation' as well as Parts 1 and 2 of Article 1 of the Republic of Lithuania Law on the Enforcement of the Law 'On the Assessment of the USSR Committee of State Security (NKVD, NKGB, MGB, KGB) and Present Activities of the Regular Employees of This Organisation' with the Constitution of the Republic of Lithuania." March 4.

2014. "On the compliance of certain provisions of the Criminal Code of the Republic of Lithuania that are related to criminal liability for genocide with the constitution of the Republic of Lithuania." March 18.

Council of the European Union 2007. "2794th Council Meeting, Justice and Home Affairs," press release, Luxembourg, April 19.

2008. *Council Framework Decision on Combating Certain Forms and Expressions of Racism and Xenophobia by Means of Criminal Law*. November 28, 2008/913/JHA.

Czarnota, Adam 2009. "Lustration, decommunisation and the rule of law," *Hague Journal on the Rule of Law*, 1: 2, 307–36.

David, Roman 2011. *Lustration and Transitional Justice: Personnel Systems in the Czech Republic, Hungary, and Poland*. Philadelphia: University of Pennsylvania Press.

Davies, Norman 2005. *God's Playground: A History of Poland in Two Volumes*, Vol. II. Oxford University Press.

Davoliūtė, Violate 2014. *The Makers and Breakers of Soviet Lithuania*. London: Routledge.

Delfi.lv 2005. "Saeima pieņem PSRS okupācijas režīma nosodījuma deklarāciju," *Delfi.lv*, May 12.

2006. "Ģenerālprokuratūrai aizrāda par gausu padomju režīma noziegumu izmeklēšanu," *Delfi.lv*, July 6.

2009. "Nodibināta Latvijas Okupācijas izpētes biedrība," *Delfi.lv/LETA*, December 18.

Dreifelds, Juris 1996. *Latvia in Transition*. Cambridge University Press.

Eesti Memento Liit no date. "Eesti Memento Liidu põhikiri," available at www.memento.ee/liidust/liidu-pohikiri/ [accessed February 20, 2014].

Eesti NSV Ülemnõukogu 1988. "Kohtuväliste massirepressioonide kohta Nõukogude Eestis 1940–1950-ndail aastail," December 7, *ENSV Teataja*, 52, 754.

1989. "Ajaloolis-õiguslikust hinnangust Eestis 1940. aastal toimunud sündmuste kohta," *Rahva Hääl*, November 14.

Eesti NSV Ülemnõukogu Presiidium 1990. "Kohtuväliselt represseeritud ja alusetult süüdimõistetud isikute rehabiliteerimisest," February 19, *Riigi Teataja*, 7, 85.

Eesti Vabariigi Riigikogu 1992. "Süümevande andmise korra kohta," July 8, *Riigi Teataja*, 31, 408.

1993a. "Ajutise komisjoni moodustamine NSV Liidu ning teiste riikide julgeoleku- ja luureorganite tegevuse uurimiseks Eestis," May 18, *Riigi Teataja*, I, 1993, 28, 496.

1993b. "Otsus 'Okupatsioonide repressiivpoliitika uurimise riikliku komisjoni küsimused,'" June 17, *Riigi Teataja* I, 1993, 40, 591.

1994a. "Eestis inimsusevastaseid kuritegusid või sõjakuritegusid toimepannud isikute kriminaalvastutuse seadus," November 9, *Riigi Teataja* I, 1994, 83, 1447.

1994b. "Eestis tegutsenud teiste riikide julgeoleku- ja luureorganite materjalide kogumise, arvelevõtmise, säilitamise ja kasutamise korra seadus," March 10, *Riigi Teataja* I, 1994, 23, 386.

1995. "Eestit okupeerinud riikide julgeolekuorganite või relvajõudude luure- või vastuluureorganite teenistuses olnud või nendega koostööd teinud isikute arvelevõtmise ja avalikustamise korra seadus," February 6, *Riigi Teataja* I, 1995, 17, 233.

1998. "Pühade ja tähtpäevade seaduse," January 27, *Riigi Teataja* I, 1998, 13, 162.

2002. "Riigikogu avaldus okupatsioonirežiimi kuritegudest Eestis," June 18, *Riigi Teataja* I, 2002, 52, 326.

2003. "Okupatsioonireziimide poolt represseeritud isiku seadus," December 4, *Riigi Teataja* I, 2003, 88, 589.

2010. "Pühade ja tähtpäevade seaduse muutmise seadus," October 21, *Riigi Teataja* I, 2010, 7, 27.

2012. "Riigikogu avaldus 'Tunnustuse avaldamine Eesti kodanikele,'" February 14, *Riigi Teataja* III, 2.

Eesti Vabariigi Riigikohu, Kriminaalkolleegium 1999. *Tartu Ringkonnakohtu kriminaalkolleegium otsus Karl-Leonhard Paulovi süüditunnistamises KrK § 101 p 1 järgi*. December 13.

Eesti Vabariigi Valitsus 2005. "Valitsuse avaldus seoses Teise maailmasõja 60. Aastapäevaga," press release, May 6.

2009. "Pühade ja tähtpäevade seaduse muutmise seaduse eelnõu seletuskiri," May 21.

Eesti Vabariigi Ülemnõukogu 1992. "Kohtuväliselt represseeritud ja alusetult süüdimõistetud isikute rehabiliteerimise kohta," February 19, *Riigi Teataja*, 1992, 7, 103.

Eesti Vabariigi Ülemnõukogu Presiidium 1992. "Otsus riikliku komisjoni moodustamisest repressiivpoliitika ja inimsusevastaste kuritegude väljaselgitamiseks," March 26, *Riigi Teataja* I, 1992, 40, 591.

Eesti Vabariik 1992. "Eesti Vabariigi Põhiseaduse Rakendamise seadus," June 28, *Riigi Teataja*, 1992, 26, 350.

Ehala, Martin 2009. "The Bronze Soldier: identity threat and maintenance in Estonia," *Journal of Baltic Studies*, 40: 1, 139–58.

Ehin, Piret and Berg, Eiki 2009. "Incompatible identities? Baltic-Russian relations and the EU as an arena for identity conflict," in E. Berg and P. Ehin (eds.), *Identity and Foreign Policy: Baltic-Russian Relations and European Integration*. Aldershot: Ashgate, pp. 1–14.

Ellis, Mark S. 1997. "Purging the past: the current state of lustration laws in the former Communist bloc," *Law and Contemporary Problems*, 59: 4, 181–96.

Elster, Jon 2004. *Closing the Books: Transitional Justice in Historical Perspective*. Cambridge University Press.

ed. 2006. *Retribution and Reparation in the Transition to Democracy*. Cambridge University Press.

ELTA 2011. "Atveriami KGB archyvai visko neatskleis," May 10.

Ergma, Ene 2004 "Riigikogu esimehe avaldus," press release, November 24.

Ezergailis, Andrew 1996. *The Holocaust in Latvia: The Missing Center*. Riga and Washington DC: The Historical Institute of Latvia/United States Holocaust Memorial Museum.

Ezergailis, Andrew 1997. *The Latvian Legion: Heroes, Nazis, Or Victims?: A Collection of Documents from OSS War-Crimes Investigation Files, 1945–1950*. Riga: Historical Institute of Latvia.

Eurasian Secret Services Daily Review 2006. "Amendments to Lithuanian law urge KGB collaborators to confess Soviet past," *Eurasian Secret Services Daily Review*, October 16.

European Commission 2007. *Europe for Citizens Programme 2007–2013*.

2010. *Report from the Commisison to the European Parliament and the Council. The memory of the crimes committed by totalitarian regimes in Europe*. COM(2010) 783, Brussels, December 22.

European Court of Human Rights 2004a. *Sidabras and Džiautas v. Lithuania*. Second Section, Appl. nos. 55480/00 and 59330/00, July 27.

2004b. *Ždanoka v. Latvia*. Chamber Judgment, Appl. no. 58278/00, June 17.

2005. *Rainys and Gasparavičius v. Lithuania*. Third Section, Appl. nos. 70665/01 and 74345/01, April 7.

2006a. *Kolk and Kislyiy v. Estonia*. Fourth Section, Appl. nos. 23052/04 and 24018/04, January 17.

2006b. *Ždanoka v. Latvia*. Grand Chamber, Appl. no. 58278/00, March 16.

2008a. *Kononov v. Latvia*. Former Third Section, Appl. no. 36376/04, July 24.

2008b. *Kuolelis, Bartoševičius and Burokevičius v. Lithuania*. Second Section, Appl. nos. 74357/01, 26764/02 and 27434/02, February 19.

2008c. *Larionovs c. la Lettonie*. Troisième Section, Appl. no. 45520/04, January 4.

2008d. *Tess c. la Lettonie*. Troisième Section, Appl. no. 19363/05, January 4.

2009a. *Žičkus v. Lithuania*. Second Section, Appl. no. 26652/02, April 7.

2009b. *Vasiliauskas v. Lithuania*. Second Section, Appl. no. 35343/05, June 17.

2010. *Kononov v. Latvia*. Grand Chamber, Appl. no. 36376/04, May 17.

European Parliament 2005. The Future of Europe Sixty Years After the Second World War, May 12, Resolution P6_TA(2005)0180.

2008. European Day of Remembrance for Victims of Stalinism and Nazism, September 23, Declaration P6_TA(2008)0439.

Europolitics 2005. "Justice and Home Affairs: MEP urge extending swastika ban to Communist symbols," *Europolitics: The European Affairs Daily*, February 1.

Feldman, Merje 1999. "Justice in space? The restitution of property rights in Tallinn, Estonia," *Cultural Geographies*, 6: 2, 165–82.

Fisher, Lynn M and Jaffe, Austin J 2000. "Restitution in transition countries," *Journal of Housing and the Built Environment*, 15: 3, 233–48.

Fridrihsone, Madara 2000a. "Krustugunīs Kononova notiesāšana izsauc starpvalstu konfliktu," *Jaunā Avīze*, January 26.

2000b. "Vēsture un taisnā tiesa," *Jaunā Avīze*, May 25.

2004. "Aicina aplest kompensāciju," *Dienas Bizness*, October 15.

Gailius, Bernardas 2005. "Lithuanian experience of the Soviet genocide investigations: problematic cases and general conclusions," available at www.genocid.lt/Spec/gailius.htm [accessed January 13, 2014].

Garton Ash, Timothy 2002. "Trials, purges and history lessons: treating a difficult past in post-communist Europe," in J.-W. Müller (ed.), *Memory and Power in Post-War Europe: Studies in the Presence of the Past*. Cambridge University Press, pp. 265–82.

Generalinės Prokuratūros STS 2008. "Generalinės prokuratūros specialiuju tyrimu skyriaus veiklos 2007 metais ataskaita." Vilnius.

2011. "Generalinės prokuratūros specialiuju tyrimu skyriaus veiklos 2010 metais ataskaita." Vilnius.

Genocide and Resistance Research Center in Lithuania n.d. *The Museum of Genocide Victims. A Guide to the Exhibition*. Vilnius: LGGRTC.

Girnius, Kestutis 2011. "Uprising of 1941: ambiguous, but very important," *The Lithuania Tribune*, July 4.

Gledhill, John 2011. "Integrating the past: regional integration and historical reckoning in Central and Eastern Europe," *Nationalities Papers*, 39: 4, 481–506.

Goldbergs, Jānis 2000. "Sociālisti atbalsta genocīdā apsūdzēto Savenko," *Neatkarīgā Rīta Avīze Latvijai*, February 29.

Grodsky, Brian K. 2009. "Beyond lustration: truth-seeking efforts in the post-communist space," *Taiwan Journal of Democracy*, 5: 2, 21–43.

2011. *The Costs of Justice: How New Leaders Respond to Previous Rights Abuses*. Notre Dame, IN: University of Notre Dame Press.

Grūtups, Andris and Krastiņš, Edmunds 1995. *Īpašuma Reforma Latvijā*. Riga: Mans Īpašums.

Haughton, Timothy 2013. "Battlefields, ammunition and uniforms: the past and politics in post-communist Central and Eastern Europe," *Comparative European Politics*, 11: 2, 249–60.

Hayner, Priscilla B. 2002. *Unspeakable Truths: Facing the Challenge of Truth Commissions*. New York: Taylor & Francis.

Hiden, John and Salmon, Patrick 1994. *The Baltic Nations and Europe: Estonia, Latvia and Lithuania in the Twentieth Century*. Rev. edn. London/New York: Longman.

Higgins, Andrew 2013. "In trial, Romania warily revisits a brutal past," *The New York Times*, September 29.

Hiio, Toomas 2005. "Kahjude ja kaotuste kokkuvõte. Raamatuarvustused." *Diplomaatia* 25 (October).

Hiio, Toomas, Maripuu, Meelis, and Paavle, Indrek, eds. 2005. *Estonia 1940–1945: Reports of the Estonian International Commission for the Investigation of Crimes Against Humanity*. Tallinn: Estonian Foundation for the Investigation of Crimes Against Humanity.

eds. 2009. *Estonia since 1944: Reports of the Estonian International Commission for the Investigation of Crimes Against Humanity*. Tallinn: Estonian Foundation for the Investigation of Crimes Against Humanity.

Horne, Cynthia M. 2009a. "International legal rulings on lustration policies in Central and Eastern Europe: rule of law in historical context," *Law & Social Inquiry*, 34: 3, 713–44.

2009b. "Late lustration programmes in Romania and Poland: supporting or undermining democratic transitions?" *Democratization*, 16: 2, 344–76.

2009c. "Lustration and trust in public institutions: a retrospective on the state of trust building in Central and Eastern Europe," *Sfera Politicii*, 142, 30–44.

Horne, Cynthia M. and Levi, Margaret 2004. "Does lustration promote trustworthy governance? An exploration of the experience of Central and Eastern Europe," in J. Kornai and S.-R. Ackermann (eds.), *Building a Trustworthy State in Post-Socialist Transition*. London: Palgrave Macmillan, pp. 52–74.

Huntington, Samuel P. 1991. *The Third Wave: Democratization in the Late Twentieth Century*. Norman: University of Oklahoma Press.

Ijabs, Ivars 2011. "The issue of compensation in Latvian–Russian relations," in Muižnieks (ed.), pp. 175–90.

IKUERK 2001. *Phase II: The German Occupation of Estonia in 1941–1944. Conclusions*. Tallinn: Estonian International Commission for Investigation of Crimes Against Humanity.

2004. *Phase I: The Soviet Occupation of Estonia in 1940–1941. Conclusions*. Tallinn: Estonian International Commission for Investigation of Crimes Against Humanity.

2008. *Phase III: The Soviet Occupation of Estonia from 1944. Conclusions*. Tallinn: Estonian International Commission for Investigation of Crimes Against Humanity.

Immigration and Refugee Board of Canada 2002. "Lithuania: treatment of former KGB agents and the availability of state protection (Jan. 1998–Oct. 2002)," available at www.unhcr.org/refworld/docid/3f7d4dc623.html [accessed May 17, 2010].

Indrikovs, Zenons 1989. "Sirds neaizmirst," *Cīņa*, June 14.

International Congress on the Evaluation of the Crimes of Communism ed. 2000. *Anti-Communist Congress and Public Tribunal (Documentation)*. Vilnius.

Jakobsone, Ieva 2001. "Decisions of domestic courts: judgment of the Supreme Court of the Republic of Latvia concerning genocide decisions of domestic courts," in I. Ziemele (ed.), *Baltic Yearbook of International Law*. Amsterdam: Brill, pp. 261–98.

Jakubčionis, Algirdas 2007. *The Unarmed Anti-Soviet Resistance in Lithuania in the 1950s and 1960s*. Vilnius: Genocide and Resistance Research Center of Lithuania.

Jambrek, P. ed. 2008. *Crimes Committed by Totalitarian Regimes: Reports and Proceedings of the 8 April European Public Hearing*. Brussels: Slovenian Council Presidency.

Jansons, Ritvars 2002. "Kara un genocīda noziegumus izmeklējot," paper presented at the conference "The Policy of Responsibility in Lithuania: Research and Evaluations of War Victims and Genocide in 1992–2002," Genocide and Resistance Research Center of Lithuania, Vilnius.

2007. "Kriminālvajāšana par pretpadomju propagandu un aģitāciju PSRS/ Latvijas PSR: 1953–1967," in Latvijas Vēsturnieku Komisija (ed.), *Latvijas vēsture 20. gadsimta 40.– 90. gados. Latvijas vēstures komisijas 2006. gada pētījumi*. Riga: Latvijas vēstures institūta apgāds, pp. 401–24.

Jaskovska, E. and Moran, J. P. 2006. "Justice or politics? Criminal, civil and political adjudication in the newly independent Baltic states," *Journal of Communist Studies and Transition Politics*, 22: 4, 485–506.

Jõks, Allar 2005. "Ettekanne Eestit okupeerinud riikide julgeolekuorganite või relvajõudude luure- või vastuluureorganite teenistuses olnud või nendega koostööd teinud isikute arvelevõtmise ja avalikustamise korra seaduse kooskõla kohta Eesti Vabariigi põhiseadusega." Eesti Vabariigi Õiguskantsler, July 12.

Juodvalkytė, Aldona 2004. "Renkami atsiminimai apie tremties ir kalinimo vietas, Laisvės kovų dalyvius," *KRONIKA*, January 30.

Kahk, Juhan 1991. *World War II and Soviet Occupation in Estonia: A Damages Report*. Tallinn: Perioodika.

Kaminski, Marek M. and Nalepa, Monika 2006. "Judging transitional justice: a new criterion for evaluating truth-revelation procedures," *Journal of Conflict Resolution*, 50: 3, 383–408.

Kaprāns, Mārtiņš, Procevska, Olga, Uzule, Laura, and Saulītis, Andris 2012. *Padomju Deportāciju Pieminēšana Latvijā: Atmiņu Politika un Publiska Telpa*. Riga: Mansards.

Karadjova, Mariana 2004. "Property restitution in Eastern Europe: domestic and international human rights law responses," *Review of Central and East European Law*, 29: 3, 325–63.

Kārkliņa, Guna 2011. "Mātes savus dēlus gaidīja visu mūžu. Mūsējie svešos karos," *Kas Jauns*, May 28.

Kasekamp, Andres 2010. *A History of the Baltic States*. New York: Palgrave Macmillan.

Katz, Dovid 2009. "On three definitions: genocide, holocaust denial, holocaust obfuscation," in L. Donskis (ed.), *A Litmus Test Case of Modernity. Examining Modern Sensibilities and the Public Domain in the Baltic States at the turn of the Century*. Frankfurt/New York: Peter Lang, pp. 259–78.

Kattago, Siobhan 2012. *Memory and Representation in Contemporary Europe: the Persistence of the Past*. Farnham: Ashgate.

Kattel, Rainer and Raudla, Ringa 2013. "The Baltic Republics and the crisis of 2008–2011," *Europe-Asia Studies*, 65: 3, 426–49.

Kesnere, Rūta 2014. "Čekas maisu liktenis joprojām neskaidrs," *Diena*, January 16.

Kincis, Jānis 2014. "VDK dokumentus plāno publiskot pēc to zinātniskās izpētes 2018.gadā," *Diena*, May 8.

Kinzer, Stephen 1991. "Lithuania starts to wipe out convictions for war crimes," *The New York Times*, September 5.

Kiss, Czilla 2013. "Hungary," in Stan and Nedelsky (eds.), II, pp. 230–36.

Koleva, Katerina 2007. "Restitution of expropriated property in Eastern Europe: the restrictive approach and available remedies with a special emphasis on the case law of the European Court of Human Rights related to restitution," in Sabine Fischer, Heiko Pleines and Hans-Henning Schröder (eds.), *Movements, Migrants, Marginalisation: Challenges of Societal and Political Participation in Eastern Europe and the Enlarged EU*. Stuttgart: ibidem-Verlag, pp. 159–72.

Kotar, Tamara 2013. "Slovenia," in Stan and Nedelsky (eds.), II, pp. 439–45.

Kritz, Neil J. 1995a. "The dilemmas of transitional justice," in Kritz (ed.), pp. xix–xxx.

ed. 1995b. *Transitional Justice: How Emerging Democracies Reckon with Former Regimes*, Vol. III: *Laws, Rulings, and Reports*. Washington, DC: US Institute of Peace Press.

Kuodytė, Dalia and Tracevskis, Rokas, eds. 2004. *The Unknown War: Armed Anti-Soviet Resistance in Lithuania in 1944–1953*. Vilnius: Genocide and Resistance Research Center of Lithuania.

Kuzio, Taras 2001. "Transition in post-communist states: triple or quadruple?" *Politics*, 21: 3, 168–77.

Kuti, Csongor 2009. *Post-Communist Restitution and the Rule of Law*. Budapest: Central European University Press.

Landsbergis, Vytautas 2012. *Rezistencijos pradžia. 1941-ųjų Birželis: dokumentai apie šešių savaičių laikinąją Lietuvos Vyriausybę*. Vilnius: Jungtinės spaudos paslaugos.

Langa, Liāna and Kalpiņa, Rudīte 2013. "Vai aicinājums turpināt 'dzīvot melos?'" *Ir*, December 23.

Langenbacher, Eric and Shain, Jossi, eds. 2010. *Power and the Past: Collective Memory and International Relations*. Washington, DC: Georgetown University Press.

Latvijas Okupācijas Izpētes Biedrība 2012. *Padomju Savienības Nodarītie Zaudējumi Baltijā*. Riga: LIOB.

Latvijas PSR Augstākās Padomes Prezidija 1989. "Par četrdesmitajos un piecdesmitajos gados no Latvijas PSR teritorijas izsūtīto pilsoņu reabilitāciju," June 8, *Ziņotājs*, 25 (661).

Latvijas PSR Ministru Padome 1988. "Par pilsoņu nepamatotu administratīvu izsūtīšanu no Latvijas PSR 1949. gadā," November 2, *Ziņotājs*, 350.

Latvijas Republikas Augstākā Padome 1990a. "Par genocīda un antisemītisma nosodījumu un nepieļaujamību Latvijā," September 19, *Ziņotājs*, 1990.

1990b. "Par Latvijas Republikas likuma 'Par nelikumīgi represēto personu reabilitāciju' spēkā stāšanās kārtību," August 3, *Ziņotājs*, 41 (172).

1990c. "Par nelikumīgi represēto personu reabilitāciju," August 3, *Ziņotājs*, 34.

1990d. "Par svētku un atceres dienām," October 18, *Ziņotājs*, 42.

1992a. "Par 5. Saeimas vēlēšanām," October 20, *Ziņotājs*, 46.

1992b. "Par grozījumiem Latvijas Republikas likumā 'Par Latvijas Republikas tautas deputāta status,'" June 30, *Latvijas Vēstnesis*, 32.

1992c. "Par konvencionālo tiesību normu izpildi Latvijā attiecībā uz noziegumiem pret cilvēci,'" March 25, *Ziņotājs*, 15.

1992d. "Par Latvijas Republikas likuma 'Par politiski represētās personas statusa noteikšanu' piemērošanu un spēkā stāšanās kārtību," May 13, *Ziņotājs*, 22.

1992e. "Par politiski represētās personas statusa noteikšanu," May 13, *Ziņotājs*, 22/23.

1993. "Par grozījumiem Latvijas kriminālkodeksā un Latvijas kriminālprocesa kodeksā," April 6, *Latvijas Vēstnesis*, 16.

Latvijas Republikas Centrālā statistikas pārvalde 2003. *Namīpašumu denacionalizācijas gaita Latvijā*. Riga: Latvijas Republikas Centrālā statistikas pārvalde.

2013. "MAG19. Namīpašumu denacionalizācija (1992–2002)," available at www.csb.gov.lv/dati/galvenie-raditaji-30424.html [last updated October 14, 2013].

Latvijas Republikas Ministru Kabinets 1995. "Par Totalitārisma seku dokumentēšanas centra rīcībā esošo Valsts drošības komitejas dokumentu izmantošanas kārtību," June 13, *Latvijas Vēstnesis*, 94 (377) 151.

1999. "Vēsturnieku komisijas nolikums." 4 May, *Latvijas Vestnesis*, 141/142 (1601/1602) 164.

2005. "Par komisijas izveidi PSRS totalitārā komunistiskā okupācijas režīma upuru skaita un masu kapu vietu noteikšanai, informācijas par represijām un masveida deportācijām apkopošanai un Latvijas valstij un tās iedzīvotājiem nodarīto zaudējumu aprēķināšanai," August 5, *Latvijas Vēstnesis*, 124 (3282).

2009. "Informatīvais ziņojums 'Par Komisiju PSRS totalitārā komunistiskā okupācijas režīma upuru skaita un masu kapu vietu noteikšanai, informācijas par represijām un masveida deportācijām apkopošanai un Latvijas valstij un tās iedzīvotājiem nodarīto zaudējumu aprēķināšanai,'" press release, November 28.

Latvijas Republikas Saeima 1994a. "Par bijušās Valsts drošības komitejas dokumentu saglabāšanu, izmantošanu un personu sadarbības fakta ar VDK konstatēšanu." 19 May, *Latvijas Vēstnesis*, 65, 196.

1994b. "Par bijušās Valsts drošības komitejas dokumentu saglabāšanu, izmantošanu un personu sadarbības fakta ar VDK konstatēšanu." June 2, *Latvijas Vēstnesis,* 65 (196).

1995a. "Grozījums likumā 'Par svētku un atceres dienām,'" April 13, *Latvijas Vēstnesis,* 58 (341).

1995b. "Par politiski represētās personas statusa noteikšanu komunistiskajā un nacistiskajā režīmā cietušajiem." 12 April, *Ziņotājs,* 10.

1996a. "Par nacionālās pretošanās kustības dalībnieka status," April 25, *Latvijas Vēstnesis,* 82 (567).

1996b. "Deklarācija 'Par Latvijas okupāciju,'" August 22.

1997. "Grozījums likumā 'Par svētku un atceres dienām,'" December 11, *Latvijas Vēstnesis* 322/323 (1037/1038).

1998a. "Deklarācija par latviešu leģionāriem Otrajā pasaules karā," October 29.

1998b. "Grozījumi likumā 'Par svētku un atceres dienām,'" July 8, *Latvijas Vēstnesis,* 199/200 (1260/1261).

1998c. Latvijas Republika 6. Saeima plenarsēžu stenogramma, March 12 and May 7.

2005. "Deklarācija par Latvijā īstenotā Padomju Sociālistisko Republiku Savienības totalitārā komunistiskā okupācijas režīma nosodījumu," May 12.

2006. "Latvijas Okupācijas muzeja likums," October 26, *Latvijas Vēstnesis,* 171 (3539).

2009a. "Grozījumi Krimināllikumā," June 10, *Latvijas Vēstnesis,* 90 (4076).

2009b. "Grozījums likumā 'Par svētku, atceres un atzīmējamām dienām,'" July 21, *Latvijas Vēstnesis,* 114 (4100).

2013. "Grozījumi publisku izklaides un svētku pasākumu drošības likumā," July 3, *Latvijas Vēstnesis,* 129 (4935).

Latvijas Republikas Satversmes Tiesa 2000. "Par Saeimas vēlēšanu likuma 5.panta 5. un 6.punkta un Pilsētas domes un pagasta padomes vēlēšanu likuma 9. panta 5. un 6.punkta atbilstību Latvijas Republikas Satversmes 89. un 101. pantam, Eiropas Cilvēka tiesību un pamatbrīvību aizsardzības konvencijas 14.pantam un Starptautiskā pakta par pilsoņu un politiskajām tiesībām 25.pantam. Spriedums Latvijas Republikas vārdā," August 30, *Latvijas Vēstnesis,* 307/309 (2218/2220).

2005. "Par 2004. gada 27. maija likuma 'Grozījumi likumā 'Par bijušās Valsts drošības komitejas dokumentu saglabāšanu, izmantošanu un personu sadarbības fakta ar VDK konstatēšanu' atbilstību Latvijas Republikas Satversmes 101. pantam, Eiropas Cilvēktiesību un pamatbrīvību aizsardzības konvencijas 14. pantam un Pirmā protokola 3. Pantam," March 22, *Latvijas Vēstnesis,* 50 (3208).

2006. "Par Saeimas vēlēšanu likuma 5. panta 5. un 6.punkta un Pilsētas domes, novada domes un pagasta padomes vēlēšanu likuma 9. panta pirmās daļas 5. un 6. punkta atbilstību Latvijas Republikas Satversmes 1., 9., 91. un 101.

pantam un Starptautiskā pakta par pilsoniskajām un politiskajām tiesībām 25. un 26. Pantam," June 15, *Latvijas Vēstnesis*, 95 (3463).

Leggewie, Claus 2008. "A tour of the battleground: the seven circles of pan-European memory," *Social Research*, 75: 1, 217–34.

2009. "Schlachtfeld Europa. Transnationale Erinnerung und europäische Identität," *Blätter für deutsche und internationale Politik*, 2, 81–93.

Lepassalu, Virkko 2005. *Süümepiinadeta: Georg ja Lennart Meri sidemetest eriteenistusega ja selle tagajärgedest*. Tallinn.

LETA 2013. "Aizliedz publiskos pasākumos izmantot PSRS un nacistiskās Vācijas simbolus," *LETA*, June 20.

Letki, Natalia 2002. "Lustration and democratisation in East-Central Europe," *Europe-Asia Studies*, 54: 4, 529–52.

Levy, Daniel and Sznaider, Natan 2010. *Human Rights and Memory: Essays on Human Rights*. University Park, PA: Pennsylvania State University Press.

Lewis, Alison 2003. "Reading and writing the Stasi file: on the uses and abuses of the file as (auto) biography," *German Life and Letters*, 56: 4, 377–97.

Lietuvos Ministrų Taryba 1989. "Dėl žalos atlyginimo reabilituotiems asmenims, suimtiems arba nuteistiems nuo 1940 m. birželio 15 d. iki 1981 m. birželio 1 d." 24 July," *Valstybės žinios*, 22–299, 160.

Lietuvos Politinių Kalinių ir Tremtinių Sąjungos 2013. "Lietuvos Politinių Kalinių Ir Tremtinių Sąjungos, Įstatai," available at www.lpkts.lt/ [accessed February 20, 2014].

Lietuvos Republikos Prezidentas 1995. "Dėl pažymėjimų apie neteisėtą represavimą išdavimo teisėtumo patikrinimo," February 24, *Valstybės žinios*, 18–422, 557.

Lietuvos Respublikos Aukščiausioji Taryba 1990. "Dėl asmenų, represuotų už pasipriešinimą okupaciniams režimams, teisių atstatymo," May 2, *Valstybės žinios*, 14–386, I-180.

1991a. "Dėl papildomų socialinių garantijų šeimoms asmenų nukentėjusių, kovojant už Lietuvos Respublikos laisvę, nuo 1991 m. sausio 11–13 d. vykdytos agresijos ir po to buvusių įvykių," January 16, *Valstybes žinios*, 3–78, I-954.

1991b. "Dėl 1940–1991 m. TSRS padarytos žalos Lietuvos Respublikai ir jos gyventojams atlyginimo," June 4, *Valstybes žinios*, 17–456, I-1403.

1992. "Dėl valstybinio Lietuvos gyventojų genocido tyrimo centro īsteigimo ir Lietuvos Respublikos įstatymo 'Dėl ypatingos reikšmės archyvų išsaugojimo' įsigaliojimo tvarkos," October 29, *Valstybės žinios*, 33–1012, I-3021.

Lietuvos Respublikos Aukščiausiosios Tarybos Prezidiumas 1990. "Dėl 1990 m. gegužės 2 d. Lietuvos Respublikos įstatymo 'Dėl asmenų, represuotų už pasipriešinimą okupaciniams režimams, teisių atstatymo' kai kurių nuostatų taikymo tvarkos'," October 31, *Valstybės žinios*, 32–780, I-735.

1991. "Dėl rezistencijos (pasipriešinimo) dalyvio pažymėjimo," October 16, *Valstybės žinios*, 30–818, I-1888.

1992. "Dėl apdovanojimo Sausio 13-osios atminimo medaliu," March 4, 9–219.

Lietuvos Respublikos Prezidentas 1998. "Dekretas 159: dėl tarptautinės komisijos nacių ir sovietinio okupacinių režimų nusikaltimams lietuvoje įvertintion," September 7.

Lietuvos Respublikos Seimas 1992a. "Dėl 1992 m. birželio 14 d. referendume priimt Lietuvos Respublikos piliečių sprendimo," June 30, 21–615, I-2683.

1992b. "Dėl atsakomybės už Lietuvos gyventojų genocidą," April 9, *Valstybės žinios*, 13–342, I-2477.

1993a. "Dėl įstatymo 'Dėl piliečių nuosavybės teisių į išlikusį nekilnojamąjį turtą atstatymo tvarkos ir sąlygų'," January 12, *Valstybės žinios*, 5–83, I-44.

1993b. "Lietuvos gyventojų genocido ir rezistencijos tyrimo centro," July 6, *Valstybes žinios*, 32–735, I-242.

1994a. "Dėl socialinės paramos asmenims, sužalotiems atliekant būtinąją karinę tarnybą sovietinėje armijoje, ir šioje armijoje žuvusiųjų šeimoms (1945 07 22 - 1991 12 31)," July 20, *Valstybės žinios*, 59–1162, I-576.

1994b. "Dėl rezistencijos (pasipriešinimo) dalyvių teisių komisijos," November 17, *Valstybės žinios*, 93–1810, I-665.

1995. "Dėl Lietuvos Respublikos įstatymo 'Dėl asmenų, represuotų už pasipriešinimą okupaciniams režimams, teisių atstatymo' pakeitimo ir papildymo," September 28, *Valstybės žinios*, 85–1915, I-1051.

1996. "Dėl Lietuvoje gyvenančių antrojo pasaulinio karo dalyvių, kovojusių antihitlerinės koalicijos pusėje, statuso," August 20, *Valstybės žinios*, 82–1966, I-1496.

1997a. "Asmenų, nukentėjusių nuo 1939–1990 metų okupacijų, teisinio statuso," June 30, *Valstybės žinios*, 66–1609, VIII-342.

1997b. "Atmintinų Dienų," July 3, *Law VIII-39*, 67–1672.

1997c. "Dėl okupacijų laikotarpio masinių represijų, genocido ir kitų nusikaltimų žmonijai ir žmoniškumui bei karo nusikaltimų tyrimo," November 6, *Valstybės žinios*, 104–2629.

1997d. "Pasipriešinimo 1940–1990 metų okupacijoms dalyvių teisinio statuso pripažinimo ir karių savanorių karinių laipsnių bei apdovanojimų prilyginimo," July 3, *Valstybės žinios*, 67–1673, VIII-398.

1997e. "Piliečių nuosavybės teisių į išlikusį nekilnojamąjį turtą atkūrimo," 1 July, *Valstybės žinios*, 65–1558, VIII-359.

1998a. "Baudžiamojo kodekso papildymo 62(1), 71 straipsniais ir 8(1), 24, 25, 26, 35, 49, 54(1), 89 straipsnių pakeitimo ir papildymo įstatymas," April 21, *Valstybės žinios*, 42–1140, VIII-708.

1998b. "Baudžiamojo kodekso papildymo aštuonioliktuoju skirsniu 'karo nusikaltimai' (333–344 straipsniai), 8(1), 24, 25, 26, 35, 49, 295 straipsnių papildymo ir pakeitimo, 219 ir 261 straipsnių pripažinimo netekusiais galios," June 9, *Valstybės žinios*, 57, 1580, VIII-776.

1998c. "Dėl SSRS valstybės saugumo komiteto (NKVD, NKGB, MGB, KGB) vertinimo ir šios organizacijos kadrinių darbuotojų dabartinės veiklos," July 16, *Valstybės žinios*, 65–1877, VIII-858.

1998d. "Įstatymo 'Dėl SSRS valstybės saugumo komiteto (NKVD, NKGB, MGB, KGB) vertinimo ir šios organizacijos kadrinių darbuotojų dabartinės veiklos' įgyvendinimo," July 16, *Valstybės žinios*, 65–1878, VIII-859.

1999. "Asmenų, slapta bendradarbiavusių su buvusios SSRS specialiosiomis tarnybomis, registracijos, prisipažinimo, įskaitos ir prisipažinusiųjų apsaugos," November 23, *Valstybės žinios*, 104–2976, VIII-1436.

2000. "Nepriklausomybės gynėjų ir kitų nukentėjusių nuo 1991 m. sausio 11–13 d. ir po to vykdytos SSRS agresijos asmenų teisinio statuso pripažinimo įstatymas," January 4, *Valstybės žinios*, 5–124, VIII-1517.

2007. Plenary Session, Plenarinių posėdžių stenogramos, posėdis nr 268, 304, March 15, June 7.

2008. "Dėl Lietuvos Respublikos Vyriausybės programos," December 9, *Valstybės žinios*, 146–5870, XI-52.

2009. "Dėl Jono Žemaičio pripažinimo Lietuvos valstybės vadovu," March 12, *Declaration*, 30–1166.

2010. "Lietuvos gyventojų genocido ir rezistencijos tyrimo centro įstatymo 5 straipsnio papildymo įstatymas," 30 June, *Valstybės žinios*, 86–4520, XI-962.

2012. "Kompensacijų asmenims, 1990–1991 m. atsisakiusiems prievartinės tarnybos sovietų armijoje ir dėl to nukentėjusiems nuo sovietų armijos veiksmų," May 10, *Valstybės žinios*, 57–2830, XI-2007.

Lietuvos Respublikos Vyriausybė 1995a. "Dėl Atminimo ženklų, simbolių ir paminklų genocido aukoms ir asmenims, represuotiems už pasipriešinimą okupaciniams režimams, sukūrimo valstybinės programos 1996–2000 metams," December 1, *Valstybės žinios*, 100–2234, 1516.

1995b. "Dėl žalos, padarytos Lietuvos Respublikai 1940–1991 metais buvusios TSRS ir 1991–1993 metais - Rusijos Federacijos kariuomenės, apskaičiavimo," April 5, *Valstybės žinios*, No. 31–726, 484.

1996. "Dėl žalos, padarytos Lietuvos Respublikai 1940 - 1991 metais buvusios TSRS ir 1991 - 1993 metais - Rusijos Federacijos kariuomenės, nustatymo darbų programos," February 13, *Valstybės žinios*, 16–424, 242.

1997. "Dėl Pasipriešinimo dalyvių (rezistentų) teisių komisijos sudėties ir nuostatų patvirtinimo," November 14, *Valstybės žinios*, 103–2597, 1244.

1998. "Dėl Tuskulėnų aukų atminimo įamžinimo komisijos sudarymo," February 2, *Valstybės žinios*, 13–314, 124.

2002a. "Dėl atminimo ženklų, simbolių ir paminklų genocido aukoms ir asmenims, represuotiems už pasipriešinimą okupaciniams režimams, tęstinės 2003–2008 metųprogramos patvirtinimo," October 8, *Valstybės žinios*, 98–4338, 1600.

2002b. "Dėl Tuskulėnų rimties parko sukūrimo programos ir tuskulėnų rimties parko sukūrimo programos įgyvendinimo priemonių patvirtinimo," June 19, *Valstybės žinios* 64–2594, 932.

2007. "Dėl Lietuvos Respublikos Vyriausybės 2002 m. birželio 19 d. Nutarimo nr. 932 'Dėl Tuskulėnų rimties parko sukūrimo programos ir tuskulėnų rimties parko sukūrimo programos įgyvendinimo priemonių patvirtinimo' pakeitimo," March 28, *Valstybės žinios* 40–1490, 322.

Lietuvos Statistikos Departamentas 2013. "Nuosavybės teisių i gyvenamuosius namus aktūrimas," available at http://osp.stat.gov.lt/rodikliai4, last updated 2011 [accessed on March 1, 2014].

Lietuvos TSR Aukščiausioji Taryba 1989. "Dėl Lietuvos TSR Aukščiausiosios Tarybos deputatų J. Kupliauskienės, J. Marcinkevičiaus, K. Motiekos, R. Ozolo ir Z. Vaišvilos paklausimo, kaip vykdomas Lietuvos TSR Aukščiausiosios Tarybos Prezidiumo 1988 m. spalio 21 d. Įsakas 'Dėl asmenį, iškeldintų iš lietuvos tsr teritorijos 1941–1952 metais, reabilitavimo'," July 5, *Vyriausybės žinios*, 20–261, XI-3085.

Lietuvos TSR Aukščiausiosios Tarybos Prezidiumas 1988. "Dėl asmenų, iškeldintų iš Lietuvos TSR teritorijos 1911–1952 metais, reabilitavimo," October 21, *Vyriausybės žinios*, 31–324, XI-2611.

Lieven, Anatol 1994. *The Baltic Revolution: Estonia, Latvia and Lithuania and the Path to Independence.* New Haven, CT: Yale University Press.

Liivoja, Rain 2013. "Competing histories: Soviet war crimes in the Baltic states," in K. J. Heller and G. Simpson (eds.), *The Hidden Histories of War Crimes Trials.* Oxford University Press, pp. 248–66.

Littoz-Monnet, Annabelle 2012. "The EU politics of remembrance: can Europeans remember together?" *West European Politics*, 35: 5, 1182–202.

2013. "Explaining policy conflict across institutional venues: European Union-level struggles over the memory of the Holocaust," *JCMS: Journal of Common Market Studies*, 51: 3, 589–604.

Ločmele, Klinta, Procevska, Olga, and Zelce, Vita 2011. "Celebrations, commemorative dates and related rituals: Soviet experience, its transformation and contemporary Victor Day celebrations in Russia and Latvia," in Muižnieks (ed.), pp. 109–38.

Ločmele, Nellija 1997. "Tiesa nekonstatē Aivara Kreitusa sadarbību ar Drošības komitēju," *Diena*, October 29.

2000. "Prezidente: Latvijai jāsastādā okupācijas zaudējumu bilance," *Diena*, June 29.

Lungescu, Oana 2005. "EU rejects Communist symbol ban," *BBC News*, February 8.

Luup 1998. "Harry Männil mustas ringis," *Luup*, June 15.

Lux, Martin, Kährik, Anneli, and Sunega, Petr 2012. "Housing restitution and privatisation: both catalysts and obstacles to the formation of private rental housing in the Czech Republic and Estonia," *International Journal of Housing Policy*, 12: 2, 137–58.

MacQueen, M. 1998. "The context of mass destruction: agents and prerequisites of the Holocaust in Lithuania," *Holocaust and Genocide Studies*, 12: 1, 27–48.

Mägi, Harri 2012. *ENSV KGB tegevuse lõpetamine*. Tallinn: Varak.

Mälksoo, Lauri 2001. "Soviet genocide? Communist mass deportations in the Baltic States and international law," *Leiden Journal of International Law*, 14, 757–87.

2003a. *Illegal Annexation and State Continuity: The Case of the Incorporation of the Baltic States by the USSR: A Study of the Tension Between Normativity and Power in International Law*. Amsterdam: Martinus Nijhoff.

2003b. "State responsibility and the challenge of the realist paradigm: the demand of Baltic victims of Soviet mass repressions for compensation from Russia," in I. Ziemele (ed.), *Baltic Yearbook of International Law*. Amsterdam: Brill, pp. 57–76.

Mälksoo, Lauri and Laaring, Mait 2011. "Judgment of the European Court of Human Rights (Grand Chamber) in the case *Kononov v. Latvia* (application No. 36376/04)," *Juridica*, 3, 232–36.

Mälksoo, Maria 2007. "The First Lady of the Baltic 'memory offence,'" *Diplomaatia*, 47 (August), 4–7.

2014. "Criminalizing communism: transnational mnemopolitics in Europe," *International Political Sociology*, 8: 1, 82–99.

Maripuu, Meelis 2001. "Eesti juutide holokaust ja eestlased," *Vikerkaar*, 8–9, 135–46.

2004. "Estonian Communist Party membership 1940 – 1990," in H. Ahonen and E. Tarvel (eds.), *Estonia's Occupation Revisited*. Tallinn: The Kistler-Ritso Estonian Foundation, pp. 42–48.

Marmei, Kristin 2001. "Estonia commemorates 14 June 1941 deportation," *Central Europe Review*, 3: 22, June 18.

Matonyte, Irmina 2013. "The elites' games in the field of memory: insights from Lithuania," in G. Mink and L. Neumeyer (eds.), *History, Memory and Politics in Central and Eastern Europe: Memory Games*. New York: Palgrave Macmillan, pp. 105–20.

Mauliņš, Jānis 1996. Plenary Session of the Saeima of the Republic of Latvia, 6. Saeimas sēžu stenogrammas, March 14.

McAdams, A. James 2001. *Judging the Past in Unified Germany*. Cambridge University Press.

Meri, Lennart 2001. "Remarks in Rakvere, 6 June," available at http://vp1992-2001.president.ee/eng/k6ned/K6ne.asp?ID=4577 [accessed January 15, 2014].

Mertelsmann, Olaf and Rahi-Tamm, Aigi 2009. "Soviet mass violence in Estonia revisited," *Journal of Genocide Research*, 11: 2–3, 307–22.

Ministry of Foreign Affairs of the Russian Federation 2003. "Information and Press Department commentary regarding a media question about passing by a Latvian Court of Sentence upon Great Patriotic War veteran Nikolai Larionov," press release, October 2.

Ministry of Foreign Affairs of the Russian Federation 2004. "Kommentarii Departamenta informatsii i pechati MID Rossii v sviazi s voprosom SMI o reshenii Verkhovnogo suda Latvii v otnoshenii veterana Velikoi Otechestvennoi voiny N.V. Tessa," press release, November 18.

Mink, Georges 2013. "Institutions of national memory in post-communist Europe: from transitional justice to political uses of biographies (1989–2010)," in G. Mink and L. Neumayer (eds.), *History, Memory and Politics in Central and Eastern Europe: Memory Games*. New York: Palgrave Macmillan, pp. 155–70.

Misiunas, Romuald J. 1994. "The archives of the Lithuanian KGB," *Berichte des Bundesinstituts für ostwissenschaftliche und internationale Studien*, 3, 1–47.

Moran, John P. 1994. "The Communist torturers of Eastern Europe: prosecute and punish or forgive and forget?," *Communist and Post-Communist Studies*, 27: 1, 95–109.

Morkus, Prana and Burauskaite, Birute 2002. *Resistance to the Occupation of Lithuania: 1944–1990*. Vilnius: The Genocide and Resistance Research Center of Lithuania.

Muciņš, Linards 1990. Plenary Session of the Supreme Council of the Republic of Latvia, Latvijas Republikas Augstākās Padomes sēžu stenogramma, July 17.

Müller, Jan-Werner 2010. "On 'European memory': some conceptual and normative remarks," in M. Pakier and B. Stråth (eds.), *A European Memory? Contested Histories and Politics of Remembrance*. New York: Berghahn Books, pp. 25–37.

Muižnieks, Nils, ed. 2011. *The Geopolitics of History in Latvian-Russian Relations*. Riga: University of Latvia Press.

Murphy, Michael 2011. "Apology, recognition, and reconciliation," *Human Rights Review*, 12: 1, 47–69.

Muuli, Kalle 1993. "Kommentaare pärast Hardo Aasmäe esinemist Riigikogus 25. veebruaril," *Postimees*, February 27.

Nacionalinė žemės tarnyba 2013a. "Informacija apie pilieciu nuosavybes teisiu atkurima kaimo vietoveje. Suvestine. 2013 m. spalio 1 d," available at www.nzt.lt/go.php/Statistika [accessed December 20, 2013].

2013b. "Informacija apie pilieciu nuosavybes teisiu atkurima miestu teritorijose. Suvestine. 2013 m. spalio 1 d," available at: http://www.nzt.lt/go.php/Statistika [accessed December 20, 2013].

Naimark, Norman M. and Gibianskii, Leonid 1997. *The Establishment of Communist Regimes in Eastern Europe, 1944–1949*. Boulder, CO: Westview Press.

Nalepa, Monika 2008. "To punish the guilty and protect the innocent: comparing truth-revelation procedures," *Journal of Theoretical Politics*, 20: 2, 221–45.

2009a. "Lustration and the survival of parliamentary parties," *Taiwan Journal of Democracy*, 5: 2, 45–68.

2009b. "The origins of competing claims to land in East Central Europe: in-kind restitution as a problem of fair division," paper prepared for the Annual Meeting of the American Political Science Association, Toronto, September 3–6.

2010. *Skeletons in the Closet: Transitional Justice in Post-Communist Europe.* Cambridge University Press.

Nedelsky, Nadya 2004. "Divergent responses to a common past: transitional justice in the Czech Republic and Slovakia," *Theory and Society*, 33: 1, 65–115.

Neimane, Lelde 2012. "OM Audiovizuālais krājums," paper presented at the conference "2000: Videoliecības ierakstam veltītajā," Riga, March 26.

Nekrosius, Ipolitas and Petrylaitė, Vida 2010. *Social Security Law in Lithuania.* Alphen aan den Rijn: Kluwer Law International.

Nollendorfs, Valters 2010. "Country Report Latvia," report presented at the international conference "The Crimes of Communist Regimes," Prague, February 24–25.

Nollendorfs, Valters and Erwin Oberländer, eds. 2005. *The Hidden and Forbidden History of Latvia under Soviet and Nazi Occupation 1940–1991.* Riga: Institute of the History of Latvia.

Norkus, Zenonas 2012. *On Baltic Slovenia and Adriatic Lithuania: A Qualitative Comparative Analysis of Patterns in Post-Communist Transformation.* Budapest: CEU Press.

2013. "Parliamentarism versus semi-presidentialism in the Baltic states: the causes and consequences of differences in the constitutional frameworks," *Baltic Journal of Political Science*, 2, 7–28.

O'Donnell, Guillermo 1992. "Transitions, continuities, and paradoxes," in S. Mainwaring, G. O'Donnell and J. S. Valenzuela (eds.), *Issues in Democratic Consolidation: The New South American Democracies in Comparative Perspective.* Notre Dame, IN: University of Notre Dame Press, pp. 17–56.

Offe, Claus 1992. "Coming to terms with past injustices," *European Journal of Sociology*, 33: 1, 195–201.

1997. *Varieties of Transition: The East European and East German Experience.* Cambridge, MA: MIT Press.

Offe, Claus and Poppe, Ulrike 2005. "Transitional justice after the breakdown of the German Democratic Republic," in A. Czarnota, M. Krygier and W. Sadurski (eds.), *Rethinking the Rule of Law after Communism.* Budapest: CEU Press, pp. 153–89.

Offe, Claus and Poppe, Ulrike 2006. "Transitional justice in the German Democratic Republic and unified Germany," in J. Elster (ed.), *Restitution and Reparation in the Transition to Democracy*. Cambridge University Press, pp. 239–75.

Õispuu, Leo 1996a. *Poliitilised arreteerimised Eestis, 1940–1988*. Tallinn: Eesti Represseeritute Registri Büroo.

Õispuu, Leo 1996b. *Poliitilised arreteerimised Eestis, 1940–1988 (§58), Köide 1*. Tallinn: Eesti Represseeritute Registri Büroo.

Õispuu, Leo 2003. *Küüditamine Eestist Venemaale: Märtsiküüditamine 1949*. Tallinn: Eesti Represseeritute Registri Büroo.

2007. *Deported, Arrested, Murdered, 1940–1990: Crimes of Soviet Occupation in Estonia, Converged Name Register R1-R6*, Tallinn: Estonian Repressed Persons' Records Bureau.

2010. *Communist Crimes in Estonia: Additional Name List 1940–1990. Supplements for Books R1-R7. Book R8/1*. Tallinn: Eesti Represseeritute Registri Büroo.

Olsen, Tricia D., Payne, Leigh A., and Reiter, Andrew G. 2010a. "The justice balance: when transitional justice improves human rights and democracy," *Human Rights Quarterly*, 32: 4, 980–1007.

Olsen, Tricia D., Leigh A. Payne, Andrew G. Reiter and Eric Wiebelhaus-Brahm 2010b. "When Truth Commissions improve human rights," *International Journal of Transitional Justice*, 4: 3, 457–476.

Onken, Eva-Clarita 2003. *Demokratisierung der Geschichte in Lettland. Staatsbürgerliches Bewusstsein und Geschichtspolitik im ersten Jahrzehnt der Unabhängigkeit*. Hamburg: Krämer.

2007a. "The Baltic states and Moscow's 9 May commemoration: analysing memory politics in Europe," *Europe-Asia Studies*, 59: 1, 23–46.

2007b. "The Politics of finding historical truth: reviewing Baltic history commissions and their work," *Journal of Baltic Studies*, 38:1, 109–16.

Padrik, Jaana 1996. "Avalikud asjad," *Eesti Raadio*, April 1.

Parliamentary Assembly 1996. "On Russia's request for membership of the Council of Europe," January 25, OPINION No. 193.

2006. Need for International Condemnation of Crimes of Totalitarian Communist Regimes. January 25, PACE Resolution 1481.

Peep, Viljar 1997. *Põhiseadus ja Põhiseaduslik Assamblee*. Tallinn: Eesti Vabariigi Justiitsministeerium.

Pelkaus, E., ed. 2001. *Aizvestie. 1941.14. jūnijs*. Riga: Nordik, State Archives.

Petersen, Roger Dale 2001. *Resistance and Rebellion: Lessons from Eastern Europe*. New York: Cambridge University Press.

Petersoo, Pille and Tamm, Marek 2008. *Monumentaalne konflikt: mälu, poliitika ja identiteet tänapäeva Eestis*. Tallinn: Varrak.

Petrenko, Dmitrij 2008. "How does the Russian community live in Latvia?" in N. Muižnieks (ed.), *Manufacturing Enemy Images? Russian Media Portrayal of Latvia*. Riga: University of Latvia Press, pp. 45–78.

Pettai, Eva-Clarita 2011a. "The convergence of two worlds: historians and emerging histories in the Baltic states," in M. Housden and D. Smith (eds.), *Forgotten Pages in Baltic History: Diversity and Inclusion*. Amsterdam: Rodopi, pp. 263–80.

2011b. "Establishing Holocaust memory in Estonia and Latvia," in O. Rathkolb and I. Sooman (eds.), *Historical Memory Culture in the Enlarged Baltic Sea Region and its Symptoms Today*. Vienna: V&R unipress/Vienna University Press, pp. 159–74.

2013a. "Center for the Documentation of the Consequences of Totalitarianism," in Stan and Nedelsky (eds.), III, pp. 26–31.

2013b. "Estonian International Commission for Investigation of Crimes Against Humanity," in Stan and Nedelsky (eds.), III, pp. 117–21.

2015. "Interactions between history and memory: historical commissions and reconciliation," in S. Kattago (ed.), *The Ashgate Research Companion to Memory Studies*. London: Ashgate, pp. 239–50.

Pettai, Vello 2001. "Estonia and Latvia: international influences on citizenship and minority integration," in A. Pravda and J. Zielonka (eds.), *International Influences on Democratic Transition in Central and Eastern Europe*. Oxford University Press, pp. 257–80.

2006. "Studying political culture in post-communist Europe," in S. Berglund, B. Henningsen and M.-B. Schartau (eds.), *Political Culture: Values and Identities in the Baltic Sea Region*. Berlin: Berliner Wissenschaftsverlag, pp. 83–97.

2007. "The construction of state identity and its legacies: legal restorationism in Estonia," *Ab Imperio*, 3, 403–26.

2012. "Lustration in den baltischen Staaten. Aktive Vergangenheitsbewältigung seit 1991," in M. Knodt and S. Urdze (eds.), *Die politischen Systeme der baltischen Staaten: Eine Einführung*. Wiesbaden: VS Verlag für Sozialwissenschaften, pp. 97–115.

2013a. "Estonia," in Stan and Nedelsky (eds.), II, pp. 161–67.

2013b. "State Commission for the Examination of Repressive Policies Carried Out During the Occupations," in Stan and Nedelsky (eds.), III, pp. 410–14.

Pettai, Vello, Auers, Daunis, and Ramonaite, Aine 2010. "Political development," in M. Lauristin (ed.), *Estonian Human Development Report*. Tallinn: Estonian Cooperation Assembly, pp. 144–66.

Pettai, Vello and Onken, Eva-Clarita 2009. *National Report on Estonia*. Commissioned by the European Commission, Direction D: Fundamental Rights and Citizenship of the Directorate-General for Justice, Freedom and Security for the project "How the Memory of Crimes Committed by Totalitarian and/or Other Repressive Regimes in Europe Is Dealt With."

Plakans, Andrejs 2009. *National Report on Latvia*. Commissioned by the European Commission, Direction D: Fundamental Rights and Citizenship of the Directorate-General for Justice, Freedom and Security for the project "How the Memory of Crimes Committed by Totalitarian and/or Other Repressive Regimes in Europe Is Dealt With."

2011. *A Concise History of the Baltic States.* Cambridge University Press.

Platform of European Memory and Conscience 2012. "Declaration, adopted on 12 January," available at www.memoryandconscience.eu/2012/05/03/declaration-2012/ [accessed February 19, 2014].

Pravda.ru 2010. "Kononov's case to test Russia's ability to defend its past and future," *Pravda*, April 6.

President of the Republic of Lithuania 2012. On the International Commission for the Evaluation of the Crimes of the Soviet and Nazi Occupation Regimes in Lithuania. October 16, Decree No 1K-1185.

Prigge, William 2004. "The Latvian Purges of 1959: a revision study," *Journal of Baltic Studies* 35: 3, 211–30.

Prikulis, Juris 2011. "*PSRS* 'parādu grāmatas' sastādīšana Latvijā: 1987.-2010," available at http://demoshistoria.lv/aktualais-arvalstis/krievija/krievija-latvija/psrs-paradu-gramatas-sastadisana-latvija-1987-2010 [accessed January 10, 2014].

Prutsch, Markus J. 2013. *European Historical Memory: Policies, Challenges and Perspectives. Note.* Brussels: Directorate-General for Internal Policies, Policy Department B: Structural and Cohesion Policies.

Pruuli, Tiit 1993. "KGB kammitsais," *Postimees*, March 18–19.

1998. "Mašonkins un mašonkini," *Lauku Avīze*, March 24.

Purs, Aldis 2012. "Soviet in form, local in content: elite repression and mass terror in the Baltic states 1940–1953," in K. McDermott and M. Stibbe (eds.), *Stalinist Terror in Eastern Europe*. Manchester University Press, pp. 19–38.

2013. *Baltic Facades: Estonia, Latvia and Lithuania Since 1945.* London: Reaktion Books.

Pušinskytė, Lijana 2008. "Žodinės istorijos metodas, jo taikymo rezistencijos tyrimuose problemos," *Genocidas ir rezistencija*, 24: 2, 12–23.

Quigley, John B. 2006. *The Genocide Convention: An International Law Analysis.* Farnham: Ashgate.

Quint, Peter E. 2000. "The border guard trials and the East German past-seven arguments", *American Journal of Comparative Law*, 48: 541, 541–72.

Rahi-Tamm, Aigi 2005. "*Human losses*," in V. Salo et al. (eds.), pp. 25–46.

Rahi, Aigi 2003. "On the current state of research into repression in Estonia," in Latvia's Occupation Museum (ed.), *Yearbook of the Occupation Museum of Latvia 2002.* Riga: Occupacijas Muzeja Fonds, pp. 13–40.

Raidla, Jüri 1991. Testimony before the plenary of the Supreme Council of Estonia, 8 May.

Raimundo, Filipa 2012. "Post-transitional Justice? Spain, Poland and Portugal compared," unpublished PhD thesis, European University Institute.

2013. "Dealing with the past in Central and Southern European democracies: comparing Spain and Poland," in G. Mink and L. Neumeyer (eds.), *History, Memory and Politics in Central and Eastern Europe*. New York: Palgrave Macmillan, pp. 136–54.

Rancāns, Klementijs 2006. "Čekas maisi – priekšvēlēšanu medusmaize," *Latvijas Avīze*, March 29.

Rask, Märt 2007. "Tänu Põhiseadusele," *Riigikogu toimetised*, no. 17.

Raude, Kuno 2013. "Kümme aastat okupatsioonirežiimide poolt represseeritud isiku seadust," *Riigikogu toimetised*, 28, 178–80.

Reconciliation of European Histories Group 2011. "Commemorating 70 years from the first mass deportations from the Baltic States: 'Your past is our past.' Tunne Kelam MEP, 9 June," available at http://eureconciliation.wordpress.com/page/3/ [accessed February 14, 2014].

Reichelt, Katrin 2010. *Lettland unter deutscher Besatzung 1941–1944: der lettische Anteil am Holocaust*. Berlin: Metropol-Verlag.

Resnais, Gunārs and Pētersons, Tālivaldis 2010. "Par politiski represētās personas statusu," *Latvijas Avīze*, September 9.

RIA Novosti 2010. "Overturning of Kononov's case 'dangerous precedent' – Russian parliament," *RIA Novosti*, May 21.

2012. "Moscow dismisses Lithuania 'occupation' claims," *RIA Novosti*, July 25.

Riekstiņš, Jānis, ed. 2000. *Represijas Latvijas laukos 1944–1949*. Rīga: Latvijas Valsts Arhīvs.

ed. 2009. *Represijas pret latviešiem PSRS. 1937–1938. Dokumentu krājums*. Rīga: Latvijas Valsts Arhīvs.

Riffler, Vera 2010. "Quantitative impact assessment in transitional justice research: no single truth in place?" *International Journal of Rule of Law, Transitional Justice and Human Rights*, 1, 16–27.

Rimšāns, Jānis 2006. "Jaunatnes pretošanās izpausmes komunistiskajam režīmam Latvijas PSR (1965 1985)," in Latvijas Vēsturnieku komisija (ed.), *Latvia and Eastern Europe in the 1960s–1980s: Conference Proceedings*. Riga: Latvijas vēstures institūta apgāds, pp. 116–32.

Rislakki, Jukki 2008. *A Case for Latvia: Disinformation Campaigns Against a Small Nation*. Amsterdam: Rodopi.

Roht-Arriaza, Naomi 2006. "The new landscape of transitional justice," in Naomi Roht-Arriaza and Javier Mariezcurrena (eds.), *Transitional Justice in the Twenty-First Century: Beyond Truth Versus Justice*. Cambridge University Press, p. 1–16.

Rozenšteine, Aija, Saulītis, Andris, Siliņa, Gita, and Zelče, Vita 2011. "16. Marts – konfrontācijas un piemiņas diena," in N. Muižnieks and V. Zelče (eds.), *Karojošā Piemiņa. 16. Marts un 9. Maijs*. Riga: Zinātne, pp. 145–72.

Rushton, Beth 2006. "Truth and reconciliation? The experience of Truth Commissions," *Australian Journal of International Affairs*, 60: 1, 125–41.

Ruska, Rita 2010. "Vilina represēto privilēģijas," *Latvijas Avīze*, March 18.

2012. "Uz represētā statusu – iesniegumu rekordskaits," *Latvijas Avīze*, April 11.

Ruzgas, Albertas 2010. *Rezistentų pogrindiniai periodiniai leidiniai: Okupacijų metai, 1940–1989 (Leidinių sąvadas)*. Vilnius: Genocide and Resistance Research Center of Lithuania.

Sadurski, Wojciech 2003. "'De-communization,' 'lustration' and constitutional continuity: dilemmas of transitional justice in Central Europe," *EUI Working Paper LAW*, 15.

2005. *Rights Before Courts: A Study of Constitutional Courts in Postcommunist States of Central and Eastern Europe*. Dordrecht: Springer.

Salo, Vello, ed. 2005. *The White Book: Losses Inflicted on the Estonian Nation by Occupation Regimes 1940–1991*. Tallinn: Estonian Encyclopedia Publishers.

Šapovālovs, Pavels 1990. Plenary Session of the Supreme Council of the Republic of Latvia, Latvijas Republikas Augstākās Padomes sēžu stenogramma, July 17.

Saskaņas centrs 2012. "Uz daudziem Otrā pasaules kara veterāniem neattieksies likuma darbība, lai gan par tā pieņemšanas mērķi tika deklarēta karojušo pušu samierināšana un sabiedrības saliedēšana," press release, November 29.

Satkauskas, Rytis 2003. "A bill for the occupants or an issue to negotiate: the claims of reparations for Soviet occupation," in I. Ziemele (ed.), *Baltic Yearbook of International Law*. Amsterdam: Brill, pp. 77–96.

2004. "Soviet genocide trials in the Baltic states: the relevance of international law," in I. Ziemele (ed.), *Yearbook of International Humanitarian Law*. Amsterdam: Brill, pp. 388–409.

Schabas, William 2000. *Genocide in International Law: The Crimes of Crimes*. Cambridge University Press.

Schedler, Andreas 2001. "Taking uncertainty seriously: the blurred boundaries of democratic transition and consolidation," *Democratization*, 8: 4, 1–22.

Schetnaya palata Rossiiskoi Federatsiya 2004. "Mezhdu Rossiei i stranami Baltii do sikh por ne resheny finansovye i imuschestvennye problem," press release, September 30.

Seimas of the Republic of Lithuania 2010. Resolution on Compensation to the Victims of the USSR Aggression Perpetrated During and After 11–13 January 1991 and to Their Families. January 19.

Semler, Christian 2004. "Lettische Geschichtspolitik," *taz, die tageszeitung*, March 26.

Senn, Alfred Erich 2007. *Lithuania 1940: Revolution from Above*. Amsterdam: Rodopi.

Shugart, Matthew Soberg and Carey, John M. 1992. *Presidents and Assemblies: Constitutional Design and Electoral Dynamics*. Cambridge University Press.

Sildam, Toomas 1996. "Kaitsepolitsei on end üles andnud ligi 1000 eriteenistuste kaastöötajat," *Päevaleht*, March 27.

Sildam, Toomas and Mattson, Toomas 1997. "Eesti NSV KGB taganemine," *Luup*, August 4.

Sizova, Jara 2000. "Birkavs apšauba okupācijas kompensācijas pieprasīšanas lietderību no Krievijas," *BNS news portal*, July 2.

Šķinķe, Iveta, ed. 2007. *Aizvestie. 1949. 25. Marts*. Riga: Nodik, State Archive.

Skucas, T. 2004. "Lithuania: a problem of disclosure," *Demokratizatsiya: The Journal of Post-Soviet Democratization*, 12: 3, 411–25.

Smith, Kathleen E. 1996. *Remembering Stalin's Victims: Popular Memory and the End of the USSR*. Ithaca, NY: Cornell University Press.

Šneidere, Irene 2005. "The first Soviet occupation period in Latvia 1940–1941," in Nollendorfs and Oberländer (eds.), pp. 33–42.

Snyder, Timothy 2003. *The Reconstruction of Nations: Poland, Ukraine, Lithuania, Belarus, 1569–1999*. New Haven, CT: Yale University Press.

2010. "The fatal fact of the Nazi-Soviet pact," *The Guardian*, October 5.

2012. *Bloodlands: Europe Between Hitler and Stalin*. London: Basic Books.

Spiegel online 2004. "Eklat bei Buchmesse-Eröffnung: 'Das höre ich mir nicht an'," *Spiegel online*, March 24.

Spohr Readman, Kristina 2004. *Germany and the Baltic Problem after the Cold War: The Development of a New Ostpolitik, 1989–2000*. Southgate: Frank Cass Publishers.

Sprūde, Viesturs 2009a. "Totalitārisma seku dokumentēšanas centra ka SAB 'piektais ritenis'," *Latvijas Avīze*, May 12.

2009b. "Ar nepadarīta darba sajūtu," *Latvijas Avīze*, August 13.

Stan, Lavinia 2006. "The roof over our heads: property restitution in Romania," *Journal of Communist Studies and Transition Politics*, 22: 180–205.

2009a. "The failed revolution. The impact of 1989 on the former Soviet republics," *Sfera Politicii*, 142, 45–60.

2009b. "Hungary," in Stan (ed.), II, pp. 102–27.

ed. 2009c. *Transitional Justice in Eastern Europe and the Former Soviet Union: Reckoning with the Communist Past*. London: Routledge.

Stan, Lavinia 2013. *Transitional Justice in Post-communist Romania*. Cambridge University Press.

Stan, Lavinia and Nadya Nedelsky, eds. 2013. *Encyclopedia of Transitional Justice*, 3 vols. Cambridge University Press.

Stankevičius, Česlovas 1996. *Enhancing Security of Lithuania and Other Baltic States in 1992–94 and Future Guidelines*. Research report available at www.nato.int/acad/fellow/94-96/stankevi/home.htm [accessed March 1, 2014].

Stašaitytė, Vytenė 2008. "Sudaryta Liustracijos komisija," *Alfa.lt*, May 4.

Stevick, E. Doyle 2007. "The politics of the Holocaust in Estonia: historical memory and social divisions in Estonian education," in B. A. Levinson and E. D. Stevick (eds.), *Reimagining Civic Education: How Diverse Societies Form Democratic Citizens*. Lanham, MD: Rowman & Littlefield, pp. 217–44.

Strauss, Tiiu 2013. *Haldusleping "Omandireformi registrite volitatud töötlemine."* Report commissioned by the Estonian Ministry of Finance, Tallinn, March 28.

Streikus, Arūnas 2012. *The Church in Soviet Lithuania*. Vilnius: Genocide and Resistance Research Center of Lithuania.

Strods, Heinrihs and Kott, Matthew 2002. "The file on operation 'Priboi': a re-assessment of the mass deportations of 1949," *Journal of Baltic Studies*, 33: 1, 1–36.

Supreme Court of the Republic of Latvia 1996. Judgement Concerning Genocide. November 4, Case#PAK-269/1996.

Suziedelis, Saulius 2007. "The perception of the Holocaust: public challenges and experience in Lithuania," paper presented at the East European Studies (EES) Noon Discussion (Meeting Report 341).

Švarca, Inga 2012. "Transitional justice mechanisms applied by Latvia in its transition from Communist regime," *Hitotsubashi Journal of Law and Politics*, 40, 59–85.

2014. *The Procedure of the European Court of Human Rights Regarding Countries in Transition: The ECtHR's Transitional Justice Cases against Latvia*. Hamburg: Kovač.

Szczerbiak, Aleks 2014. "Explaining patterns of lustration and Communist Security Service file access in post-1989 Poland," *Sussex European Institute Working Paper* No. 133.

Taagepera, Rein 1989. "Estonia's road to independence," *Problems of Communism*, 38: 6, 11–27.

Tamm, Marek 2013. "In search of lost time: memory politics in Estonia, 1991–2011," *Nationalities Papers*, 41: 4, 1–24.

Tarto, Enn 1994. Plenary Session of the Riigikogu of the Republic of Estonia, VII Riigikogu stenogramm, V Istungjärk, December 14.

Teitel, Ruti G. 2000. *Transitional Justice*. Oxford University Press.

Tėvynės sąjunga – Lietuvos Konservatoriai 1996. "Lietuvos Sėkmė: Tėvynės sąjungos (Lietuvos Konservatorių) 1996 m. Seima rinkimų programa," Vilnius.

Tēvzemei un Brīvībai/LNNK 2000. "Likumprojekts 'Par PSRS okupacijas nodaritu zaudejumu kompenzaciju.'" *Latvijas Republikas Saeima likumprojektu registers*, 706.

Tismăneanu, Vladimir 2009. *Stalinism Revisited: The Establishment of Communist Regimes in East-Central Europe*. Budapest: Central European University Press.

Titavs, Dans 1997. "Genocīda noziegumu izpēte – vēsturnieku vai juristu darbs?" *Diena*, October 21.

Tracevskis, Rokas 2000a. "Landsbergis asks Russia for billions," *The Baltic Times*, May 18.

2000b. "Tribunal on communism announces its verdict," *The Baltic Times*, October 5.

2003. "A grave fit for whom?," *Transitions Online*, March 5.

Troebst, Stefan 2010. "Halecki revisited: Europe's conflicting cultures of remembrance," in M. Pakier and B. Strath (eds.), *A European Memory?: Contested Histories and Politics of Remembrance*. Amsterdam: Berghahn Books, pp. 145–54.

Truska, Liudas and Vareikis, Vygantas 2004. *Holokausto prielaidos: antisemitizmas Lietuvoje / The Preconditions for the Holocaust: Anti-Semitism in Lithuania*. Vilnius: Margi Raštai.

Tsenkova, Sasha 2000. *Riga: Housing Policy and Practice – A Framework for Reform*. Report commissioned by Canadian International Development Agency, Baltic Initiative Program "Latvian-Canadian Housing Cooperation Project."

Tsenkova, Sasha and Turner, Bengt 2004. "The future of social housing in Eastern Europe: reforms in Latvia and Ukraine," *International Journal of Housing Policy*, 4: 2, 133–49.

Tucker, Aviezer 2006a. "Paranoids may be persecuted: post-totalitarian transitional justice," in J. Elster (ed.), *Retribution and Reparation in the Transition to Democracy*. Cambridge University Press, pp. 181–205.

2006b. "Rough justice: rectification in post-authoritarian and post-totalitarian regimes," in J. Elster (ed.), *Retribution and Reparation in the Transition to Democracy*. Cambridge University Press, pp. 276–98.

TVnet 2013a. "Atjauno okupācijas režīma nodarīto zaudējumu aprēķināšanas komisiju," *TVnet*, November 5.

2013b. "DP uztic vērtēt Rubika izteikumus par 1949.gada represijām," *TVnet/LETA*, May 3.

United Nations Human Rights Committee 1995. "Concluding observations of the Human Rights Committee: Estonia." November 9, *UN Treaties Bodies Database*, CCPR/C/79/Add.59.

United Nations Secretary General 2004. *The Rule of Law and Transitional Justice in Conflict and Post-Conflict Societies*. Report commissioned by United Nations Secretary General.

Upleja, Ieva and Titavs, Dans 1998. "Vai pienācis laiks vētīt čekas maisus Latvijā?," Diena, October 26.

US Department of Justice 2001. "Justice Department welcomes WWII genocide conviction in Lithuania of former Florida resident," press release, February 16.

Vaher, Ken-Marti and Pärna, Priidu 2003. "Seletuskiri okupatsioonirežiimide poolt represseeritud isiku seaduse eelnõu juurde." Justiitsministeerium, November 5.

Vaičaitis, Vaidotas A. 2012. "Konstitutionelle Verfasstheit der baltischen Staaten," in M. Knodt and S. Urdze (eds.), *Die politschen Systeme der baltischen Staaten*. Wiesbaden: Spinger VS, pp. 155–72.

Valenzuela, J. Samuel 1992. "Democratic consolidation in post-transitional settings: notion, process, and facilitating conditions," in S. Mainwaring,

G. O'Donnell and J. S. Valenzuela (eds.), *Issues in Democratic Consolidation: The New South American Democracies in Comparative Perspective*. Notre Dame, IN: University of Notre Dame Press, pp. 57–104.

Valentukevičius, Rimvydas 2004. "Nusikaltimų žmoniškumui tyrimo problemos," paper presented at the conference "Crimes Against Humanity and War Crimes Research Problems," Genocide and Resistance Research Center of Lithuania, Vilnius.

Van Der Merwe, Hugo, Baxter, Vicki and Chapman, Audrey R. 2009. *Assessing the Impact of Transitional Justice: Challenges for Empirical Research*. Washington, DC: US Institute of Peace Press.

Van Elsuwege, Peter 2003. "State continuity and its consequences: the case of the Baltic states," *Leiden Journal of International Law*, 16: 2, 377–88.

Van Schaak, B. 1996. "Crime of political genocide: repairing the Genocide Convention's blind spot," *The Yale Law Journal*, 106, 2259–91.

Vihalemm, Triin 2011. "Language space and human capital in the Baltic states," in M. Lauristin (ed.), *Estonian Human Development Report*. Tallinn: Estonian Cooperation Assembly, pp. 116–43.

Vīksne, Rudīte 2005. "Members of the Arajs Commando in Soviet court files: social position, education, reasons for voluteering, penalty," in Nollendorfs and Oberländer (eds.), pp. 188–206.

Vilnius District Court 1998. *Nuosprendis Lietuvos Respublikos Vardu, K. Kurakino byla – nuosprendis*. Vilnius District Court, December 2.

Volzhskaya, Mariya S. 2011. "Kononov v. Latvia: a partisan and a criminal – The European Court of Human Rights takes a controversial stance on war crimes," *Tulane Journal of International and Comparative Law*, 19, 651–68.

Waldorf, Lars 2012. "Anticipating the past: transitional justice and socio-economic wrongs," *Social & Legal Studies*, 21: 2, 171–86.

Weiss-Wendt, Anton 2005. "Hostage of politics: Raphael Lemkin on 'Soviet genocide,'" *Journal of Genocide Research*, 7, 551–59.

2008. "Why the Holocaust does not matter to Estonians," *Journal of Baltic Studies*, 39: 4, 475–97.

Welsh, Helga A. 1994. "Political transition processes in Central and Eastern Europe," *Comparative Politics*, 26: 4, 379–94.

Wezel, Katja 2013. "Latvia," in Stan and Nedelsky (eds.), II, pp. 273–80.

Wiebelhaus-Brahm, Eric 2010. *Truth Commissions and Transitional Societies: The Impact on Human Rights and Democracy*. London: Routledge.

Williams, Kieran, Fowler, Brigid, and Szczerbiak, Aleks 2005. "Explaining lustration in Central Europe: a 'post-communist politics' approach," *Democratization*, 12: 1, 22–43.

Wolff, David 2006. "The KGB reports from Lithuania," *Acta Slavica Iaponica*, 23, 219–40.

Zake, Ieva 2010. "Politicians versus intellectuals in the lustration debates in transitional Latvia," *Journal of Communist Studies and Transition Politics*, 26: 3, 389–412.

Žalimas, Dainius 2010. "Crimes committed by the communist regimes from the standpoint of international legislation: Lithuanian case study," paper presented at the international conference "The Crimes of Communist Regimes," Prague, February 24–25.

Zālīte, Indulis 1997. "Galvenās nevardarbīgās pretošanās formas un slēptais nacionālisms kā iekšējā nepakļaušanās padomju režīmam Latvijā (70. – 80.gadi)," *Latvijas Vēsture*, 79: 4, 79–89.

1998. "Radošā inteliģence – VDK kontroles objekts un propagandas ierocis (70. – 80. gadu atspoguļojums VDK dokumentos)," *Latvijas Vēsture*, 55: 3, 55–61.

Žilinskas, Justinas 2009. "Broadening the concept of genocide in Lithuania's criminal law and the principle of nullum crimen sine lege," *Jurisprudencija*, 118: 4, 333–48.

2011. "The Kononov case and the Baltic states," *Jurisprudence: Research Journal*, 18: 3, 859–70.

2012. "Introduction of 'crime of denial' in the Lithuanian criminal law and first instances of its application," *Jurisprudence: Research Journal*, 19: 1, 315–29.

Zimmermann, Michael 2008. "The Nazi period in the Baltic states," in Council of Europe (ed.), *Project Education of Roma Children in Europe: Fact Sheets on Roma History*, available at www.coe.int/education/roma [accessed February 27, 2014].

Zirnīte, Māra 2006. "National oral history: Time of Change Project," *Elore*, 13: 1, 1–6.

Zuroff, Efraim 2002. "Holokausti Päev Eestis oleks suur samm edasi," *Eesti Päevaleht*, August 7.

2011. *Operation Last Chance: One Man's Quest for Bringing Nazi Criminals to Justice*. New York: Palgrave Macmillan.

INTERVIEWS AND COMMUNICATIONS

Arpo, Martin, interview, Tallinn, October 4, 2013
Hänni, Liia, interview, Tõravere, January 10, 2014
Hänni, Uku, interview, Tõravere, January 10, 2014
Jansons, Ritvars, interview, Riga, September 27, 2013
Kuodytė, Dalia, interview, Vilnius, May 8, 2013
Lane, Nicholas, email correspondence, May 31 and June 2, 2011
Lane, Nicholas, interview, Tallinn, June 9, 2011
Liblik, Eve, interview, Tallinn, May 14, 2013
Mälksoo, Lauri, communication, Tartu, June 13, 2013
Marcinkevičienė, Elžbieta Jūratė, interview, Kaunas, May 9, 2013
Muciņš, Linards, interview, Riga, January 15, 2014
Niglas, Aivar, interview, Tallinn, October 4, 2013
Nollendorfs, Valters, email correspondence, September 16, 2009
Saueauk, Meelis, interview, Tallinn, October 4, 2013
Šidlauskas, Gintaras, interview, Vilnius, May 8, 2013
Strupinskienė, Lina, interview, Vilnius, May 7, 2013
Tarto, Enn, interview, Tartu, September 6, 2013
Urmonas, Algimantas, interview, Vilnius, May 7, 2013
Valentukevičius, Rimvydas, interview, Vilnius, May 6, 2013
Venclauskas, Linas, personal communication, Kaunas, May 9, 2013
Zālīte, Indulis, interview, Riga, September 27, 2013

INDEX